Filming the First

POLITICS, LITERATURE, & FILM

Series Editor: Lee Trepanier, Assumption University

The Politics, Literature, & Film series is an interdisciplinary examination of the intersection of politics with literature and/or film. The series is receptive to works that use a variety of methodological approaches, focus on any period from antiquity to the present, and situate their analysis in national, comparative, or global contexts. Politics, Literature, & Film seeks to be truly interdisciplinary by including authors from all the social sciences and humanities, such as political science, sociology, psychology, literature, philosophy, history, religious studies, and law. The series is open to both American and non-American literature and film. By putting forth bold and innovative ideas that appeal to a broad range of interests, the series aims to enrich our conversations about literature, film, and their relationship to politics.

Advisory Board

Recent Titles

Filming the First: Cinematic Portrayals of Freedom of the Press by Helen J. Knowles-Gardner, Bruce E. Altschuler, and Brandon T. Metroka
A Prophet of Modern Delusions: Tolstoy's Critique of Modernity by John P. Moran
Political Wisdom in Late Shakespeare: A Way Out of the Wreck by Nicolas McAfee
Film and Faith: Modern Cinema and the Struggle to Believe edited by Carson Holloway and Micah Watson
Dark Places: Crime and Politics in the Personal Noir of James Ellroy edited by Darrell A. Hamlin and Joseph Romance
The Architecture of Survival: Setting and Politics in Apocalypse Films by Erik Trump and Jake Parcell
Come With Me If You Want to Live: The Future as Foretold in Classic Sci-fi Films by Michael Harris

Filming the First

Cinematic Portrayals of Freedom of the Press

Helen J. Knowles-Gardner, Bruce E. Altschuler, and Brandon T. Metroka

LEXINGTON BOOKS
Lanham • Boulder • New York • London

Published by Lexington Books
An imprint of The Rowman & Littlefield Publishing Group, Inc.
4501 Forbes Boulevard, Suite 200, Lanham, Maryland 20706
www.rowman.com

86-90 Paul Street, London EC2A 4NE

British Library Cataloguing in Publication Information Available

Library of Congress Cataloging-in-Publication Data

Names: Knowles, Helen J., author. Altschuler, Bruce E., author. Metroka, Brandon T., 1984- author.
Title: Filming the first : cinematic portrayals of freedom of the press / Helen J. Knowles, Bruce E. Altschuler, and Brandon T. Metroka.
Description: Lanham, Maryland : Lexington Books, [2024] | Includes bibliographical references and index. | Series: Politics, literature, & film.
Identifiers: LCCN 2024013905 (print) | LCCN 2024013906 (ebook) | ISBN 9781793650443 (cloth) | ISBN 9781793650450 (ebook)
Subjects: LCSH: Freedom of the press in motion pictures. | Journalism in motion pictures.
Classification: LCC PN1995.9.F8255 K66 2024 (print) | LCC PN1995 (ebook) | DDC 791.43/653
LC record available at https://lccn.loc.gov/2024013905
LC record available at https://lccn.loc.gov/2024013906

Contents

Acknowledgments

To borrow the title of a Beatles song, this book has taken a "long and winding road." We first pitched our ideas for the volume to Lexington in 2020 and signed the contract with them in January 2021. In the intervening years, one of us left academia, departing a twenty-year professorial career for a research directorship at a nonprofit think tank; one of us successfully worked toward and earned promotion to associate professor with tenure; and the other one faced the challenges of living in New York City during the height of the global COVID pandemic. And then, beyond these significant bumps in the road to manuscript completion, we all experienced the everyday trials and tribulations, and highs and lows, of what is known as "life." As a result, deadlines came and went for the submission of this manuscript. Throughout it all, Lexington has been unbelievably patient, acceding to our numerous requests for further time to complete our work. Having worked with this publisher before, this patience is unsurprising. Nevertheless, we remain forever indebted to them for bearing with the three of us.

A special debt of gratitude is owed the two anonymous reviewers solicited by Lexington to read through a draft of a manuscript that was, by our collective admission, in much need of thoughtful and constructive critical feedback. We hope the reviewers will agree with us that the book you are holding in your hands is a vastly improved product. Of course, all remaining errors are our own.

HELEN'S ACKNOWLEDGMENTS

In May 2022, Rylee Collea sent me an email. Just about to receive her undergraduate degree in political science from the State University of New York at Oswego, Rylee wanted me to know that "it was nice to have a professor who would allow for us to speak freely and openly about how we felt. I learned so much but most importantly I learned that it's important to speak up . . .

that's something that I will carry with me the rest of my life and I thank you for that." The spring 2022 semester had been particularly rough for me, in large part because of the way in which true expressive freedom on campus was dying an increasingly rapid death. I had begun to realize just how much my *colleagues* did not share my "commitment to the principle that debate on public issues should be uninhibited, robust and wide-open" (to borrow the words of Justice William J. Brennan, Jr.).[1] Therefore, it was heartening to know that my *students* understood that "commitment" and appreciated why I had taken very vocal stands in support of positions that neither they nor I considered unpopular or controversial, but which were very much deemed as such by authorities on campus. I am forever grateful to Rylee for sending me that email; her words are ones that I treasure, and they embody a viewpoint that I wear as a badge of pride.

What happened on campus during the spring 2022 semester, accompanied by other factors that had been building in the workplace for several years, greatly hastened my desire to leave the career I had known for almost two decades. I have had the privilege of teaching, and learning from, many wonderful students in my free speech/free speech movies classes over the years, but it was time to leave.

I am beyond grateful to the Institute for Free Speech (IFS) for giving this "recovering academic" the perfect home. Sincere thanks go to my colleagues David Keating, Tom Garrett, Tiffany Donnelly, Sarah Fisher, Peter Russo, and Doug Granger (Doug produced the fantastic cover art for this book) for making the IFS a truly wonderful place to work. This work reflects my own views rather than those of the IFS.

Of course, this book would not have taken shape without my superb coauthors. I have now had the great good fortune to work with both of them on multiple volumes.

I also extend my gratitude to the feline and equine menagerie who used their paws and hooves to keep me grounded—loving meows to Toffee, Smokey, Faith, Clementine, Fiona, Everton, Samantha, and Winston, and loving neighs to Doc.

Finally, this book is dedicated to John, who, on February 11, 2023, made the wonderful decision to interrupt his longtime partner's watching of that lunchtime's televised English Premier League soccer game. I was stirred from my comfort on the sofa with a marriage proposal; our beautiful spring wedding followed three months later. It is beyond delightful to be able to dedicate this book to my *husband* John, the center of my world.

BRUCE'S ACKNOWLEDGMENTS

Writing can be solitary work, but the pandemic made it far more so. I would like to thank my friends for their support and encouragement, which sometimes meant listening patiently to my ideas as I wrote. The anonymous outside readers of our earlier manuscript contributed useful ideas for improving my work and making the final version more consistent. Thanks also to the New York Public and SUNY Oswego libraries for their remote collections that allowed me to do much of my research without leaving my apartment. Last but not least, I appreciate being able to collaborate with my coauthors/coeditors Helen Knowles-Gardner and Brandon Metroka, whose suggestions made my work better.

BRANDON'S ACKNOWLEDGMENTS

I would like to express appreciation for the many individuals who offered ideas, patience, and support during the writing of this volume. Special thanks to Leslie Todd for research support through the Mabee Library at University of the Incarnate Word, exceptional coauthors and coeditors Helen Knowles-Gardner and Bruce Altschuler for their insights, Rafael Saavedra and Laura Cannon for their assistance in editing, and Lorraine Ewers, Rosalinda Villarreal, Flor Rodriguez, Angelica Khorram, and Kathy Allwein for ongoing (and too often, thankless) administrative support of faculty.

Heartfelt thanks and recognition to the friends and colleagues who provided laughs and comfort, asked questions, and gave needed refuge throughout the writing process. Without them—and without exaggeration—completion of this project would not have been possible: James R. Alexander, Stefanie Boswell, Laura Cannon, Greg Clines and Jakob Rinderknecht, Maria Felix-Ortiz, Ron "R. J." Gathagan and Linh Le, Mike (RIP) and Tracey Henry, Rafael Hoyle, Abraham (and Luna!) Jara, John Kainer, Jonathan Marian, Robert and Lisa Matson, Blaise and Brittany Metroka, Ryan Metroka, Ash and Ben Miele, Jason A. Piccone, Jose Angel Rodriguez III, Brady L. Root, Gabriel Saxton-Ruiz, Teresa Taylor-Partridge, Alex Villarreal, Sean Viña and Amanda Stephens, and Ray Wrabley.

Finally, to Jackson-Jackson: loyal doggo and the goodest boy of nearly thirteen years. RIP, Jacko.

NOTE

1. *New York Times v. Sullivan*, 376 U.S. 254, 271 (1964).

Introduction

The Fundamental First Amendment

Helen J. Knowles-Gardner, Bruce E. Altschuler, and Brandon T. Metroka

On Saturday, June 19, 1971, US district court judge Murray Gurfein issued his ruling on the motion for a preliminary injunction that was being sought by the federal government in its lawsuit against the *New York Times*.[1] That lawsuit, known as the Pentagon Papers case, was ultimately decided by the US Supreme Court with a short *per curiam* opinion—an unsigned opinion that spoke for the court:

> We granted certiorari in these cases in which the United States seeks to enjoin the New York Times and the Washington Post from publishing the contents of a classified study entitled "History of U.S. Decision-Making Process on Viet Nam Policy." . . . "Any system of prior restraints of expression comes to this Court bearing a heavy presumption against its constitutional validity." . . . The Government "thus carries a heavy burden of showing justification for the imposition of such a restraint."[2]

Quite simply, the court held, the federal government had failed to meet that burden, and freedom of the presses was restored to its rightful constitutional place. The *New York Times*—and all the nation's other newspapers—were once again free to publish the classified study, which was never the national security threat that the Nixon administration deemed it to be.

Although the decision in *New York Times v. United States* was momentous, the opinion itself ultimately "lacked . . . rhetorical passion."[3] The same could never have been said of the instantly famous sentence that sprung forth from the pages of Gurfein's June 19 ruling: "A cantankerous press, an obstinate press, an ubiquitous press must be suffered by those in authority in order to preserve the even greater values of freedom of expression and the right of the people to know."[4]

- cantankerous (*adj.*): "quarrelsome"
- obstinate (*adj.*): "stubborn, intractable"
- ubiquitous (*adj.*): "present everywhere or in several places simultaneously"[5]

As Thomas Jefferson stressed when he wrote to a friend in 1786, we need to "suffer" such a press because "[o]ur liberty depends on the freedom of the press, and that cannot be limited without being lost."[6]

It is not that simple, though. For example, two decades later, near the end of his presidency, Jefferson reversed course, believing that—after almost eight years of dealing with the way in which he thought the press treated his leadership—"[n]othing can now be believed which is seen in a newspaper. Truth itself becomes suspicious by being put into that polluted vehicle."[7] Increasingly, today, this sounds eerily familiar. There is a sense that many of "those in authority" do not want to "suffer" (or, in any way tolerate) a "cantankerous . . . obstinate . . . [and] ubiquitous press." Instead, they want media coverage on their own terms (to paraphrase the movie *Citizen Kane*). As two of us have observed elsewhere, this has ironically resulted in social and sociopolitical rhetoric that is divisive by design; dialogue can easily dissolve into something more akin to a monologue, wherein one shuts down, or shouts down, one's opponents (often by employing the "fake news" epithet).[8]

Surveys show that Americans remain broadly committed to the basic First Amendment principles of freedom of speech and freedom of the press. Approximately 90 percent of the voters surveyed in one prominent 2023 poll expressed support for constitutional protection of these principles.[9] This would seem to be good news, a positive democratic response to the partisan politicking of politicians. Once again, however, there is an important caveat. Support for freedom of the press in particular often shrinks significantly when it comes to specific cases. A 2020 poll, for example, found that 89 percent of respondents agreed that "freedom of the press is essential for American democracy," yet 41 percent described the news media as the "enemy of the people." And 40 percent agreed that the president should have the authority to close news outlets engaged in bad behavior, with 29 percent believing that "President Trump should close down news media like CNN, the *Washington Post*, and the *New York Times*."[10]

Is there a ray of hope within all this ambiguity? Absolutely. People might want to bash (or even muzzle) the press. However, *the free press provision of the First Amendment protects the press against the whims of public opinion and attempts by public officials to prevent embarrassing media coverage.*

At first glance, the First Amendment does this with very simple and straightforward language—"Congress shall make no law . . . abridging the freedom of speech, or of the press." If only it were truly that simple. The free speech and press clauses of the First Amendment have generated considerable controversy ever since the Bill of Rights was ratified in 1791. Over the course of US history, many questions have been asked about the scope and meaning of the First Amendment's expressive freedom language. For example, does "no law" actually mean "*no* law"? If Congress cannot make a law abridging speech and press freedoms, are state and local governments similarly constrained? And do we actually need a separate guarantee of freedom of the press? If so, then why single the press out? Neither commentators nor courts have arrived at conclusive answers to these questions, and they probably never will.

Enter the films discussed in this book.

VISUAL TEXTS

The First Amendment is ripe for cinematic treatment because films—"visual texts"—can and do make important contributions to the *conversation* about legal issues in society. Indeed, films contribute significantly to the social construction of knowledge about media, knowledge that often (and for good reason) transcends a legalistic way of approaching the subject matter. As Robert Kolker has explained, "[t]he reason that attention must be paid to film is that most of us get our stories—our narratives and myths—from it. . . . In other words, from the late-nineteenth century onward, people have turned to film as entertainment, escape, and (however unconsciously) education—as an affirmation of the way they live or think they ought to live their lives."[11]

The law is, in many ways, just like the movies. It is a storytelling enterprise; it is a business of narratives and of myths. American law is an adversarial system; the principal goal is to zealously represent one's client. Maybe the truth will come out in the process, but the pursuit of the truth is not the lawyer's goal. The telling of stories is an integral component of the pursuit of zealous representation.[12] When we learn about the lives of those involved in and affected by the law, we learn about far more than just those cases. That process of learning also enhances our knowledge about the society in which we live, the one in which previous generations lived, and/or the society that we hope to bestow upon future generations.[13] Indeed, movies often perform that civic educational function—conveying complex legal principles—better than scholars and commentators. Often, the telling of interesting and entertaining stories necessitates an approach—and a medium—that is worlds apart from the dry academic discussion found in the pages of academic journals. Movies can do this in many different ways, and as readers work through the chapters in this book, they are encouraged to note, for example, the specific use of comedy, satire, and music, and even phrases that have become iconic (such as "Follow the money" or "I'm mad as hell and I'm not going to take this anymore") in storytelling.

Filmmakers—even those who create documentaries—do so through the use of various cinematic and character-building techniques. Chief among these techniques is centering a historical episode or important substantive idea around a main character or protagonist. Having a protagonist audiences can root for enhances box office appeal. Furthermore, by telling fictional or fictionalized stories, movies often present a subtext that relates an issue of the past to current conditions. For example, in *The Post* (analyzed in chapter 3), director/producer Steven Spielberg sought to use the *Washington Post*'s legal fight to publish the Pentagon Papers to show the importance of a free press at a time it was under attack, particularly in the rhetoric of President Donald Trump.

Of course, even films that embark on a faithful retelling of a true story (and most of the films in this book are in some shape or form related to real events) are bound to take some sort of cinematic license with the facts. As E. Michele Ramsey observes, filmmakers must often make choices in the construction of life stories to fit the constraints and expectations of the modality. Beyond the need to fit lifetimes within a roughly two-hour exposition, the general desire to please audiences and the financial bottom line can encourage filmmakers to sacrifice historical fact "in favor of an audience pleasing saga."[14] Deviations from historical truth, to varying degrees, have the potential to reinforce various myths held by a society or culture. With reference to films that focus on or are adjacent to legal issues, Ramsey points out that such productions add an additional layer of legitimacy or myth to the films' principal subjects.

The chapters in this book show how culture has affected portrayals of the press in film. In turn, movies both reflect and educate viewers on myriad aspects of media freedoms and the subjects covered by media. Two important features of film underscore this point. First, films allow viewers to experience unfamiliar events, ideas, identities, and trades via pseudoexperience. For example, "[i]f members of an audience have no direct experience with the work of bomb technicians, then their notion of how they operate and their demeanor might come from watching a film."[15] Second, films create intensely sensory narratives, combining sound, imagery, and dialogue to create uniquely immersive experiences: "It is through this representation of reality that moviegoers can witness history, understand seminal world events, and learn about other cultures."[16] In sum, films are important agents of socialization and are therefore appropriate units of analysis in any effort to describe and illustrate the extent of legal and social constructions of press freedom.

TEN CHAPTERS, EIGHTEEN FILMS—A NOTE ON METHODS

This book focuses specifically on cinematic treatment of *press* freedoms rather than expressive freedom in general. The films selected for the book are the units of analysis that illustrate how "the press" (a term that now includes various forms of media established since the Founding Generation) has changed in form and purpose. Each film or set of films illustrates a discrete aspect of this important evolution, including the potential or documented defects of a free press; the role of the press in altering the trajectory of governments and society, as well as the liberties taken with the accuracy of depictions of that role; the negative depictions and effects of modern media on historically marginalized identities, including BIPOC and LGBTQIA+; media serving as a voice for historically marginalized identities and those historically without a voice; war coverage in foreign theaters and the limitations on press freedom in that context, including attempts at censorship; and the need for the media to make a profit.

The primary objective of the book is to provide readers with an accessible (and enjoyable) applied analysis of how contemporary culture, as reflected in film, tells stories that depict press and media freedoms during a time when various forms of institutional media are under sustained attack. We also believe, consistent with previous scholarship, that films can facilitate active learning in the university classroom through compelling depictions of new and existing concepts via the narrative form.[17]

This book discusses—and provides some initial answers—to the following set of loosely interrelated questions:

- Historically, how have the media been portrayed in film (i.e., positively or negatively, and with an institutional or individual focus)?
- To what extent are movies able to tell compelling and commercially viable stories about free speech law?
- What press freedom narratives have appeared in film, and how do they reflect the historical legal and social constructions of those freedoms?
- What are the political, social, and historical eras (and assumptions of those eras) in which the films are embedded?
- What visual and audio techniques do films employ to create or evoke narratives about the media and its subjects?
- What do depictions of the media in film suggest or reveal about cultural (and media) attitudes toward various social identities, particularly the historically minoritized (i.e., women, BIPOC, LGBTQIA+)?

- How, if it all, do film depictions of the media construct—or reflect—the attitudes of the public and journalists themselves?
- How do filmmakers use subtext such that past or fictional events function as commentary about contemporary controversies?

In discussing these questions, the book employs a variant of the case study method. The case study approach is a valuable qualitative research method because of its tendency toward rich, thick descriptions of events, ideas, institutions, artifacts, and various other units of analysis, and its ability to build upon existing theory. Here, the visual texts featured in each chapter allow for both "within-case" and comparative case study of the questions posed above and the additional elements identified below (and in each chapter). We follow Alexander George and Andrew Bennett in defining a case "as an instance of a class of events."[18] Each film selected is an instance of a cultural portrayal of an element of the media as well as a portrayal of the subjects of media coverage (such as wars, criminal trials, abused children, and BIPOC and LGBTQIA+ identities). And, each film illustrates an important aspect or implication of the exercise of press freedoms under the First Amendment.

To evaluate how and when films construct media and its subjects—or, as Richard Howells describes it, to "[d]emonstrate how texts may be examined in order to expose the underlying ideas, values and beliefs they embody about society and politics"—this book searches for and assesses the background cultural patterns of thought and assumptions reflected in those constructions.[19] As visual texts, the eighteen films/documentaries analyzed in the chapters that follow can be evaluated in their social rather than just their "internal" context. In other words, each film explored in the book incorporates an understanding of "all of the social and historical conditions in which texts are produced" as well as "the way they are received by real people," which is in addition to evaluations limited to the "familiar, close analys[es] of the text under discussion."[20]

In constructing our analyses of the chosen films, we apply some of the techniques and emphases offered by Howells in *Visual Culture.* Doing so required careful and multiple viewings of each film selected, recording and evaluating dialogue in light of the images presented as well as the presentation techniques of each film (in other words, the significance of scene construction and camera cuts; long, medium, and short-range shots and the editing techniques employed; lighting and character orientation toward the camera; and the use of sound, including music). We also offer some insight into the origins of the films and the intentions of their principal creators.

Moving beyond summaries of cinematic techniques requires an assessment and incorporation of the social, political, and other historical conditions in which the visual texts are produced. To do this, we situate the films within their respective contemporary contexts, relying on secondary sources (the written word, as revealed in historical texts and other scholarly assessments) and primary sources (firsthand accounts of contemporary events). In addition, we must account for films presenting past events and evaluate them for accuracy—or take note of the assumptions the present may impose upon the past. If history is a controlled act of the imagination due to our inability to directly experience it, then the types of sources described above represent the controls. The reader will also find that in order to explore and assess how films are consumed by the public—the effects of films on society—we also rely on extant scholarship evaluating how and when visual texts affect attitudes as well as available polling data to assess contemporary attitudes toward any subjects featured in the films.

When combined, all these elements provide the reader with analysis of eighteen films over the course of ten chapters, wherein we explore the myriad ways in which the movie industry has filmed the complexities of the First Amendment's free press clause.

NOTES

1. 328 F. Supp. 326 (1971).
2. *New York Times v. United States*, 403 U.S. 713, 714 (1971).
3. Ronald K. L. Collins and Sam Chaltain, *We Must Not Be Afraid to Be Free: Stories of Free Expression in America* (New York: Oxford University Press, 2011), 84. In order to get the agreement of six justices, it also lacked specifics, providing little guidance for future judges and the media.
4. 328 F. Supp. at 331.
5. *The Oxford American Dictionary and Language Guide* (New York: Oxford University Press, 1999), 136, 683, 1091.
6. Letter from Thomas Jefferson to James Currie, January 28, 1786, Library of Congress, https://www.loc.gov/resource/mtj1.005_0216_0218/?sp=1 (last accessed May 24, 2023).
7. Letter from Thomas Jefferson to John Norvell, June 11, 1807, Library of Congress, https://www.loc.gov/resource/mtj1.038_0592_0594/?sp=1&st=pdf&pdfPage=1 (last accessed December 29, 2023).
8. Helen J. Knowles and Brandon T. Metroka, "Introduction: Why Free Speech Theory Matters," in *Free Speech Theory: Understanding the Controversies*, ed. Helen J. Knowles and Brandon T. Metroka (New York: Peter Lang, 2020), 1–32. It is important to note that "fake news" claims are hardly new. They did not magically come into being with the presidential campaign and presidency of Donald J. Trump. See Keith J. Bybee and Laura E. Jenkins, "Free Speech, Free Press, and Fake News: What if the Marketplace of Ideas Isn't About Identifying Truth?" in *Free Speech Theory*, 95–118.

9. Carl M. Cannon, "POLL: Is Censorship a Partisan Issue?" RealClear Opinion Research, September 22, 2023, https://www.realclearpolitics.com/real_clear_opinion_research/poll_is_censorship_a_partisan_issue_149790.html.

10. Everette E. Dennis and Klaus Schoenbach, "Trust in U.S. News Media," Harris Poll/Northwestern Medill, July 2020, https://magazine.medill.northwestern.edu/wp-content/uploads/2020/07/NUQ-Trust-in-U.S.-Media-Report_09July2020.pdf.

11. Robert P. Kolker, *Film, Form, and Culture*, 4th ed. (New York: Routledge, 2015), 1.

12. Instructive, here, is Stephen Paskey, "The Law Is Made of Stories: Erasing the False Dichotomy between Stories and Legal Rules," *Legal Communications and Rhetoric: JALWD* 11 (2014): 51–82.

13. One of us discusses this extensively in the context of the US Supreme Court's landmark labor law decision *West Coast Hotel v. Parrish*, 300 U.S. 379 (1937). See Helen J. Knowles, *Making Minimum Wage: Elsie Parrish versus the West Coast Hotel Company* (Norman: University of Oklahoma Press, 2021).

14. E. Michele Ramsey, "Protecting Patriarchy: The Myths of Capitalism and Patriotism in *The People vs Larry Flynt*," *Feminist Media Studies* 5, no. 2 (2005): 197.

15. Michelle C. Pautz, "*Argo* and *Zero Dark Thirty*: Film, Government, and Audiences," *PS: Political Science & Politics* 48, no. 1 (2015): 121.

16. Pautz, "*Argo* and *Zero Dark Thirty*," 121.

17. Cheryl Bluestone, "Feature Films as a Teaching Tool," *College Teaching* 48, no. 4 (2000): 141.

18. Alexander L. George and Andrew Bennett, *Case Studies and Theory Development in the Social Sciences* (Cambridge, MA: MIT Press, 2005), 17.

19. Richard Howells, *Visual Culture*, 3rd ed. (Medford, MA: Polity Press, 2019), 70–71.

20. Howells, *Visual Culture*, 88.

Chapter 1

Censorship in a Time of War

Good Morning, Vietnam

Helen J. Knowles-Gardner

"Censorship reflects a society's lack of confidence in itself. It is a hallmark of an authoritarian regime."[1] Historically, freedom of speech and freedom of the press have found themselves under the greatest attack—under the greatest threat of censorship—during times of war. Such times are, to borrow the title of Geoffrey R. Stone's book, "perilous."[2] The "lack of confidence" a society has in itself—or, more specifically, the "lack of confidence" the government has in its citizens—intensifies during wartime. The unique nature of wartime threats to expressive freedom lends itself to analysis, in this chapter, of only one film—*Good Morning, Vietnam*. That analysis is centered around a set of important questions:

- Why does the government treat freedom of the press differently during wartime?
- Is there ever any constitutional justification for imposing special limits on press freedoms during a time of war? And if yes, how far can such limits go?
- Why are prior restraints particularly problematic threats to freedom of the press? Are they ever justified?

Although the wartime setting makes *Good Morning, Vietnam* distinguishable from the other films analyzed in this book, it does have one important thing in common with most of those other movies: It is based (albeit very loosely) on a true story. This factor compels consideration of additional aspects of cinematic depictions of freedom of the press:

- Changing aspects of a real-life character, and actual events that occurred, in order to enhance audience appeal.
- The use of music to create historical context and to elicit specific feelings from the audience.
- The use of "standpoint" to convey stories in movies.
- The use of comedy to make serious points.

As subsequent chapters in this book further emphasize, the most invidious governmental efforts to limit freedom of the press are those that seek to impose prior restraints. These are limits imposed before something can be published (thereby preventing the material from seeing the light of day); they are restrictions imposed *prior* to publication. They differ from the more prevalent type of restrictions that seek to punish speakers after they have uttered and/or published something. Regarding the oppressive nature of prior restraints, consider the words of legal scholar Alexander M. Bickel (who represented the *New York Times* in the Pentagon Papers case; see *The Post* analysis in chapter 3):

> Prior restraints fall on speech with a brutality and a finality all their own. Even if they are ultimately lifted they cause irremediable loss—a loss in the immediacy, the impact, of speech. . . . The violator of a prior restraint may be assured of being held in contempt; the violator of a statute punishing speech criminally [after its utterance] knows that he will go before a jury [who will learn—as other audiences have already—exactly what he said], and may be willing to take his chance, counting on a possible acquittal. *A prior restraint, therefore, stops speech more effectively. A criminal statute chills, prior restraint freezes.*[3]

Prior restraints that are defended by the government as ways of protecting national security during a time of war are featured in 1987's *Good Morning, Vietnam* (hereafter GMV), the solitary film analyzed in this chapter. The prior restraints in GMV differ from those that appear in other movies examined in this volume. For example, in *The Post* (chapter 3), the efforts at prior restraint fail. By contrast, in GMV the prior restraints successfully limit press freedom. For reasons that will become clear, however, this does not mean that GMV is a movie about failures of press freedom.

Governments often make disingenuous and dangerous attempts to defend restrictions of press freedom by issuing bogus cries of "national security." (The Pentagon Papers case—see *The Post*—is a perfect example.) In light of the fact that such restrictions are typically directed at limiting speech because of the content of that speech, courts require the government to show that it has a "compelling" reason for imposing the limits and that the end cannot be achieved through any other means that places less restriction on speech. This is the strict scrutiny standard of judicial review. This means that restrictions in the name of "national security" face steep constitutional hurdles. However, for reasons outlined below, when "national security" is the justification, and the nation is at war, those hurdles are far less difficult for the government to overcome than is the case during a secure time of peace.

As we will see, GMV features examples of censorial malfeasance. What the film showcases, however, are noble efforts to strike back at the governmental hand that believes it "can hold back the mighty traffic of life with a tin whistle and a raised right hand."[4] Yes, disc jockey Airman Adrian Cronauer (and, to a lesser extent, his assistant, Private Edward Garlick) both encounter government censorship. Ultimately, however, their actions are best interpreted as those of crusading members of the media seeking to prevent the dominant narrative of war from becoming nothing more than "a bright shining lie" (to borrow the title of Neil Sheehan's Pulitzer Prize–winning book about the Vietnam War).[5]

WAR IS DIFFERENT, AND SO IS *GOOD MORNING, VIETNAM*

Before engaging in an in-depth analysis of GMV, a short author note is necessary because by focusing on only one film, this chapter departs from the others in this volume. War is different. It imposes different pressures upon society, and in order to relieve those pressures, society is often more willing than it otherwise would be to accept limitations on civil liberties, including expressive freedom. As Chief Justice William H. Rehnquist acknowledged in his book on the subject, the "Roman legal maxim" *inter arma silent leges* (in times of war, the law falls silent) takes its broadly accepted "validity" in part from its "descriptive" meaning: "It speaks first simply as a truism: in time of war the government's authority to restrict civil liberty *is* greater than in peacetime."[6] However, there is also the reality that in times of war when the government wants to limit civil liberties, it does indeed feel less constrained to do so. As Francis Biddle (President Franklin D. Roosevelt's attorney general, 1941–1945) once wrote, "The Constitution has not greatly bothered any wartime President."[7] Similarly, the courts have historically exhibited a "reluctance . . . to decide a case against the government on an issue of national security during a war."[8] As Stone observes,

> War creates a powerful mass psychology. Emotions run high. Spies, saboteurs, and terrorists lurk around every corner. *Our* way of life is imperiled. Anything that increases the danger to *our* troops—*our* sons and daughters—is feared and despised. The thought that a loved one or friend has put life and limb at risk for

> an unworthy cause is intolerable. We are just; our enemy is cruel, immoral, inhuman. Loyalty is the order of the day. In such an atmosphere, the line between dissent and disloyalty is elusive, and often ignored.[9]

GMV is by no means the only film to address press freedom, and the work of journalists, in a time of war. Other important examples include *Foreign Correspondent* (1940), *The Year of Living Dangerously* (1982), and *Salvador* (1986). Similarly, GMV is certainly not the only cinematic treatment of the Vietnam War to address the freedom of the press (or lack thereof). *The Killing Fields* (1984) and *Full Metal Jacket* (1987) both explore that topic in their own distinct ways. However, the narrative in GMV is driven, to a far greater extent than in the other movies mentioned here, by the theme of government censorship during wartime.

In *Vietnam on Film*, Gilbert Adair identifies a staggering sixty films about myriad aspects of that conflict, released over a twelve-year time period (1968–1979)—on average, five every year.[10] The attractiveness of Vietnam to filmmakers did not abate once the calendar turned over into the 1980s—twenty-eight Vietnam War–related movies were made during that decade.[11] Indeed, over the course of sixteen months between 1987 and 1988 alone, the market was "saturated" with six movies about Vietnam.[12]

According to one commentator, this cinematic "study of Vietnam—like virtually every other war era—is rich with differing perspectives and redolent with many 'truths.'"[13] Unfortunately, that point was lost on many reviewers of GMV, who were critical of what they perceived to be the film's lack of serious attention to US policymaking vis-à-vis Vietnam. William J. Palmer, whose review is discussed in more detail below, concludes that the film not only "trivializes the war and the issues of the war" but "does not even qualify as a movie."[14] In her retrospective look at GMV thirty-five years on, Danielle Solzman very effectively rebuts the "GMV is bad because it is not about the war in Vietnam" critique. "War comedies are not an easy feat to make," she observes. "There's a fine line when it comes to presentation." She acknowledges the fact that in GMV the "[f]ootage of troops fighting or under attack is few and far between," but then concludes that this is "for the best of the film." Yes, "it doesn't sell the full portrait of the Vietnam War." However, "[i]f you want a film that depicts the war's full portrait, there are plenty of films out there."[15] This is the key point. GMV is not a film about the Vietnam War. Of the aforementioned six "major Vietnam War films" released between 1987 and 1988, "only *Platoon*, *Full Metal Jacket*, *Hamburger Hill*, and *Off Limits* are really about the Vietnam War. *Gardens of Stone* and *Good Morning, Vietnam* are not really about the war itself."[16] GMV is a film set in Vietnam during that conflict that does, in places, "stress . . . that the United States is fulfilling a French imperialist design," but that "notion . . . goes unexplored" because that is not one of the principal themes of the movie.[17] In the pages that follow, this chapter argues that it is the very fact that US intervention in Vietnam is not the focus of the film that makes it a stronger freedom of the press movie.

GOOOOOOOOOOOD MORNING, VIETNAM!

Airman Adrian Cronauer (Robin Williams) arrives in Saigon from Crete in 1965. He is the embodiment of irreverent tendencies: out of military uniform (dressed "to blend into a crowd of drunken Greeks") and politically incorrect (having "been on a Greek island with a lot of women who look like Zorba," he "never thought" he'd "find women attractive ever again"), he is unafraid of breaking—or even giving the middle finger to—military protocol. The movie's depiction of his time in Vietnam is "based ever-so-loosely" on the real Cronauer's "experiences in Vietnam," from 1965 to 1966, as the disc jockey for the *Dawn Buster* program on Armed Forces Radio Saigon (AFRS).[18] As Cronauer (who "co-authored the original story" for the film) has written, "[Y]es, I was a disc jockey in Vietnam. . . . Yes, I did teach English during my off-duty time; no, I did not teach my class how to swear and use New York street slang; and no, I was not teaching because I was trying to meet this particular, beautiful Vietnamese girl. At least, not one particular, beautiful Vietnamese girl." Continuing, Cronauer observes, "[Y]ou could name any character in the film, and I'd probably be able to think of at least half-dozen people I knew during my four years in the Air Force who fit that stereotype."[19] And although "[t]he film was never intended to be a point-by-point accurate biography,"[20] what it tells us about wartime censorship, and the dangers attached to that practice, is certainly not lost in the translation from reality to the world of cinema.

"THE GUYS IN THE REAR, WITH THE BEER"

GMV uses a particular "standpoint" to convey the way in which press freedom can prevail even when the government successfully imposes prior restraints and heavy-handed wartime censorship. As Carla A. Fellers explains, in film theory "[a] standpoint is a point of view exhibiting distinctive, contextually derived values and 'from which particular features of reality are brought into sharp perspective and other features are obscured.'"[21] Standing in direct contrast to the "official standpoint [that] encompasses unquestioning allegiance to conventional warfare" is Cronauer's "unofficial" standpoint that "represents innovative, imaginative, and unconventional conduct during war."[22]

Technically speaking, as a noncombat member of the military, Cronauer was what many Vietnam veterans, the "grunts" who did see combat, would derisively describe as a REMF—rear-echelon motherfucker.[23] "The guys in the rear, with the beer,"[24] who made up the overwhelming percentage of troops deployed to Vietnam, were viewed with disdain by large numbers of grunts. "If you lived behind wire, you were in the rear echelon," observes Vietnam veteran George "Sonny" Hoffman. "If you slept in a bed, ate hot food, took hot showers, used a flush toilet, and got laid regularly, you were a Mother Fucker."[25] Of course, we should be cautious about generalizations—about both the REMFs and the grunts' opinions of them. Regardless, these points are helpful regarding analysis of GMV and freedom of the press, because Cronauer harnesses the power of the microphone, using it to give the normally muted enlisted grunts a "voice." And as discussed later in this chapter, this becomes particularly clear after Cronauer's own voice, on the radio, is temporarily silenced.

There are two ways in which Cronauer gives the grunts a voice. First, he literally gives them something to listen to; he is a voice they would not otherwise get to hear. Second, he idiomatically gives their fears, concerns, and other such views a voice, one they would not otherwise get to express.

It is not until fairly late in the film that Cronauer feels the full impact of the censorship his programming choices trigger. However, when he takes to the air for the first time, he does so fully aware that his is the voice of an outsider. It is a voice that pierces the otherwise heavily sanitized broadcasts that typically accompanied the dawn's early light when, as Cronauer proclaims on air, the 0 in 0600 "stand[s] for . . . Oh my God, it's early."

A SUPPORTING CAST OF INANIMATE OBJECTS

From the film's outset, the audience is made aware of the role of censorship through a series of closeup shots of two important pieces of technology. As shown in chapter 3, in *All the President's Men*, the typewriter—often depicted using close-up, full-frame shots—is used to great cinematic effect, essentially giving the typewriter character status in the film. Barry Levinson and cinematographer Peter Sova use the same technique in GMV. Indeed, the first "character" we see is a microphone. As the opening credits roll, the microphone fills the screen; a shallow depth of field ensures the background is blurred. We hear two things: dulcet-toned "champagne music"[26] and the voice of a radio announcer. Neither is entertaining or engaging. And the announcer is just that, a man reading military messages in a monotonous tone. (He is reading seemingly verbatim—because he has to correct himself, after the fact, when he reads the typo-ridden script that has been set in front of him.) When we eventually see the face of the announcer, it is heavily blurred behind a glass screen. This leaves the audience with the impression that the person reading what the military has instructed him to read is a faceless automaton. Before Cronauer arrives on the scene, this is how the grunts get their news, the programming choices deliberately "anesthetizing the airwaves."[27] None of this "fit[s] the expected character of a war zone anymore than the tidy office does," and this suits the government just fine.[28]

Cinematic use of another piece of technology underscores this. Intermittently, we see close-up shots of a volume level meter whose needle moves back and forth in small increments but always stays in the middle range as the announcer speaks. In other words, there is nothing loud or "off the charts" about this broadcast. All of a sudden, that changes. We hear a loud screeching noise that sounds like static, and the needle slams to the maximum volume level end of the meter. Immediately the scene moves from the interior of the radio studio to an airport taxiway. It becomes clear that the loud static is actually the roar of an airplane's engines as the screen is filled—again very deliberately—with a truck bearing a large "Follow Me." We, the audience, are being asked to visually follow the taxiing aircraft that is heeding the truck's instructions. Cinematically, this is how Adrian Cronauer arrives in GMV.

As the plane taxis, we again hear the radio announcer's colorless broadcast. Only when the film returns to the studio does the announcer come into focus. However, his appearance is fleeting, thereby emphasizing that the focus has shifted, from him and his carefully government-scripted broadcast to the out-of-uniform (unless you consider "Cretan camouflage" to be a "uniform") Cronauer descending the stairs of the airplane. Sergeant Major Dickerson (J. T. Walsh) is never going to like Cronauer, whose reputation for irreverent tendencies and irreverent broadcasts precedes him. "United States Air Force. The hat does give you away," Dickerson sarcastically—and with a significant note of disgust in his voice—says when confronting Cronauer for the first time. The fact that Cronauer is going to encounter resistance (understood in myriad ways) is demonstrated as Garlick (Forest Whitaker) drives their jeep into the compound of military buildings where the two men will live and work. Having salivated over the Vietnamese women during the drive from the airport, Cronauer exclaims, excitedly, that he "feel[s] like a fox in a chicken coop." This is immediately followed by the filling of the screen with a large red-and-white "STOP" sign affixed to the barrier. The irony of this moment should not be lost on the audience.

Before Cronauer takes to the air for the first time, Levinson and Sova again use a close-up of an inanimate object to remind us—and, by extension, Cronauer—of the omnipresent censorship imposed upon all who work for the AFRS. As Cronauer and Garlick walk down the corridor toward the broadcast booths (and away from the audience), there is a cut to a close-up, full-frame image of a teletype machine churning out short news flashes. Garlick warns Cronauer that he is not permitted to air any of the "news" headlines the machine produces until they are approved by the film's rather comical (in appearance and mannerisms) but very serious (in their work) pair of censors (played by identical twins Don and Dan Stanton). After Cronauer meets the two men—known in the credits only as "Censor #1" and "Censor #2—he and Garlick walk into the radio booth. The camera—which gives us the point of view of the censors—follows Cronauer and Garlick, swivel panning from behind the large glass windows of the censors' office. Big Brother is constantly watching.

WAR, UNSCRIPTED

Although the real Cronauer is undoubtedly right that GMV "was intended to be a piece of entertainment,"[29] censorship and press freedom in a time of war remains a powerful and instructive subplot, and continues to be evident from the moment Cronauer and Garlick set foot in that booth. (Although the point of view has now subtly shifted, we the audience still find ourselves watching from the same position as the censors.) As Cronauer begins to rifle through and make his own musical selections from shelves of records, Garlick gets concerned; he shows Cronauer a stack of preselected 45s (presumably those sanctioned by the military brass).

What happens next is perhaps the most famous moment in the film. Cronauer dons his headphones, flips the switch to "transmit," and opens his broadcast with the memorable line "Goooooooooood morning, Vietnam!" William Palmer argues that the film "fails" because of a "'dependen[ce] completely on monologue rather than the kind of dialogue which can explore such a complex issue as . . . the Vietnam War.'"[30] As observed above, this sort of critique misses the point, and ignores the message—about wartime threats to press freedom—that Cronauer's radio booth monologues make.

Those monologues were the result of Williams's comic genius along with Levinson's astute decision to cast him in the role and his equally astute decision to let his leading star loose on those monologues unscripted. As Owen Gilman explains, "Improvisation is a dark art because it maximizes the use of uncertainty." Yes, of course "we know that filmed improvisation can be reshot if it fails to produce the desired results," but that does not detract from the effectiveness of its use in GMV.[31] Gilman makes the important point that "the Vietnam War placed people, sooner or later, in situations where control from any authority was virtually nonexistent. By having Robin Williams go into the radio broadcast booth without a script, Levinson represented a fundamental truth of the war."[32] And this was a truth the government did not want to see the light of day—namely, that things were happening chaotically, not with the "order and reasonableness" to which the government was laying "claim." In GMV, "improvisation stands for the horror of chaos."[33]

One particular scene in the film shows the reality of this, and the way in which Williams's (and Levinson's) use of improvisation to illustrate the "horror of chaos" elicited a governmental censorial reaction. Jimmy Wah (Cu Ba Nguyen) owns a saloon in Saigon that is a favorite watering hole for the American troops. Enticed by Tuan (Tom T. Tran) to go and visit Tuan's sister Trinh (Chintara Sukapatana), who Cronauer lusts after, the airman leaves the bar just seconds before the place explodes. This is a seminal moment in the film for myriad reasons—not the least of which being that Tuan is (unbeknownst to Cronauer at this point in the film) a member of the Vietcong, and Cronauer's friendship with him ultimately costs the airman his posting in Vietnam after it almost costs him his life.

As the journalist Stanley Karnow observes in his definitive history of the country and its conflicts, "there were no secure areas in Vietnam"—whether one was a grunt or a REMF. "A GI assigned to an office [or a radio station] in Saigon or a warehouse in Danang could be killed or injured at any moment of the day or night." Of course, the experience was very different for the "infantryman" who "during his one-year tour . . . humping the bush was in combat almost continually."[34] But the bottom line remains important: "[T]here were no secure areas in Vietnam," and the bombing at Jimmy Wah's demonstrates this.

The scene cuts abruptly from an ash-covered Cronauer looking back at the burning building to the teletype machine at the radio station; the machine is reporting the news flash of the explosion. The film cuts back to the confusion, mayhem, and blood of the bomb site, and the dead and injured servicemen and Vietnamese. Another cut back to the teletype (with a tight focus on the words being printed); back to the victims; back to the machine's text: "THREE GIS WERE WOUNDED TWO WERE KILLED"; then immediately back to outside the bar, where some dead, blood-soaked GIs are being carried away. As one lies in the dirty wet street, Cronauer pleads with two military policemen (MPs). Move them to somewhere dignified, he cries; ultimately, he enlists the help of some MPs, and they move the dead GIs.

Immediately, we—the audience—are transported back to the sanitized surroundings of the teletype room, and now Cronauer has joined us. Clearly traumatized—shell-shocked—Cronauer rips the paper out of the machine and storms into the radio booth, ignoring one of the censors who runs after him. The censor rips the paper out of his hands and reminds him that he can't read uncensored news. The cameras are positioned to show the standoff between the two men. Cronauer, says, "It's the truth. I just want to report the truth. It'd be a nice change of pace." The background is blurred, but we can see

Dickerson walking toward the men. The focus now shifts to the sergeant major; he is flanked by Cronauer in one corner of the scene and the censor in the other, both now out of focus. Dickerson takes the sheet of teletype paper from the censor.

> Dickerson: This is not official news, Airman. As far as I'm concerned it didn't happen.
>
> Cronauer: What are you afraid of, Dickerson? People might find out there's a war going on?

When Cronauer changes his tone and apologizes to the officer, Dickerson is satisfied—perhaps skeptical of the airman's sincerity, but nevertheless satisfied enough to leave. If the audience is also caught off-guard by Cronauer's uncharacteristic acceptance of military authority and censorship, that does not last long.

When Cronauer goes into the booth to do his afternoon broadcast, cinematic techniques ensure that we the audience are aware of two things. First, Big Brother continues to watch, because we again see Cronauer take his seat and don his headphones from the perspective of the censors behind the glass window; indeed, the booth is partially obscured by the out-of-focus Dickerson in the foreground, giving us the effect of watching over Dickerson's shoulder. Second, as the camera angle changes, focusing now on a tight full-screen image of Cronauer's face and the microphone, the deejay's body language is uncharacteristically concerned and hesitant. Before launching into his trademark greeting, there is momentary silence as Cronauer looks around the room. After that greeting, and when he starts his broadcast, the camera angle changes again as we see Cronauer give the thumbs up to Dickerson (over whose shoulder we are still looking). Before returning to focus on Cronauer, Dickerson's emotionless face fills the screen as he stares through the glass at the irreverent airman. Cronauer makes some improvised jokes about stories involving Princess Margaret and Elizabeth Taylor, but his heart is not in it. The exhausted and traumatized Cronauer's head slumps, hitting the microphone. This seems to jolt him out of his temporary state, and he sits back upright. What he says next rounds out the importance of this scene to the film's messages about freedom of the press in a time of war: "In Saigon today, according to official sources, nothing actually happened. One thing that didn't officially happen was a bomb didn't officially explode at 1430 hours, unofficially destroying Jimmy Wah's café."

As we hear the words "bomb didn't officially explode," the camera pivots to see a livid Dickerson screaming (silently, because he is separated from us and Cronauer by the glass window) and slamming his palm against the window. Reluctantly, the staff are forced to cut the transmission of the broadcast midsentence, but not before Cronauer has reported more details, including the "unofficial" death toll. As Cronauer looks, perhaps with a degree of inevitable resignation, at the panel of dials in front of him that are no longer illuminated, the camera angle again changes. We are once again Dickerson, looking at the booth from behind the window. Then another cut puts us back in the booth as we, but not Cronauer, now look out—and up—at Dickerson, who gives one final look at the airman—is it a look of smug satisfaction?—and walks away. Finally, the camera focuses on Cronauer as he silently removes his headphones, pushes the microphone away, and lowers his head into his hand with defeated dejection. Reminiscent of scenes in *Good Night, and Good Luck* (chapter 5) and *All the President's Men* (chapter 3), the camera pulls back, slowly, and Cronauer diminishes in size, swallowed by his surroundings. The feeling of a "near-solitary confinement, an existence of interior space, space that brought the individual face to face with chaos"—a feeling of censorship—is complete.[35]

In his *Washington Post* review of GMV, Hal Hinson is deeply critical of the film, and in particular the scenes that followed Cronauer's suspension from the airwaves for this refusal to adhere to military protocol. "Once Levinson establishes that Cronauer is an embattled genius, the movie loses whatever starch it might have had," writes Hinson, and "the film's tone shifts from irreverent to serious and suddenly the subject becomes 'How I Went to Vietnam and Had My Consciousness Raised.'"[36] This critique completely ignores the importance of the freedom of the press narrative in the film.

NOT ALL CENSORSHIP IS UNCONSTITUTIONAL

There are two ways in which the fallout from this bombing censorship incident emphasizes the freedom of the press narrative in GMV. First, it reminds us that although Cronauer is ultimately a heroic figure in this film who in many ways triumphs over the unreasonable governmental efforts to muzzle him, not all of these instances of censorship should be considered unreasonable.

Although prior restraints are very rarely constitutional, those that *genuinely* advance national security have long been viewed by the courts as consistent with the First Amendment. The US Supreme Court established this in 1931, in one of its most famous decisions regarding freedom of the press. In his majority opinion in *Near v. Minnesota*, Chief Justice Charles Evans Hughes emphasized that it would be wrong to consider every prior restraint automatically unconstitutional; "in exceptional cases" such limitations on speech would be tolerated—but "*only* in exceptional cases."[37] Hughes quoted from Justice Oliver Wendell Holmes Jr.'s famous opinion in *Schenck v. United*

States (1919), observing that "[w]hen a nation is at war, many things that might be said in time of peace are such a hindrance to its effort that their utterance will not be endured so long as men fight."[38] Hughes provided a short list of examples of "exceptional cases,"[39] but the only example that remains good law today is his first. "No one," he wrote, "would question but that a government might prevent actual obstruction to its recruiting service or the publication of the sailing dates of transports or the number and location of troops."[40]

When the speaker is a member of the military community, governmental restrictions on, or punishments of, that speaker's utterances are afforded considerable deference by the courts, whether during a time of war or peace. As Rehnquist explained in his opinion for the court in *Parker v. Levy* in 1974, "the different character of the military community and of the military mission requires a different application of those protections. The fundamental necessity for obedience, and the consequent necessity for imposition of discipline, may render permissible within the military that which would be constitutionally impermissible outside it."[41] Indeed, as Elizabeth Beaumont explains, "the Court consistently treats the military *as a special and separate context or environment in which standard First Amendment protections do not apply.*" Speech by military personnel falls into one of the "major categories of special contexts" together with speech by "schoolchildren, incarcerated prisoners, and public employees."[42] Even strong defenders of First Amendment freedoms have accepted this status quo. For example, Thomas I. Emerson concluded, without contention, that "[t]he military system is outside the Civilian system of freedom of expression and is subject to different rules."[43] Period.

Of course, that is true—and not in an abstract theoretical sense. As Beaumont reminds us, the "military has always operated as a somewhat distinct society governed by its own criminal code" because it does indeed have its own criminal code—the Uniform Code of Military Justice (UCMJ).[44] Today, the UCMJ has an article devoted to "provoking speech or gestures" that reads as follows: "Any person subject to this chapter [the UCMJ] who uses provoking or reproachful words or gestures towards any other person subject to this chapter shall be punished as a court-martial may direct."[45] This clearly affords military personnel a *very different* level of speech protection from that which civilians enjoy under the First Amendment. Additionally, related articles address the use of "contemptuous words" against certain officials,[46] and "violat[ing] or fail[ing] to obey" orders and regulations.[47]

The UCMJ's "General Article" 134—which, among other things, can be and historically has been used to bring "indecent language" charges—is very broad. Its language, as defined in the *Manual for Courts-Martial United States*, addresses speech "which is grossly offensive to modesty, decency, or propriety, or shocks the moral sense, because of its vulgar, filthy, or disgusting nature, or its tendency to incite lustful thought. Language is indecent if it tends reasonably to corrupt morals or incite libidinous thoughts. The language must violate community standards."[48] This definition underscores the very different ways in which restrictions of speech are addressed in the military and civilian worlds.

These broad provisions apply to all service members, including those who are serving in media-related positions for the military (for, example, the American Forces Network, which operates the American Forces Radio and Television Service). Therefore, although no mention is made of the UCMJ in GMV, it should be very clear that bringing UCMJ violations charges against Cronauer for his actions—as portrayed in the film—would not have been difficult.[49]

MONTAGE

As we have seen, Cronauer's reaction to the bombing at Jimmy Wah's emphasizes the freedom of the press narrative in GMV by reminding us that not all censorship is inherently unreasonable. However, with some of the scenes that follow Cronauer's temporary suspension, we are also reminded of the very reason why censorship is inherently problematic—namely, its silencing of voices. This is achieved to great effect using montage, "a basic" but powerful cinematic "technique."[50]

After General Taylor (Noble Willingham)—who has more sympathy for Cronauer's style than any of the other commanding officers in the film—informs Lieutenant Steven Hauk (Bruno Kirby) that Cronauer has been taken off the air (Hauk and Dickerson share a contempt for the airman), there is a rapid cut from Hauk leaving through a door to an upward camera angle looking over a toilet stall door. From the point of view of Cronauer seated on the toilet, we see Garlick enter the frame. The point of view then changes, and from over Garlick's shoulder we look down at Cronauer. Garlick delivers the news that Cronauer has been reinstated. Cronauer does not care. He is defiant; he is not going back on the air. The conversation continues elsewhere in the bathrooms, and Cronauer emphasizes that the reason he won't get back behind the microphone is the censorship. Garlick will not let the issue drop. He later finds Cronauer in a restaurant and emphasizes that it is not just Cronauer's voice that has been silenced by the suspension.

Recall that there are two main ways that Cronauer gives the men in the field—the grunts—a voice in GMV. First, he literally gives them something to listen to; he is a voice that they would not otherwise get to hear. Although Garlick is concerned about this, he exhibits justifiably greater anguish at the way in which the suspension has not only silenced the airman's broadcasts but in doing so has also silenced the voice that aired the fears, concerns, and other such views of the soldiers—views they would not otherwise get to express.

As the two men leave the restaurant, Garlick won't let the matter drop. He drives himself and Cronauer out into the streets in a military-issue jeep. We begin to see troop transport trucks slowly moving through the congested thoroughfare, and at one point the jeep is surrounded by the trucks as traffic grinds to a halt. Most of the soldiers in the trucks—whose vantage point is deliberately higher than that of Cronauer and Garlick—are from the 1st Infantry Division of the US Army; their "Big Red One" shoulder patches identify them as such. To the initial embarrassment of Cronauer, Garlick stands up in the jeep and directs the soldiers' attention to the man beside him. In order to convince them that the passenger really is Cronauer, one of the soldiers asks him to do his trademark broadcast opening. "*Goooooooooood morning, Vietnam*!"—from the moment these words burst forth from his mouth, Cronauer the reluctant airman is suddenly transformed into Cronauer the irreverent disc jockey. It is as though he has taken his show on the road, into the fields.

This brings Cronauer "face-to-face with the reality of war." It is a profound—and profoundly important—moment in the film: "Nothing filters what he sees. These soldiers need to hear what he says. His irreverent ranting from the borderline between the sanitized view of the war and the unedited reality of battle experience serves a purpose beyond personal expression. He is speaking not just *to* the soldiers in the field; he is speaking *for* them."[51] As the trucks pull away, Cronauer sincerely and emotionally says, "Well, you guys take care of yourselves. I won't forget you." The point of view shifts; we now see the jeep from the perspective of the soldiers in the lead truck, as Cronauer and Garlick are left behind. As the other trucks pass by, close to the camera and out of focus, in the background we see Cronauer's in-focus face. This creates the dramatic effect of hemming Cronauer in, a prisoner to the hopes, dreams, and needs of the men he must once again give voice to.

The poignance of Cronauer's first dawn-busting broadcast after meeting these men—a broadcast that is very specifically "speaking *for* them" (Cronauer dedicates it to them)—is cinematically captured using a forty-one-shot montage sequence accompanied by Louis B. Armstrong's incredibly powerful song "What a Wonderful World." Through this montage, Levinson captures at least fifteen different aspects of the war, unsanitized and uncensored, flipping back and forth between the lives of the American GIs and the lives of the Vietnamese: transportation of soldiers; families sleeping on the streets; troops being loaded onto planes; workers in the fields and washing clothes in the rivers; military helicopters patrolling the skies; Lieuenant Hauk, pictured from a distance, a small and lonely figure in the confines of the radio station;

carpet bombing of Vietnamese villages and the accompanying death and destruction; Vietnamese people being rounded up by soldiers and summarily shot; GIs trying to pick up local women; Vietnamese protesters being beaten; members of the media being targeted for covering these events; and American troops wading through muddy jungles. As the song comes to an end, there is one final shot in the field—of two soldiers at a lookout post, listening to the radio that is hanging up next to them. There is a cut back to the booth, and the screen is filled with Cronauer's face and the microphone. His solemn expression speaks volumes.

Here, as in so many places in GMV, "[b]eneath the humor, tensions between song melodies, lyrics, and screen images," there is "create[d] a story of the conflict between official and unofficial versions of the Vietnam War."[52] And inextricably intertwined with that story is the narrative of press freedom. Although wartime and military censorship of expressive freedom is generally given *far* more legal and judicial deference than that which occurs during peacetime and with civilians, it is also important to remember that regardless, the work of someone like Cronauer is profoundly important.

WAR, OFF SCRIPT

Despite the aforementioned proliferation of Vietnam movies released in 1986 and 1987, GMV was a box office success. It was one of only seven films released in 1987 to reach a total gross in excess of $100 million (its total gross income was $123,922,370). Its 1987 release was *very* limited; it played in only four theaters until January 15, 1988. Once its run expanded to 785 theaters, its revenue increased by over 6,000 percent. It grossed $11,752,913 over the weekend of January 15–17 alone.[53]

By contrast, critical reactions to GMV were mixed, in large part because the movie bore little in common with "Hollywood's Vietnam"[54] as depicted in the other four 1986–1987 movies (*Platoon, Full Metal Jacket, Hanoi Hilton,* and *Hamburger Hill*). It "depart[ed] from expectations created by its subject matter, production era, and ostensible genre,"[55] and critics could not help but make their assessments comparative in nature. Henry A. Giroux's evaluation of the film is based upon the assumption, as he writes, that "[i]t is impossible to separate" GMV "from the context and content of Vietnam films that preceded it."[56] Unwilling to review the film objectively or solely on its merits, he concludes that it "willfully expunges the discourses of history, politics, and ethics from its narrative in order to appeal to a generation of youth raised on the affective energies of high-tech rock, 1980s yuppie buffoonery, and a narcissistic assertion of whiteness as the singular referent for intelligence, manhood, and sensuality."[57] Similarly, in his *Washington Post* review, Hinson concludes that GMV went "wrong in ways that are maddeningly obvious," and that cinematically the film failed, in part, because of "the flat, soft-focus view" used to shoot some of the scenes of Vietnamese villages and their residents, scenes that came "across as too uncomplicated, too tidy. Looking at Levinson's shots of both the countryside and the city," laments Hinson, "you can't help but think that the worst has happened—that he's turned Vietnam into a suburb."[58]

For similar reasons, Hinson also takes aim at Levinson's decision to make Williams's improvisation such an important element of the film. To Hinson, the actor's "free associative riffs seem[ed] whoppingly anachronistic. The attitudes towards gays, toward blacks, toward the war itself, come across as too hip for 1965." He contends that the film was "[v]isually . . . stultifyingly uninteresting, especially when Williams is stuck in his chair monologuing into the mike."[59] This ignores the point made earlier in this chapter about the way in which the deliberately restrictive confines of the radio booth make an important statement about the censored nature of the AFRS in Saigon in 1965. And it also—very significantly—ignores the rise of multiple protest movements throughout the 1960s.

Hinson does not hide his contempt for Williams's performance and Levinson's direction, concluding that "[i]t's one thing to want to turn Robin Williams into a star—it's another to turn him into Bob Hope."[60] In their reviews, Giroux and Hinson both seem to entirely miss the point of the film. They crave a Vietnam War film that is scripted in a particular way. This is unrealistic. After all, "What a Wonderful World" was used to ironic effect. And many of the points made in the film might be viewed for what they are—comedy. For example, the character Phil McPherson (one of the AFRS employees, played by Juney Smith) observes, "Well, we originally wanted Bob Hope" as entertainment for the troops, "but it turns out he won't come." "Why not?" asks Hauk. Garlick replies, "He doesn't play police actions, just wars. Bob likes a big room, sir." This, of course, is not accurate, because Hope, a comedian and entertainer beloved by the troops, did indeed make numerous tours to Vietnam, including in 1965.[61] Nevertheless, the criticism of Giroux and Hanson's reviews still stands, because they both craved a serious Vietnam *War* film set in the big theater of the battlefield, not a comedic movie set during the Vietnam War in a radio booth. They craved something other than *Good Morning, Vietnam*.

WAR *IS* DIFFERENT, BUT THE FIRST AMENDMENT STILL EXISTS

In the final passage of *Perilous Times*, Geoffrey Stone writes: "Freedom can endanger security, but it is also the fundamental source of American strength."[62] As this chapter makes clear, "freedom [of the press] can endanger security" during a time of war, and because of the significant national and international implications of that threat to security, governmental limits on freedom of the press are treated with considerable deference by the courts. The pages above also demonstrate, however, that freedom of the press is very much "the fundamental source of" the country's "strength."

Of particular importance is the way in which *Good Morning, Vietnam* emphasizes the role of a free press in ensuring that unpopular views see the light of day—even within the confines of the military community, and even during a time of war. The film achieves this through Cronauer's character; he might be a REMF, but he instinctively knows how to give the grunts a voice by (a) giving them something to listen to that would otherwise be censored, and (b) giving voice to their views and concerns that would otherwise go unheard.

In *When the Press Fails*, W. Lance Bennett, Regina G. Lawrence, and Steven Livingston write that "[t]here is little doubt that reporting which challenges the public pronouncements of those in power is difficult when anything deviating from authorized versions of reality is met with intimidating charges of bias."[63] This astute observation serves as a useful transition from the case study of *Good Morning, Vietnam*, the only film in this book that directly addresses freedom of the press during a time of war (*Citizenfour*, analyzed in chapter 8, discusses surveillance state activities in the context of the amorphous "War on Terror"), to the movies analyzed in the chapters that follow. As noted above, GMV achieves many of its freedom of the press goals through the use of a particular standpoint—"a point of view exhibiting distinctive, contextually derived values and 'from which particular features of reality are brought into sharp perspective and other features are obscured.'"[64] Bennett and colleagues observe that in the twenty-first century, "[f]inding the independent journalistic standpoints from which to speak truth to power"—as Cronauer did—"or at least to balance the talk of high-status officials with reasonable challenges" has become increasingly difficult because we live "in an information environment muddled by the conditions that increasingly define the U.S. public communication system."[65] The three most troubling conditions identified by Bennett and colleauges are (1) "*[t]he rise of a dominant class of communication professionals who manage most-high-level political situations*"; (2) "*[t]he decline of public debate on the democratic responsibilities of the media*"; and (3) "*[t]he spiral of public disconnection with and antagonism toward both politicians and the press*."[66]

Although these conditions are now, in the twenty-first century, accentuated and particularly problematic, they are by no means new problems (as their existence in GMV shows). Indeed, an overwhelming majority of the movies analyzed in the chapters that follow were either made in the 1900s or depict events from the twentieth century. Consequently, going forward readers are encouraged to consider the extent to which media conditions have either evolved or stayed the same over time. In so doing, readers will gain a comprehensive historical understanding of these cinematic representations of press freedom.

NOTES

1. *Ginzburg v. United States*, 383 U.S. 463, 498 (1966) (Stewart, J., dissenting).
2. Geoffrey R. Stone, *Perilous Times: Free Speech in Wartime, from the Sedition Act of 1798 to the War on Terrorism* (New York: Norton, 2004).
3. Alexander M. Bickel, *The Morality of Consent* (New Haven, CT: Yale University Press, 1975), 61.
4. Heywood Broun, quoted in Ezra Goodman, *The Fifty-Year Decline and Fall of Hollywood* (New York: Simon and Schuster, 1961), 423.
5. Neil Sheehan, *A Bright Shining Lie: John Paul Vann and America in Vietnam* (New York: Random House, 1988). Here it is worth noting that Sheehan was the *New York Times* journalist—briefly mentioned in chapter 3—who obtained the Pentagon Papers from Daniel Ellsberg.
6. William H. Rehnquist, *All the Laws but One: Civil Liberties in Wartime* (New York: Vintage, 1998), 224, italics added.
7. Francis Biddle, *In Brief Authority* (New York: Doubleday, 1962), 219.
8. Rehnquist, *All the Laws but One*, 221. Here, readers may find Mel Urofksy's article about the US Supreme Court's decision-making during World War II instructive. Melvin I. Urofsky, "The Court at War and the War at the Court," *Journal of Supreme Court History* 1996, no. 1 (1996): 1–18.
9. Stone, *Perilous Times*, 4–5.
10. Gilbert Adair, *Vietnam on Film: From The Green Berets to Apocalyse Now* (New York: Proteus, 1981), 173–90.
11. Gilbert Adair, *Hollywood's Vietnam* (London: Heinemann, 1989), 203–22.
12. Peter C. Rollins, "Using Popular Culture to Study the Vietnam War: Perils and Possibilities," in *Why We Fought: America's Wars in Film and History*, ed. Peter C. Rollins and John E. O'Connor (Lexington: University Press of Kentucky, 2008), 374; William J. Palmer, *The Films of the Eighties: A Social History* (Carbondale: Southern Illinois University Press, 1993), 25.
13. Rollins, "Using Popular Culture to Study the Vietnam War," 368.
14. Palmer, *Films of the Eighties*, 55.

15. Danielle Solzman, "Good Morning, Vietnam Turns 35 Years Old," *Solzy at the Movies*, December 23, 2022, https://www.solzyatthemovies.com/2022/12/23/good-morning-vietnam-turns-35-years-old/.

16. Palmer, *Films of the Eighties*, 25.

17. Rollins, "Using Popular Culture to Study the Vietnam War," 374.

18. Adrian Cronauer, "The Twenty-Third Charles L. Decker Lecture in Administrative and Civil Law," *Military Law Review* 183 (2005): 176, 76n1.

19. Cronauer, "Charles L. Decker Lecture," 176n1, 77.

20. Cronauer, "Charles L. Decker Lecture," 177.

21. Carla A. Fellers, "'What a Wonderful World': The Rhetoric of the Official and the Unofficial in *Good Morning, Vietnam*," *War, Literature & the Arts: An International Journal of the Humanities* 17, no. 1/2 (November 2005): 232.

22. Fellers, "What a Wonderful World," 233. Several of the characters in the movie, and then the television series, *M*A*S*H*, most notably Hawkeye Pierce, can similarly be described as representative of this "unofficial" standpoint.

23. Over the years, during different times of combat, they have also been called, variously, "pogues, chair-borne rangers . . . People Other Than Grunts (POGs), and Fobbits." Richard Faulkner, *Pershing's Crusaders: The American Soldier in World War I* (Lawrence: University Press of Kansas, 2017), 349. The latter term, "Fobbits," was particularly used during Operation Iraqi Freedom (2003–2011).

24. Kara Dixon Vuic, "The Guys in the Rear, with the Beer," *Reviews in American History* 41, no. 1 (March 2013): 140–44.

25. George "Sonny" Hoffman, quoted in Meredith H. Lair, *Armed With Abundance: Consumerism & Soldiering in the Vietnam War* (Chapel Hill: University of North Carolina Press, 2011), 63.

26. Fellers, "What a Wonderful World," 233.

27. Palmer, *Films of the Eighties*, 55.

28. Fellers, "What a Wonderful World," 233.

29. Cronauer, "Charles L. Decker Lecture," 177.

30. Quoted in Owen W. Gilman Jr., "Vietnam, Chaos, and the Dark Art of Improvisation," in *Inventing Vietnam: The War in Film and Television*, ed. Michael A. Anderegg (Philadelphia: Temple University Press, 1991), 235–36.

31. Gilman, "Vietnam, Chaos, and the Dark Art of Improvisation," 236.

32. Gilman, "Vietnam, Chaos, and the Dark Art of Improvisation," 244.

33. Gilman, "Vietnam, Chaos, and the Dark Art of Improvisation," 236.

34. Stanley Karnow, *Vietnam: A History*, 2nd ed. (New York: Penguin, 1997), 33.

35. Gilman, "Vietnam, Chaos, and the Dark Art of Improvisation," 235–36.

36. Hal Hinson, "'Good Morning, Vietnam,'" *Washington Post*, January 15, 1988.

37. 283 U.S. 697, 716 (1931), italics added.

38. *Schenck v. United States*, 249 U.S. 47, 52 (1919), quoted in 283 U.S. at 716.

39. 283 U.S. at 716.

40. 283 U.S. at 716. In 2003, after extensive pressure from the military, Fox News recalled its correspondent Geraldo Rivera from Iraq after the journalist included details of troop movements plans in his broadcast. David Carr, "Pentagon Says Geraldo Rivera Will Be Removed from Iraq," *New York Times*, April 1, 2003.

41. 417 U.S. 733, 758 (1974).

42. Elizabeth Beaumont, "Rights of Military Personnel," *First Amendment Encyclopedia*, updated July 29, 2023, https://firstamendment.mtsu.edu/article/rights-of-military-personnel/ (last accessed October 30, 2023).

43. Thomas I. Emerson, *The System of Freedom of Expression* (New York: Random House, 1970), 57.

44. Beaumont, "Rights of Military Personnel."

45. "917. ARTICLE 117. Provoking Speeches or Gestures," https://ucmj.us/917-article-117-provoking-speeches-or-gestures/ (last accessed March 31, 2023).

46. "888. ARTICLE 88. Contempt toward Officials," https://ucmj.us/888-article-88-contempt-toward-officials/ (accessed March 31, 2023).

47. "892. ARTICLE 92. Failure to Obey Order or Regulation," https://ucmj.us/892-article-92-failure-to-obey-order-or-regulation/ (accessed March 31, 2023).

48. Joint Service Committee on Military Justice, *Manual for Courts-Martial United States* (2019), IV-148, https://jsc.defense.gov/Portals/99/Documents/2019%20MCM%20(Final)%20(20190108).pdf?ver=2019–01–11–115724–610 (last accessed June 11, 2024).

49. An interesting point to note here is about the military newspaper *Stars and Stripes*, which is "partly funded by the military" but is also "editorially independent." The military has, in recent years, sought to remove funding from the newspaper in a manner that suggested the decision was motivated by censorship, not financial, concerns. See J. P. Lawrence, "*Stars and Stripes* Evades Cuts as the Military Embraces Secrecy," *Columbia Journalism Review*, December 9, 2020, https://www.cjr.org/first_person/stars-and-stripes-evades-cuts-as-the-military-embraces-secrecy.php.

50. Rollins, "Using Popular Culture to Study the Vietnam War," 385.

51. Fellers, "What a Wonderful World," 236.

52. Fellers, "What a Wonderful World," 232.

53. "Domestic Box Office for 1987," Box Office Mojo, https://www.boxofficemojo.com/year/1987/ (last accessed October 30, 2023); "Good Morning, Vietnam," Box Office Mojo, https://www.boxofficemojo.com/release/rl3713304065/weekend/ (last accessed October 30, 2023).

54. Rollins, "Using Popular Culture to Study the Vietnam War," 374.

55. Don Kunz, "Barry Levinson's Good Morning, Vietnam," *War, Literature & the Arts: An International Journal of the Humanities* 14, no. 1/2 (March 2002): 230.

56. Henry A. Giroux, "Memory and Pedagogy in the 'Wonderful World of Disney': Beyond the Politics of Innocence," in *From Mouse to Mermaid: The Politics of Film, Gender, and Culture*, ed. Elizabeth Bell, Lynda Haas, and Laura Sells (Bloomington: Indiana University Press, 1995), 50.

57. Giroux, "Beyond the Politics of Innocence," 51.

58. Hinson, "Good Morning, Vietnam."

59. Hinson, "Good Morning, Vietnam."

60. Hinson, "Good Morning, Vietnam."

61. Generally, see "Bob Hope," Vietnam Veterans Memorial Fund, https://www.vvmf.org/topics/Bob-Hope/ (last accessed April 11, 2023).

62. Stone, *Perilous Times*, 557.

63. W. Lance Bennett, Regina G. Lawrence, and Steven Livingston, *When the Press Fails: Political Power and the News Media from Iraq to Katrina* (Chicago: University of Chicago Press, 2007), 13.

64. Fellers, "What a Wonderful World," 232.

65. Bennett, Lawrence, and Livingston, *When the Press Fails*, 3.

66. Bennett, Lawrence, and Livingston, *When the Press Fails*, 3–4, italics in original.

Chapter 2

A Media Mogul Battles against His Fictional Doppelganger

Citizen Kane *and* RKO 281

Bruce E. Altschuler

As discussed in the introduction, filmmakers are storytellers. One of their favorite genres is the biopic, short for "biographical picture." Although the term was originally defined as a movie based on the life of a real person, Anna Baccanti argues that it can also include certain films with a fictional protagonist, because what distinguishes this type of film is "the narrative structure and the thematic focus on a person's life story." She specifically cites *Citizen Kane* (1941), with its title character's strong resemblance to real life newspaper magnate William Randolph Hearst.[1] This allows the film to depict the nineteenth-century transformation of newspapers into a mass medium through the life of Charles Foster Kane.

Because the purpose of a biopic is to expose the "real person" hidden behind their public facade, Rafaela Bassili explains that "the challenge for the filmmaker is to use artifice to reveal the person behind the persona—in other words, using fiction to reveal truth."[2] One of the main reasons *Citizen Kane* is so acclaimed is its use of novel techniques to accomplish this goal.

This chapter discusses the following cinematic key points:

- How *Citizen Kane* depicts its main character, who is based on a real-life media mogul.
- Director Orson Welles's use of deep focus and other innovations to tell his story.
- Welles's use of multiple narrators to force the audience to play the role of a reporter judging their credibility.

- How more recent films such as *RKO 281* and *Mank* depict the making of *Citizen Kane* and Hearst's attempts to prevent movie theaters from showing it.

Is a 1941 film relevant in today's age of twenty-four-hour television news and social media? Charlotte Rawlings believes that its "black and white depiction of journalism may be nearly a century old, but its relevance is yet to fade." She points to the film's depiction of what today might be termed "fake news" in its account of Kane's coverage of Cuba; Kane's statement that "the news goes on for 24 hours a day" to explain why he put a bed in his office; and the fictional editor's asking the reporter writing about Kane's final word, "Rosebud," to use multiple sources to ascertain the truth (something that will be crucial in the next chapter's discussion of *All the President's Men*).[3] This chapter will also discuss the following legal questions:

- Did the transformation of the press into a true mass medium affect how the First Amendment was interpreted?
- As media moguls consolidated ownership by acquiring competitors, how did their pursuit of profit affect whether they served the public interest that the First Amendment was designed to protect?
- How well does the concept of the "marketplace of ideas" help the public distinguish between accurate and false information?
- Does the First Amendment protection of the media against government interference create a loophole that allows wealthy private individuals and powerful corporations to attempt censorship? Or, as has often been stated, does freedom of the press apply only to those who can afford to own one?
- How should the law deal with "fake news"?

THE REVOLUTION OF THE PENNY PRESS

In an age where print media has lost so much of its readership, why should viewers care about the rise and fall of a newspaper baron? Laura Mulvey argues that the influence of Rupert Murdoch demonstrates the continuing importance of media moguls, even if the media has changed significantly since *Kane*'s heyday.[4] Other modern-day potentates, most notably Mark Zuckerberg of Facebook, also have outsized influence over public opinion.

Because the fictional Charles Foster Kane (Orson Welles) bears such an uncanny and not coincidental resemblance to the real-life mogul William Randolph Hearst, it is important to understand the context of American newspapers in the era of the "yellow press" when Hearst was at his most influential. In the 1790s, when the First Amendment was added to the Constitution, newspaper readership consisted of those who could afford to purchase mail subscriptions at the price of six cents per issue. As Michael Schudson has written, "[R]eadership was confined to mercantile and political elites." This changed during the 1830s, a decade that "marked a revolution in American journalism" when the penny press reached more of a mass audience.[5] The invention of the cylinder press in the 1830s allowed for the printing of fifteen hundred copies per hour. During the same period, the growth of cities created an audience for these inexpensive newspapers. The first of the penny press newspapers was the *New York Sun.* It prospered by featuring crime news, but its reporting standards were low until Charles Dana took over after the Civil War with the promise of "a daily photograph of the whole world's doings in the most luminous and lively manner."[6]

In 1830, there were 650 weekly newspapers and 65 dailies, with a total circulation of 78,000. Ten years later the number had increased to 1,141 weeklies and 138 dailies, with a circulation of 300,000, while the American population only increased from about 13 million to 17 million. Because success depended on a circulation large enough to attract advertisers to make up for their low price, these newspapers, writes Schudson, "began to reflect, not the affairs of an elite in a small trading society, but the activities of an increasingly varied, urban and middle class society."[7] They expressed "the culture of a democratic market society, a culture which had no place for social or intellectual deference."[8] This almost perfectly describes the philosophy of Charles Foster Kane, the fictional subject of *Citizen Kane*.

James Gordon Bennett's *New York Herald* covered the news, particularly crime news, in an even more sensational manner than his rivals. In his most famous stunt, he sent Henry Stanley to Africa to find Dr. David Livingstone. Horace Greeley's *New York Tribune* set higher standards, including the establishment of an editorial page, but when he ran as the Democratic candidate against President Ulysses S. Grant, he lost badly.

In 1883, Joseph Pulitzer bought the failing *New York World.* According to James McGrath Morris, "Pulitzer was part of a new order of journalism—lively, independent and crusading."[9] Before coming to New York, he had transformed the bankrupt *St. Louis Post* into a popular and profitable newspaper. The *World*'s spectacular headlines and entertaining stories soon made it the most widely read newspaper in the United States. Pulitzer believed that his paper "should be more powerful than the president."[10]

After turning the *San Francisco Examiner* into a profitable publication, Hearst, supplied with funds by his mother, entered the highly competitive New York market with his purchase of the *New York Morning Journal*, one of the weakest of the city's eight morning papers. According to David

Nasaw, Hearst used the infusion of cash "to ruthlessly strip Pulitzer of his remaining talent."[11] His acquisitions even included the comic character the Yellow Kid, which gave the style used by newspapers of the time the appellation of "yellow journalism." According to Morris, the fight between the two men "sucked the newspapers into a spiraling descent of sensationalism, outright fabrications and profligate spending that threatened the survival of both."[12] Eventually, writes Nasaw, Hearst "built the nation's first media conglomerate by extending his newspaper empire horizontally into syndicated feature, photo, and wire services; magazines; newsreels; serial, feature and animated films; and radio."[13]

CITIZEN KANE

The idea of making a film whose protagonist strongly resembled Hearst came from screenwriter Herman Mankiewicz, who knew Hearst quite well. After studying all the available scripts, Robert Carringer believed that the first draft was "by and large a literal reworking of specific incidents and details from Hearst's life."[14] Simon Callow has written that because "Hearst was absolutely, unmistakably and actionably the central character," it would not be legally possible to shoot that draft. Instead, director Orson Welles rewrote the script to make Kane more complex, telling an interviewer that "one of the authors hated Kane and one of them loved him."[15] Kane resembles several prominent newspaper publishers, but none as much as Hearst.

The 2020 movie *Mank* suggested that Mankiewicz wrote the original draft as revenge against Hearst for the Hollywood-financed newsreel campaign to defeat the socialist Upton Sinclair's candidacy for governor of California, but this seems far-fetched at best. According to Greg Mitchell, "[T]here's not a shred of proof that Hearst actually financed those phony newsreels . . . nor that Mankiewicz objected," although Hearst's newspapers regularly attacked Sinclair.[16]

The Rise of Charles Foster Kane

Citizen Kane opens on a dark night with somber music as the camera encounters a "No Trespassing" sign. As undeterred as a reporter seeking to expose the secrets of the powerful, the camera continues on through a fence to Charles Foster Kane's palatial estate of Xanadu, where it shows him dropping a snow globe as he utters his dying word: "Rosebud." The tone is set for the audience to interpret the inconsistent stories told by those who knew Kane best in order to try and understand his life.

The movie provides the basic details of Kane's life in a newsreel, *News on the March*. At the time *Kane* was made, newsreels often preceded the theater's feature film. Because few could afford television sets, these short films provided the only way to see the news for an audience estimated at 40 million in the United States and more than 200 million worldwide.[17] The film's newsreel is so much a parody of Henry Luce's *March of Time* that Welles wanted to hire its narrator, but because that would have cost too much, he instead used William Alland, who also played reporter Jerry Thompson. To give the newsreel an authentic look, the film was dragged across the floor and stepped on.[18]

The facts of Kane's life presented by the newsreel, however, are not enough to understand him. In a dark screening room when the newsreel ends, Thompson is given the job of learning the meaning of Kane's final word in hopes that it will provide the key to understanding his life. As Thompson's boss explains, "All I saw on that screen is that Charles Foster Kane is dead." By not showing the face of either Thompson or his colleagues throughout the film, Welles forces the audience into his role of decoding the interviews of those who knew Kane the best. As Mulvey puts it, the viewer has to "interpret clues and symptoms on the screen as might a detective or a psychoanalyst"[19]—or, especially, a reporter. This was clearly Welles's intention. As he told an interviewer, Kane "is never judged with the objectivity of an author and the point of the picture is not so much the solution of the problem as its presentation."[20]

In contrast to Hearst, whose father was a wealthy man who made his fortune through mining and served as a United States Senator from California, Kane came from far humbler origins. However, young Charles's life was transformed when an apparently worthless deed to a mine given to his mother to pay the rent in her rooming house turned out to be worth a fortune after gold was discovered on the property. In a crucial scene, Charles's parents turn over his upbringing to banker Walter Thatcher (George Coulouris), who will bring him to the East from Colorado. Welles's and cinematographer Gregg Toland's use of deep focus allows us a clear view through the window of Charles playing in the snow at the same time as his parents are negotiating with Thatcher, rather than having to cut from one to the other. The rebellious Charles hits the banker with his sled and unsuccessfully attempts to run away. Later, we will see snow piling up on that sled, followed by a dissolve to Thatcher presenting him with a more expensive one as a Christmas present. The audience will understand the importance of these scenes only at the very end of the movie. This is one reason that it takes more than a single viewing to understand the movie fully.

After Kane's second wife, Susan Alexander (Dorothy Comingore), rebuffs Thompson's attempt to interview her, his next stop is the Thatcher Memorial

Library, an intimidating institution dominated by a huge statue of its late founder. Thatcher's memoir, presented in flashback (as are the stories of the other witnesses), jumps from his removal of Charles from his parents to Kane's coming of age when, after showing no interest in most of his extensive holdings, he informs Thatcher that it could be "fun" to run a newspaper. A montage shows the banker angrily reading a series of articles from Kane's newspapers denouncing his businesses.

When Thatcher tries to explain that this muckraking is damaging to Kane's own financial interests, Kane replies that as a businessman, he fully agrees and would even donate funds to opposing these articles, but he is also a second person, a newspaper publisher dedicated to exposing the truth. This answer skips over the fact that newspapers are also businesses with their own financial interests. As Sarah Street points out, the film exposes the contradictions between monopoly journalists and their political rhetoric.

Despite Kane's start as an antitrust crusader, he quickly buys rival newspapers in order to build a media empire. While claiming to represent the public, he is opposed to labor unions.[21] In recent years, the creation of media conglomerates has accelerated dramatically, including the consolidation of newspapers. In 2019, New Media Investment Group purchased the Gannett newspaper chain, including *USA Today*. The merged companies owned 260 daily papers and more than 300 weeklies in forty-seven states. A year later, when McClatchy Newspapers, which had been family owned for 163 years, filed for bankruptcy, it was purchased by a hedge fund, Chatham Asset Management. Between 2006 and 2018, McClatchy cut its workforce from 15,000 to 3,300.[22] As of 2018, ten companies owned 1,500 newspapers, including 572 of 1,283 dailies in the United States. About half of all newspapers changed ownership in a fifteen-year period, most family owned or small regional chains selling to larger conglomerates.[23] The result has been a dramatic reduction in employment and the closing of numerous local newspapers, reducing expensive, labor-intensive investigative reporting. The First Amendment may have been designed to protect newspapers against government interference, but it was no safeguard against the pursuit of profit that has put so many newspapers out of business.

Typical of Kane's "yellow journalism" is a story told in Thatcher's narrative about a Cuba correspondent who reports on the absence of war. "You provide the prose poems," Kane replies, "I'll provide the war." This is an echo of an incident in which Hearst reportedly telegraphed photographer Frederick Remington, who asked to return home because of a lack of action, "You furnish the pictures and I'll furnish the war." However, Hearst's biographer, David Nasaw, was unable to find a record of either telegram.[24] Because no other prominent reporters were on the scene, this "fake news" would likely have been accepted as truth by many of Kane's readers, much as a considerable amount of today's disinformation is believed by those whose news comes from a single ideologically biased source.

The story is then picked up by Bernstein (Everett Sloane), Kane's loyal chief assistant, who is referred to only by his surname. Accompanied by Jed Leland (Joseph Cotten), he and Kane take over the *Inquirer*, a staid newspaper whose circulation of 26,000 is a fraction of its more sensationalist competitor, the *Chronicle*. When the previous editor opposes an increase in crime stories based on speculation and innuendo, Kane tells him, "If the headlines are big enough, the stories will be." As circulation rises to nearly 500,000, Kane hires his competitor's best reporters, increasing readership to nearly 700,000. These events are quite similar to Hearst's buildup of the *New York Morning Journal*, discussed earlier in this chapter. The big headlines can be seen as analogous to modern "clickbait."

Kane balances this by publishing a Declaration of Principles, promising readers to "present all the news immediately and honestly" and to be "a fighting and tireless champion of their rights as citizens," on the front page. Hearst's New York newspaper, during its third year, similarly declared in a front-page editorial that "a new force has appeared on the side of good government." Leland, who serves as the conscience of the film, asks to keep the handwritten copy, but because Kane's face is in shadow during this scene and he pauses before signing, the film appears to be questioning his sincerity. Welles told Peter Bogdanovich that Kane's smile at Leland's skepticism was "the smile of somebody deeply embarrassed; being caught out. . . . He doesn't believe in anything."[25]

Later in the film, explaining Kane's political ambitions, Leland puts this thought somewhat differently: "He never believed in anything except Charlie Kane. He never had a conviction except Charlie Kane in his life." Benjamin Huffbauer believes that this is why Donald Trump, in 1992 and 2016 interviews, identified *Citizen Kane* as his favorite movie. (Huffbauer points to Trump's many changes of position.)[26] A good example would be Trump's frequent changes of party affiliation. In 1987 he registered as a Republican, then switched to the Independence Party in 1999 when he ran for its presidential nomination in the California primary the next year. He became a Democrat in 2001, reregistered as a Republican in 2009, registered in 2011 as unaffiliated with a party, then finally returned to the Republican Party in 2012.[27] Huffbauer also notes the palatial estates—Xanadu for Kane and Mar-a-Lago for Trump—owned by both.[28] In addition, despite their very different upbringings, Kane and Trump began their careers with substantial bequests from their parents. So fascinated is Trump with *Citizen Kane* that he filmed a short interview on the subject with famed documentary filmmaker Errol Morris in 2002. However, his answer to Morris's final question, which asked what advice he would have for the fictional Kane, suggests limited insight into the movie's main themes. Without pausing for thought or indicating any irony, Trump replied, "Get yourself a different woman."[29]

When Kane heads off to Europe, he gets engaged to marry Emily Norton (Ruth Warrick), the president's niece. Contrary to Bernstein's quip that she could before too long become a president's wife, their marriage slowly deteriorates. The film presents this cleverly and economically in a breakfast montage that begins with the loving couple seated side by side. The distance between them increases over the years as, through the use of whip pans, the table elongates. When Emily states her dislike of Kane's paper's criticism of the president, stating, "People will think—" he interrupts: "what I tell them to think." By the end of the scene, Kane is seated at one end of the table with the *Inquirer* while Emily, at the other end, peruses the *Chronicle*.

Meanwhile, the *Inquirer* is celebrating its success with a party that was originally set in a brothel. Because movies were "voluntarily" censored at the time, production code administrator Joseph Breen demanded the scene be removed as a violation of the code. Welles filmed it anyway, but a second warning forced him to delete it. After Breen also required that there be "an absolute minimum of drinking and drunkenness," the final version shows champagne being poured but no one actually consuming it.[30] There is considerable irony in the censorship of a movie about the press. Fortunately, Welles didn't mind the deletion because he thought the scene "wasn't that good."[31]

The Fall of Charles Foster Kane

After Leland takes over the story at the height of Kane's success, the film indicates his decline by changing from bright, high-contrast lighting to something harsher as he abandons his early idealism to pursue more selfish ends. In a crucial scene, Kane, literally and symbolically splattered by mud on his way to a warehouse to retrieve his late mother's possessions,[32] meets Susan Alexander, a young woman suffering from a toothache who lives nearby. This begins a romance that will end Kane's first marriage and lead to his second. Kane's political ambitions convince him to run for governor on a reform platform. At a rally, speaking in front of a larger-than-life poster of himself, Kane promises that his first act in office will be to prosecute political "boss" Jim Gettys (Ray Collins). Unfortunately for Kane, Gettys learns of his affair with Susan and arranges a confrontation at her apartment. The exposure ends both Kane's political career and his marriage. The "yellow press" that Kane was so influential in creating proved the instrument of his defeat.

Hearst's political ambitions to be governor of New York and president were also derailed, but not because of an extramarital affair. He was elected to Congress in 1902 and 1904 as a progressive Democrat. However, when he ran for mayor of New York City in 1905, it was as a third-party reform candidate.

Opposition by the Democratic Party organization resulted in a narrow defeat, possibly tainted by fraud. He continued to run unsuccessfully for office: for governor as a Democrat in 1906, for mayor as an independent in 1909, and for governor again in 1922, when he lost the Democratic nomination to Al Smith. As the years passed, Hearst's politics became more conservative. Although he grudgingly supported Franklin Roosevelt in the 1932 presidential election, as New Deal laws increasing taxes on the wealthy and favorable to trade unions were enacted his newspapers began referring to the "Raw Deal." By 1936, Hearst contributed $30,000 (the equivalent of approximately $675,000 in 2023) to Roosevelt's opponent, Alf Landon.

By showing the *Inquirer* replacing its planned headline of "Kane Elected" with "Fraud at the Polls," the film wittily comments on the partisanship of the media in a way that is still relevant in light of the 2020 presidential election. After the election, a drunken Leland confronts Kane, warning him that workers want rights, not gifts from above.

With his political ambitions frustrated, Kane marries Susan and throws his energies into making her a successful opera singer, using his newspapers to promote her career, whether she likes it or not. Declaring that "we're going to be a great opera star," he even builds an opera house in Chicago for her debut. Welles denied that Susan was modeled on Hearst's mistress Marion Davies, a successful comic actress who appeared in some forty films. According to Welles, "Marion was much better than Susan—whom people wrongly equated with her."[33] Because Hearst's wife refused a divorce, he remained married for forty-seven years, living with Davies, quite happily, at his San Simeon castle for much of that time. In the movie, Emily Kane and her son die in an automobile accident not long after the divorce, leaving Kane childless for the remainder of the movie, while Hearst was a devoted father to five sons all his life.

Susan's debut is an unmitigated disaster. Welles shows this creatively by having the camera slowly rise to show two workers, high above the stage, holding their noses. Kane, however, has arranged rave reviews in his newspapers—but there is one exception: Jed Leland. When an inebriated Leland passes out before completing his negative review, Kane takes over, completing the review just as the critic had intended, then firing his friend. Leland tells Thompson that this was Kane's way of demonstrating his own honesty. Like Leland, screenwriter Mankiewicz once passed out drunk while writing a review, in his case for the *New York Times* in 1925, but no one ever completed it.[34]

Susan's description of these events differs from Leland's, focusing on her resistance to Kane pushing her to become an opera diva. She berates her husband after learning that he had given Leland a $25,000 severance check, only to see him opening an envelope with the check torn into small pieces accompanied by the original handwritten Declaration of Principles. He rips it up, describing the document as "an antique." Pushed to continue her tour, Susan is able to stop it only by attempting suicide. Kane retreats to his lavish Xanadu estate, overstuffed with statues and other items he has accumulated over the years. A bored and isolated Susan, consoled only by completing jigsaw puzzles, eventually leaves him.

In a final effort to decode "Rosebud," Thompson approaches Kane's butler, Raymond (Paul Stewart), who asks to be paid $1,000 for the secret, an early example of what would later be termed "checkbook journalism," although Raymond's information proved so unimportant that he never received any payment.[35] Raymond's account shows Kane, in a fit of anger, smashing Susan's room and remaining possessions after she leaves him. As the audience watches Kane's largely worthless trove of possessions incinerated, Thompson concludes that no single word can explain the life of someone as complex as Kane. The audience, however, learns one fact that neither the reporter nor anyone else in the film is aware of as it watches the remnants of young Charles's sled Rosebud burn up, lost in the other detritus of his life. This leaves open the question of whether Thompson is correct, or whether Kane's final word suggests that his entire life has been an attempt to compensate for the loss of his parents by accumulating power and searching for love. The movie's final shot, showing the camera exiting from Xanadu as it again passes the "No Trespassing" sign, echoes the opening. Rosebud turned out to be less a key to Kane's life than a device to tell his life story to the audience.

Profits versus Personal Ambition

When Thatcher warned Kane that his attacks on corporations were harming his own financial holdings, Kane replied that he was rich enough that this would make little immediate difference to his finances. Although one theme of this chapter is the potential conflict between privately owned media making a profit and the public service obligation that is the justification for singling the press out for First Amendment protection, for media moguls there is a third factor: The influence of their media empires gives them a platform to advance their own ambitions and policy preferences. For Kane this meant his unsuccessful campaign for governor, which he hoped would eventually lead to the presidency. His newspapers also provided an opportunity to promote his wife's singing career even if she lacked the talent and desire to succeed.

Modern moguls have become so wealthy that they can pursue their personal ends at even less relative cost than Kane. Rupert Murdoch and Elon Musk provide examples of how considerations of personal influence and ambition can override the pursuit of profit. When the Australian Murdoch bought the *New York Post* in 1976, he started what would eventually become a media empire in the United States, most notably the cable network Fox News. Because of federal regulations limiting cross-ownership of newspapers and television stations in the same city, he sold the newspaper in 1988, but he bought it back five years later, after these regulations were eased, and has owned it ever since. If the pursuit of profit is so important, why would Murdoch so stubbornly hold on to this local newspaper? The *Post* "has never made a penny," Jonathan Mahler points out, "but it has been a powerful cultural force."[36] Having an important voice in New York City, the cultural and media capital of the United States, is important to Murdoch. Eric Alterman notes that although the *Post* loses between $30 million and $50 million per year, all of Murdoch's newspapers taken together generate only 14 percent of News Corp's income. "What they cost in cash," he believes, "they more than make up in political and propaganda value."[37]

Musk, famous as the entrepreneur behind Tesla and SpaceX, only became a media magnate when he purchased the social media company Twitter, which he soon renamed X, in 2022 for $40 billion. As Twitter/X's value declined, Musk himself admitted that he paid at least twice what it was worth. Even though the changes Musk made have failed to improve the company's bottom line, David Nasaw believes that this "makes perfect sense," because "the platform provides him with a guaranteed, controlled, uncensorable, unedited outlet to market himself and his products" to tens of millions of users. Much like Murdoch, the money he loses is a fraction of his $180 billion net worth.[38]

RKO 281

After Hearst learned about *Citizen Kane*, he devoted extraordinary efforts to preventing its release. These actions, which contributed to the film's failure at the box office despite numerous rapturous reviews, are the subject of the 1999 movie *RKO 281* and will make up much of the rest of this chapter.

Citizen Kane has not only inspired the creativity of filmmakers who came after, it has also been the subject of several movies such as *Mank*, about the role of Herman Mankiewicz in writing the script, which was discussed earlier in this chapter. A 1995 Oscar-nominated documentary, *The Battle over Citizen Kane*, examined Hearst's attempted suppression of *Citizen Kane* and led to a fictionalized film about these events, *RKO 281*, whose title was the studio's code name for *Citizen Kane*.

The documentary's portrayal of Welles's fight for artistic freedom spurred Ridley Scott to try to make a dramatic film on the subject, but no Hollywood studio was interested in financing his project.[39] Coincidentally, at the same time, David Fincher was pitching *Mank*, which would take another two decades to get made.[40] Scott convinced HBO to fund his movie, but its lower budget forced him to make changes from the original cast of Edward Norton as Welles, Marlon Brando as Hearst, and Madonna as Marion Davies, and to turn over directing to Benjamin Ross. He remained as executive producer.[41]

RKO 281 opens with two scenes that attempt to mimic the style of *Citizen Kane*. The first briefly shows young Orson's mother on her deathbed telling him he will have just one chance at greatness. This is followed by a newsreel laying out Welles's pre-*Kane* career. Several other scenes are also pale imitations of counterparts in *Kane*. *RKO 281* signals that it will take significant liberties with the facts by telling the audience that it is "based in part" on the documentary *The Battle over Citizen Kane*.

These opening scenes are followed by Welles (Liev Schreiber) and Mankiewicz (John Malkovich) attending a huge party thrown by Hearst (James Cromwell) at San Simeon, the counterpart of Kane's Xanadu. Welles's story about bullfighting charms everyone except Hearst, who believes the sport to be barbaric. Welles is offended by the straitlaced Hearst. Although the visit inspires him to create a film about the newspaper magnate, Mankiewicz resists, fearing Hearst's power, but he later shows Welles notes on the subject that he has been accumulating over the years and agrees to write the script.

This scene has been criticized because it is entirely fictional. Although Mankiewicz was a frequent guest of Hearst's, Welles never was. Ross believes that his invention was justified: "I don't think that sort of liberty is a disgraceful one, because it doesn't go against any fundamental truths about Welles."[42] However, the scene also misrepresents the beginning of *Kane* in another way: It was Mankiewicz, not Welles, who originated the idea of making a movie about a fictionalized version of Hearst, with the title *American*.[43] As discussed earlier, the original script modeled Kane so closely on Hearst that Welles had to make significant modifications.

RKO 281 emphasizes the role played by gossip columnists Hedda Hopper (Fiona Shaw) and Louella Parsons (Brenda Blethyn) in informing Hearst about *Kane* and pressuring RKO not to release the film. Welles tries to court both, denying that his movie is about Hearst, but Hopper demands to see an early version, even if it is only a rough cut. After the screening, she slaps Welles, then calls Hearst to tell him that he is the movie's subject. Hearst angrily confronts Parsons, asking why she was not as well informed as her rival. Although *RKO 281* shows Hearst turning off a projector showing *Kane*, there is no evidence that he ever saw the movie.

Because no film can be comprehensive, *RKO 281* covers only some of Hearst's efforts to prevent the release of *Kane*. Hearst used several tactics to achieve this goal: personal attacks on Welles, putting pressure on theater owners and studios to prevent screenings, and convincing other studios to try to buy all copies of *Kane* in order to destroy them. The film shows Louis B. Mayer (David Suchet) meeting with other studio heads to arrange a purchase of all *Kane* prints, but doesn't mention why RKO was unwilling to accept their offer of $800,000. One reason was that Welles threatened to sue for breach of contract. Instead, the studio heads simply agreed not to book *Kane* in any of their thousands of theaters.

Parsons took three weeks off from her column to work against *Kane* by threatening to expose misdeeds of actors that she had been covering up as well as fanning the flames of anti-Semitism against the studio heads, most of whom were Jewish. On January 9, 1940, Hearst's newspapers removed mention not only of *Kane*, but of all RKO films. The ban on other RKO films only lasted about two weeks, but the one on *Kane* continued for eight months.

Hearst went so far as to call Welles a communist, leading to an FBI report that concluded that *Kane* was "an extension of the Communist Party's campaign to smear one of its most effective and consistent opponents."[44] These attacks went too far when Hearst criticized, and labeled as communist propaganda, a Welles radio program supporting free speech. The backlash caused the audience for the rest of the series to double.[45] Although early drafts of the *RKO 281* script include the FBI's investigation of Welles, the final version dropped this topic as a distraction from the main plot.[46]

Welles fought back, with greater support from George Schaefer (Roy Scheider), his studio's head, than *RKO 281* suggests. On January 22, Welles spoke at a screening of studio holding company executives and their attorneys, followed by a series of private screenings for other important Hollywood figures. The quality of the film proved an antidote for many, although Hearst's pressure continued to make finding theaters willing to show *Kane* difficult.

Nor did other media outlets uniformly support Hearst's campaign. Magazine magnate Henry Luce was one of the first to view Welles's film. Amused by the parody of his own newsreel and not particularly fond of Hearst, he ran favorable stories in both *Time* and *Life*.[47] In *Newsweek*, *Time*'s main rival, John O'Hara, told readers to "go to your neighborhood exhibitor and ask him why he isn't showing *Citizen Kane*."[48]

Finally, the film shows Welles's plea to RKO executives to stand up for free speech at a time when Adolf Hitler is threatening Europe. Schaefer explains that it was a "pretty speech," but that RKO will release *Kane* because Hearst's serious financial difficulties have reduced his leverage. *RKO 281* shows Marion Davies (Melanie Griffith) selling her jewelry for $1 million, but considering that Hearst's debt was about $125 million, that had no more than a symbolic impact.

To make for a more dramatic conclusion, *RKO 281* takes significant liberties with the facts. At *Kane*'s premiere, Schaefer tells Welles he made a great movie, but that Schaefer had been fired as head of RKO. In fact, Schaefer was fired two years later because of problems with *The Magnificent Ambersons*

(Welles's next picture) and poor overall box office results at RKO. Welles was so satisfied with his support from Schaefer that he called him "an absolute hero. He was marvelous to me."[49]

Also embellished is an anecdote about Welles encountering Hearst in a hotel elevator the day the movie opened in San Francisco. As Welles told Bogdanovich, after introducing himself, he invited Hearst to the premiere. Receiving no reply, he told Hearst that "Charles Foster Kane would have accepted." Hearst silently exited the elevator.[50] The *RKO 281* version invents a debate between the two as Hearst rebukes Welles for "the damage you have done." He then prophetically summarizes their future lives: "My battle with the world is over. Yours is only beginning." The scene ends with Welles's actual speculation about what Kane would have done. The audience then sees Welles and Mankiewicz having a drink, Hearst and Davies dancing, and the *Citizen Kane* premiere.

Finally, a series of titles tells us what happened to the principals and that despite strong reviews, *Kane* did poorly at the box office but is considered a great movie. Surprisingly unmentioned is that it received nine Oscar nominations but won only one, for best screenplay.

Despite winning best picture awards from the New York Film Critics Circle and the National Board of Review, *Citizen Kane* lost $150,000 and was withdrawn from circulation by RKO in 1942. David Nasaw concluded that because of the film's unconventional structure, "it is doubtful that the film would have been a box-office hit even had Hearst's associates not interfered with its distribution," citing the decline of business in New York City even after a strong opening.[51] Similarly, Robert Carringer believes that even though difficulties finding theaters hurt, "it is unlikely that they made a crucial difference" because *Kane* was not a movie designed to appeal to a commercial audience.[52]

It was television that revived *Kane* after RKO sold its film library to that medium during the 1950s. At about the same time, to take advantage of Welles's starring role in a Broadway production of *King Lear*, the film was rereleased in theaters. By the 1960s, *Kane* was ranked first in polls of great films by *Sight and Sound* and other publications.

CITIZEN KANE AND CENSORSHIP

If the First Amendment seems largely absent from *Citizen Kane*, it is; constitutional protection for freedom of the press "did not become the cornerstone of the law of the press until the twentieth century" when the Supreme Court held that the First Amendment applied to the states as well as the federal government.[53] When it came to defending *Citizen Kane* from Hearst's attempts to prevent its being shown, government may not have been involved, but Welles invoked the symbolic value of the First Amendment in his defense.

The Supreme Court's lack of freedom of the press cases during the nineteenth century does not mean that there were no important legal developments. Even before the Constitution was adopted and the First Amendment added, Thomas Jefferson wrote to a friend in 1786 that "our liberty depends on the freedom of the press and that cannot be limited without being lost."[54] The first crisis after the approval of the Constitution and Bill of Rights came with the passage of the 1798 Sedition Act, which criminalized the publication of "false, scandalous, and malicious" material that would bring Congress or the president into "contempt or disrepute." The seventeen indictments and ten convictions were mostly of journalists. Jefferson made the law an important issue in his successful presidential campaign, after which it was repealed and those convicted were pardoned by the newly elected president. These actions prevented any cases from reaching the Supreme Court for review. In his inaugural address, Jefferson stressed the importance of preserving the right of citizens "to think freely and to speak and to write what they think."[55] By 1964, despite the lack of a definitive Supreme Court ruling, Justice William J. Brennan's majority opinion in *New York Times v. Sullivan* concluded that "[a]lthough the Sedition Act was never tested in this Court, the attack upon its validity has carried the day in the court of history." Justice William O. Douglas came to a similar conclusion five years later.[56]

Despite justified praise of Jefferson for his statements supporting a free press, the criticism he received during his presidency weakened that support. In an 1807 letter, he wrote "nothing can now be believed which is seen in a newspaper, truth itself becomes suspicious by being put into that polluted vehicle."[57] Presidents since Jefferson have often come to similar conclusions. In his study of relations between presidents and the media, Harold Holzer concluded that "no American President has ever counted himself fully satisfied with his press coverage."[58]

One approach adopted by the court during the twentieth century has been termed the "marketplace of ideas." As explained by Justice Oliver Wendell Holmes Jr., it proposes "the free trade in ideas" because "the best test of truth is the power of the thought to get itself accepted in the competition of the market." While this hardly guarantees that truth will prevail, it "is the theory of our Constitution. It is an experiment as all life is an experiment."[59] Jared Schroeder explains that this approach "assumes that given access to a full range of ideas that are generally not limited by the government, rational citizens will accept ideas that are true and reject those that are false," at least in the long run. However, he argues that because so many Americans live in information bubbles that largely control what reaches them, and because deep fakes have become so convincing, marketplaces are more like niche stores with a few preapproved ideas.[60] This important argument will be discussed in detail in the analysis of *The Social Network* in chapter 4.

Hearst's unsuccessful attempt to suppress *Citizen Kane* shows that although the First Amendment may provide the media with protection against government censorship, there remains a significant danger from private entities not constrained by the Constitution. There is considerable irony in Hearst using his First Amendment–protected media empire to try to prevent someone else's expression of views he disliked.

All the studios had "voluntarily" agreed in 1934 to abide by the Production Code, whose administrator was Joseph Breen. When Breen demanded that a party scene set in a brothel be removed from the film, Welles complied. His resistance was minimal because the scene was unimportant and, in his view, not particularly good. In contrast, when aides to Hearst asked that *Kane* be held in violation of the code's rule against movies about living persons, Breen concluded that it was not a film about Hearst and therefore not a violation. Interestingly enough, about a year later, Breen was put in charge of RKO productions, a job he held only briefly before returning as code administrator the following year.[61]

What is scary about Hearst's efforts is just how close they came to preventing the showing of one of the greatest films ever made, and perhaps even literally destroying it. Welles believed that without Schaefer's strong support, RKO might have decided to never open the film at all. Welles's unusually favorable contract prevented the other studios from buying the film for $800,000 and destroying all prints. *Citizen Kane* is such a great film that when it was screened for critics and others influential in the industry, strong positive reaction and favorable articles in non-Hearst publications made the film impossible to suppress, which would not have been the case for a movie of lower quality. Even then, nearly all the most prominent theater owners declined to show it. Finally, Hearst's own financial weakness made it easier to resist him.

CONCLUSION

Charles Silver wrote that "Charles Foster Kane, America's most powerful newspaper publisher . . . aspires to be a profit-making prophet, and . . . this seems all too relevant to today's uber-capitalist America."[62] To David Thomson, Kane represents "the American recipe of public charm and actual demagoguery."[63] Even in an age where technology has gone well beyond the print media of Kane's day, these quotes suggest that there are still contemporary counterparts of Charles Foster Kane. Ted Turner expanded his Atlanta television station into the Turner Broadcasting System, an empire that included CNN, the first twenty-four-hour cable news channel. Rupert Murdoch got his start with newspapers in Australia and the United Kingdom before moving into cable news and other broadcasting outlets as well as film. The *New York Post* may be a small part of his media empire in financial terms, but it remains a visible one with significant political impact in New York City, and the political influence of Fox News in the United States is immense, especially within the Republican Party. Even if Mark Zuckerberg began Facebook to connect college students and make money rather than out of any political motivation, social media has become the single most important source of news for many Americans. (See chapter 4's discussion of *The Social Network*.) Elon Musk purchased Twitter, making numerous changes, including renaming it and reinstating Donald Trump's account. Jeff Bezos used some of his profits from Amazon to buy the *Washington Post*. And Donald Trump transformed his notoriety as a reality television host into a victory in the 2016 presidential election, something that eluded both the real William Randolph Hearst and the fictional Charles Foster Kane.

That these media magnates are all white men tells us something that will be considered in later chapters. A rare exception was Katharine Graham, who presided over the *Washington Post* from 1963 to 1991, becoming the first female CEO of a *Fortune* 500 company when she took that position with the Washington Post Company, which also owned *Newsweek* and television stations. The discussion of the film *The Post* in chapter 3 examines her struggle to assert herself in a male-dominated media business. Chapters 9 and 10 also analyze the depiction of marginalized groups by the media.

Both Hearst and Kane began their careers claiming to be populist reformers, but that did not prevent each from being a "profit-making prophet." Kane's sarcastic response to Thatcher's rebuke that the damage to corporations attacked by the *Inquirer* will cost Kane's own portfolio a million dollars a year is to conclude that it will take another sixty years before this results in his bankruptcy. One of his first acts is to publish a Declaration of Principles on his front page. However, as discussed earlier, the film strongly suggests that Kane was less than sincere in these beliefs. These positions were both good for the circulation of the newspaper, and therefore good business, crucial to the success of Kane's political aspirations. When faced with a conflict between sensational news coverage that would boost circulation and accurate reporting, as in its coverage of crime stories and the Spanish-American War, Kane's newspapers opted for the former. Nor did Kane hesitate to marry the niece of a president for whom he expressed contempt, for motives that appear to be more practical than romantic. Kane's opposition to trade unions demonstrates that any conflict between the financial interests of his newspaper and his sympathies with the working class would be resolved in favor of the former. According to Ruth Warrick, the actress who played Emily Norton Kane,

Welles told the cast that the movie "is about the kind of man that Americans tend to make their heroes, when actually they are the despoilers of their country."[64] Whether this applies to specific media figures who run for political office will be left to the judgment of our readers. Welles also believed that people like Kane "tend toward the newspaper and entertainment world. They combine a morbid preoccupation with the public with a devastatingly low opinion of the public mentality and moral character."[65]

Because films are expensive to make, those in charge of financing them decide what the public sees. Welles was lured to Hollywood by a contract that gave him unprecedented control over his first film. Without this contract, a film with the unconventional structure of *Citizen Kane* might never have been made. Because it lost money, it was withdrawn from circulation in 1942. Only because the advent of television returned *Kane* to public attention did its reputation grow to where many consider it the greatest movie ever made.

The fight over the release of *Citizen Kane* suggests that censorship by private citizens and businesses can present as great a danger as efforts by the government. In the end, persistence by a few people and fortunate circumstances have allowed us to see a great motion picture.

NOTES

1. Anna Baccanti, *Screening the Creative Process: Genius, Gender, and the Contemporary Biopic* (Germany: Brill | Fink, 2023), 1–2.
2. Rafaela Bassili, "Sofia Coppola's Subversive Search for Truth in 'Pricilla,'" *New York Times Magazine*, November 15, 2023, https://www.nytimes.com/2023/11/15/magazine/sofia-coppola-priscilla-movie.html?searchResultPosition=1.
3. Charlotte Rawlings, "Five Reasons Why *Citizen Kane* Is Still Relevant to Journalism," *XCity Plus*, May 4, 2021. https://xcityplus.com/culture/8123/five-reasons-citizen-kane-still-relevant-journalism/.
4. Laura Mulvey, *Citizen Kane*, 2nd ed. (London: British Film Institute, 2012), 7–8.
5. Michael Schudson, *Discovering the News: A Social History of American Newspapers* (New York: Basic Books, 1978), 14–15.
6. Peter Andrews and Edward Sorel, "The Press," *American Heritage*, October 1994, 36.
7. Schudson, *Discovering the News*, 18, 22–23.
8. Schudson, *Discovering the News*, 60.
9. James McGrath Morris, "Man of the World," *Wilson Quarterly* 34, no. 1 (2010): 28.
10. Morris, "Man of the World," 32.
11. David Nasaw, *The Chief: The Life of William Randolph Hearst* (Boston: Houghton Mifflin, 2000), 105.
12. Morris, "Man of the World," 32.

13. Nasaw, *The Chief*, xiii–xiv.

14. Robert L. Carringer, *The Making of Citizen Kane* (Berkeley: University of California Press, 1985), 21.

15. Simon Callow, *Orson Welles, Vol. 1: The Road to Xanadu* (New York: Viking, 1996), 493, 495.

16. Greg Mitchell, "*Mank* and Politics: What Really Happened in 1934 California," *New York Times*, December 7, 2020.

17. Leah Weinryb Grohsgal, "Newsreel or Not Real," *Humanities* 40, no. 2 (Spring 2019), https://www.neh.gov/article/newsreel-or-not-real.

18. Callow, *Orson Welles*, 523–24.

19. Mulvey, *Citizen Kane*, 33.

20. André Bazin, *Orson Welles: A Critical View* (Venice, CA: Acrobat Books, 1992), 58.

21. Sarah Street, "Citizen Kane," *History Today*, March 1996, 48–52.

22. Marc Tracy, "Gannett, the Owner of USA Today, Is About to Get a Whole Lot Bigger," *New York Times*, August 6, 2019; Marc Tracy, "Chatham Hedge Fund Has the Winning Bid for McClatchy Newspapers," *New York Times*, July 13, 2020.

23. Penelope Muse Abernathy, "The Expanding News Desert," Hussman School of Journalism and Media, 2023, https://www.usnewsdeserts.com/reports/expanding-news-desert/loss-of-local-news/bigger-and-bigger-they-grow/ (last accessed June 11, 2024).

24. Nasaw, *The Chief*, 127–28.

25. Orson Welles and Peter Bogdanovich, *This Is Orson Welles* (New York: Da Capo Press, 1998), 50–51.

26. Benjamin Huffbauer, "How Trump's Favorite Movie Explains Him," *Politico*, June 6, 2016, https://www.politico.com/magazine/story/2016/06/donald-trump-2016-citizen-kane-213943/.

27. Joshua Gillen, "Bush Says Trump Was a Democrat Longer Than a Republican 'In the Last Decade,'" PolitiFact, August 24, 2015, https://www.politifact.com/factchecks/2015/aug/24/jeb-bush/bush-says-trump-was-democrat-longer-republican-las/.

28. Huffbauer, "How Trump's Favorite Movie Explains Him."

29. Tim Murphy, "The Trump Files: Donald Has One Piece of Advice for Citizen Kane," *Mother Jones*, September 29, 2020, https://www.motherjones.com/politics/2020/09/trump-files-donald-has-weirdest-reaction-citizen-kane/.

30. Harlan Lebo, *Citizen Kane: A Filmmaker's Journey* (New York: Thomas Dunne, 2016), 51.

31. Welles and Bogdanovich, *This Is Orson Welles*, 81.

32. Probably including his childhood sled.

33. Lebo, *A Filmmaker's Journey*, 221.

34. Ben Kenigsberg, "Who Wrote 'Citizen Kane'? It's No Mystery," *New York Times*, December 6, 2020.

35. For an informative discussion of this practice, see Robert S. Boynton, "Checkbook Journalism Revisited," *Columbia Journalism Review* 46, no. 5 (January/February 2008): 12–14.

36. Jonathan Mahler, "What Rupert Wrought," *New York*, April 11, 2005, 28–36.
37. Eric Alterman, "All Rupert, All the Time," *Nation*, August 13, 2007, 10.
38. David Nasaw, "Elon Musk Makes Sense, Really," *New York Times*, May 12, 2023.
39. Sarah Lyall, "When a Magnate Tried to Play Movie Censor," *New York Times*, July 4, 1999.
40. J. Hoberman, "RKO 281," *Film Comment*, January/February 2000, 75–77.
41. Bernard Weinraub, "Orson Welles Gives Them the Willies," *New York Times*, November 17, 1999.
42. Lyall, "When a Magnate Tried."
43. Richard Brody, "Herman Mankiewicz, Pauline Kael, and the Battle over 'Citizen Kane,'" *New Yorker*, November 14, 2020, https://www.newyorker.com/culture/the-front-row/herman-mankiewicz-pauline-kael-and-the-battle-over-citizen-kane.
44. Callow, *Orson Welles*, 570.
45. Callow, *Orson Welles*, 556–57.
46. Weinraub, "Orson Welles Gives Them the Willies."
47. Lebo, *A Filmmaker's Journey*, 203.
48. Callow, *Orson Welles*, 549.
49. Welles and Bogdanovich, *This Is Orson Welles*, 87.
50. Welles and Bogdanovich, *This Is Orson Welles*, 49–50.
51. Nasaw, *The Chief*, 572.
52. Carringer, *The Making*, 117.
53. C. W. Anderson, Leonard Downie Jr., and Michael Schudson, *The News Media: What Everyone Needs to Know* (New York: Oxford University Press, 2016), 10–11; *Gitlow v. New York*, 268 U.S. 652 (1925).
54. Quoted in Stephen J. Wermiel, "Freedom of the Press: Challenges to this Pillar of Democracy," *Social Education* 83 (March/April 2019): 68.
55. Larry Gragg, "Order vs. Liberty," *American History* 33 (October 1998): 24.
56. *New York Times v. Sullivan*, 376 U.S. 254 (1964); *Watts v. United States*, 394 U.S. 705 (1969).
57. "Selected Quotations from the Thomas Jefferson Papers," Library of Congress, https://www.loc.gov/collections/thomas-jefferson-papers/articles-and-essays/selected-quotations-from-the-thomas-jefferson-papers/.
58. Harold Holzer, *The Presidents vs. the Press* (New York: Dutton, 2020), xiv.
59. *Abrams v. United States*, 250 U.S. 616, 624 (1919) (Holmes, J., dissenting).
60. Jared Schroeder, "Marketplace of Ideas Turns 100—It's Not What it Used to Be," *The Hill*, November 9, 2019, https://thehill.com/opinion/judiciary/469715-as-marketplace-of-ideas-turns-100-truth-is-not-what-it-used-to-be/.
61. Callow, *Orson Welles*, 534–35.
62. Charles Silver, *An Auteurist History of Film* (New York: Museum of Modern Art, 2016), 103.
63. David Thomson, *The New Biographical Dictionary of Film*, 6th ed. (New York: Knopf, 2014), 1106.

64. Alex Chadwick, "Citizen Kane" Actress Lets Out "Secret," Weekend All Things Considered (April 27, 1991).

65. Callow, *Orson Welles*, 497.

Chapter 3

Heroic Newspaper Reporters, Editors, and Publishers Battle the President

All the President's Men *and* The Post

Bruce E. Altschuler

Bill Nichols has written that "narrative is the great storytelling device" that .plays a critical role "in the construction of any social reality." He believes that Hollywood films adhere to certain storytelling conventions: Individuals are central to problem solving, there is a basic coherence of the social fabric, time and history are progressive forces, and resolving social conflict is a desirable and laudable goal.[1] All these conventions are on display in the two films analyzed in this chapter. In *All the President's Men* (hereafter ATPM), reporters Bob Woodward and Carl Bernstein are the individuals who heroically expose the Watergate cover-up that led to the 1974 resignation of President Richard M. Nixon. And in *The Post*, also depicting a real-life aspect of the Nixon administration's antagonistic relationship with the press, *Washington Post* publisher Katharine Graham makes the decision to publish the Pentagon Papers, risking the newspaper's business in order to vindicate freedom of the press. From these cinematic depictions, the following questions emerge:

- To what extent does investigative reporting contribute to the media's checking function in American constitutional democracy?
- As the media continues to undergo significant changes, to what extent does it depend upon journalists undertaking rigorous investigative journalism?

- How does the relationship between national security and press freedoms shape the stories in *The Post* and *All the President's Men*?
- How does the need to make a profit affect news coverage?

In addition to asking the reader to consider the answers to these questions, the cinematic analysis in this chapter highlights the following key points:

- How films choose to tell real stories.
- The use of subtext in cinematic storytelling.
- The cinematic portrayal of women in journalism.
- The creation of suspense using lighting, camera angles, and sound.

Although made four decades apart—*All the President's Men* in 1976 and *The Post* in 2017—both films raise these questions and make these points by depicting the same powerful person and the journalistic efforts to reveal his political misdeeds. In both films, Nixon is trying to hide something and failing to do so in large part due to the work of the men and women of the *Washington Post*.

INVESTIGATIVE JOURNALISM

Vincent Blasi believes that the authors of the First Amendment "placed great emphasis on the role that free expression can play in guarding against breaches of trust by public officials."[2] Investigative reporting has been a crucial part of this checking function. Even though such reports have never been more than a small fraction of the news, James T. Hamilton argues that they "have outsized influence because they generate new information about issues of importance" that powerful people are trying to hide.[3] Although there is no universally accepted definition of investigative reporting, David Kaplan suggests there is agreement on certain basic elements, one of which is "systemic in-depth and original research and reporting, often involving the unearthing of secrets." He adds that some would also include an emphasis on social justice and accountability.[4] The nonprofit Investigative Reporters & Editors defines it as "the reporting through one's own initiative and work product, of matters of importance to readers, viewers or listeners."[5] One definition—that investigative journalism is "fact-checking political speech, digging into digital data, and aggressive beat coverage to reveal as much as possible about what is really going on in every aspect of American society"—very much describes the work of Woodward and Bernstein in ATPM.[6]

Modern investigative journalism began to emerge in the early twentieth century. In 1906, Theodore Roosevelt coined the term "muckraker" to criticize journalists for damaging the country through reporting that emphasized corruption and scandal.[7] Among the most famous muckrakers were Ida Tarbell, who wrote a history of the Standard Oil monopoly that led to its dissolution, and Lincoln Steffens, whose articles exposing urban corruption were later collected into a book, *The Shame of the Cities*. By the time ATPM was made, muckraking, which we now call investigative reporting, had become institutionalized. One of the prime examples was the *Boston Globe*'s spotlight team, begun in 1970 and featured in the 2015 film *Spotlight* (see chapter 9). It demonstrates that investigative journalism remains a crucial element of the press and an important reason why robust press freedoms must be defended.

The market works against the type of investigative reporting depicted in ATPM and *The Post* because "it is costly to create, hard to translate its social benefits into revenues, and easy to stymy by keeping information hidden inside government agencies."[8] Hamilton cites the example of the media mogul Rupert Murdoch, who, after acquiring the *Wall Street Journal* in 2007, advocated an end to "having people write articles to win Pulitzer Prizes," suggesting that they instead "[g]ive people what they want to read."[9] Although it was not immediately apparent that the American public *wanted* to read about Watergate and the Pentagon Papers, it soon became clear that for the sake of preserving American democracy it was what they *needed* to read.

ALL THE PRESIDENT'S MEN

Unlike Charles Foster Kane, the protagonists of *All the President's Men* are unambiguously portrayed as media heroes battling to inform the public on issues of national importance, issues the Nixon administration would do almost anything to keep hidden. In a 2011 survey of practitioners and academics, ATPM was universally rated as the best film about journalism, despite all the technological developments since it was made in 1976.[10] In a more nuanced but equally enthusiastic evaluation, Ken Ringle writes that "even though it over-glamorizes reporting, [and] oversimplifies editing . . . *All the President's Men* remains the best film ever made about the craft of journalism."[11] Indeed, as we will see in chapter 7, the film heavily influenced and shaped the making of *Shattered Glass* (2003). Even more recently, Johnny Restall declared in 2021 that "the film remains incisively topical today and not just in the US."[12]

In 1974, *Washington Post* journalists Bob Woodward and Carl Bernstein published *All the President's Men*, their book-length account of how they investigated, uncovered, and reported on the events that led to the resignation of President Nixon. In June 1972, a group of men broke into the Watergate offices of the Democratic National Committee in Washington, DC, triggering what became known as the Watergate scandal. The reporting of Woodward and Bernstein uncovered the fact that the burglars worked for the Nixon reelection campaign. The administration's efforts to cover up this and other related illegal activities ultimately involved numerous administration officials—"the president's men"—including Nixon himself.

Although movies based on books usually mirror the themes of their original sources, for ATPM it was Robert Redford's idea for the film that transformed the book. Originally, Woodward and Bernstein (often referred to as Woodstein) planned to write about *the story of Watergate*.[13] When Redford contacted them to suggest instead that *they and their investigation* were a better story, they eagerly embraced his idea. According to Jordan Orlando, "Redford had very precise—and very cinematic—ideas about how the story should be told," and a major function of William Goldman's film script was "reinventing the reporters as movie heroes."[14] As is clear throughout this book, films make arguments, often indirectly, not only because of what they include in their storytelling but also as a result of what they exclude. Both films discussed here omit some facts that make their main characters less than perfect while exaggerating others that flatter the narrative's heroes.

ATPM embraces Blasi's point that freedom of the press is a necessary check on government overreach. Despite the enormous power of the government, two young scrappy reporters expose the wrongdoing that has come to be known as the Watergate scandal. The pen—or in this case, the typewriter and the landline phone—can be mightier than the proverbial sword. The opening scene makes this point dramatically. After seventeen seconds of white paper that may seem to the audience like an eternity, typewriter keys loudly strike one huge letter at a time, dominating the screen. This shot took a hundred separate cuts, overlaid with the sound of cannon shots and whip cracks,[15] giving it equality to the scene that follows of Nixon's helicopter landing to take him to a joint session of Congress where he will deliver a speech.

ATPM adds to its credibility by telling its story in a documentary style. As in *Goodnight, and Good Luck*, discussed in chapter 5, where Senator Joseph McCarthy plays himself through the use of news programs on television screens, President Richard Nixon and his top aides are seen only on television rather than being played by actors. The "actor" who plays Frank Wills, the security guard who discovered the Watergate break-in while it was in progress, is Wills himself. The *Post* allowed cameras in its building entrance, elevators, and parking lot, but decided that filming in its newsroom would have been too disruptive for both its employees and the filmmakers. Instead, an exact replica of the newsroom was built in California for $450,000, a very high cost in 1976 dollars (the equivalent in 2023 of approximately $2.4 million).[16]

"Woodstein" Is on the Case

Because the Watergate break-in initially was viewed by the *Washington Post* as a local story, recently hired Bob Woodward (Robert Redford), the newspaper's lowest-paid reporter, is sent to cover the arraignment, which was filmed in the actual courtroom where it occurred.[17] When he notices a seemingly out-of-place lawyer observing the proceedings, along with such other curious anomalies as high-priced private attorneys whom the defendants did not have the opportunity to contact replacing their court-assigned counsel, Woodward realizes the story may have national implications. His initial impression is reinforced when he hears defendant James McCord (Richard Herd) whispering to the judge that he is a retired CIA employee. Soon, Carl Bernstein (Dustin Hoffman), another local reporter, fights his way onto the story. Ben Bradlee, the *Post*'s executive editor at the time, has described Bernstein as the "Peck's Bad Boy of the Metro Staff."[18] In fact, Bradlee was about to fire Bernstein because of his erratic work habits, his irresponsible expense accounts, and his decision to abandon a rental car in a parking lot. It was Bernstein's Watergate reporting that saved his job.[19]

The movie is a detective story with an ending the 1976 audience already knew because they had recently lived through the depicted events, and it lacks any information about its heroes' personal lives. So how could the filmmakers attract an audience large enough to make a profit? One answer was to add some humor by presenting Woodward and Bernstein as an odd couple who did not particularly like each other when first forced to work together. Woodward was Ivy League educated; Bernstein never attended college. Woodward was a Republican; Bernstein, a liberal. Woodward was a WASP; Bernstein, a Jew. Unsolicited, Bernstein, the better writer of the two, rewrites Woodward's original story. In one humorous moment, after Bernstein lights a cigarette in an elevator, Woodward asks, "Is there any place you don't smoke?" As the two work together, however, they learn each other's strengths and become a highly effective team.

The newspaper's Metro section editor, Harry Rosenfeld (Jack Warden), successfully resists pressure to replace Woodstein with more experienced and better-known national reporters because their ambition makes them "hungry." The movie presents the pair as workaholics who will do anything, even using some questionable methods, to obtain information. The only scene of either man's personal life, showing Bernstein with a woman, was cut from the movie.[20] According to Woodward and Bernstein themselves, they were able to devote all their waking hours to their task because, at the time, Woodward was divorced and Bernstein separated.[21]

Dramatizing the Story

Director Alan J. Pakula needed to find a way to dramatize scenes in the newsroom where Woodward and Bernstein's activity consisted primarily of making phone calls. His solution was to have cinematographer Gordon Willis use a dioptic lens with split focus to divide the scene in two, with one side showing the phone call while the other, equally in focus, shows unrelated activity elsewhere in the newsroom or important developments in the outside world. This has much the same result as the deep focus used in *Citizen Kane*. One particularly effective use of the split diopter shows Woodward phoning Nixon campaign donor Kenneth Dahlberg to ask how a check he signed wound up deposited in the bank account of one of the Watergate burglars. Simultaneously, on the other side of the screen, everyone else in the newsroom gathers around a television set to watch a report on Thomas Eagleton's withdrawal as George McGovern's running mate in the 1972 presidential election.

Much of the film's suspense comes from the small details, most of which are unknown to the audience, gathered by Woodstein. One reason the movie is so revered by today's reporters is its depiction of the routine nature of news gathering. Woodward and Bernstein are constantly knocking on the doors of potential sources, only to have those doors slammed in their faces. Those called on the telephone often either hang up, lie, or deny knowing anything. The enormity of the task facing Woodstein is dramatized visually by showing them as small figures set against Washington's monumental architecture. The most dramatic contrast is in a scene set in the Library of Congress where, as the two reporters fruitlessly work their way through thousands of library patron call slips, the camera slowly rises to the very high ceiling, showing Woodward and Bernstein as tiny figures among a crowd of researchers. Later in the film, as they drive through the city, the camera moves gradually upward to show an aerial view of Washington, whose buildings dwarf the pair's car. This is an example of subtext, an implicit theme that may have an impact on viewers.

The film uses lighting to show how governmental secrets in the dark outside world are brought into the bright fluorescent light of the newsroom. The darkness of those outside world scenes, many occurring at night, adds to the sense of menace felt by Woodstein and communicated to the audience. Most suspenseful are the three scenes of Woodward meeting with the confidential source nicknamed "Deep Throat" by a *Post* editor.[22] Deep Throat (Hal Holbrook) instructs Woodward to take a circuitous route (using several cabs to avoid possible surveillance) to a dimly lit, largely empty parking garage late at night. Deep Throat's face is largely in shadow, while Woodward's is better lit. Deep Throat's most memorable line—the suggestion that the reporters "follow the money"—was an invention of screenwriter Goldman.[23]

In this scene, and the one immediately following, the film makes dramatic use of sound. In the parking garage, direct sound ensures that the audience hears every detail, including Deep Throat's nervous swallowing and the scuffing of the two men's shoes as they shift their weight anxiously. That scene ends with the enshadowed Deep Throat saying to Woodward, "Your lives are in danger." There is an abrupt cut to the next scene, where Bernstein opens the door of his home to a visibly stressed Woodward, who immediately silences him with the gesture of putting a finger to his lips. Woodward then turns on the stereo, using music by Vivaldi to drown out any other sounds. As the classical music continues, it begins to compete with—or perhaps to be accompanied by—the sound of the typewriter's keystrokes as Woodward conveys Deep Throat's warning; the typewritten message adds that Bernstein's apartment may be bugged. The cutting back and forth, between one shot showing the two men hunched over the typewriter and another looking over their shoulders but tightly focused in on the paper as their typed words appear on the page, symbolizes the way in which Woodstein and their principal instrument of presidential downfall are truly united.

Sources and Shield Laws

Woodward kept the identity of Deep Throat secret from even his colleagues and editors. When asked by Bradlee (Jason Robards) about his source, he satisfies the editor by assuring him that everything Deep Throat told him proved accurate and was confirmed by other sources. According to Woodstein, they and their editors developed an "unwritten rule" that two sources would be required for any of their stories that suggested possible criminal activity.[24] This rule has since become the gold standard of investigative reporting. Woodward only revealed the identity of Deep Throat to Bradlee after the follow-up book to ATPM, *The Final Days*, was published in 1976, and he never told *Post* publisher Katharine Graham. It was not until 2005[25] that ninety-one-year-old Mark Felt, who had been deputy director of the FBI during the Watergate scandal, revealed to the public that he was Deep Throat.[26]

Woodward's ability to conceal the identity of Deep Throat in order to obtain crucial information about the culpability of the Committee to Re-elect the President (CRP, mocked by Democrats as CREEP) has become a strong piece of evidence in favor of providing legal protection for the ability of reporters to keep the identity of confidential sources secret, even if they are subpoenaed in a legal proceeding. The argument is that the checking value behind the First Amendment's protection of a free press provides the basis for the claim. However, the Supreme Court rejected this reasoning in 1972 in

Branzburg v. Hayes.[27] Thirty-nine states have passed shield laws that give reporters protection, although that protection varies in strength from one state to another. In addition, according to Gene Policinski of the Freedom Forum, with the exception of Wyoming all the remaining states "have a judicial opinion that substitutes for a state law."[28] Despite numerous bills introduced in Congress over the years since *Branzburg*, there is no federal shield law. In one of the most notable cases, in 2005 *New York Times* reporter Judith Miller served eighty-five days in jail after refusing to name her source for a story about the exposure of Valerie Plame as a CIA agent. She would have served longer except that her source released her from their confidentiality agreement.[29]

Discussed in more detail in the next chapter, changes in the media have created new complications regarding defining who is a reporter qualifying for protection. What about a blogger? A freelance writer hoping to write a story to sell to a newspaper, a magazine, or even an online publication? An organization like WikiLeaks? Legislators and judges have to address this and other problems as new forms of media emerge. The most recent Department of Justice guidelines, a revision of those originally adopted in 1970, do little to address this problem. Instead, they protect members of the traditional news media while giving the department almost total discretion over whether to include newer forms of journalism such as blogs and newsletters.[30]

Following the Money Pays Off

Eventually Woodstein's persistence begins to bear fruit. While today's reporters can view most documents digitally, Woodward and Bernstein were forced to travel to wherever physical copies were available. Bernstein has to fly to Miami to view a local investigator's files, but it pays off when he discovers checks deposited in Watergate burglar Bernard Barker's bank account. The six weeks it took for him to trace the serial numbers of hundred-dollar bills found by the police when they searched the burglars after the break-in to Barker's bank account[31] was likely a bit too much routine for the movie to include.

Woodstein works to tie this money to a CRP slush fund. Bernstein convinces the sister of CRP's bookkeeper to allow him into their house, where he spends six hours coaxing bits of information out of the reluctant bookkeeper (Jane Alexander). The camera switches back and forth between Bernstein and the bookkeeper, avoiding close-ups, to build tension. When Bernstein later meets with Woodward, the film switches to a lighter tone as Bernstein, heavily caffeinated from using refills of his coffee as an excuse to stay, manically explains what he has learned as he frantically pulls scraps of paper, with notes on them, from every pocket.

An even bigger breakthrough comes when former CRP treasurer Hugh Sloan (Stephen Collins) agrees to talk to Woodstein. Upset by the unethical activities the CRP was engaged in, Sloan's wife had convinced him to resign, freeing him to speak openly and honestly to the reporters. Because his information implicates former attorney general John Mitchell, they phone Mitchell in his hotel room at 11:30 at night, apparently waking him up. As Bernstein reads him the article they intend to publish the next day, a startled and angry Mitchell colorfully threatens the publisher of the *Post*: "Katie Graham's gonna get her tit caught in a big fat wringer if that's published." This shocked even Bernstein, who called Bradlee to ask whether to publish Mitchell's remark. Bradlee tells Bernstein to cut the reference to Graham's "tit," but otherwise go ahead and print.

An Uncertain Ending

Unlike the book's ending, with Nixon's 1974 State of the Union address declaring that "one year of Watergate is enough," and the beginning of the House Judiciary Committee impeachment inquiry,[32] the *film* concludes 138 pages earlier, with Woodstein's one serious error. Sloan told them that top Nixon aide H. R. Haldeman was one of the men who controlled the CRP slush fund. When Sloan appeared before the grand jury, he was asked about four of those who had access to this money and answered yes, but because Haldeman was not one of those he was questioned about, Sloan never named Haldeman in his testimony. Because the reporters misunderstood this distinction, or perhaps because Sloan failed to communicate it clearly to them, Woodstein's story named Haldeman as implicated in Sloan's testimony. When Haldeman issued a public denial, Nixon and his aides used the error to damage the *Post*'s credibility. Nevertheless, Bradlee defended the accuracy of the newspaper's reporting. Screenwriter Goldman decided to end the movie this way because the audience would know that this error didn't stop Woodstein from eventually succeeding.[33] Redford liked the idea of finishing the movie with doubt by the reporters of their success, which suggested an important question: "Can it [history] repeat itself?"

"Nothing's riding on this except the First Amendment, the Constitution, freedom of the press and maybe the future of the country."

The film concludes with an epilogue. After a final meeting with Deep Throat, who upbraids Woodward for his reporting error while agreeing that it was, in fact, all a "Haldeman operation," Woodward and Bernstein meet with Bradlee in his backyard, again worried about electronic surveillance. Bradlee tells them to take a brief break, then get right back to work, ending with the memorable line, a slightly more dramatic version of what he actually said: "Nothing's riding on this except the First Amendment, the Constitution, freedom of the press and the future of the country." Bradlee believed that when Walter Cronkite devoted fourteen minutes to the Watergate story on October 27, 1972, and eight minutes the next night, "it validated the *Post*'s stories in the public's mind."[34]

In the *Post* newsroom, the camera closes in on a television showing Nixon's inauguration on the left side of the screen as Woodward and Bernstein are typing furiously on the right, followed by teletype machines hammering out *Post* stories about Nixon's downfall, ending in his resignation and Gerald Ford's succession to the presidency. In an echo of the film's opening, the film ends with the sound of these machines overpowering the twenty-one-gun salute at Nixon's inauguration.

Had the movie continued the story, Woodstein might have seemed less heroic. After the election, Nixon's landslide victory made it easier for the administration to clamp down on information and, as Graham writes, "the Watergate story dried up."[35] Woodward and Bernstein were so desperate for sources that they sought out the identities of grand jurors, hoping they would provide information. This was of such questionable legality that Judge John Sirica reprimanded them in open court, although he did not mention their names.[36] By March 23, 1973, when the Senate Watergate committee revealed that it had interviewed James McCord, a Watergate burglar who had contacted Sirica, with a willingness to tell all, "the days when the *Post* had dominated the Watergate story were over."[37] In the end, Nixon's own recordings of his conversations provided the evidence that led to his impeachment and resignation.

ATPM was a critical and financial success. Its first-week gross of $7 million led all other films, while total receipts of $70.6 million far exceeded its budget of $8.5 million. It won best picture awards from the National Society of Film Critics, the New York Film Critics Circle, and the British Academy of Film and Television Arts, but lost to *Rocky* for the Oscar. In 2015, the *Hollywood Reporter* polled hundreds of past Academy Award voters, asking them to recast their ballots in historic votes. In the revote, ATPM was the winner, with *Network*, a film discussed in chapter 4, finishing a close second.[38]

THE POST

The Post, released in 2017, grossed $82 million in the United States and another $98 million in the rest of the world, a solid profit compared to its budget of approximately $50 million, but far short of *Star Wars Episode VIII: The Last Jedi*, which took in $620 million domestically and $712 million elsewhere, according to Box Office Mojo.[39] The film dramatizes the *Washington Post*'s decision to publish the top-secret Pentagon Papers after the courts temporarily prevented the *New York Times* from publishing them. Such a prior restraint had long been considered the most dangerous restriction on freedom of the press and therefore nearly always a violation of the First Amendment because it deprives the public of information. The question in this case was whether there was a national security exception, and if there was, how broad or narrow it should be. Because these events occurred a year before those in ATPM, *The Post* is effectively a prequel to that movie, even including some of the same characters, most notably Ben Bradlee.

The Pentagon Papers were a study of what went wrong during the Vietnam War, commissioned during the Lyndon B. Johnson administration by Secretary of Defense Robert McNamara. Although the documents only covered events that took place before and during the presidency of Johnson (who left office in January 1969), by the time one of their authors, Daniel Ellsberg, shared them with the *Times*, Nixon had been elected president. It was his administration that went to court seeking to halt publication.[40]

At first glance, the decision to make *The Post* seems a curious one. By 2017, when the movie was released, more than forty-five years had passed. Because the *Times* was the first to publish the Pentagon Papers, the *Post* merely played a secondary role in the litigation. It is not surprising that James Goodale, writing in the *Times*, said that because the film minimizes the role of his newspaper and exaggerates that of the *Post*, it is "good drama but bad history."[41] Similarly, Manohla Dargis observed in her *Times* review that it was "more than a little corn and wishful thinking" because "movies like either to glorify or demonize journalists. Yet given the recent assaults on journalism and the truth, this heroizing is also irresistible."[42] These are not merely sour journalism grapes: they make valid points.

The film was made in the relatively short time period of nine months because director Steven Spielberg saw similarities between its events and President Donald Trump's conflicts with the media. Spielberg explained that "the level of urgency to make the movie was because of the current climate of this administration, bombarding the press and labelling the truth as fake if it suited them."[43] Trump's attacks on the media had been a feature of his presidential campaign and accelerated after he took office. One month into his presidency, referring to the *New York Times*, network news, and CNN, he tweeted that "the FAKE NEWS MEDIA is not my enemy, it is the enemy of the American People."[44] He was quite open about the reason for his assault, telling reporter Lesley Stahl, "I do it to discredit you all and demean you all, so that, when you write negative stories about me, no one will believe you."[45]

Trump's attacks accelerated a decline in public trust of the media. According to a 2017 Gallup Poll, in 1976, when ATPM was released, 72 percent of the public trusted the mass media a great deal or a fair amount. By 2017, this had declined to 41 percent. The loss of faith was particularly strong among Republicans, only 14 percent of whom gave the media one of these two positive ratings, compared to 51 percent of Democrats. Even more troubling, 42 percent of Republicans agreed that "accurate news stories casting a politician or a group in a negative light" are "always fake news." So badly weakened was the credibility of the news that 28 percent of all 2017 respondents, and even 17 percent of Democrats, agreed.[46] In essence, the subtext of *The Post* was a defense of a free press as a critique of Trump's attacks on it. Spielberg hoped to help reverse the decline in public support for press freedom by telling a story about one of its great successes in checking the abuse of presidential power.

If this was the main rationale for the film, then a movie about the *Times*'s fight to publish would seem to have been more logical. However, the original idea of Liz Hannah, who would become one of the two screenwriters for *The Post*, was to create a script about the newspaper's publisher, Katharine Graham, who had long fascinated her. Hannah chose the Pentagon Papers because, referring to Graham, "that's the moment where she came of age."[47] According to Hannah, producer Amy Pascal "saw that it was important to tell a story about a woman standing up," but it soon "became very important to tell a story about the press standing up."[48] The result was a film combining the two stories, although Hannah insisted that "[i]t is not about, necessarily, the Pentagon Papers. It is about this woman and how this event ended up that changed her."[49] Viewers of the film should keep this second subtext in mind.

Invisible Women

A major weakness of ATPM is its treatment of women, who are either invisible or depicted as open to easy manipulation. The most glaring omission is Katharine Graham, who, as the *Post*'s publisher, had the final say over whether to print any article. Geraldine Page was originally cast to play her in just one scene, but even that was cut from the script prior to filming.[50] Redford told Graham that this was because explaining what a publisher does would be too complicated. The reason Pakula gave was that Graham was a marginal figure in the book.[51] The only time she is mentioned in the film is John Mitchell's off-color remark about her.

The few women who do appear in ATPM do not come across as strong individuals. CRP's bookkeeper undergoes an excruciating six-hour session with Bernstein during which he coaxes bits of information from her. Bernstein tricks a secretary into leaving her desk so that he can sneak into her boss's office to obtain documents about the sources of financing of the Watergate burglary in a fictional scene that was added to the script over the objection of screenwriter William Goldman, who believed it to be "a phony Hollywood moment."[52]

Female *Post* reporters are portrayed as lacking the aggression of the film's heroes. Woodward and Bernstein ask one of these women to obtain information about CRP employees from a former boyfriend. Although troubled by the ethics of this request, the reporter reluctantly obtains a document that she turns over to them. When another reporter tells them that Nixon aide Ken Clawson admitted to her that he had written the so-called Canuck letter, Woodstein uses the information that this conversation took place in the woman's apartment to induce Clawson to speak further. The reporter, given the pseudonym Sally Aiken in the film (and played by Penny Fuller), explains to them that she doesn't have "the taste for the jugular that you guys do."

By making Katharine Graham their hero, the makers of *The Post* hoped to correct the record as it was portrayed in ATPM. A more recent film, *She Said*, shows how much has changed since the events depicted in these two films by telling the story of how two *New York Times* reporters, Jodi Kantor (Zoe Kazan) and Megan Twohey (Carey Mulligan), uncovered the story of movie mogul Harvey Weinstein's long history of sexual misconduct. Weinstein, a cofounder of the entertainment company Miramax, won an Oscar for producing *Shakespeare in Love* as well as seven Tony awards before eventually being forced to resign in disgrace. After Kantor and Twohey's exposés, he was convicted in New York of two felonies and sentenced to twenty-three years in prison; he was later sentenced to sixteen more years for a rape and sexual assault conviction in Los Angeles.[53]

Much like Woodstein, these two reporters had to penetrate a wall of silence created by intimidation and legal maneuvering. However, *She Said* is not simply a mirror image of ATPM with the modern technology of cellphones and computers replacing landlines and typewriters. Unlike Woodward and Bernstein, whose lack of wives and children gave them the freedom to pursue the story during all their waking hours, as Peter Bradshaw has written, "Twohey and Kantor have to deal with motherhood, babies and exhaustion which never worried Woodward and Bernstein."[54] With camera shots of Twohey and Kantor surrounded by other women, the film also makes the point that any woman can be the victim of sexual assault or harassment. Because Weinstein was the head of a private corporation, the film demonstrates that a free press is necessary not only to expose government misconduct, but also as a check on the power of private corporations that have increasing sway over our lives. This is discussed in more detail in the next chapter's analysis of *Network* and *The Social Network*.

The *Post* Decides to Publish

The Post opens with a prologue in Vietnam as Daniel Ellsberg's assignment to observe a military unit turns into actual combat. On the return flight, Secretary of Defense McNamara (Bruce Greenwood) agrees with Ellsberg's assessment that the situation is worsening. However, when the plane lands, McNamara tells reporters the very opposite, that great progress is being made. After the Pentagon Papers have been written, Ellsberg (Matthew Rhys) covertly takes a copy home. He and his friends make duplicates, to the accompaniment of suspenseful music, in a scene that intersperses footage of presidents Harry S. Truman, Dwight D. Eisenhower, John F. Kennedy, and Lyndon B. Johnson minimizing the possibility of war in Vietnam.

Cinematographer Janusz Kaminski used older lenses to give the film a period look. He told an interviewer that he "did not want the images to be too crisp or sharp."[55] In order to solve the problem of livening up a movie that spent so much time indoors during which "people are talking and talking," he employed a very active camera to follow the characters.[56]

A major theme of the film is the relationship and possible conflict between the *Post*'s need to make a profit and its coverage of the news. The movie switches between two plot strands: (1) the newspaper's stock offering and (2) its obtaining of the Pentagon Papers and the subsequent process of deciding whether to publish them. Starting with the first, it shows Graham (Meryl Streep) telling the *Post* company's chairman of the board, Fritz Beebe (Tracy Letts), how the stock offering would net $3 million, which would be enough to pay twenty-five reporters for five years. The movie omits the fact that a majority of the stock offering would be used to pay estate taxes for Graham and other stockholders.[57] Beebe tries to buck up the less than confident Graham. When she goes to a board meeting, the camera follows her as she walks a gamut of men to get to her seat. As the only woman in the room, she is largely ignored even though she is, at least nominally, in charge. When someone asks how many reporters the stock offering will finance, Graham's answer is ignored while Beebe's identical response, which immediately follows, is accepted by those present. Graham lets him consult her notes, allowing him to make her points. One board member asserts that stock "buyers are obviously skittish about having a woman in charge." The board members continue to discuss issues, including criticism of management, as if she were not there. The men seem to consider it wholly irrelevant that she has been the company's president for eight years.

Graham's father, Eugene Meyer, bought a bankrupt *Washington Post* in 1933, outbidding William Randolph Hearst. In 1946, he named Graham's husband Phil associate publisher even though Phil, an attorney, had no previous newspaper experience, unlike his wife, who had taken a job as a reporter in California upon graduating from college, later returning to Washington to work on the *Post*'s editorial page. According to Katharine, "it never crossed my mind that he [her father] might have viewed me as someone to take on an important job at the paper."[58] When ownership was transferred to the Grahams in 1948, Phil received the larger share because Meyer believed that no man should have to work for his wife. "Curiously," Katharine wrote in her autobiography, "I not only concurred but was in complete accord with this idea."[59] After her husband died by suicide in 1963, Graham was elected president of the Washington Post Company, but saw her role as a "silent partner . . . supporting the strong men" who had been "running things."[60] She added the title of publisher in 1969. The film suggests that the decision to publish the Pentagon Papers was a galvanizing event in changing her self-perception.

When Graham meets with Ben Bradlee (Tom Hanks), he wonders why *Times* reporter Neil Sheehan has not written anything for the past few months. The audience soon learns that Sheehan is part of a team of reporters analyzing the Pentagon Papers. Bradlee sends an intern to spy on the *Times* in hopes of discovering what they are up to.

Bradlee was hired by the *Post* in July 1965, then promoted to managing editor a few months later with the goal of increasing the prestige of the publication from that of a newspaper with a predominantly local orientation to one with a national focus comparable to the *New York Times*. David Remnick believes that compared to the *Times* and even the Associated Press, the *Post*'s coverage of the Vietnam War was at that time "nearly an embarrassment."[61] By the time of the film, Bradlee had made substantial improvements, including more critical coverage of the war, but still had a long way to go to catch up to the *Times*.

At Graham's house, a dinner with influential friends shows both her connections to the Washington establishment and the constraints of those friendships. When the conversation turns serious, the men and women separate. Later in the evening, after her friend McNamara tells her that a *Times* article that will be published the next day is "not flattering," Graham calls Bradlee to inform him about the forthcoming major *Times* story. The paper's intern returns from New York, having seen a mock-up of the next day's front page with a large empty space labeled NEIL, which the audience knows is

Sheehan's Pentagon Papers story. The film then switches to its portrayal of Nixon. As in ATPM, the filmmakers chose to have Nixon play himself. This time they show a silhouette of a stand-in shot through a window while the actual tape-recorded voice of the president discusses the Pentagon Papers with his top aides. An angry Bradlee demands that his reporters obtain a copy of the Papers. Graham's daughter, referring to her mother's influential friends involved in making the crucial decisions about the Vietnam War, points out that "these were your people."

Suspecting that Ellsberg was the *Times* source, *Post* reporter Ben Bagdikian (Bob Odenkirk) contacts him using cloak-and-dagger techniques such as calling from a pay phone. (This would be the equivalent today of using a burner phone to prevent being overheard or traced.) When Bagdikian obtains a copy of the Papers, he is surprised that they consist of thousands of pages, far too much to carry in the suitcase he brought. This forces him to buy a second seat on the return flight from Boston, but this conspicuous appearance somehow does not lead to a leak of what he is doing.

By this time, a federal court has issued a temporary restraining order forbidding the *Times* from further publication of its Pentagon Papers stories. When Bradlee informs Graham that the *Post* now has a copy of the Papers, he tells her that she will likely go against McNamara, who cannot be both a friend and a story subject. Nevertheless, Graham seeks McNamara's advice on whether to publish. He opposes publication, which is an invention of the film to add to Graham's courage in eventually deciding to publish. McNamara has written that when James Reston of the *Times* informed him of Mitchell's request to halt publication, he advised that the newspaper should "continue printing them but [it] should hedge its position by making clear it would obey any order issued by the Supreme Court."[62] Graham's autobiography tells a similar story.[63]

A group of reporters, including Meg Greenfield (Carrie Coon), gather at Bradlee's house with only ten hours (compared to three months for the *Times*) to analyze more than 4,000 unnumbered, out-of-order pages. They need to meet an exceptionally tight deadline in order to publish a Pentagon Papers story in the next day's edition of the newspaper. Bradlee's ten-year-old daughter relieves some of the tension—for the *Post*'s staff and the film's audience alike—by selling the reporters lemonade. This cute detail may seem to have been created in Hollywood, but it actually happened.[64]

The *Post*'s lawyers argue against publication. Not only do they fear possible prosecution for violating the Espionage Act and defying the court order against the *Times*'s publication of the Papers, they are also concerned about potentially serious business consequences should they publish. The underwriting agreement for the newspaper company's stock offering permitted cancellation in case of "disaster" or a "catastrophic event" during the week following, although it also noted that "substantial expenses" could be incurred "to achieve and maintain editorial excellence and independence."[65] As Graham told NPR in 1997, when the *Post* obtained the Papers, the stock had not yet been sold, "so we were particularly liable to any kind of criminal prosecution."[66] The company owned three very profitable television stations whose licenses had to be renewed periodically by the Federal Communications Commission (FCC). Challenges to these licenses had been encouraged by the Nixon administration, but none succeeded.[67]

The reporters strongly support publication, with some threatening to resign if the story is suppressed. Graham is called away from an employee's farewell party in the middle of a speech to take a phone call from Beebe asking her for a final decision. Bradlee joins the call, dramatically declaring that "the only way to assert the right to publish is to publish." Asked his advice, Beebe hesitantly replies, "I guess I wouldn't publish." Graham, interpreting Beebe's response as equivocal, takes a deep breath, then says, "Let's go, let's publish," just minutes before the deadline to go to press. In case the audience doesn't realize the courage this took, Bradlee's wife points out that whatever happens, his reputation will be burnished, while Graham is risking her fortune and the newspaper that is her life. Kaminski lit Graham as "bigger than life because that's what she represented."[68] To dramatic music, copies of the *Post* roll off the presses.

The Supreme Court Rules

While the Supreme Court considers the arguments in *New York Times v. United States*,[69] in which the justices are asked to assess the constitutionality of prohibiting the publication of the Pentagon Papers, highlights are shown in a montage. Bradlee lays out copies of other newspapers that received portions of the Pentagon Papers and chose to publish them. "No matter what happens tomorrow," he declares triumphantly, "we are not a little local paper anymore." At the Supreme Court, a young woman who works for the Justice Department confidentially tells Graham that she hopes the *Post* wins. As Graham leaves the courthouse after the decision in favor of the newspapers is announced, she passes by a large group of onlookers consisting entirely of women looking up admiringly.

Peter Bradshaw criticizes this invented scene as "conferring on" Graham "a feminist status that may not have been apparent at the time."[70] One reason for this conclusion is that the year before these events, forty-six female employees of *Newsweek*, which was owned by the Washington Post Company, filed a discrimination complaint with the federal Equal Employment Opportunity Commission. As Graham later wrote, "eventually we started to remedy the situation—but not enough."[71] In 1972, fifty-nine women, after having their complaints ignored, wrote a letter to the *Post*'s leadership, including Bradlee and Graham, contending that the newspaper had failed to live up to past promises of equality. Graham confessed in her 2002 autobiography that "though it took me a long time to throw off some of my early and ingrained assumptions, I did come to understand the importance of the basic problems of equality in the workplace."[72]

An epilogue to *The Post* plays Nixon's taped voice emphasizing that he will never again allow another *Post* reporter in the White House. This is followed by a shadowy scene of the Watergate burglary and security guard Frank Wills reporting it to the police. Because this epilogue would serve as an effective transition to ATPM, those who have never seen either film would do well to see *The Post* first. Graham herself later expressed the belief that publication of the Pentagon Papers—and the ensuing legal battles—prepared the *Post* for its coverage of Watergate, while Bradlee thought it put the *Post* into the top ranks of newspapers by getting "the world to refer to the *Post* and the *New York Times* in the same breath."[73]

INVESTIGATIVE JOURNALISM HAS NOT DIED

The years covered by *All the President's Men* and *The Post* "became the glory period of American journalism." Whether in reality or on the fictional big screen, "[r]eporters presented themselves as fighting for truth and justice."[74] ATPM helped burnish the image of crusading reporters, even if it exaggerated their heroism and overlooked some of their faults. Woodward and Bernstein certainly deserved their acclaim for calling the government to account, as did Graham and Bradlee. However, this proved to be the height of public approval of the media in general, and "Watergate was the glorious last stand of print" in particular.[75] The prestige of the media began to decline significantly thereafter. "By the late 1990s," write Paul Gronke and Timothy Cook, "the news media were no longer so favorably viewed."[76] Indeed, as the public moved away from print and network television as its main sources of information about government and politics, faith in the media dropped even further, and faster. Despite Spielberg's hopes, *The Post* had no effect on this decidedly long-term trend. Indeed, confidence in the press has fallen from 41 percent in 2017, when his film was made, to a record low of 34 percent in 2022.[77]

Even though print newspapers are no longer what they were during the 1970s, leading newspapers such as the *Washington Post* and the *New York Times* have adapted to the digital age. After Katharine Graham's death in 2001, ownership of the *Post* remained in the Graham family until 2013, when

Jeff Bezos of Amazon bought the newspaper. Rather than trying to maximize the revenue per subscriber, Bezos moved to increase the number of digital subscribers dramatically. By 2019, his newspaper had 1.5 million such subscribers and "went from hemorrhaging advertising to becoming a profitable business in 2016."[78] The *Times* has been even more successful in its move away from print. Of its 8.8 million subscribers at the end of 2021, 5.9 million were for digital news and 2 million were for other digital products, but less than 800,000 for print. The company's fourth quarter profit of $109 million was a 12 percent increase over the previous year.[79]

These descriptions help to explain why, as discussed above, although the media has undergone significant changes in recent decades, investigative reporting "has become an enduring ideal in American journalism, persisting in shrinking newsrooms and being adopted with enthusiasm in many online start-ups."[80] As Beth Knobel found in her study of the front pages of nine newspapers between 1991 and 2011, despite decreased budgets investigative stories increased from 1 percent to nearly 5 percent. Editors told her that such reporting increased readership and sales, especially among midsize metropolitan papers.[81] If this were not the case, investigative journalism would not have found itself compelled to adapt to new forms of media. Nonprofits such as the Marshall Project, which writes about the criminal justice system and won a Pulitzer Prize in 2016 for "An Unbelievable Story of Rape," have found creative ways of financing, often partnering with traditional media.[82] A larger nonprofit, ProPublica, sets its goal as "shining a light on abuses of power and betrayals of public trust."[83] It has won six Pulitzers, including the first ever for an online source. Investigative journalism may have changed since ATPM, but reports of its imminent demise seem, at the very least, to be premature.

The Post considered the constraints capitalism's necessity for profit placed on the media's First Amendment function of holding the government accountable. Will the increasing concentration of media ownership place certain points of view off-limits? Will reporting such as that celebrated in these two films be able to penetrate the partisan bubbles that characterize today's information environment? *The Post* touched upon some of these concerns and began to raise some of these questions in the mind of twenty-first century audiences. John Street asks whether the faith the authors of the First Amendment placed in the press was justified: "Are they independent, servants of the political truth and the public interest? Or are they the hired guns of particular political and commercial interests?"[84] The next chapter's examination of *Network* and *The Social Network* addresses these questions in light of changes in television news and the emergence of social media.

NOTES

1. Bill Nichols, *Engaging Cinema: An Introduction to Film Studies* (New York: Norton, 2010), 136, 237.

2. Vincent Blasi, "The Checking Value in First Amendment Theory," *American Bar Foundation Research Journal* 3, no. 3 (July 1977): 527.

3. James T. Hamilton, *Democracy's Detectives: The Economics of Investigative Journalism* (Cambridge, MA: Harvard University Press, 2016), 9.

4. David E. Kaplan, *Global Investigative Journalism: Strategies for Support*, Report to the Center for International Media Assistance, 2nd ed., January 14, 2013, 10, https://www.cima.ned.org/wp-content/uploads/2015/01/CIMA-Investigative-Journalism-Dave-Kaplan.pdf.

5. Hamilton, *Democracy's Detectives*, 13.

6. C. W. Anderson, Leonard Downie Jr., and Michael Schudson, *The News Media: What Everyone Needs to Know* (New York: Oxford University Press, 2016), 112.

7. Anderson, Downie, and Schudson, *The News Media*, 34.

8. Hamilton, *Democracy's Detectives*, 279.

9. Hamilton, *Democracy's Detectives*, 314.

10. Brian McNair, "Journalism at the Movies," *Journalism Practice* 5, no. 3 (2011): 366–75.

11. Ken Ringle, "Journalism's Finest 2 Hours and 16 Minutes," *Washington Post*, June 14, 1992.

12. Johnny Restall, "Celebrating the Continued Relevance of 'All The President's Men,'" *Film Cred*, April 5, 2021, https://film-cred.com/all-the-presidents-men-relevant-woodward-bernstein-nixon/.

13. *Telling the Truth About Lies: The Making of All the President's Men*, feature included with 2006 DVD of *All the President's Men*.

14. Jordan Orlando, "William Goldman Turned Reporters into Heroes in *All the President's Men*," *New Yorker*, November 27, 2018, https://www.newyorker.com/culture/cultural-comment/william-goldman-turned-reporters-into-heroes-in-all-the-presidents-men.

15. Steve Wulf, "On the Record," *Entertainment Weekly*, February 22, 2002, 74.

16. Katherine Graham, *Personal History* (New York: Vintage, 2011), 942–43; Mark Feeney, *Nixon at the Movies: A Book about Belief* (Chicago: University of Chicago Press, 2004), 263.

17. *Telling the Truth* feature and Redford 2006 DVD commentary.

18. Ben Bradlee, *A Good Life: Newspapering and Other Adventures* (New York: Simon and Schuster, 1995), 326. "Peck's Bad Boy" is an 1883 fictional character whose name has come to mean someone whose behavior leads to embarrassment.

19. Graham, *Personal History*, 870.

20. Alan J. Pakula and Richard Thompson, "Mr. Pakula Goes to Washington," *Film Comment* 12, no. 5 (September–October 1976): 12–19.

21. Bob Woodward and Carl Bernstein, *All the President's Men* (1974; repr. New York: Simon and Schuster, 2012), 51.

22. Named after a pornographic film of the same title.
23. Orlando, "William Goldman Turned Reporters into Heroes."
24. Woodward and Bernstein, *All the President's Men*, 79.
25. Bradlee, *A Good Life*, 365.
26. David Von Drehle, "FBI's No. 2 Was 'Deep Throat': Mark Felt Ends 30-Year Mystery of the Post's Watergate Source," *Washington Post*, June 1, 2005, https://www.washingtonpost.com/politics/fbis-no-2-was-deep-throat-mark-felt-ends-30-year-mystery-of-the-posts-watergate-source/2012/06/04/gJQAwseRIV_story.html.
27. 408 U.S. 665 (1972).
28. Hank Nuwer, "Understanding Shield Law," *Quill*, March 26, 2021, https://www.quillmag.com/2021/04/08/understanding-shield-law/.
29. *In re Grand Jury Subpoena, Judith Miller*, 438 F.3d 1138 (DC Cir. 2006).
30. Anna Diakun and Trevor Timm, "For the Biden Administration, Who Counts as News Media," *Columbia Journalism Review*, June 9, 2021. https://www.cjr.org/opinion/trump-biden-justice-department-media-guidelines.php.
31. Bradlee, *A Good Life*, 329.
32. Woodward and Bernstein, *All the President's Men*, 335–36.
33. William Goldman, *Adventures in the Screen Trade: A Personal View of Hollywood and the Screenwriting* (New York: Warner Books, 1983), 347.
34. Bradlee, *A Good Life*, 342.
35. Graham, *Personal History*, 892.
36. Woodward and Bernstein, *All the President's Men*, 222–4.
37. Woodward and Bernstein, *All the President's Men*, 277.
38. "Recount! Oscar Voters Today Would Make 'Brokeback Mountain' Best Picture over 'Crash,'" *Hollywood Reporter*, February 18, 2015, https://www.hollywoodreporter.com/news/general-news/recount-oscar-voters-today-would-773522/.
39. "Domestic Box Office for 2017," Box Office Mojo, https://www.boxofficemojo.com/year/2017/.
40. More on these events and the court case can be found in Sanford J. Ungar, *The Papers & the Papers: An Account of the Legal and Political Battle over the Pentagon Papers* (Boston: Dutton, 1972); Bruce E. Altschuler, "Is the Pentagon Papers Case Relevant in the Age of WikiLeaks?" *Political Science Quarterly* 130 (Fall 2015): 410–23.
41. James C. Goodale, "Spielberg's The Post: Good Movie, Bad History," *Daily Beast*, December 22, 2017, https://www.thedailybeast.com/spielbergs-the-post-good-movie-bad-history.
42. Manohla Dargis, "In *The Post*, Democracy Survives the Darkness," *New York Times*, December 21, 2017.
43. Richard Turner, "How Spielberg's Post Came to Life at Lightning Speed," *Wall Street Journal*, November 30, 2017, https://www.wsj.com/articles/how-spielbergs-post-came-to-life-at-lightning-speed-1512061678. The quote comes from Jonathan Freedland, "Steven Spielberg: 'The Urgency to Make *The Post* was because of Trump's Administration,'" *Guardian*, January 19, 2018, https://www.theguardian

.com/film/2018/jan/19/steven-spielberg-the-urgency-to-make-the-post-was-because-of-this-administration.

44. Lindsey Meeks, "Defining the Enemy: How Donald Trump Frames the News Media," *Journalism & Mass Communication Quarterly* 97, no. 1 (2020): 211.

45. David Remnick, "The Cost of Trump's Assault on the Press and the Truth," *New Yorker*, November 29, 2020, https://www.newyorker.com/magazine/2020/12/07/the-cost-of-trumps-assault-on-the-press-and-the-truth.

46. Gallup, "American Views: Trust, Media and Democracy," 2018, https://knightfoundation.org/wp-content/uploads/2018/01/KnightFoundation_AmericansViews_Client_Report_010917_Final_Updated-2.pdf (last accessed March 26, 2013).

47. Amy Nicholson, "How a Writer Defied 'One in a Million' Odds to Get Her First Movie Made by Steven Spielberg," *Washington Post*, December 21, 2017.

48. Ash Carter, "Truth to Power," *Esquire*, December 1, 2017, https://classic.esquire.com/article/2017/12/1/truth-to-power.

49. Thomas Vinciguerra, "Hell Hath No Fury Like the *New York Times* Scorned by Hollywood," *Columbia Journalism Review*, May 1, 2017, https://www.cjr.org/the_feature/tom-hanks-meryl-streep-new-york-times-washington-post.php.

50. Michael Koresky, "Liberty Films," *Film Comment* 54, no. 1 (January–February 2018): 56.

51. Graham, *Personal History*, 943–45; Anna Diamond, "What *The Post* Gets Right (and Wrong) about Katharine Graham and the Pentagon Papers," *Smithsonian*, December 29, 2017, https://www.smithsonianmag.com/smithsonian-institution/what-the-post-gets-right-wrong-katharine-graham-pentagon-papers-180967677/.

52. Goldman, *Adventures in the Screen Trade*.

53. Anna Tsioulcas, "Harvey Weinstein Will Likely Spend the Rest of His Life in Prison after LA Sentence," NPR, February 23, 2023, https://www.npr.org/2023/02/23/1158207425/harvey-weinstein-los-angeles#. For more details about Harvey Weinstein and the charges against him, see "Harvey Weinstein Timeline: How the Scandal Has Unfolded," BBC News, February 24, 2023, https://www.bbc.com/news/entertainment-arts-41594672.

54. Peter Bradshaw, "*She Said* Review: Breaking the Silence around Harvey Weinstein," *Guardian*, November 24 2022, https://www.theguardian.com/film/2022/nov/24/she-said-review-breaking-the-male-silence-around-harvey-weinstein.

55. Ron Prince, "Truth Will Out," *British Cinematographer*, April 29, 2018, https://britishcinematographer.co.uk/janusz-kaminski-asc-the-post/.

56. Matt Grabar, "Cinematographer Janusz Kaminsi on 'The Post': 'I Wanted to Make It Feel like Someone Else Shot It,'" *Deadline*, January 4, 2018. https://deadline.com/2018/01/the-post-janusz-kaminski-cinematography-interview-news-1202230114/.

57. Goodale, "Good Movie, Bad History."

58. Graham, *Personal History*, 293.

59. Graham, *Personal History*, 353.

60. Graham, *Personal History*, 644.

61. David Remnick, "Citizen Kay," *New Yorker*, January 12, 1997), https://www.newyorker.com/magazine/1997/01/20/citizen-kay.

62. Robert S. McNamara, *In Retrospect: The Tragedy and Lessons of Vietnam* (New York: Crown, 1995), 281.

63. Graham, *Personal History*, 839–40.

64. Ungar, *The Papers & The Papers*, 146.

65. Ungar, *The Papers & The Papers*, 145.

66. Mahita Gajanan, "The True Story behind *The Post*," *Time*, December 26, 2017, https://time.com/5079506/the-post-true-story/.

67. Graham, *Personal History*, 841–45.

68. Grabar, "Cinematographer Janusz Kaminski on 'The Post.'"

69. 403 U.S. 713 (1971).

70. Peter Bradshaw, "*The Post* review," *The Guardian*, December 6, 2017, https://www.theguardian.com/film/2017/dec/06/the-post-review-steven-spielberg-tom-hanks-meryl-streep-washington-post.

71. Graham, *Personal History*, 801.

72. Graham, *Personal History*, 809.

73. Graham, *Personal History*, 861–63.

74. Darrell M. West, *The Rise and Fall of the Media Establishment* (New York: Palgrave, 2001), 64.

75. Feeney, *Nixon at the Movies*, 258.

76. Paul Gronke and Timothy Cook, "Disdaining the Media: The American Public's Changing Attitudes toward the News," in *Media Power in Politics*, 6th ed., edited by Doris A. Graber (Washington, DC: CQ Press, 2011), 102.

77. Megan Brenan, "Americans' Trust in Media Remains Near Record Low," Gallup, October 18, 2022, https://news.gallup.com/poll/403166/americans-trust-media-remains-near-record-low.aspx.

78. Francesca Giuliani-Hoffman, "How the *Washington Post* Has Changed under Jeff Bezos," CNN Business, August 16, 2019, https://www.cnn.com/2019/08/16/media/jeff-bezos-donald-graham/index.html.

79. Marc Tracy, "*The Times* Hits Its Goal of 10 Million Subscriptions with the Addition of *The Athletic*," *New York Times*, February 2, 2022, https://www.nytimes.com/2022/02/02/business/media/nyt-earnings-q4–2021.html.

80. Anderson, Downie, and Schudson, *The News Media*, 36.

81. Beth Knobel, "The End of Investigative Journalism? Not Yet," *Columbia Journalism Review*, April 13, 2018, https://www.cjr.org/analysis/newspapers-financial-crisis.php.

82. The Marshall Project, https://www.themarshallproject.org/.

83. Pro Publica, https://www.propublica.org/.

84. John Street, *Mass Media, Politics & Democracy*, 2nd ed. (London: Red Globe Press, 2019), 185–86.

Chapter 4

Technology Transforms the Press into the Media

Network *and* The Social Network

Bruce E. Altschuler

"Congress shall make no law . . . abridging the freedom . . . of the press." Although this language has stayed the same since the ratification of the First Amendment on December 15, 1791, it has been (and continues to be) susceptible to multiple competing interpretations. The two films analyzed in this chapter focus our analytical and interpretive attention on the word "press." When the First Amendment was adopted, freedom of the press meant the printed press, primarily newspapers. Today "press" has become a virtual anachronism, replaced by "media." Although *Network* (1976) and *The Social Network* (2010; hereafter TSN) were released more than three decades apart, both feature the "press" as "the media"—albeit different iterations of "the media." As "the media" continues to evolve, these two films provide us with a valuable opportunity to consider how technology can change the meaning of "the media," and the effect of these changes on the constitutional protection afforded members of the fourth estate. They examine modern information sources, television news, and social media, respectively. The argument of these two films is that the development of television and social media as the main sources of news for much of the United States, especially younger Americans, has coarsened the political dialogue while polluting it with misinformation. In so doing, these films, and the accompanying analysis, raise the following questions:

- How has the transformation from the printed press to the modern mass media, particularly television and social media, affected the public's sources(s) of news?
- How does the First Amendment protect these new sources of information?
- What laws exist to protect or regulate television and social media?
- Who is a journalist? (And who should decide the answer to that question?)
- How should interpretations of the free press clause change as technology changes?
- To what extent does the need to attract audiences and make a profit affect the content of the media?

The two films discussed in this chapter tell their stories in very different ways. *Network* is a sharply satirical critique of television news. Satire can be defined as a work of art "in which prevailing vices are held up to ridicule," often but not always using humor.[1] The courts have held that "despite its literal falsity, satirical speech enjoys First Amendment protection."[2] The analysis of *The People vs. Larry Flynt* in chapter 8 will discuss this in more detail.

The Social Network tells the story of the origins of Facebook using flashbacks of testimony in legal proceedings. Because the conflict inherent in adversary settings enhances the drama, courtroom confrontations have long been popular features in movies. By flashing back during the testimony of each witness, the film exposes the audience to different viewpoints, requiring it to judge the credibility of each. Readers are encouraged to consider the following cinematic elements of the two films:

- *Network*'s use of satire to criticize television news.
- How lighting is used in *Network* to show media corruption.
- How Facebook became a media empire.
- How Mark Zuckerberg evolved from a rebellious college student into a media mogul.
- The role of women in *Network* and *The Social Network.*

A CHANGING PRESS (MEDIA) LANDSCAPE

A 2022 *New York Times* poll revealed that only 7 percent of respondents got most of their news from a major newspaper; just 1 percent from a local one.[3] Additionally, in October 2023 recent polling from the Pew Center showed that 58 percent of those questioned "prefer[red]" to get their news on a digital device, television was a distant second with 27 percent, and radio (6 percent) and print (5 percent) trailed significantly. Among those aged eighteen to twenty-nine, the trend was even more pronounced, with 83 percent preferring digital.[4] Even the readership of leading newspapers has become largely digital. For example, only 761,000 of the 9 million subscribers to the *New York Times* receive the print edition; the rest are entirely digital.[5] These trends are expected to hit local newspapers with devastating force. As Sara Fischer reported for Axios in November 2023, "[t]the decline of local newspapers accelerated so rapidly in 2023 that analysts now believe the U.S. will have lost one-third of the newspapers it had as of 2005 by the end of next year [2024]—rather than in 2025, as originally predicted."[6] The First Amendment might protect the freedom of these newspapers to publish, but it cannot protect them from the forces of capitalism and technological change.

If this demise of the print media is inevitable, is it inevitable that—as many critics suggest—the *quality* of media coverage will also suffer? Today, it is easy to think about answers to this question by focusing on the effects of social media on the dissemination of "news." However, *Network* asks us to think about the question with regard to television. Ezra Klein has written that "television turned everything into entertainment and social media taught us to think with the crowd."[7] *Network* makes this argument about television through biting satire. It is so different from *All the President's Men* (discussed in chapter 3) that it is hard to believe that both films were released in the same year, 1976.

At that time, most television entertainment and national news programming was produced by just three networks: ABC, NBC, and CBS. These programs were broadcast by local stations owned by or affiliated with the national networks. Although the First Amendment prevents government from requiring licenses for newspapers and magazines, television stations must have a license before they can broadcast over the airwaves to the public. The Federal Communications Commission distributes licenses "based on its determination of the public interest."[8] The Federal Radio Commission (FRC) was created by the Federal Radio Act of 1927 to issue licenses to radio stations. The Federal Communications Act of 1934 turned the FRC into the FCC, adding television stations to its jurisdiction. This statute declared the broadcast spectrum to be a public resource. The FCC was allowed to set conditions in exchange for allowing television and radio stations to use this resource. The Fairness Doctrine, established by the FCC in 1948, required stations "to devote a reasonable percentage of broadcast time to the coverage of public issues" and to be fair by presenting "contrasting points of view."[9] When these requirements were challenged as violating the First Amendment, they were unanimously upheld by the Supreme Court because if two stations try to broadcast on the same frequency "the result is chaos."[10] As explained below, deregulation during the 1980s (including the elimination of the Fairness Doctrine and the easing of licensing requirements), together with the widespread availability of cable networks, which do not require licenses, removed the underpinning of this "spectrum scarcity" argument.

Joseph Turow writes that during the latter part of the twentieth century, the Supreme Court "adopted an increasingly broad view of 'the press' that included factually truthful advertising and many forms of entertainment in film, television, and radio as well as print media."[11] A good example is the evolution of the Equal Time rule which was established in the 1934 law to require stations that give or sell airtime to a political candidate to make comparable time available to all rival candidates for the same price. In 1959, Congress added an exemption for news programming. Since then, the FCC has included what many would consider entertainment programming, even *The Howard Stern Show*, which regularly featured strippers and porn stars. As one official told Andrew Serros, it is no longer clear whether any television program is covered by the provision.[12]

Social media fits into this framework as well. The crucial question is whether the First Amendment is up to the challenge of protecting freedom of this greatly expanded "press" while confronting a new set of dangers.

NETWORK

The screenwriter of *Network*, Paddy Chayefsky, and its director, Sidney Lumet, were both veterans of television's "golden age" of dramas who had successfully transitioned to film. As Howard Gottfried, the movie's producer, explains, he and Chayefsky were inspired when they learned that a major global corporation was considering acquiring ABC. Chayefsky realized that this would compel the network to change its news division from a loss leader into a profit-making entity.[13] As chapter 5's analysis of *Good Night, and Good Luck* shows, even during the 1950s there were pressures on Edward R. Murrow to generate more revenue and avoid offending commercial sponsors. During the late 1960s, individual stations had already discovered that their own local news could generate considerable revenue. As Daniel Hallin observes, by the late 1970s such programming generated 60 percent of station profits, making it "'too important' to leave to journalists." The result? "[A] heavily entertainment oriented form of programming began to evolve."[14] *Network* makes a strong cinematic statement about this evolution, and its relationship to freedom of the press.

At first, Chayefsky's script ran into studio reservations. They worried that its highly critical view of television would make it difficult to sell broadcast rights, which were an important revenue source at that time. Some thought the dialogue contained too much coarse language.[15] Additionally, according to Lumet, there was concern that several lengthy monologues would bore the audience. (Readers are encouraged to compare the use of monologues in *Good Morning, Vietnam*, which is analyzed in chapter 1.) Lumet countered that "the scenes were visually arresting and brilliantly acted."[16] Despite the studio misgivings, Chayefsky was paid $300,000 for his script, which at the time was a very significant amount of money (approximately $1.5 million in 2023).[17] The opening credits describe *Network* as "by Paddy Chayefsky," making it clear that he was far more influential in the making of this film than screenwriters usually are.

The film begins by dividing the screen into four quadrants, three of which show television monitors with actual news broadcasts of the three major networks. On the fourth, Howard Beale (Peter Finch) of the fictional network UBS is also delivering the evening news. An offscreen narrator then chronicles the personal and professional decline of Beale, who, because of his excessive drinking and low ratings, has been given two weeks' notice that he will be fired.

The movie's lighting parallels its story. As director Lumet explained, "The movie was about corruption. So we corrupted the camera," starting with mostly natural light that slowly became more artificial as the film progressed.[18] Cinematographer Owen Roizman has provided more detail. The film was shot in three phases: naturalistic or "ultra-real," realistic, and commercial. The first used existing location light and the second augmented it to make it more pleasing, while in the third, "I'd create my own sources and my own moods." Active, frantic camera movement in the early scenes increased excitement, then gradually slowed down.[19]

Also worth noting is that, except for the introductory music to *The Howard Beale Show*, the film lacks a score, which is one of several ways in which it makes even some of its most apparently outrageous scenes seem realistic. As Lumet put it, *Network* tries "to stretch realism past its limit, but never to violate the truth."[20] Satire exaggerates reality to make its points, but Lumet believed that the worlds of reality and satire were colliding.

After the news broadcast, Beale goes out drinking with his boss and best friend, news director Max Schumacher (William Holden). An old-school journalist, Schumacher is the conscience of the film, often stating what seem to be Chayefsky's opinions of the decline of news values on television. When Beale declares his intention to blow his brains out on the air, Schumacher, taking the remark as gallows humor, proposes a series titled *The Death Hour*, which would be guaranteed to receive great ratings. The film soon shows this to be more prophetic than Schumacher could have imagined.

There has been some debate about whether Beale's suicide threat was inspired by the actual 1974 on-air suicide of Sarasota morning show anchor Christine Chubbuck, who shot herself after declaring, that "in keeping with Channel 40's policy of bringing you the latest in blood and guts in living color, you are going to see another first: an attempted suicide." Brian Eggert believes that because this event was a national news story, it "could not have been missed by Chayefsky."[21] After finding no specific evidence that Chayefsky was influenced by this event, however, Dave Itzkoff countered that it is unclear whether the screenwriter was aware of this incident at the time he wrote the screenplay.[22] Nevertheless, evidence of Chayefsky's prescience is that two films about Chubbuck's suicide, the docudrama *Christine* and the documentary *Kate Plays Christine*, were released in 2016, four decades after both Chubbuck's death and the release of *Network*.

The next evening, Howard's on-air announcement of his suicidal intentions makes it clear that he was neither joking nor entirely rational. In a nice touch, the control room crew is so preoccupied with their routine that, at first, they fail to notice what he has said. It only sinks in during a commercial break, after which, with the cameras still rolling, the panic-stricken crew pulls him out of his chair, drags him away, and takes the program off the air. This seemingly outrageous scene is made more realistic by having been shot in an actual Toronto news studio, using its technical facilities and some of its personnel.[23] When the program ends, UBS vice president Frank Hackett (Robert Duvall) angrily confronts Schumacher, telling him the network will no longer tolerate the news division's multimillion-dollar losses. He is more concerned with profit and loss than with either the integrity of the news or Beale's well-being, underlining a key theme of the film.

Meanwhile, programming executive Diana Christensen (Faye Dunaway) is watching film taken by the Ecumenical Liberation Army (ELA) as they robbed a bank. The ELA resembles the real life Symbionese Liberation Army, best known for kidnapping William Randolph Hearst's granddaughter Patricia. It even has its own kidnapped heiress, Mary Ann Gifford, played by Kathy Cronkite, the niece of famed CBS anchor Walter Cronkite. As if to further underscore the film's message about the corrupting element of capitalism, Christensen, who is seeking "angry shows," finds the ELA film so fascinating, she begins to negotiate with Communist Party leader Laureen Hobbs (Marlene Warfield).

The film holds the audience's attention by cutting between this over-the-top plot thread and an apparently contrite Beale's request to return briefly to his program for an apology and a final farewell. However, the film's key narrative motifs continue, because when Beale is allowed to go on the air, he abandons his prepared script to explain that his previous behavior was because he "just ran out of bullshit."

At a corporate meeting, Hackett, without having consulted Schumacher, proposes ending the independence of the news division. In these corporate scenes, additional light is added, beginning the "corruption" of the lighting meant to demonstrate the perversion of television news. Schumacher, upset by the changes since Communications Corporation of America (CCA) took over the network, ignores Hackett's demand to take Beale off the air. As a result, Schumacher is told to turn in his resignation. Christensen, however, is so excited by the broadcast and Beale's subsequent news conference that she dismisses her partner in the midst of sexual relations in order to check Beale's ratings. Not only have they soared, Beale has knocked all other stories off the front pages of the newspapers. Christensen sees Beale as "a modern-day prophet" who is "articulating a national rage." Her excited nonstop remarks contrast with other executives, who fear that Beale is having a nervous breakdown.

As a result of her victory, Christensen is put in charge of the news, which, appropriately for the film's storyline and messages, has become part of the entertainment division. However, Beale's ratings spike (which greatly contributed to Christensen's promotion) proves temporary.

"Mad as Hell"

A few days later, Beale is awakened by a voice telling him that the truth will be put into his mouth to enable him to pass it along to his audience. Throwing a coat over his pajamas, he rushes out into a rainstorm, wandering aimlessly until he arrives soaking wet at the studio in time for his program, where he delivers one of the long speeches the film is noted for. After telling the audience that "we know things are bad, worse than bad," he urges them to go to their windows and shout, "I'm mad as hell and I'm not going to take this anymore!" Watching this, Christensen gets more and more excited as she foresees ratings gold. Looking out the window of their apartment, Schumacher's daughter sees large numbers of people yelling Beale's new mantra.

This scene, and Beale's slogan, have become iconic, foreshadowing the anger that has become a major part of American politics. Ihman Rahman-Jones believes that "Beale's populist anger resonates with audiences in the film, as it would in real life now."[24] Despite consisting largely of a long speech of the kind feared by many who read Chayefsky's original script, the well-acted, emotional scene holds the audience's attention. It had thirty edits, including nine reaction shots of Christensen's growing delight.[25] Peter Finch became so emotional during filming that he had to stop halfway through the second take, telling Lumet, "I can't do it anymore." The director improvised by combining that take with the second half of the first in the final version of the film.[26]

Christensen transforms the news into an entertainment program with host Beale billed as "the mad prophet of the airwaves," accompanied by a soothsayer and applauded by a studio audience. Its high ratings mean financial salvation for the previously struggling UBS, which has now been taken over by CCA. She also develops *The Mao Tse-Tung Hour*, which, anticipating today's reality shows, uses film taken by the ELA after each of their crimes to introduce a dramatization of the events. Hobbs agrees to be a liaison between the network and the ELA after she is guaranteed editorial control over the prime-time show.

A comically satirical scene of a farmhouse meeting of Hobbs, ELA leaders, and network executives demonstrates that the profit motive can even buy off supposedly anticapitalistic radicals. *The Mao Tse-Tung Hour* has become so successful that an angry Hobbs demands to renegotiate every detail of the contract, using the language of a corporate lawyer. "I'm making a lousy two-fifteen per segment," she declares, "and I'm already deficiting twenty-five grand a week with Metro." ELA leader Great Ahmed Kahn (Arthur Burghart) dramatically ends the discussion by firing his weapon into the air. Satire often works by taking otherwise ordinary actions to an apparent extreme. In this case, the audience is induced to both laugh and consider the paradox of a communist behaving as a capitalist entrepreneur.

Stereotypical Women?

As these events unfold, Schumacher and Christensen begin an unlikely affair. Even during their sexual encounters, she talks excitedly about the success of her programs, which have moved the audience ratings of UBS from fourth place to first. When Schumacher tells his wife, Louise, that he is in love with Christensen, she responds with a speech so dramatic that, even though it was one of only two scenes that the actress Beatrice Straight appears in, she won an Oscar as best supporting actress. After six months of living together, Schumacher breaks off the affair, telling Christensen that she has been so influenced by television that she is incapable of expressing real emotion. Her reply to his request that all he wants is for her to love him is that she does not know how. According to the script, as Schumacher leaves, "the CLICK of the door being opened and the CLACK of the door closing" can be heard, leaving Christensen "alone in arctic desolation."[27]

Although these two Academy Award–winning roles make *Network* quite different from the nearly all-male ATPM, discussed in the previous chapter, the film can still be criticized for its portrayal of women, albeit on different grounds. Christensen is the workaholic career woman unable to establish real emotional relationships. As Barbara Walters, the first female anchor of a network evening news broadcast, bluntly put it, "the leading woman had to be a bitch. And that was typecasting of a woman working." Walters's own problems at ABC were due not to a lack of toughness, but because those in charge felt that she was "not one of us."[28]

Louise Schumacher is essentially Christensen's opposite: the wife who devoted her life to raising a family in support of her husband's career only to be cast aside for a younger woman. At the end of the film, she is so depressed that her adult daughter has to fly to New York from the West Coast to care for her. Is the film suggesting that women must choose between these two extremes and that those wishing to be successful in the television business must choose Diana's path?

Howard's End

The corporate success of UBS hits a snag when Beale denounces the acquisition of its parent company, CCA, by a Saudi-controlled group. He beseeches his viewers to contact the White House to express opposition to the merger. Because this generates millions of telegrams, CCA head Arthur Jensen (Ned Beatty) urgently summons Beale for a meeting. Like the other long speeches in *Network*, Jensen's is exceptionally well written and acted, but what makes it memorable is the setting and the lighting. After the New York Stock Exchange withdrew permission to film in its boardroom because of the script's criticism of corporate power, the scene was relocated to the New York Public Library's conference room, which proved to be a fortuitous accident.[29] A standing Jensen and a seated, barely lit Beale are at opposite ends of a long table lit by green bankers' lamps and a candelabra. Because of library lighting restrictions, the only other light source is directly behind Jensen's head so that, according to Roizman, it "was glowing like he might be God—as he was stating that he was."[30] Jensen's apocalyptic speech explains how nations and democracy have been replaced by "a college of corporations." Globalization will end war, famine, and all other serious problems. Jensen's gospel, preached by a converted Beale on his television program, proves so depressing that its ratings drop precipitously, but Jensen is so pleased that it proves impossible to cancel the show.

As these huge global corporations acquire constitutionally protected news companies, they are able to use them to soften stories about their other businesses. For example, when an alligator attack at Walt Disney World left a two-year-old dead, according to Brian Stelter, coverage on Disney-owned ABC "excluded an angle that NBC and CBS explored in detail": whether there should have been signs warning of the danger of alligators.[31] This is hardly the independent press the First Amendment gives special protection to.

Their jobs at risk because of the $45 million loss, UBS executives meet to decide on a course of action. Even Hobbs, now as bottom-line oriented as any capitalist, is upset because Beale's program has become such a poor lead-in for hers. The satirical comedy in this scene is that those present discuss murdering Beale with the same matter-of-fact tone as any ordinary business decision, calmly weighing the costs and benefits. Corporate morality, the film argues, is simply a matter of profit and loss. Completing the corruption of the network is the increased artificiality of the lighting, which, according to Lumet's DVD commentary, has become as bright as "a Ford commercial" in this and the next scene.[32]

The film climaxes as ELA assassins in Beale's audience rush the stage to kill him. The ending is an echo of the opening, with four television screens showing news stories about the murder interspersed with commercials. A final voiceover tells the audience that this was "the first known instance of a man being killed because he had lousy ratings." The last image is of Beale's corpse.

The Continuing Significance of *Network*

Network was a great success at the box office, with a gross of $20 million that made it one of the most profitable films of the year.[33] Despite the movie's bitter criticism of television, selling the broadcast rights proved no problem as CBS paid $5 million for three showings of an edited version.[34] The filmmakers themselves did the editing because Chayefsky feared that "otherwise they'll butcher it."[35]

The film generated some extreme reactions from reviewers. While Vincent Canby of the *New York Times* praised it as "brilliantly, cruelly funny, a topical American comedy that confirms Paddy Chayefsky's position as a major new American satirist," Frank Rich described Chayefsky in the *New York Post* as "a cranky paranoid who's overstacked his polemical deck."[36] Roger Ebert was more measured, finding it "a supremely well-acted, intelligent film that tries for too much."[37] *Network* was nominated for nine Oscars, winning four—three for acting (Dunaway, Finch, and Straight) and one for Chayefsky's screenplay. However, it (and ATPM) lost for best picture to *Rocky*.

The network news establishment predictably rejected the premise of the film entirely. Walter Cronkite countered that "since the birth of television, all of us have known how we could hype our ratings almost instantly . . . but you don't see any hint of things like that."[38] Barbara Walters claimed that there would not be "that kind of show-biz approach to the news because we will never let it happen."[39] Chayefsky strongly defended his work: "*Network* is a farce, but once the idea is there, it's all real, every bit. . . . Television will do anything for a rating. Anything! . . . Television is democracy at its ugliest. Give the people what they want."[40]

Developments since then have confirmed many of Chayefsky's fears. Jim Edwards wrote in 2012 that "the movie predicts everything about modern media in the 21st Century . . . and it did so 20 years before the internet even existed."[41] Aaron Sorkin, the screenwriter for our next film, *The Social*

Network, believes that "[n]o predictor of the future—not even Orwell—had ever been as right as Chayefsky was when he wrote *Network*."[42]

These changes were facilitated by the FCC's deregulation of broadcasting during the 1980s followed by the dramatic growth of unregulated cable television, particularly cable news networks. The FCC eliminated the Fairness Doctrine in 1987 and has also eased licensing requirements for local stations and rules against concentration of ownership of those stations. Television viewers, whose choice had been largely limited to programming of the three networks, now have hundreds of channels to choose from, weakening the argument that "spectrum scarcity" justified government regulation of broadcasting. This fragmentation reduced the nightly network news audience from Beale's 60 million to 7.5 million for ABC, the highest rated of the three programs, despite population growth in the United States of more than 100 million people.[43]

Cable news discovered that the best way to attract viewers was to express opinions rather than attempting to report the news objectively. According to Stelter, before the pandemic the conservative Fox News was approaching $2 billion in profits.[44] Matt Taibbi believes that the focus of cable news has become "making sure your viewer came back the next day. We sold anger and we did it mainly by feeding audiences what they wanted to hear."[45] CNN, the most mainstream of the cable news networks, has been the most financially troubled. In December 2022, it laid off hundreds of employees after shutting down its new streaming service earlier in the year. Its sister network HLN (formerly Headline News) ended all live programming in order to become more entertainment oriented. As the *Washington Post* put it, "the network now mostly airs unscripted shows focused on crime and mystery."[46]

The fictional cinematic takeover of USB by CCA foreshadowed real-world acquisitions of ABC, NBC, and CBS by giant media corporations. ABC was purchased by Disney in 1996 and NBC by Comcast in 2013; CBS merged with Viacom in 2018 to create ViacomCBS.

When George Clooney showed *Network* to a group of young people in 2005, none realized that it was a satire, demonstrating to him "that everything Chayefsky wrote about had happened."[47] However unscientific, this may be as good evidence as any of *Network*'s foresight.

THE ORIGINS OF *THE SOCIAL NETWORK*

Yet another revolution in communications occurred with the development of the internet during the 1990s and the introduction of social media early in the twenty-first century. The largest of these sites has been Facebook (FB), renamed as Meta in 2021. Launched by Mark Zuckerberg in 2004 on just one college campus, FB, according to captions at the end of *The Social Network*, had 500 million members in 207 countries and a value of $25 billion when the film was released in 2010. At the time FB was launched it seemed more a site for social connection than part of the press, but it has become a major source of news for much of the public and qualifies for First Amendment press protection, thereby raising numerous legal questions. This chapter's concluding sections discuss how this transition occurred and analyze these legal issues.

Nominally based on *The Accidental Billionaires* by Ben Mezrich, TSN tells the origin story of FB. Mezrich's book has been widely criticized for taking major liberties with the facts. For example, Janet Maslin wrote that it was "so clearly unreliable, that there's no mistaking it for a serious document."[48] In an author's note, Mezrich admits that he "changed or imagined" details, names, and personal descriptions while re-creating "some conversations and scenes."[49] Mezrich was first contacted in 2008 by Eduardo Saverin, who asked him to write about how Saverin and "his best friend had co-founded Facebook and no one had ever heard about him."[50] Because Zuckerberg refused to be interviewed, the book is largely Saverin's story. Mezrich's original proposal for that story attracted attention not only from publishers but also from movie studios. Aaron Sorkin, who eventually wrote the screenplay for TSN, has said it was based primarily on Mezrich's proposal, as it was nearly completed before he even read the book. Rather than telling the story from Saverin's or any other point of view, he "dramatized the fact that there were conflicting stories."[51] Once again, we see the importance of *how* a film tells a story.

Mark Zuckerberg's Rosebud

In a precredit sequence, we first hear the voice of Zuckerberg (Jesse Eisenberg), then see him and his girlfriend Erica Albright (Rooney Mara) with their faces in shadows in a noisy dark bar, arguing. With quick cuts between the two and rapid-fire dialogue, this conversation immediately grabs the viewer's attention. The ambient noise in the bar requires the audience to pay careful attention in order to understand the dialogue. The film's editors took three weeks to combine nearly a hundred takes into a single scene.[52] When Albright tells Zuckerberg that she has to leave to study, Harvard student Zuckerberg makes a condescending reference about her attending the less prestigious Boston University. Finding this the last straw, she breaks up with him. Despite his apology, Albright leaves. As the bar conversations become quieter, the soundtrack, written by Trent Reznor and Atticus Ross, the composers of the film's score, plays a melancholy piano melody to emphasize

Zuckerberg's loneliness. This melody repeats twice in the film as Zuckerberg separates himself from others close to him, most notably Saverin.

After walking back to his dorm room, Zuckerberg posts a rant against Albright on his blog. Obtaining pictures of students from their dormitory facebooks, he sets up FaceMash, a website to evaluate the attractiveness of Harvard students, particularly women. As he wrote in his blog, "I'm a little intoxicated. . . . The Kirkland [dorm] facebook is open on my desktop and some of these people have pretty horrendous facebook pics."[53] After FaceMash generated twenty-two thousand hits in just two hours, Harvard's computer network crashed.

A major problem in making the film was that so much of the action took place on computer screens. In order to create a visually interesting film, explained cinematographer Jeff Cronenweth, "we played around with focus, things falling off, and the letters coming into frame . . . anything we could to kind of change it up visually, so it didn't become stagnant."[54] For example, one scene is made more cinematically interesting by cutting quickly between screen shots of Zuckerberg's blog explaining how he set up the website, computer screens with women's pictures, a fraternity party, and student reactions to what they are seeing on their computers. The pulsing rhythm of the song "In Motion" adds to the momentum of these cuts.

The film's thesis is that these events are the key to understanding Zuckerberg's invention and development of FB. Robert Sklar compared this to *Citizen Kane*, arguing that Albright, the lost girlfriend, functions as "Zuckerberg's unattainable past, his lost chance for simple happiness, his Rosebud."[55] However, the movie's Mark Zuckerberg differs in significant ways from his real-life counterpart. Erica Albright is not the real name of anyone he dated. According to David Kirkpatrick, Zuckerberg had little interest in Harvard fraternities. Before founding Facebook, he was dating Priscilla Chan, whom he married in 2015.[56] Zuckerberg maintains that the assertion that he developed Facebook because of a failed romance is "not true."[57] Nevertheless, it works as a storytelling device to hold several elements of the plot together.

Inventing Facebook and Fighting for Credit

The rest of TSN is structured as a series of flashbacks from proceedings during lawsuits against Zuckerberg by twins Tyler and Cameron Winklevoss (both played by Armie Hammer, using a body double with Hammer's face later added by computer) and Eduardo Saverin (Andrew Garfield) the company's original chief financial officer (CFO). This allows the movie's viewers to compare its main characters as college-age young adults with their older versions contesting who deserves credit and financial compensation for the multibillion-dollar corporation that FB has become. It also gives voice to each of the antagonists with minimal evaluation of anyone's credibility. According to Sorkin, the first line he wrote for Zuckerberg in this section of the film is, "That's not what happened," as a signal that there will be several unreliable narrators.[58] Much of the language in the movie's deposition scenes is taken verbatim; although, according to Kirkpatrick, Zuckerberg's "snide put-downs of the lawyers, the twins and Saverin are largely invented and uncharacteristic."[59]

The first scene in the film's present day depicts the rebuttal by Zuckerberg of a claim in Saverin's deposition crosscut with Albright's first sight of his blog and a party of Harvard's most prestigious final club. The movie then shifts to Harvard's administrative board hearing to determine whether Zuckerberg should be disciplined for FaceMash. Zuckerberg's lack of respect for the board is depicted visually by having the camera move below the table to show that he is wearing flip-flops. His casual apology is undercut by a claim that Harvard should thank him for discovering holes in its cyber-security. Nevertheless, the board imposed a minimal penalty by placing Zuckerberg on probation and requiring him to meet with a counselor. Jim Rutenberg has written that the film shows Zuckerberg's constant pattern from this point on of responding to Facebook's mistakes by cooling things off with a promise to do better until another mishap begins a new cycle. TSN portrays "the budding tech magnate as someone more interested in growing his creation than in who might be hurt by it."[60]

The publicity around these events leads the Winklevoss twins to ask him to help program their proposed social network, the Harvard Connection. Although they cannot pay him, they suggest it would help rehabilitate his reputation, to which he sarcastically replies, "You guys would do that," but agrees anyway. However, he continually puts the twins off, frequently failing to answer their inquiries before quitting several months later.

Meanwhile, Zuckerberg had begun working on FB, stating in his deposition that he first approached Saverin about it at a dull Jewish fraternity party. Harvard's print facebooks consisted of headshots of each student captioned with their names, class years, and residences. Although the university began developing an electronic version in 2004, when Zuckerberg learned the project would take years to complete he decided, "I can do it better than they can and I can do it in a week."[61] Rather than a dating website, which is how he saw the Harvard Connection, FB would instead allow Harvard students to share pictures and personal information with friends. Its original mission statement described what was then called "TheFacebook" as "an online directory that connects people through social networks at colleges."[62] The exclusivity of limiting FB to Harvard students would be a major attraction. As president, Zuckerberg had a 70 percent share while Saverin, who eventually invested $18,000, would be CFO, owning the remaining 30 percent. Within a month of the January 2004 start, half of all Harvard students had signed up. FB quickly expanded to Columbia, Stanford, and Yale, with a separate network for each school.[63]

The film then shifts to an encounter between Zuckerberg and Albright in a bar, where she rebuffs his attempt to tell her about FB, instead complaining that he insulted her on the internet. Dismissing him, she wishes Zuckerberg "good luck with your video game."

The twins decide to bring a complaint that Zuckerberg stole their social network idea to Harvard president Lawrence Summers (Douglas Urbanski). At their meeting, he disdainfully rejects their request as asking for "special treatment" for a dispute that is not a university issue. When they later learn, after rowing in the Henley Regatta in England, that FB has expanded to Europe, they decide to sue.

Meanwhile, Sean Parker (Justin Timberlake) learns about FB from a female Stanford student. Explaining that despite founding the music file sharing app Napster, he is now broke, Parker decides to find Zuckerberg. Zuckerberg's excitement at the prospect of meeting Parker is countered by Saverin, whose skepticism is based on Parker's problematic history. Parker urges them to move the business to Silicon Valley, arguing that rather than a goal of a million dollars, "you know what's cool? A billion dollars." This memorable line has been debunked by Steven Levy as "a screenwriter's fantasy."[64] Zuckerberg takes a leave of absence from Harvard in order to relocate to Palo Alto, but Saverin remains in Boston to complete his degree and solicit advertising from East Coast businesses. Zuckerberg invites Parker, who suggests he make up business cards declaring, "I'm CEO bitch," to join FB in California.

Parker quickly arranges a meeting with venture capitalist and PayPal founder Peter Thiel (Wallace Langham). When Saverin complains that handling the business side of FB is his job, Zuckerberg warns him that he will be "left behind" if he fails to move to California. An angered Saverin foolishly freezes the FB bank account, but Thiel not only agrees to begin financing FB with $500,000, he also suggests incorporating in Delaware with a new company structure.

The portentous music during the meeting with Thiel predicts how large sums of money would cause problems for Zuckerberg and FB. After the restructuring results in the dilution of Saverin's shares from 30 percent of the company to .03 percent, he decides to sue. Actor Andrew Garfield sees the character he played as "the conscience of that whole enterprise at the beginning . . . by exiling the heart Mark ended up in all the trouble he's ended up in."[65] This claim is somewhat undercut by the fact that Saverin, who only spent six months as CFO, eventually settled for a 5 percent share, which made him a billionaire.[66] The twins' settlement was $65 billion. Both settlements included a nondisclosure agreement.

After his arrest at a party at which the police find cocaine, Parker leaves his FB position. By this time, FB has reached a million users. The film shows Zuckerberg, alone in his cubicle, pulling out one of his newly printed business cards, which use Parker's suggested language.

A meeting between Zuckerberg and one of his attorneys, Marilyn Delpy (Rashida Jones), provides a summary for the film's audience. As the only lawyer who is Zuckerberg's age, Delpy is a bridge between FB's founders and the other, more experienced attorneys as well as serving as a surrogate for the movie's audience. She explains that despite his reluctance to settle, the result will be favorable to him, as the cost will be the equivalent of "a speeding ticket." When Zuckerberg tries to justify himself as "not a bad guy," she replies, "You're not an asshole, Mark. You're just trying so hard to be."

As in ATPM, the world of TSN is a largely male one, with Delpy's brief role the most significant one played by a female other than girlfriends, sexual partners, or an older female lawyer asking a deposition question. FB did, however, hire Sheryl Sandberg as its chief operating officer in 2008, several years after the events depicted in the film. She served in that position until stepping down in 2022. During that tenure, she was, in many ways, the public face of the company. Despite her prominence, Cecilia Kang and Erin Griffith write that the tech "industry's record on female leadership trails that of other industries," citing a 2020 study that found that the largest Silicon Valley companies had the same percentage of women leaders (less than 5 percent) in 2020 as they had two years earlier.[67]

The final scene returns to the opening motif as Zuckerberg looks up Albright on FB, perhaps trying to "friend" her, while the film score plays the Beatles song "Baby, You're a Rich Man," illustrating the irony that Zuckerberg has achieved fame and great financial success at the cost of his personal relationships, the sort of connections that FB promises to nourish. In his DVD commentary, director David Fincher explains that the movie's theme is "a loss of innocence for everyone involved."

The film was a critical and box office success. During the first week of release, its $22.4 million gross led all films. Eventually TSN totaled $97 million in the United States and $225 million worldwide.[68] Although some critics expressed reservations about the movie's factual inaccuracies, most reviews were enthusiastic. Manohla Dargis praised it as a "fleet, weirdly funny, exhilarating, alarming and fictionalized look at the man behind the social media phenomenon Facebook," while Mick LaSalle called the movie "a major American story and an important cautionary tale."[69] Nominated for eight Academy Awards, it won three, for best adapted screenplay, original score, and editing.

From Social to News Media

Tim Wu has described FB's original appeal as "the need to see what old friends or family were up to without the burden of talking to them."[70] However, by 2021, it had become a media company from which a third of Americans obtained their news. It had a market value of nearly a trillion dollars, and owned data on more than a third of the world's population.[71] Several innovations facilitated this change.

In 2006, FB introduced a News Feed page on which users determined which posts they would see, beginning with items that mentioned them, followed by those about friends, then about pages and groups they had joined.[72] The Like button came three years later. When users "liked" a post, similar ones would appear on their News Feeds. The filtering out of uncomfortable ideas created preference bubbles that grew as other users with similar beliefs shared their values. Wu explains the result as providing free information to advertisers who could microtarget users with "advertising that people actually wanted to see."[73] Even more dangerous is FB's use of tracking to collect data on its users who "were simply handing over a treasure trove of detailed demographic data."[74]

Because FB membership is free, the company depends on advertising for its profits. The larger its audiences are, and the more time they spend on the platform, the more appealing it is to advertisers and the more user data they can accumulate. Editorial judgment is largely left to algorithms that aim to maximize use. This rewards controversy and disinformation because, as Becca Rothfeld explains, "the more divisive a meme or a story, the more engagement it generates," resulting in more time spent online, which, in turn, allows advertisers to target users better by accumulating data about their browsing habits.[75] Sheera Frankel and Cecilia Kang believe that "Facebook was at its heart an advertising company. By 2017, its advertising revenue exceeded the total of all newspapers."[76]

Maya Phillips suggests that TSN "feels grimly prophetic" because despite FB's creating an impression of human connection, "it has become a medium best known for invasions of privacy and the dissemination of false information, hate speech and propaganda."[77]

The most notable of a series of FB scandals was the considerable number of far-right stories, conspiracy theories, and false information, particularly about Hillary Clinton's emails, during the 2016 presidential campaign. Special Counsel Robert Mueller indicted thirteen Russian citizens and three of their organizations as part of his investigation into foreign interference with that election. However, shortly after the election Zuckerberg told an interviewer that "the idea that fake news on Facebook, of which it's a very small amount of the content, influenced the election in any way, I think, is a pretty crazy idea."[78]

NEW MEDIA, THE FIRST AMENDMENT, AND THE LAW

Despite all the criticisms of news on television and social media, both are protected by the First Amendment so that they can provide the public with the information necessary for good citizenship. However, social media companies seem to want this protection without the responsibility that goes with it. Zuckerberg has claimed that "[w]e're a technology company. . . . We do not produce content."[79] The law gives social media companies extra protection by recognizing this distinction in Section 230 of the 1996 Communications Decency Act, which differentiates between publishers, who can be held liable for harmful content, and platforms, which, because they are simply conduits for third-party-produced material, cannot be. This law permits platforms such as FB to remove any harmful posts while giving them immunity should they fail to remove such material.[80] Although this allowed social media platforms to grow to their current state, it also protected them even when material posted on their platform led to violence, was rife with disinformation and conspiracy theories, or allowed foreign governments to interfere in elections.

But is Section 230 still relevant in a social media world? As Michael Smith and Marshall Van Alstyne have argued, the law was written "during a long-gone age of naïve technological optimism and primitive technological capabilities" and it is badly in need of updating.[81] Democrats and Republicans generally agree on the need for change but disagree sharply on the nature of necessary remedies, in large part because of the existence of the free press clause of the First Amendment.[82] The uncertain state of the relationship between the law and social media will likely stay just that—uncertain—regardless of future legislative and judicial developments.

One of the founders of FB, Chris Hughes (played by Patrick Mapel in TSN), believes that its dominance of the market is so great that the only solution is to break it up. He notes that FB is so unaccountable that even after it was fined $5 billion by the Federal Trade Commission in 2019, its stock price increased by 7 percent. He estimates that since the government allowed it to buy rivals WhatsApp and Instagram, its revenues have grown to 80 percent of the entire world's total. The only solution is to break up the company and set up a new agency to regulate tech companies.[83]

In 2020, FB opted for self-regulation when it established an Oversight Board, "a council of sage advisers" from around the world, who would review decisions about what speech should be allowed on the platform. Zuckerberg's justification was that "there are some calls that just aren't good for the company to make for itself."[84] One of its first major cases was a review of the indefinite ban of Donald Trump after the January 6 insurrection. Although the board found the ban justified because of the continuing threat of violence, it ruled that rather than an open-ended ban, FB would have six months to institute a defined penalty. In January 2023, FB ended its ban on Trump.

THE MEDIA AND THEIR MESSAGE

When accepting the Oscar for his TSN screenplay, Sorkin connected the themes of the two films discussed in this chapter and expressed his debt to Chayefsky. "It's impossible to describe what it feels like to be handed the same award that was given to Paddy Chayefsky thirty-five years ago," he declared. "I'm accepting this on his behalf as well."[85]

Despite the message of these films that replacing the printed press with television and social media as the public's main source of news has led to more but worse information, it would be futile to wish for a return to a mythical golden age of newspapers, even if it were possible. As *Citizen Kane* made clear long ago, the pursuit of larger audiences and profits could corrupt the idealism of Kane's Declaration of Principles as much as have television news and social media. Even the heroic Edward R. Murrow was not immune from sponsor pressures and the need to please audiences with uncritical celebrity profiles. Today, the respected *New York Times* has been described as no longer just "a newspaper anymore. . . . It's a games company and a podcast producer, all with a side of news."[86]

Tristan Harris of the Center for Humane Technology stated the dilemma well. What makes technology confounding is that "it is simultaneously utopian and dystopian." He believes that it is the business model, not technology, that is the problem.[87] Both films argue that the pursuit of profits, by taking precedence over early idealism, was the cause of the problems portrayed. Finding solutions consistent with the First Amendment will not be easy.

NOTES

1. Margaret Drabble, ed., *The Oxford Companion to English Literature*, 5th ed. (Oxford: Oxford University Press, 1985), 868.
2. *Farah v. Esquire Magazine*, 736 F.3d 528 (DC Cir. 2013).
3. Reid J. Epstein, "As Faith Flags in U.S. Government, Many Voters Want to Upend the System," *New York Times*, July 13, 2022.

4. Pew Research Center, "News Platform Fact Sheet," updated November 15, 2023, https://www.pewresearch.org/journalism/fact-sheet/news-platform-fact-sheet/ (last accessed November 26, 2023).

5. Katie Robertson, "New York Times Reports a Gain of 180,000 Digital Subscribers," *New York Times*, August 3, 2022.

6. Sara Fischer, "One-third of U.S. Newspapers as of 2005 Will Be Gone by 2024," Axios, November 16, 2023, https://www.axios.com/2023/11/16/newspapers-decline-hedge-funds-research.

7. Ezra Klein, "Opinion: I Didn't Want It to Be True, But the Medium Really Is the Message," *New York Times*, August 7, 2022.

8. Jonathan Weinberg, "Broadcasting and Speech," *California Law Review* 81 (1993): 1106.

9. "The Awareness Doctrine," *Harvard Law Review* 135 (2022): 1909.

10. *Red Lion Broadcasting v. FCC*, 396 U.S. 367, 388–89 (1969).

11. Joseph Turow, *Media Today: Mass Communication in a Converging World* (New York: Routledge, 2017), 127.

12. Andrew Serros, "All Things Not-So Equal," *News Media & the Law* (Fall 2003), https://www.rcfp.org/journals/the-news-media-and-the-law-fall-2003/all-things-not-so-equal/.

13. "The Making of *Network*: The World and Words of Paddy Chayefsky," featurette on *Network* DVD, 2006.

14. Daniel Hallin, "Whatever Happened to the News?" *Media & Values* 50 (Spring 1990): https://www.medialit.org/reading-room/whatever-happened-news.

15. Dave Itzkoff, *Mad as Hell: The Making of Network and the Fateful Vision of the Angriest Man in Movies* (New York: Times Books, 2014), 64–65.

16. Sidney Lumet, *Making Movies* (New York: Vintage, 1996), 36–37.

17. Brian Eggert, "*Network*," Deep Focus Review, May 1, 2016, https://deepfocusreview.com/definitives/network/.

18. Lumet, *Making Movies*, 85.

19. Herb A. Lightman, "*Network* and How It Was Photographed," *American Cinematographer*, December 6, 2021, https://theasc.com/articles/network-how-it-was-photographed.

20. Itzkoff, *Mad as Hell*, 164.

21. Eggert, "*Network*."

22. Itzkoff, *Mad as Hell*, 42.

23. Lightman, "*Network* and How It Was Photographed."

24. "'I'm as mad as hell, and I'm not going to take this any more!'" February 17, 2017, https://medium.com/@IRahmanJones/im-as-mad-as-hell-and-i-m-not-going-to-take-this-any-more-18758ebbe55f (last accessed April 3, 2023).

25. Itzkoff, *Mad as Hell*, 109.

26. Itzkoff, *Mad as Hell*, 110.

27. Paddy Chayefsky, *The Collected Works of Paddy Chayefsky: The Screenplays*, vol. 2 (New York: Applause Books, 2000), 216.

28. Itzkoff, *Mad as Hell*, 161.

29. Itzkoff, *Mad as Hell*, 119.

30. Lightman, "*Network* and How it Was Photographed."

31. Brian Stelter, "How ABC Covered the Awful News Involving Its Parent Disney," CNN Business, June 15, 2016, https://money.cnn.com/2016/06/15/media/abc-news-disney-orlando-coverage/index.html.

32. *Network* (Blu-ray), Warner Brothers, 2011.

33. Itzkoff, *Mad as Hell*, 174.

34. Itzkoff, *Mad as Hell*, 211–12.

35. Susan Horowitz, "Paddy Chayefsky Speaks Out," *Saturday Review*, November 13, 1976, 45.

36. Vincent Canby, "Chayefsky's 'Network' Bites Hard as a Film Satire of TV Industry," *New York Times*, November 15, 1976; Itzkoff, *Mad as Hell*, 165.

37. Robert Ebert, *Roger Ebert's Movie Home Companion: 1988 Edition* (Kansas City, MO: Andrews McMeel, 1987), 570.

38. Itzkoff, *Mad as Hell*, 157.

39. Rob Nixon, "*Network*," Turner Classic Movies, August 23, 2003, https://www.tcm.com/tcmdb/title/342/network/#articles-reviews?articleId=1185.

40. Joan Samuel, "Paddy Chayefsky: 'TV Will Do Anything for a Rating. Anything!'" *New York Times*, November 14, 1976.

41. Jim Edwards, "SPOOKY: The 1976 Movie 'Network' Predicted YouTube and 'Two and a Half Men,'" Business Insider, February 15, 2012, https://www.businessinsider.com/spooky-the-1976-movie-network-predicted-youtube-and-two-and-a-half-men-2012-2.

42. Itzkoff, *Mad as Hell*, 226.

43. A. J. Katz, "Week of Aug. 8 Evening News Ratings: World News Tonight Remains No. 1 with Gains Driven by Busy News Cycle," TVNewser, August 16, 2022, https://www.adweek.com/tvnewser/week-of-aug-8-evening-news-ratings-world-news-tonight-remains-no-1-with-gains-driven-by-busy-news-cycle/512579/.

44. Brian Stelter, *Hoax: Donald Trump, Fox News, and the Dangerous Distortion of Truth* (New York: One Signal, 2020).

45. Matt Taibbi, *Hate Inc.: Why Today's Media Makes Us Despise One Another* (New York: OR Books, 2019), location 3029.

46. Jeremy Barr and Elahe Izadi, "CNN Makes Massive Staff Cuts as News Industry Prepares for a Dark Winter," *Washington Post*, December 1, 2022.

47. Roger Fristoe, "Pop Culture 101-*Network*," March 5, 2014, https://www.tcm.com/tcmdb/title/342/network/#articles-reviews?articleId=962185.

48. Janet Maslin, "Harvard Pals Grow Rich: Chronicling Facebook without Face Time," *New York Times*, July 19, 2009.

49. Ben Mezrich, *The Accidental Billionaires: The Founding of Facebook: A Tale of Sex, Money, Genius and Betrayal* (New York: Doubleday, 2009), 1–2.

50. Mark Harris, "Inventing Facebook," *New York*, September 17, 2010, https://nymag.com/movies/features/68319/.

51. Harris, "Inventing Facebook."

52. Abdullah Al-Ghamdi, "Why *The Social Network*'s Opening Scene Took Three Weeks to Edit," ScreenRant, September 23, 2020, https://screenrant.com/social-network-movie-opening-scene-editing-why-explained/.

53. Alex Horton, "Channeling *The Social Network*, Lawmaker Grills Zuckerberg on His Notorious Beginnings," *Washington Post*, April 11, 2018.

54. Anhar Karim, "10 Years Later, 'The Social Network' Cinematographer Jeff Cronenweth On Finding Art In Compromise," *Forbes*, October 24, 2020, https://www.forbes.com/sites/anharkarim/2020/10/24/10-years-later-the-social-network-cinematographer-jeff-cronenweth-on-finding-art-in-compromise/?sh=370039506939.

55. Robert Sklar, "Review," *Cinéaste* 36, no. 1 (2010): 46–47.

56. David Kirkpatrick, "Facebook and Mark Zuckerberg in *The Social Network* Aren't Real," *Daily Beast*, July 14, 2017, https://www.thedailybeast.com/facebook-and-mark-zuckerberg-in-the-social-network-arent-real.

57. Steven Levy, *Facebook: The Inside Story* (New York: Blue Rider Press, 2020), 6.

58. Harris, "Inventing Facebook."

59. Kirkpatrick, "Facebook and Mark Zuckerberg."

60. Jim Rutenberg, "The Facebook Movie Told Us What We Needed to Know about Mark Zuckerberg," *New York Times*, November 18, 2018.

61. Tim Wu, *The Attention Merchants: The Epic Scramble to Get Inside Our Heads* (New York: Knopf, 2016), 379.

62. Jill Lepore, "Facebook's Broken Vows," *New Yorker*, July 26, 2021, https://www.newyorker.com/magazine/2021/08/02/facebooks-broken-vows.

63. Levy, *Facebook*, 64–65.

64. Levy, *Facebook*, 82.

65. Kara Swisher, "Why This Hollywood Actor Stays Off Social Media (Mostly)," *New York Times*, March 14, 2022.

66. Kirkpatrick, "Facebook and Mark Zuckerberg."

67. Cecilia Kang and Erin Griffith, "What Sheryl Sandberg's Exit Reveals about Women's Progress in Tech," *New York Times*, June 3, 2022.

68. "The Social Network," Box Office Mojo, https://www.boxofficemojo.com/release/rl1802536449/ (last accessed November 8, 2022).

69. Manohla Dargis, "Millions of Friends, but Not Very Popular," *New York Times*, September 23, 2010; Mick LaSalle, "Review: 'The Social Network,'" *San Francisco Chronicle*, October 1, 2010.

70. Wu, *Attention Merchants*, 386.

71. Lepore, "Facebook's Broken Vows."

72. Sheera Frenkel and Cecilia Kang, *An Ugly Truth: Inside Facebook's Battle for Domination* (New York: Harper, 2021), 32.

73. Wu, *Attention Merchants*, 387.

74. Wu, *Attention Merchants*, 392.

75. Becca Rothfeld, "The Shaming-Industrial Complex," *New Yorker*, March 21, 2022, https://www.newyorker.com/magazine/2022/03/28/the-shaming-industrial-complex-cathy-oneil-the-shame-machine-owen-flanagan-how-to-do-things-with-emotions.

76. Frenkel and Kang, *An Ugly Truth*, 163.

77. Maya Phillips, "'The Social Network' 10 Years Later: A Grim Online Life Foretold," *New York Times*, October 5, 2020.

78. Andrew Marantz, *Antisocial: Online Extremists, Techno-Utopians, and the Hijacking of the American Conversation* (New York: Viking, 2019), 209.

79. Marantz, *Antisocial*, 70.

80. Michael D. Smith and Marshall Van Alstyne, "It's Time to Update Section 230," *Harvard Business Review*, August 12, 2021, https://hbr.org/2021/08/its-time-to-update-section-230.

81. Smith and Van Alstyne, "It's Time to Update Section 230."

82. Generally, see Danielle Keats Citron, *The Fight for Privacy: Protecting Dignity, Identity, and Love in the Digital Age* (New York: Norton, 2022); Sara Morrison, "Section 230, the Internet Law That's under Threat, Explained," *Vox*, February 23, 2023, https://www.vox.com/recode/2020/5/28/21273241/section-230-explained-supreme-court-social-media; Adam Candeub and Eugene Volokh, "Interpreting 47 U.S.C. §230(C) (2)," *Journal of Free Speech Law* 1 (2021): 175–90.

83. Chris Hughes, "Opinion: It's Time to Break up Facebook," *New York Times*, May 9, 2019.

84. Kate Klonick, "Inside the Making of Facebook's Supreme Court," *New Yorker*, February 12, 2021, https://www.newyorker.com/tech/annals-of-technology/inside-the-making-of-facebooks-supreme-court.

85. Aaron Sorkin, Academy Awards Acceptance Speech for Best Screenplay, February 23, 2011.

86. Ben Strauss, "At the *Athletic* and *New York Times*, a Marriage with Promise and Tension," *Washington Post*, October 7, 2022.

87. Quoted in the 2020 documentary *The Social Dilemma*.

Chapter 5

"How Can We Possibly Approve and Check the Story . . . ?"

Good Night, and Good Luck *and* The China Syndrome

Helen J. Knowles-Gardner

"Your show airs tomorrow. How can we possibly approve and check the story that you are running in the limited amount of time you have given us?" This is the question that Colonel Anderson (Glenn Morshower) asks Fred Friendly (George Clooney) in the 2005 movie *Good Night, and Good Luck*. It is October 1953, and the CBS television news show *See It Now*, produced by Friendly, is about to air a program regarding the decision of the United States Air Force to dismiss Milo Radulovich, a lieutenant in the Air Force Reserve. In response to Anderson's question, Friendly says, "With all due respect, you have been invited to participate in this piece, not to approve this piece." CBS went ahead and aired the piece without the approval of the government (the military).

"Mr. Gibson, if there's nothing to hide let him speak. Whose place is it? Whose place is it, Mr. Spindler?" Kimberly Wells (Jane Fonda), a television news reporter for KXLA, asks this question during the final scene of the 1979 thriller *The China Syndrome*. Bill Gibson (James Hampton) is a public relations spokesperson for the Ventana nuclear power plant. He is trying to prevent one of the technicians, Ted Spindler (Wilford Brimley), from telling the gathered media the truth about what just happened inside the plant. Wells's journalistic efforts are successful; the industrial cover-up of a nuclear accident is thwarted.

As these two paragraphs suggest, in both *Good Night, and Good Luck* (hereafter GNGL) and *The China Syndrome* (hereafter TCS) the media ultimately resist efforts by elements of the military-industrial complex to engage in corruption and/or malfeasance. In both films, "the media," or "the press," if we are considering the extent of First Amendment protections, is television. Consequently, readers will see some thematic similarities to the previous chapter's analysis of *Network*. This includes the way in which the role played by the small screen can be both negative and positive; in large part the ability of the press to perform its invaluable democratic function disappears if the funding goes away. (Even NPR and PBS rely, in part, on corporate sponsors and donations from listeners/viewers "like you.") For both of the networks portrayed in the films in this chapter, the revenue from commercials is essential; sponsors must be kept happy.

Both films ask the following questions:

- Why is it important, in the United States, to ensure that the press has the freedom to inquire about the decency—or dignity, or morality, or legality—of the actions of those who, in the broad sense of the word, *govern* our everyday lives?
- To what extent is "collective responsibility" an important element of press freedom?
- To what extent did the forces of capitalism and anticommunism shape the way in which the press exercised its constitutionally protected freedom in the 1950s?

When considering the answers to these questions, readers of this chapter are encouraged to consider the following elements of the two films under discussion:

- The use of black and white to set the tone of, and shape the messages conveyed by, a film.
- The portrayal of gender roles in films.
- The cinematic use of dialogue to convey both tension and facts.

As both of the films analyzed in this chapter demonstrate, the fact of constitutionally protected freedom of the press in the United States is frequently accompanied by myriad tensions. Nevertheless, as Justice Hugo L. Black wrote in 1971 in *New York Times v. United States* (the lawsuit at the center of *The Post*; see chapter 3), this is a constitutionally protected freedom that enables the press "to fulfill its essential role in our democracy." It is "[t]he press" that "serve[s] the governed, not the governors." The First Amendment's free press clause ensures that the press can "bare the secrets of government and inform the people."[1] In both GNGL and TCS, the people are informed by the journalistic revealing of secrets that those who govern our lives try to protect.

However, as we will see, the two films have something else in common. Neither the real-life CBS (in GNGL) nor the fictional KXLA (in TCS) achieve their noble journalistic goals through entirely noble means. When CBS went after Senator Joseph McCarthy, it did not engage in strictly objective reporting, and many of the internal repercussions of the *See It Now* broadcasts were driven not by a desire to enhance press freedom but rather by a push to increase network revenue. Similarly, for much of TCS, Wells and her cameraman Richard Adams (Michael Douglas) face the capitalist reality that their employer cannot afford to spite the corporate hand that feeds the network (in the form of advertising).

GOOD NIGHT, AND GOOD LUCK

GNGL takes its title from the famous phrase with which the legendary radio and television journalist Edward R. Murrow signed off from his *See It Now* broadcasts in the 1950s. Murrow was deeply committed to maintaining a high standard of journalism.[2] He studiously sought to keep coverage of "Hollywood celebrities" out of his *news*casts, and often expressed his concerns "about attractive personalities drawing 'huge television audiences regardless of the violence that may be done to truth or objectivity' and coverage consisting of 'bathing girls on surf boards.'"[3]

The film depicts the famous 1953–1954 on-air clashes between Murrow (David Strathairn) and Friendly, and Senator Joseph R. McCarthy (R-WI). In 1953, McCarthy turned his communist-hunting attention to the actions of the United States Army. This was, in the senator's mind, a perfectly logical extension of his efforts, over the past three years, to seek out and destroy the "nest of Communists and Communist sympathizers who are helping to shape our foreign policy."[4] This was, in McCarthy's opinion, a nest feathered by the State Department, to comfort and aid anyone and everyone who deigned to be "different."

For McCarthy, however, it was the beginning of the end of his Senate career. The Army subsequently accused the Senator of asking for preferential treatment for a former staff member of the Senate Permanent Subcommittee on Investigations, of which McCarthy was chair. The Senate then conducted investigative hearings that ABC television covered live. On June 9, 1954, during those hearings, McCarthy sparred with Joseph Welch, the lawyer representing the Army. Predictably, McCarthy had sought to attach the "Red" label to one of Welch's colleagues. Under the full glare of the television lights, Welch memorably hit back: "Until this moment, Senator, I think I never really gauged your cruelty or your recklessness. . . . Let us not assassinate this lad further, Senator. You have done enough. Have you no sense of decency?" McCarthy's fall from political grace had begun, in earnest, several months earlier, but there is no doubt that this famous encounter accelerated that downfall and led to the Senate censuring him on December 2.[5]

Paying a Heavy Price for "Go[ing] Right at" McCarthy

"You ever spend any time in Detroit, Fred?" asks Murrow early in GNGL. In October 1953, Murrow brought to Friendly's attention a newspaper story from Dexter, Michigan, about Milo Radulovich, an Air Force Reserve lieutenant who was dismissed because of accusations that his family members were communist sympathizers. (No one, including Radulovich and his lawyer, was ever permitted to see the evidence—if any existed—that supported these charges.) Murrow and Friendly had long been concerned about McCarthy's witch hunt. However, the October 20 broadcast of *See It Now*—dealing directly with the Radulovich dismissal—was the first time they aired their concerns on national television. The airing came with a heavy price tag—literally and metaphorically.

Take, for example, Don Hollenbeck (Ray Wise). Murrow's protégé, Hollenbeck becomes a tragic figure in the movie. Seventy minutes into the ninety-minute film, in a room filled with joy, sarcastic comments (at McCarthy's expense) abound as the *See It Now* staff rejoice at the news that the Senate has begun to investigate the Senator. The camera moves to focus upon Friendly's face as he answers the phone. There is a stark contrast between the gravity of his facial expression and the background noise of joking and laughing. After Friendly replaces the receiver and walks over to Murrow, the audience instantly knows something is very wrong. If GNGL were in color, we would see the blood drain from Murrow's face as Friendly whispers into his ear. The background sounds are replaced with silence, and one feels the oxygen being sucked out of the room. The film moves to a neighboring room—a music studio at CBS—where Dianne Reeves sings the soft, decidedly melancholy "somewhere there's music."[6] There follows another swift change of scene as we see and hear Joe Wershba (Robert Downey Jr.) reading a newspaper article. On June 22, 1954, the forty-nine-year-old Hollenbeck committed suicide. As the music and Wershba's voice continue in the background, we are taken to Hollenbeck's home (one of only two scenes in the film that take place outside the CBS headquarters). We witness him calmly turn on the gas of his stove, settle into an armchair, and wait to die. While myriad factors influenced his decision to take his own life, there is little doubt—as GNGL importantly makes clear—that the journalistic attacks he suffered for purported communist sympathies affected his state of mind. Most notably, these attacks came, relentlessly and mercilessly, from the pen of Jack O'Brian, who frequently attacked Hollenbeck in the pages of the *New York Journal American*.[7]

Earlier in the film, at the end of his landmark March 9, 1954, broadcast, Murrow says of McCarthy that "he didn't create this situation of fear, he merely exploited it, and rather successfully." Alluding to Shakespeare's *Julius Caesar*, Murrow goes on to say, "Cassius was right; the fault, dear Brutus, is not in our stars, but in ourselves." One cannot help but think that this definitive speech, from this definitive broadcast, was used, in part, to foreshadow Hollenbeck's suicide later in the film. This is because the *See It Now* broadcast is immediately followed by programming featuring Hollenbeck offering a glowing, full-throated endorsement of everything Murrow has just said. O'Brian destroyed Hollenbeck in the Hearst newspapers the next morning. (It is instructive here to recall *Citizen Kane*, discussed in chapter 2.)

One of the most famous ways in which anticommunist conformity was demanded in the 1950s was through the use of loyalty oaths. Although GNGL suggests that it did not happen until 1953—at around the same time that Murrow and Friendly decided to take on McCarthy—CBS actually began requiring its employees to sign such oaths in December 1950. This was the same sort of loyalty oath as federal civil servants were obliged to swear allegiance to. Based on what it described as "the unique nature of broadcasting," CBS said the oaths would help to guarantee "that there be no question concerning loyalty to our country of any C. B. S. employe [*sic*]." One was required to answer questions attesting to whether one was "now, or [had] ever been a member of the Communist party . . . or any Communist organization" or any other similarly subversive entity.[8] Consequently, when *See It Now* did, in the words of Friendly, "go right at" McCarthy, the network already had in place an important internal restriction that had the *potential* to limit press freedoms by generating self-censorship in the form of *not* "go[ing] right at" McCarthy.

As the staff of *See It Now* prepare their landmark March 9, 1954, program, which was a no-holds-barred attack on McCarthy, Murrow responds to his colleagues' concerns: "We're gonna go with the story because the terror is right here in this room." The reality of the "terror" faced by those individuals becomes clear very early on in GNGL when Joe and Shirley Wershba (Patricia Clarkson) discuss the CBS loyalty oath. "It's simply a loyalty oath," Joe remarks. His wife reacts quite differently. She is deeply concerned, and Joe's efforts to assuage her fears by listing the people (including Murrow) who have signed the document do not help. We never find out whether the couple signed the document, but ultimately that does not matter. The film has already made its point.

And it has made its point about a very bleak time in the history of expressive freedom in the United States. As Geoffrey Stone observes, "The Cold War generated unprecedented First Amendment activity for the Supreme Court. As a consequence of World War I, the Court handed down six decisions involving the First Amendment. As a result of the Cold War, it handed down *sixty* such decisions. For roughly a decade, this was the dominant issue on the Court's docket."[9] And during "an era of rampant McCarthyism, government at all levels hunted down 'disloyal' individuals and denounced them for past or present beliefs or associations."[10] The government witch-hunting was facilitated and defended by a series of Supreme Court decisions, notably *Dennis v. United States* in 1951.

In *Dennis*, the court sustained the convictions of Communist Party leaders who had been found guilty of advocating the violent overthrow of the government. The court "adopt[ed]" a lower court judge's subtle but important adaption of the "clear and present danger" test, which meant that "[i]n each case" the judges "must ask whether the gravity of the 'evil,' discounted by its improbability, justifies . . . invasion of free speech [such] as [is] necessary to avoid the danger" caused by the speech.[11] This test, which all but assumed that communist speech was dangerous, "provided a green light to Red hunters."[12]

Although there is much truth to Stone's statement that "June 17, 1957 marked the end of the Cold War in the Supreme Court" because "[o]n that day, the Court handed down" a series of "decisions that reversed the course of constitutional history,"[13] his analysis of those decisions also shows that the real post–Cold War expressive freedom came in their progeny (which began to appear in the 1960s).[14]

Geopolitical developments and changes of personnel on the Court facilitated this,[15] but not before the Court made another significant, and unfortunate, freedom of speech decision to close out the 1950s. In *Barenblatt v. United States*, a bare majority of the justices upheld the contempt of Congress conviction of a college professor who refused to answer House Un-American Activities Committee (HUAC) questions about his political beliefs. Writing for a five-justice majority, Justice John Marshall Harlan concluded—in line with *Dennis* and the decade—that there was a "close nexus between the Communist party and violent overthrow of government" and that the court could not "blind itself to world affairs which have determined the whole course of our national policy since the close of World War II." Therefore, the Court determined to strike a "balance between the individual and the governmental interests here at stake," a balance that "must be struck in favor of the latter."[16]

Justice Hugo Black could not have disagreed more, and spent forty-five minutes announcing the content of his dissenting opinion, which Chief Justice Earl Warren and Justice William O. Douglas joined.[17] It is a dissent that is rightly hailed as a major defense of expressive freedom. As the free speech scholar Alexander Meiklejohn described it, the dissent "will be honored and heeded so long as Americans seek to understand what their Political Freedom is."[18] Where the *Barenblatt* majority thought it was refusing to "blind itself to world affairs," the dissenters could clearly see what the court "fails to see"—and indeed, "what is here for all to see—that exposure and punishment is the aim of this committee and the reason for its existence." Continuing, Black explained that "[a]s disclosed by its many reports," HUAC existed

> to try witnesses and punish them because they are or have been Communists or because they refuse to admit or deny Communist affiliations. The punishment imposed is generally punishment by humiliation and public shame. There is nothing strange or novel about this kind of punishment. It is, in fact, one of the oldest forms of governmental punishment known to mankind; branding, the pillory, ostracism and subjection to public hatred being but a few examples of it.

But this should not be the work of the Supreme Court; "drumhead courts" maybe, but not the courts of the United States. "I cannot believe," wrote Black, "that the nature of our judicial office requires us to be so blind."[19] This was a "judicial sermon" that Black brought to a close "with the choice of perdition or perfection."[20] The final sentence of the dissent read as follows: "Ultimately, all the questions in this case really boil down to one—whether we as a people will try fearfully and futilely to preserve democracy by adopting totalitarian methods or whether, in accordance with our traditions and our Constitution, we will have the confidence and courage to be free."[21]

Such was the combined word length of Harlan and Black's opinions that the *New York Times* declined to print their full text. Lamenting this editorial decision, the newspaper's Supreme Court correspondent Anthony Lewis noted in a letter to Washington, DC, bureau chief James "Scotty" Reston that "[t]he Times' policy on texts was summarized succinctly and good-naturedly as: Nothing gets more than 6,000 words except the Second Coming."[22] Lewis found this explanation to be entirely unsatisfactory and inconsistent with recent precedent. He was particularly concerned about the absence from the pages of the paper of the text of Black's dissent, the "greatest expression of his libertarian First Amendment view. Everyone I talked to around the Court yesterday [June 8, 1959—the day *Barenblatt* was decided] considered the Barenblatt case one of the really big ones."[23]

In 2015, when the *Washington Post* ran an opinion piece written by Lee C. Bollinger (a noted First Amendment scholar who was at the time president of Columbia University), it did so under a very appropriate headline: "Americans only figured out free speech 50 years ago." For as Bollinger accurately observed, "[c]ontrary to what most people think, our modern conception of freedom of speech and press is a relatively recent phenomenon—one not fully formed until the 1960s."[24] This did not happen until the Court's free speech jurisprudence evolved, replacing many of the 1950s decisions.[25] As discussed in the next chapter, an important part of this jurisprudential shift—especially for freedom of the press—was *New York Times v. Sullivan* (1964),[26] which Meiklejohn famously described as "an occasion for dancing in the streets."[27]

Objectivity or Editorializing?

If McCarthyism left a trail of judicial destruction, it also left a trail of victims, including Don Hollenbeck. However, the blame cannot simply and solely fall upon the shoulders of the Senator from Wisconsin and those who fanned his flames of hysteria. It must also fall upon the shoulders of those who failed to hold McCarthy accountable for his destructive actions even when they knew (or had good reason to know) that his actions were grounded in nothing more than wild speculation and discriminatory innuendo. Writing in the *New York Times* on the twenty-fifth anniversary of the March 1954 *See It Now* broadcast, the real Joseph Wershba observed that "[i]n the cold-war climate of fear that the Senator was exploiting and exacerbating, the careers of many eminent men and women were being destroyed on the basis of hearsay evidence—or no evidence at all—and McCarthy's rampage seemed unstoppable."[28] It was this "climate of fear" that generated the decision in *Barenblatt*. The media was frequently complicit in making the "rampage" seemingly "unstoppable." As Edwin R. Bayley notes, numerous factors help to explain why the media frequently failed to cover McCarthyism in the way they should have done.[29] However as both Wershba's article and GNGL indicate, one very important factor was corporate fear of lost revenue.

Returning to GNGL, one finds Sig Mickelson (Jeff Daniels), who oversees news and public affairs programming for CBS, watching footage of the Radulovich interview. He expresses his concern (to Murrow and Friendly) about a lack of neutrality in the piece. Murrow forcefully and defiantly says that he "simply cannot accept that there are two equal and logical sides" to every story (the validity of Murrow's observation is something the film *Denial*—analyzed in the next chapter—also asks the audience to consider). Mickelson relents, but not without making Murrow very aware of the financial implications of going after McCarthy. "Do you know how many *Person to Persons* you're going to have to do to make up for this?" Hosted by Murrow, *Person to Person* was the kind of "interviewing the rich and famous" entertainment television that Murrow wanted to keep very separate from his *news*casts. Yet, as GNGL makes very clear, when *See It Now* hurt the revenues of CBS, that negative financial impact was not confined to coverage of the news; it hurt the entire network. At the time, unlike today, the news division was a money loser designed to gain prestige and help stations meet their public interest licensing obligation. *Person to Person*, on the other hand, was a money maker. Today, the news is profitable (partly for reasons anticipated in *Network*—see chapter 4) and the licensing requirement has become largely pro forma.

Like Mickelson, William Paley (Frank Langella)—the head of CBS—is very concerned about the consequences of taking on McCarthy. He repeatedly emphasizes that he is not placing restrictions on the editorial content of the Murrow/Friendly broadcasts. However, after CBS airs McCarthy's one-man rebuttal, we see Paley walk into one of the broadcasting booths. As he looks around the room, one gets the sense that he is expecting the walls figuratively to come crashing down. As if to emphasize that concern, the scene abruptly cuts to a commercial for ALCOA (Aluminum Company of America). Murrow's attacks on McCarthy jeopardized the commercial well-being of CBS, as major sponsors such as ALCOA threatened to take their advertising money elsewhere. Toward the end of the film, even though Paley continues to state that he has not intruded upon the content of Murrow's broadcasts, it becomes clear that commercial pressure is indeed going to limit *what* Murrow says. Citing ALCOA and other *former* sponsors of, and diminishing ratings for, *See It Now*, Paley informs Murrow that the show is being changed from sixty minutes prime-time on a Tuesday evening to thirty minutes on Sunday afternoons.[30]

The Importance of Cinematic Techniques in *Good Night, and Good Luck*

"[T]he responsibility of American network news to speak truth to power"—even in the face of corporate pressures—is a "theme" that simply will not (and should not) go away. This is because government-created fearmongering will not go away. However, Phillip Lopate is right when he says that focusing on it "risks overshadowing any discussion of the . . . aesthetic merits" of movies such as GNGL.[31] Writing for the *New Statesman*, a British political and cultural magazine, Victoria Segal said of the film that it "is everything Hollywood normally isn't—black and white, intimate, compact, cheap."[32] This provides a useful way in which to frame this chapter's remaining analysis of the film.

Black and White

One of the reasons GNGL makes such a powerful statement about press freedom is that it does not simply portray the Murrow-led CBS as a silver knight in shining armor, slaying the evil dragon McCarthy. Instead, almost from the very beginning the movie is careful to ensure that the audience is aware of the shortcomings of CBS (and television more generally) when it took on McCarthyism. As Clooney and Grant Heslov explain in their DVD special features commentary on the movie, one way in which they achieved this was through fidelity to the actual details of the events conveyed—as much as this is possible in Hollywood. For example, no actor played Senator McCarthy;[33] instead, he was only seen through archival footage—the McCarthy that the audience sees on television screens in GNGL is the same McCarthy that people saw come into their homes, via the small screen, in the 1950s.[34] Consequently, had GNGL been made in color, with intermittent shots of that black-and-white footage, the film would have sent a disjointed (and inaccurate) message about the real roles played by McCarthy, Murrow, and the media.[35] The black-and-white film—and the fact that the movie only runs to ninety minutes—enhances the feeling that GNGL is just as much a documentary as it is a feature film (as does the fact that none of the men in the film wore makeup).[36] As Clooney explains, this was deliberate. The desire to make GNGL, and to give the film the feeling of a documentary, was driven in part by Clooney's experience growing up as the son of a television news anchorman.[37]

Intimate

Hear It Now was the short-lived (December 1950–June 1951) radio predecessor of *See It Now*. Both Hollenbeck and Wershba were staff members for the show, which paved the way for its television successor by joining "Friendly's innovative production techniques with Murrow's take on the major events and figures of the day." As Matthew C. Ehrlich observes, "rather than being 'oppositional,'" the radio show "stressed collective responsibility and reason, much as *See It Now* later would."[38]

In GNGL, that "collective responsibility and reason" is conveyed to the audience in numerous ways, but none perhaps quite as effective as the use of spatial intimacy. Writing in *Sight and Sound*, Geoffrey Macnab observes that "[a]s in the great cinéma verité documentaries *Primary* and *Crisis* (which Clooney has acknowledged as influences), there is often a sense that we are eavesdropping on momentous events."[39] The spatial intimacy that generates this feeling of "eavesdropping" comes, in large part, from the fact that with the exception of three scenes—Hollenbeck's suicide, the gathering of the *See*

It Now staff in a bar after one of the broadcasts, and the ballroom scenes—GNGL takes place solely in the offices and studios of CBS. There are no outside scenes. Everything occurs between walls in generally (and thereby further confining) smoke-filled rooms.

Although the scenes shot in a ballroom setting—scenes with which the film opens and closes—could have generated an atmosphere that was anything but "intimate" (because ballrooms are generally cavernous spaces), ultimately these scenes accentuate the intimacy of the film and strongly emphasize the theme of "collective responsibility and reason." When we first see Murrow, he is waiting in the wings, ready to take the stage after being introduced by Mickelson. Murrow is in darkened profile, with a cloud of cigarette smoke enveloping his face. He stands (literally and figuratively) in stark contrast to all the other individuals we have heretofore seen, for in the preceding first three minutes of the film, the camera has taken the audience on a relaxed and jovial journey around the softly lit ballroom; men and women, in formal evening attire, laugh, joke, drink, smoke, take photographs together, and generally have a very good time. The occasion is the October 1958 "Salute to Edward R. Murrow" by the Radio-Television News Directors Association and Foundation.[40] When Murrow takes the stage, there is no customary "thank you, I'm honored, etc." Instead, he begins by saying, "This might just do nobody any good." Continuing, he states, "At the end of this discourse a few people may accuse this reporter of fouling his own comfortable nest, and your organization may be accused of having given hospitality to heretical and even dangerous ideas." Murrow unapologetically continues, "We are currently wealthy, fat, comfortable, and complacent . . . unless we get up off our fat surpluses and recognize that television in the main is being used to distract, delude, amuse, and insulate us, then television, and those who finance it, those who look at it, and those who work at it, may see a totally different picture too late."[41] GNGL gives the viewer the impression that this speech—and its speaker—have taken over (giving a sense of intimacy) the ballroom; the theme of "collective responsibility and reason" is now front and center as these words are met with the silence of a rapt audience.

Compact

Lopate writes of the "air of restraint" present in GNGL.[42] Cinematically, this was achieved in two important ways. First, and most significantly, the film was shot exclusively using long lenses. Cinematographer Robert Elswit used only two lenses for the entire movie—two 11–100mm zoom lenses.[43] As Sina Nitzsche observes, "[T]hroughout the movie" the effect of using these lenses is to put "the audience . . . [in] the position of a silent observer"—a fly on the wall, so to speak. "The use of telephoto lenses permits close-up shots of the CBS members and their fight against injustice. *The cinematic spectator therefore is an immediate witness of the unfolding narrative*," which "enables a *direct and authentic viewing experience*,"[44] an experience that is an important part of GNGL's "compact" nature.

The film also assumes a "compact" nature because of the frequent presence of small screens. GNGL captures the way in which Murrow and McCarthy only "fought each other through the media." The two men "never squared off in the same room," and this, as Lopate observes, "is accentuated by the many shots of Murrow watching his adversary holding forth on a tv monitor."[45] To borrow Marshall McLuhan's famous phrase, in GNGL the "medium" really "is the message."[46]

Cheap

When the nominees were announced for the 2006 Academy Awards, the combined budgets of the five movies vying to take home the coveted Best Motion Picture Oscar totaled less than the entire budget spent to make the film that topped the domestic box office ranking in 2005. Approximately $113 million was spent to make the latest installment of the *Star Wars* franchise. By contrast, four of the five movies that received the critical acclaim that comes with a Best Picture Oscar nomination were made with far more modest budgets. Those four included GNGL, which Segal is right to describe as a "cheap" movie.

Yet there is no doubt that GNGL had the last laugh. Although it did not win any Oscars, it received many other high-profile awards, and significantly, at the box office in 2005 it grossed more than three times its budget. Indeed, as the 2006 Oscars demonstrated, a film could achieve the distinction of being nominated for (and winning, as *Crash* did) the ultimate award while retaining the "cheap" production label.[47]

THE CHINA SYNDROME

Accounting for inflation, *The China Syndrome* was considerably more expensive to make than GNGL. The approximate budget for Clooney's 1995 film was $7 million; in 1979, the equivalent budget would have been approximately $3.3 million. That year, the budget for TCS was $5.9 million. Interestingly, however, in terms of gross income and recouping the money spent to make the two films, TCS was considerably more successful, and it was released in a year that proved that small budget films could hit it large (indeed, very large in the case of *The Amityville Horror* and *Rocky II*) at the box office.[48]

Much of the literature about TCS discusses the *timeliness* of the film. In order for twenty-first-century readers to understand that timeliness, it is first necessary to briefly explain what the film is *not* about. The reference to China in the movie's title only very indirectly relates to China, and not in any way that is intended to reflect positively or negatively upon that country. As the physicist Dr. Lowell (Donald Hotton) explains in the movie,

> If the core [of a nuclear reactor] is exposed for whatever reason, the fuel heats beyond core heat tolerance in a matter of minutes. Nothing can stop it. And it melts down right through the bottom of the plant, theoretically to China. But of course, as soon as it hits ground water, it blasts into the atmosphere and sends out clouds of radioactivity. The number of people killed would depend on which way the wind is blowing. Render an area the size of Pennsylvania permanently uninhabitable, not to mention the cancer that would show up later.

Although there are several reasons why TCS—a thriller about such an "accident" (and the cover-up of that "accident") at a nuclear power facility—was likely to be a box office success upon its release in March 1979,[49] what gave the movie "an astounding timeliness" was the fact that twelve days later there was an accident (partial meltdown of a reactor) at the Three Mile Island nuclear power station in Pennsylvania.[50] As one of the movie's stars, Jane Fonda, observed, this was "the most shocking synchronicity between real-life catastrophe and movie fiction ever to have occurred."[51] This synchronicity becomes even more important when one realizes that the name of the movie was not revealed in advance of the release of the film so as to ensure that the nuclear power industry remained in the figurative dark about the film's actual arguments.[52]

The literature also emphasizes the film's anti–nuclear power/anti–nuclear power industry message. Often, however, it does so by contending that the nuclear power industry is not the only antagonist that should draw our ire in this movie. According to these commentators, the film spotlights *two* corrupt bogeymen: the nuclear industry and the media. For example, Wayne J. McMullen contends that the film's "primary message is that large corporations use excessive amounts of power, and use it ruthlessly," and he includes KXLA, the network television station featured in TCS, in the list of "large corporations" to which he refers.[53] Similarly, Tony Shaw argues that the film "brought together the themes of media and nuclear power . . . as a true '*complex*,'" and "highlighted the intimate connection, and *collusion*, between nuclear energy and television—both relatively new technologies that lent themselves to centralized control and that needed to appear infallible."[54]

While valid, these commentaries overlook an incredibly important aspect of TCS. To be sure, KXLA is not a perfect media entity (as discussed below, this is for many of the same corporate bottom line reasons that were evident in GNGL). However, this does not mean that it is devoid of redeeming qualities. On the contrary, TCS demonstrates that even a ratings-hungry television station can rise above its often flawed approach to the pursuit of stories and play that oh-so-essential role of a free press in a democracy, the "vigorous" and "oppositional" role of confronting and exposing.[55]

"This Is Coverage, Not Controversy." Well, Not Yet Anyway.

In Oliver Stone's 1987 film *Wall Street*, the lead character—Gordon Gekko—famously proclaimed that "greed . . . is good." This was a role for which Michael Douglas won a Best Actor Oscar. It was a "portrayal . . . which captured the spirit of greed that appeared to consume the financial markets in the 1980s." It was not the first time that Douglas had starred in a film that was a "bellweather [*sic*]" for a particular period in time. TCS (which Douglas produced as well as starred in) sent important messages about America at the end of the 1970s.[56] Indeed, when one focuses on the freedom of the press aspect of the film, it becomes clear that those messages are not so much *timely* as they are *timeless*—much like those of *All the President's Men* from three years earlier (see chapter 3).

At the beginning of TCS, however, the audience is not given the impression that they are about to watch a cinematic portrayal of crusading journalism in action. TCS opens with television news reporter Kimberly Wells preparing to report from the field. As she struggles to get the attention of the production crew back in the studio, the audience clearly realizes that this is not a moment of 1970s women's liberation. Wells does journalistic puff pieces (on this occasion, reporting about singing telegrams); as KXLA network executive Don Jacovich (Peter Donat) later bluntly tells her, "Let's face it. You didn't get this job because of your investigative abilities. Kimberly, don't fight it. Don't try to be anything else." Despite her excitement at being told (after finishing with the singing telegrams) that there has been a change of plans and she is now headed to do a piece at Ventana nuclear power plant, near Los Angeles, what she first encounters at Ventana confirms what Wells has been told about her ultimate role. She emphasizes to her cameraman Richard Adams (Douglas), who is goofing around before the pair are taken on the plant tour: "Don't blow it for me Richard. *This is coverage, not controversy*."

How appropriate, and prescient, those words will prove to be, because it is during the tour that an "accident" takes place. For reasons either directly or indirectly associated with corporate greed, the employees of California Gas & Electric (the owner/operator of Ventana, and hereinafter CGE) spend the remainder of the film attempting to at best downplay the significance of the "accident" and at worst deny that it ever took place. The lengths to which CGE will go to ensure a successful cover-up seemingly know no bounds, including what the audience might interpret as the attempted murder of KXLA soundman Hector Salas (Daniel Valdez), and the murder (at the second attempt) of Jack Godell (Jack Lemmon) a shift supervisor/chief engineer at Ventana.

The cover-up starts with Bill Gibson, the plant's public relations person who has been conducting the tour. He assures Wells, Adams, and Salas that the tremors they felt, and the blaring alarms and subsequent message from the loudspeaker on the wall (that all personnel need to head to safety areas), are no cause for concern. This is only fifteen minutes into the two-hour film, and what happens next demonstrates that TCS is very much a film about the importance of a free press. McMullen writes that in the film, "James Crabe's cinematography is remarkable" for what it does *not* do. It "does not draw attention to itself, but subtly and unobtrusively creates a variety of moods."[57] Crabe's cinematic techniques shine in this scene. Godell remains calm, asking his staff to "relax" because everything is "perfectly normal"; however, the audience knows, from a previous abrupt cut to Godell's face, that everything is far from "perfectly normal." From their vantage point in the visitors' room, whose large windows afford a clear view down into the Ventana control room, Wells, Adams, and Salas probably did not see Godell's furrowed brow, and they did not hear his words. They nevertheless know what we, the audience, know—there is reason for concern.

What Adams does next clearly indicates that there is a desire to bring this "accident" to the light of the public—consistent with the "illuminating" role of television to which Murrow referred in GNGL. Adams is in the foreground of the shot, slightly out of focus, and Wells is in the center of the screen in sharp focus. She carefully glances over, a look of concern on her face, and whispers, "Are you taping this?" The audience cannot really hear this, but Adams does. Stone-faced and looking straight ahead at the window, he nods ever so slightly. The camera then moves slowly and deliberately down to show us that he is holding his video camera, aiming it down at the control room, and using his hand to quietly adjust the focus. Building the tension, the scene cuts back and forth between close-ups of a sweating, agonizing Godell, a stoic Wells, and the lens of Adams's camera (which fills the entire screen). Just as in GNGL, a scene with minimal sound, or silence, adds to the tension in TCS; all the audience hears, for seventy seconds, is the faint whirring of machines and computer printouts as Godell and his colleagues wait—with the audience—to see whether the "event" they are witnessing will end safely.

The film immediately cuts from a close-up of the computer printer spitting out the news that the "Event ends 15:36:00.3" to Wells and Adams's car racing into the KXLA parking lot. Therein begins the network's complicity in

CGE's efforts to cover-up the "event" at Ventana, in large part to avoid jeopardizing the licensing of another of the company's plants, Point Conception. With urgency, Wells and Adams dash into the film processing room and tell the employee they have "got a rush." They need the film ready to show the station's executives immediately because "it's hot"—metaphorically and literally. It is hot news of an incident at a nuclear power plant, an incident that left the plant's supervisor visibly shaken. To the amazement of everyone, Jacovich stalls, citing a need to find out more details before airing the footage. On one level, this seems like a sensible decision of responsible journalism—a decision designed to ensure that the film is not taken out of context. That illusion crumbles, however, when the audience and Wells spy Jacovich talking (conspiring?) with Gibson.

Perhaps this is the "media and nuclear power . . . '*complex*'" to which Shaw referred.[58] However, that "*complex*" argument is flawed, because KXLA's antidemocratic cover-up is largely the work of Jacovich alone (and thus, it represents an important example of the internal self-policing practices—and structures—of the media). Later, when Godell quasi-rhetorically asks, "You wouldn't be asking questions just to get a story would you?" Wells answers, "No, I wish I were. I'm not an investigative reporter." Although this suggests that Wells is still consciously conforming to the gendered role that her profession seeks to confine her to,[59] everything Wells does from this point onward demonstrates that she is in fact exactly what she has just professed not to be. The very fact that she has gone to a bar frequented by the Ventana workers in order to seek out and question Godell about "the accident" speaks volumes.

It is during these scenes at the bar that another important cinematographic element of the film shines—namely, the strategic use of pointed dialogue to build tension in this thriller and to underscore the importance of the freedom of the press messages conveyed in TCS:

> Godell: I don't like reporters . . . I think most of them feel the only good news is bad news.
>
> Wells: Don't you think that reporters serve a public function . . . Woodward and Bernstein?
>
> Godell: Well, why don't you ask me a public function question and I'll tell you whether I do or I don't.
>
> Wells: All right. Was the public at any time in any danger as a result . . . of the accident?

From this point onward, Wells acts as the very model of a modern investigative journalist.

Many of Wells's colleagues at the network have yet to see this in her, though. They still consider her nothing more than a pretty woman to put in front of a camera. She independently changes her schedule in order to do a short piece from the Point Conception hearing after talking with Godell at the bar and instinctively knows there is an important story that has to be told. Before she goes live, however, we are taken inside the studio production booth, where we see a bank of television screens showing different shots from different camera angles. At the center of our focus, as we look over the shoulder of two technicians, is a screen showing Pete Martin (Stan Bohrman), a suave KXLA anchor. We hear him say to his crew, "Okay, let's see what's gonna happen now; we're gonna go with the redhead out to the beach as she does a whale story." When the "whale story" becomes a "nuclear story" as Wells interviews protesters outside the Point Conception hearing, we hear one of the studio technicians say (as the shot continues to focus on the bank of screens), "I hope Jacovich is nowhere near a set." The phone immediately rings; we already know who is on the other end of the line.

"He'll Get Himself Shot . . . "

Later, as the complexities of the cover-up mount, we see the Ventana security guards close the plant gates behind Godell, who has just evaded the pursuers intent on running him off the road in order to stop him from exposing the industrial corruption. The camera immediately cuts from a wide shot to a close-up of Godell stopping his car and looking behind him. The camera then turns to show what he sees: the closed chain-link gate, and another car screeching to a halt a few yards away in a cloud of dust. "He'll get himself shot, driving up here like that," says one of the guards. Readers are encouraged to consider the irony of that remark when they watch the movie.

For the remaining thirty-five minutes, the tension builds as Godell exhibits nothing but extreme concern—a concern that his colleagues dismiss; as his control room coworker Ted Spindler says, sadly and gently, "Go home, why don't you just go home?" In disbelief at their lack of concern about the safety of the plant, Godell feels as though he has no other option. Does he know the fate that awaits him? Perhaps—perhaps, as he grabs the gun from the holster of a security guard, orders everyone to leave, and locks himself in the control room, he knows that the plant will be his final "home."

By now, both Godell and the film's audience are aware that Wells is a very capable investigative reporter. The supervisor and journalist share a desire to tell the truth, which is why Godell asks for her to be brought to the plant. Yet, as a shot of Adams and a television crewman running down a corridor of the Ventana plant lugging camera equipment immediately cuts to gun-toting members of a SWAT team running up a flight of stairs of the very same building, we know this will not end well. But for whom will it not end well? The tension continues to build as we go from seeing pliers cut a wire, to Godell's agonized face as the cutting of the wires triggers a major, blaring alarm, to yet another power cable being cut—but this time, it is the feed to the television camera. Just as soon as the news coverage of the control room dies, the SWAT team breaks through the door and kills Godell. It is no accident that they shoot him in the back.

"Don't deviate, just stick to the prepared script." This is the order Gibson receives as he prepares to read a statement to the gathered journalists. Unsurprisingly, that "prepared script" accounts for the events of the day by downplaying everything that has happened and describing Godell as "an emotionally disturbed employee [who] was humored just long enough to get the situation under control"—an employee who "had been drinking." When Gibson turns the microphone over to Spindler, Wells grabs her own microphone and barges over to the pack of journalists. The exchange that follows is profound and poignant, and Wells does everything that the American people should hope that a dedicated member of the fourth estate will do in order to expose a threat to the nation's democratic well-being: "Let's just hope it doesn't end here. This is Kimberly Wells, live on Channel 3."

TCS closes with the only instance where Jacovich praises Wells—right after her last broadcast. Not only did he never praise her in person, but the only time he complimented her was from the confines of the control room at the studio (Wells is still at Ventana) and after KXLA has gone to a commercial break. The viewer is left to ponder how Wells would have reacted upon receiving this compliment in person, for what Jacovich says is, "She did a hell of a good job. I must say I'm not surprised." As he finishes speaking (and we only hear him, thus depriving us of his facial expressions), we see a shot of two television monitors, side by side. One shows the wrapping up of the Ventana coverage, while the other shows a commercial—a commercial for a microwave oven. The irony is quite deliberate, and should not be lost on the viewer, or the reader, as the entire screen switches to a color test card, then fades to black as the credits roll in complete silence.

"Reporters" *Do* "Serve a Public Function"

In the late 1950s, Pacific Gas and Electric Company (PG&E) made a television commercial that highlighted the growing importance, to Californians, of the electric power generated by its Vallecitos nuclear power plant and its under-construction power plant at Humboldt Bay (which opened in 1963). "Creative engineering, research, and pioneering development like this help keep your PG&E service your best bargain," proclaimed announcer Hank Simms.[60] In TCS, California Gas & Electric, the operators of the fictional power plant at Ventana and the one under construction at Point Conception, relied on cutting corners in order to deliver their "best bargain" to their Golden State customers. As a corporate entity, KXLA was also impacted by the corporate profit and loss columns. Ultimately, however, as a result of the tenacious journalism of Wells and Adams, the station exposed that industrial corruption, thereby performing an invaluable democratic function for its viewers who—like the television network—were important consumers of the product being generated at Ventana.

Of course, in TCS the constitutionally protected freedom of the press is not being employed to hold the government directly accountable. Instead, it serves as a check upon something broader—the military-industrial complex that governs our lives, albeit in a different way than the government does. However, it is important to note that the power-generating industry, often referred to as a *public utility*, is heavily regulated by the government; in that respect, therefore, the actions of the media in TCS ultimately can be said to have checked (albeit indirectly) the actions of elected officials. Indeed, it is worth noting that following the accident at Three Mile Island less than two weeks after the release of the film, the federal government implemented new governmental regulations pertaining to the nuclear industry, and since that accident no new nuclear power plant has been built in the United States.

When Wells asked Godell if he thought "reporters serve[d] a public function" like "Woodward and Bernstein," she never received a response. As this chapter suggests, TCS unequivocally answers that question for him, in the affirmative.

Checking Power

In his *New York Times* review of *Good Night, and Good Luck*, David Carr observes that "government needs a vigorous, even oppositional press to find its best nature."[61] This point is conveyed with crystal clarity in not only the George Clooney and Grant Heslov film reviewed by Carr, but also in *The China Syndrome*. Together, these two films demonstrate the democratic importance of ensuring that the press has the freedom to expose corruption and/or governmental/industrial malfeasance. More broadly, the films showcase the speaking of truth to power (even to nongovernmental institutions or quasi institutions); as such, they are important examples of the checking power of the press (as is discussed in chapter 3). Otherwise, the "absolute power" of which Lord Acton famously wrote will inevitably "corrupt . . . absolutely."[62] Ultimately, however, the two films also emphasize the fundamental truth of Murrow's 1958 speech. When the television media is used to "teach," "illuminate," and "inspire," it becomes so much more than "merely wires and lights—in a box."

NOTES

1. *New York Times v. United States*, 403 U.S. 713, 717 (1971) (Black, J., joined by Douglas, J., concurring).

2. For an excellent, concise study of Murrow's journalism career, see Bob Edwards, *Edward R. Murrow and the Birth of Broadcast Journalism* (New York: Wiley, 2004).

3. Matthew C. Ehrlich, "Radio Prototype: Edward R. Murrow and Fred Friendly's Hear it Now," *Journal of Broadcasting and Electronic Media* 51, no. 3 (2007): 450.

4. This language appeared in a February 11, 1950, telegram McCarthy sent to President Harry S. Truman. Quoted in Robert J. Donovan, *Tumultuous Years: The Presidency of Harry S. Truman, 1949–1953* (Columbia: University of Missouri Press, 1996), 162.

5. Larry Tye, *Demagogue: The Life and Long Shadow of Senator Joe McCarthy* (Boston: Houghton Mifflin Harcourt, 2020), 435–37, 379–80.

6. Reeves's songs, such as "TV Is the Thing This Year" and "I've Got My Eyes on You," provide an ironic commentary throughout the movie.

7. For an excellent overview of the complexities of Hollenbeck's life and death, see Loren Ghiglione, *CBS's Don Hollenbeck: An Honest Reporter in the Age of McCarthyism* (New York: Columbia University Press, 2008).

8. Jack Gould, "C.B.S. Demanding Loyalty Oaths from Its 2,500 Regular Employes," *New York Times*, December 21, 1950.

9. Geoffrey R. Stone, *Perilous Times: Free Speech in Wartime, from the Sedition Act of 1798 to the War on Terrorism* (New York: Norton, 2004), 395.

10. Stone, *Perilous Times*, 313.

11. 341 U.S. 494, 510 (1951).

12. Stone, *Perilous Times*, 411.

13. Stone, *Perilous Times*, 413.

14. Especially see Stone, *Perilous Times*, 418.

15. Stone, *Perilous Times*, 413.

16. 360 U.S. 109, 128, 129, 134 (1959).

17. Court Calendar, Monday June 8, 1959, Box 125, Agendas for the Court, O.T. 1956–1960, Earl Warren Papers, Manuscript Division, Library of Congress (hereinafter LOC), Washington, DC.

18. Alexander Meiklejohn, "The Barenblatt Opinion," *University of Chicago Law Review* 27 (1960): 330.

19. 360 U.S. at 153–54, 162 (Black, J., joined by Warren, CJ., and Douglas, J., dissenting).

20. Peter Irons, *The Courage of Their Convictions: Sixteen Americans Who Fought Their Way to the Supreme Court* (New York: Penguin, 1988), 92.

21. 360 U.S. at 162 (Black, J., joined by Warren, CJ., and Douglas, J., dissenting).

22. Letter from Anthony Lewis to Scotty Reston, June 9, 1959, Papers Part II: Box 8, Annual File, Supreme Court, General, 1955–1964 (2 of 4), Anthony Lewis Papers, LOC.

23. Lewis to Reston.

24. Lee C. Bollinger, "Opinion: Americans Only Figured out Free Speech 50 Years Ago. Here's How the World Can Follow Our Lead," *Washington Post*, February 12, 2015.

25. Generally, see Helen J. Knowles, and Steven B. Lichtman, eds. *Judging Free Speech: First Amendment Jurisprudence of US Supreme Court Justices* (New York: Palgrave Macmillan, 2015), especially chapters 3–5.

26. 376 U.S. 254 (1964).

27. Quoted in Harry Kalven Jr., "The New York Times Case: A Note on 'The Central Meaning of the First Amendment,'" *Supreme Court Review* 1964 (1964): 221 n125.

28. Joseph Wershba, "Murrow vs. McCarthy: See It Now," *New York Times*, March 4, 1979.

29. Edwin R. Bayley, *Joe McCarthy and the Press* (Madison: University of Wisconsin Press, 1981).

30. In the film, a significant goof is the fact that Langella gets this the wrong way round, saying the thirty-minute show is being extended to sixty minutes.

31. Phillip Lopate, "The Medium and Its Conscience: George Clooney's Good Night, and Good Luck Recreates One of the Most Dramatic Chapters in Television History," *Film Comment*, September–October 2005, 31.

32. Victoria Segal, "Small-Screen Hero: A Tale of Anti-McCarthy Pluck Sets High Standards for TV," *New Statesman*, February 20, 2006, 48. By comparison, *Syriana*, the disappointing December 2005 film starring Clooney, is everything that Hollywood normally is.

33. Clooney and Heslov observe in their DVD commentary on the movie that 20 percent of test audiences had not heard of McCarthy and that many individuals asked for the identity of the actor portraying the senator. See "Commentary by Director/Screenwriter George Clooney and Producer/Screenwriter Grant Heslov," *Good Night, and Good Luck*, Warner Brothers DVD, 2005. As discussed in chapter 3, *All the President's Men* did the same thing for Richard Nixon. *The Post* did something similar, using Nixon's actual voice while showing the back of an actor "playing" Nixon.

34. Clooney feared that an actor would be either too tepid or too harsh. In test screenings, audience members criticized the "actor" playing McCarthy as over the top. See Geoffrey Macnab, "Good Night, and Good Luck," *Sight and Sound* 15, no. 11 (2005): 26; Sukhdev Sandhu, "When Television Took a Stand," *Telegraph* (London), February 17, 2006.

35. The movie was shot on color stock, printed in black and white, and then transferred to black-and-white stock. "Commentary by Director/Screenwriter George Clooney and Producer/Screenwriter Grant Heslov."

36. "Commentary by Director/Screenwriter George Clooney and Producer/Screenwriter Grant Heslov."

37. "Commentary by Director/Screenwriter George Clooney and Producer/Screenwriter Grant Heslov."

38. Ehrlich, "Radio Prototype," 438.

39. Macnab, "Good Night, and Good Luck," 26.

40. Although the movie says that event was on October 25, 1958, the "Salute" was actually on October 15, 1958.

41. The film used the verbatim text of Murrow's 1958 speech. The audio of the actual speech can be found/heard here: https://www.americanrhetoric.com/speeches/edwardmurrowrtnda.htm (last accessed August 7, 2021).

42. Lopate, "The Medium and its Conscience," 31.

43. Jacqueline B. Frost, *Conversations With Contemporary Cinematographers: The Eye behind the Lens* (London: Routledge, 2021), 44.

44. Sina Nitzsche, "'The Tube is Flickering Now': Aesthetics of Authenticity in *Good Night, and Good Luck*," *Current Objectives of Postgraduate American Studies* 8 (2007), https://copas.uni-regensburg.de/article/view/98/122, italics added.

45. Lopate, "The Medium and its Conscience," 31.

46. Marshall McLuhan, *Understanding Media: The Extensions of Man* (New York: McGraw Hill, 1964), chap. 1.

47. Data taken from "Domestic Box Office for 2005," Box Office Mojo, https://www.boxofficemojo.com/year/2005/ (last accessed December 10, 2023).

48. "Top Grossing Movies of 1979," The Numbers, https://www.the-numbers.com/market/1979/top-grossing-movies (last accessed December 10, 2023).

49. See Tony Shaw, "'Rotten to the Core': Exposing America's Energy-Media Complex in *The China Syndrome*," *Cinema Journal* 52, no. 2 (Winter 2013): 105.

50. Wayne J. McMullen, "*The China Syndrome*: Corruption to the Core," *Literature/Film Quarterly* 23, no. 1 (1995): 56.

51. Quoted in Dov Greenbaum, "Is It Really Possible to Do the Kessel Run in Less than Twelve Parsecs and Should It Matter: Science and Film and Its Policy Implications," *Vanderbilt Journal of Entertainment and Technology Law* 11, no. 2 (2009): 285. Indeed, despite the fact that many of the people who worked on the film were openly antinuclear, the principal boost to the antinuclear narrative of the film came not from the initial reviews but instead from Three Mile Island. Greenbaum, "Science and Film and Its Policy Implications," 282–83.

52. Greenbaum, "Science and Film and Its Policy Implications," 282.

53. McMullen, "Corruption to the Core," 62. There are two types of "network" stations. One is owned and operated by a national network; the other is simply affiliated with a national network, which means much of its programming is supplied by the network. To complicate matters, there is now a real KXLA, an independent station, founded in 2000 as KVMD and changing to KXLA the next year. It broadcasts a variety of "ethnic" programming, including Japanese and Spanish language shows.

54. Shaw, "'Rotten to the Core,'" 112, italics added.

55. David Carr, "A Ringside Seat for Murrow versus McCarthy," *New York Times*, September 18, 2005.

56. Christian C. Day, Michael P. Walls, and Lisa A. Dolak, "Riding the Rapids: Financing the Leveraged Transaction Without Getting Wet," *Syracuse Law Review* 41, no. 2 (1990): 667 n19.

57. McMullen, "Corruption to the Core," 56.

58. Shaw, "'Rotten to the Core,'" 112, italics added.

59. It is worth noting that the original script cast this part with Richard Dreyfus in it. Aljean Harmetz, "Fallout from 'China Syndrome' Has Already Begun," *New York Times*, March 11, 1979, https://www.nytimes.com/1979/03/11/archives/fallout-from-china-syndrome-has-already-begun-the-china-syndrome.html.

60. PG&E Nuclear Power, YouTube Vintage TV Commercials, https://www.youtube.com/watch?v=Ao5P0jVbO1o (last accessed December 27, 2021).

61. Carr, "A Ringside Seat for Murrow Versus McCarthy."

62. For an insightful discussion of Acton's words, see Sydney E. Ahistrom, "Lord Acton's Famous Remark," *New York Times*, March 13, 1974, https://www.nytimes.com/1974/03/13/archives/lord-actons-famous-remark.html.

Chapter 6

Testing the Limits of Freedom

Denial *and* Deliberate Intent

Helen J. Knowles-Gardner

In his message to the Booksellers of America in 1942, President Franklin D. Roosevelt observed that during World War II, books were being used as "weapons." It was, he observed, "part of your dedication always to make them weapons for man's freedom."[1] While this sounds like a laudable goal, it also generates a set of thorny questions:

- Is it ever morally and/or constitutionally permissible to suppress the publication of books that are considered the antithesis of "weapons for man's freedom"?
- To what extent does/should the First Amendment protect the publication of lies?
- To what extent does/should the First Amendment protect the publication of speech that incites violence?

The two emotionally demanding films analyzed in this chapter—both based on true stories—challenge us to think carefully about these questions. *Denial* (2016), a British-made major motion picture, addresses the censorship question indirectly. In her 1993 book *Denying the Holocaust*, Deborah E. Lipstadt, an American historian, devoted a relatively short section to criticizing the books written by Holocaust denier David Irving.[2] The film examines the libel suit that Irving brought, and questions (a) whether Irving could legally prevent her from publishing her criticisms, and (b) whether some books that are repositories of hate and lies—like Irving's works—have any legitimate place in the world of expressive freedom. By contrast, the made-for-television movie *Deliberate Intent* (2000) tackles the censorship question directly. It asks the audience to consider whether the publisher of *Hit Man: A Technical Manual for Independent Contractors* could (and should) be held legally liable after it became clear that the individual who committed a gruesome triple homicide followed, almost to the letter, the hit man instructions in the book.

In addition to confronting the above questions, these two films ask us to consider these additional aspects of cinematic depictions of freedom of the press:

- The taking of dramatic license when making a movie about a true story.
- Adhering to the facts of a true story at the expense of critical acclaim and commercial success.
- Using a movie to explain complex elements of the law of press freedoms.

Just as the answers to the above questions may not be the same regarding *Denial* and *Deliberate Intent*, readers may well find that these aspects of cinematography are treated differently in these two films.

DENIAL

Consider the following. Fact: Watergate happened, and the Nixon administration tried to cover it up. Fact: Senator Joseph McCarthy wrongly tarred many individuals with the red brush of communism. Question: Would either of these *facts* have come to light in a world that did not value expansive freedom of the press? Answer: extremely doubtful. And so it is with *Denial*. Fact: The Holocaust happened. Fact (as expressed by Justice Charles Gray in his judgment for Lipstadt and Penguin in 2000): David Irving's "falsification of the historical record" in his works denying the Holocaust "was deliberate and . . . motivated by a desire to present events in a manner consistent with his own ideological beliefs even if that involved distortion and manipulation of historical evidence."[3] Question: Would this *fact* about Irving's work have come to light in a world that did not value Lipstadt's expansive and expressive freedom to write a book (and Penguin's freedom to publish it) showing that Holocaust deniers are deniers of the truth? Answer: extremely doubtful.

In *Denying the Holocaust*, there are references to Irving on sixteen of the book's almost three hundred pages. However, on twelve of those sixteen, Irving's name only appears because Lipstadt is discussing others' factual statements about him and his activities.[4] Three other pages do no more than provide factual statements and information about Irving's work *as described by others*.[5] That leaves *one* page—181—on which appear the following sixty-three words:

> Irving is one of the most dangerous spokespersons for Holocaust denial. Familiar with historical evidence, he bends it until it conforms with his ideological leanings and political agenda. A man who is convinced that Britain's great decline was accelerated by its decision to go to war with Germany, he is most facile at taking accurate information and shaping it to confirm his conclusions.[6]

Three years later, contending that she was part of a conspiracy to damage his reputation, Irving sued Lipstadt and Penguin, alleging they had libeled him—that is, that Lipstadt had made false written statements about him and that Penguin had published those false statements. (The broad area of the law that addresses making false statements is defamation; within the law of defamation, libel relates to false written statements, slander to false spoken statements.) There was no denying that Lipstadt's book was critical of Irving, but most of the references were just that, references. Only these sixty-three words represented a substantive expression of *Lipstadt's* own views about the man. However, as Anthony Julius—the English lawyer who represented Lipstadt in this litigation—observed in *Denial*, the 2016 movie depiction of this legal fight, "England's a club, Deborah; and he [Irving] wants to join." As we will see, Irving viewed the label "Holocaust denier" as essentially denying him entry to that club.

The Opening Salvo

Timothy Spall was praised for his depiction of Irving as the "perfect smarmy embodiment of the banality of evil."[7] The actor "all but walked off with the movie," providing a "sly, jovial portrayal" that was "a model of how to play a bad man without resorting to a lot of wink-wink actor's tricks."[8] We see this "banality of evil" and acting masterclass on display from the moment the film opens—with a vivid demonstration of the horror of Irving's views. The screen is black for the first few seconds; audience laughter can be heard, but before we see him, we hear a man say, "I don't see any reason to be tasteful about Auschwitz." More laughter. Then the audience sees him—albeit on a television screen. Text tells us that this man is "British Historian David Irving" giving a talk to a general and very sympathetic audience at the Travelport Airport Inn in Alberta, Canada, on September 29, 1991. Irving continues, "I say to you quite tastelessly that more women died on the backseat of Senator Edward Kennedy's car at Chappaquiddick than ever died in a gas chamber at Auschwitz."[9] Irving's television audience responds with much laughter and applause.

The film's audience immediately despises the character. This is largely because of Spall's self-assured body language and the tone he uses to deliver the lines.

The screen again fades to black and for a few seconds we *see* nothing. However, we do *hear* a woman say authoritatively, "Holocaust denial rests on . . . " This is Lipstadt (Rachel Weisz), who, when the setting is revealed, is in a classroom of college students. She is educating them about the "basic assertions" of Holocaust deniers. Cinematically, the decision briefly to introduce us to the *words* of Irving and Lipstadt (via black screens) before we see these two individuals is important. It forces us to focus on their audible, rather than bodily and facial, expressions. In other words, it forces us to focus on what they are saying.

At one point in the classroom scene, Lipstadt turns to ask her students for answers to the question "How do we know the Holocaust happened?" Although we all know the Holocaust happened, it quickly becomes clear that proving it is not as easy as either the students or we, the audience, think. This transitions to the next scenes, which depict what several reviewers referred to as the opening scene in *Denial*.[10] Although not the opening as such, these scenes do indeed "set . . . the stage for the real-life drama that unfolds."[11]

The setting for the beginning of that drama is DeKalb College in Atlanta, Georgia, in 1994. Lipstadt is giving a talk about her book. A member of the audience (composed primarily of students) asks if it is true that she declines to debate Holocaust deniers. She emphasizes, in response, that she "won't debate fact." One of the big questions *Denial* asks is, how should we respond to people who lie (or, put a different way, who embrace "alternative facts")? In her book, Lipstadt explains that while she "once was an ardent advocate" of ignoring Holocaust deniers, she now believes that this "is no longer an option." This does not mean the alternative strategy is to debate them. "In fact," she writes, "it means *not* doing that. We cannot debate them for two reasons, one strategic and the other tactical. . . . [D]eniers long to be considered the 'other' side. Engaging them in discussion makes them exactly that. Second, they are contemptuous of the very tools that shape any honest debate: truth and reason."[12]

As the DeKalb scene in *Denial* suggests, however, purveyors of alternative facts can command a sense of intrigue. The next person (possibly an Irving sympathizer planted in the audience) to ask a question of Lipstadt wants to know why she denigrates the work of Irving in particular. Right before this, we see Irving quietly slip into the back of the auditorium after surreptitiously taking a copy of Lipstadt's book from a table and immediately turning to consult the index. The camera is focused on Lipstadt as she speaks to the audience; she denies denigrating Irving, and matter-of-factly states that she does not "think he's worth my time." The camera then swings round to focus on a man in the audience who raises his hand and stands up. Although *we* know it is Irving, neither Lipstadt nor the DeKalb audience are yet aware of this fact.

As she calls on him to ask his question, the camera changes perspective. Now behind Lipstadt, it shows her looking out at the audience. To great effect, and making us feel like we are Lipstadt, cinematographer Haris Zambarloukos shifts the camera angle so that, because of Irving's placement in the auditorium, Lipstadt is not only forced to look up to her questioner (placing Irving in a position of power) but also has to shield her eyes from the bright lights, making her (and us) very uncomfortable. As Irving introduces himself, the entire audience seems to be drawn to him (and therefore away from the camera). The fact that he is seated toward the rear of the auditorium means most of them are indeed, like Lipstadt, looking up at him.

Putting on a show, Irving pulls $1,000 out of his pocket (this actually happened), offering it to anyone who can show a document proving Hitler ordered the Holocaust. To compound the anger and isolation Lipstadt is feeling, Irving also gives away his books for free at the end of Lipstadt's event (which he has hijacked). The camera is no longer looking up at him: instead, we look down from a high vantage point as people flock to get a copy of his book; we hear Irving saying that it is "real history." The camera cuts to a shot of Lipstadt's face, the full-screen close-up accentuating her bitterness and anger.

These scenes provide a sense of Irving as the victor. Thus, they serve as an effective means of ensuring the audience will be disoriented by what happens next: Irving decides to sue Lipstadt for libel. For Irving, the victorious DeKalb confrontation could never be anything more than the opening salvo, because it simply reinforced what he already believed to be true—that Lipstadt was out to get him.

New York Times v. Sullivan

In 1964, the US Supreme Court decided "arguably the most important First Amendment case in history."[13] *New York Times v. Sullivan* reshaped American libel law.[14] The court struck down an Alabama libel law that did not require someone to show that an individual's speech had actually harmed them (damaged their reputation). Under these *libelous per se* laws, if a jury found "words were . . . 'of and concerning'" someone (which was exceptionally easy to prove), then there was "'implie[d] . . . legal injury from the bare fact of publication itself,'" and it was thus legally presumed that the words were false *and* malicious.[15] This essentially made it impossible to escape legal liability for saying, for example, something as innocuous as an elected official was not a nice person, or for saying/writing something about a public official that got the smallest details wrong. As the legal scholar Harry Kalven, Jr. observed in his famous article about *Sullivan*, "Political freedom ends when government can use its powers and its courts to silence its critics."[16]

In *Sullivan*, the court unanimously established a far more speech-protective standard for libel cases involving a plaintiff who is a public official. The individual now had to prove that someone's statement about them was "made with 'actual malice'—that is, with knowledge that it was false or with reckless disregard of whether it was false or not."[17] As Justice Arthur J. Goldberg eloquently emphasized in a separate opinion,

> The theory of our Constitution is that every citizen may speak his mind and every newspaper express its view on matters of public concern and may not be barred from speaking or publishing *because those in control of government think that what is said or written is unwise, unfair, false, or malicious*. In a democratic society, one who assumes to act for the citizens in an executive, legislative, or judicial capacity must expect that his official acts will be commented upon and criticized. *Such criticism cannot, in my opinion, be muzzled or deterred by the courts at the instance of public officials under the label of libel.*[18]

Three years later, the court issued its decision in another libel case, *Curtis Publishing Co. v. Butts*.[19] This time, the justices were confronted with a case involving "'public figures'" (as distinct from "public officials") who "were involved in issues in which the public has a justified and important interest."[20] In a fractured decision, the justices indicated that they thought it should be easier for such individuals to prevail in libel cases. Ultimately, however, over time the *Sullivan* test has essentially become the de facto legal standard in cases involving "public figures" as well as "public officials." This is why Irving did not sue Lipstadt in the US courts; as Lipstadt observes, he "would have to prove I lied."[21] The law of libel is *very* different in England, different in a way that made Irving confident he would prevail against Lipstadt *in the English judicial venue*.

US Versus English Libel Law

Toward the end of *Denying the Holocaust*, Lipstadt wrote the following prophetic passage:

> When we witness assaults on truth, our response must be strong, though neither polemical nor emotional. We must educate the broader public and academe about this threat and its historical and ideological roots. . . . The effort will not be pleasant. Those who take on this task will sometimes feel—as I often did in the course of writing this work—as if they are being forced to *prove* what they know to be fact.[22]

Such is the nature of English libel law that this was essentially what Lipstadt's legal team had to do: (a) prove that Irving deliberately falsified history, his own personal anti-Semitic beliefs driving him to deny the Holocaust; and, to a lesser extent, (b) prove that the Holocaust happened. In legal parlance, Lipstadt's team claimed "justification," which was the only legal strategy it could adopt in the case. "Justification" meant showing that what Lipstadt had written was true; even if her words hurt Irving's reputation, she was legally *justified* in writing them.[23]

Although Lipstadt did indeed write the truth, it is the very fact that her lawyers would be compelled to prove this that spurred Irving to bring his case in the English courts. In short, even today, "English defamation law tilt[s] the scales dramatically towards plaintiffs,"[24] and Irving was certain Lipstadt would be unable to prove that his Holocaust denial was nothing but a pack of anti-Semitic lies.

In *Denial*, over lunch in Atlanta, Julius (Andrew Scott) educates Lipstadt—and the movie's audience—about the litigation strategy chosen by Irving and the fundamental differences between American and English libel law. As she notes in her book, Julius gave her "a crash course in British libel law."[25] To be sure, much of American law is based on English common law. For example, the American absolutist understanding of the law of prior restraint (a concept on display in *The Post*; see chapter 3) was inherited from English common law. And not until *Sullivan* did English and American *libel* law take divergent paths. Yes, in the famous colonial-era 1735 case the New York printer John Peter Zenger was acquitted of "seditious libel." (Zenger had published newspaper columns criticizing the royal governor of New York.)[26] However, that outcome was very much an anomaly. Until *Sullivan*, England and the United States had very similar legal approaches to defamation.[27] After *Sullivan*, "[s]o great are the differences that in recent decades United States courts have refused to enforce English judgments arising from claims for libel and slander."[28] This is because English libel law remains rooted in the same *libelous per se* approach rejected in *Sullivan*. While the Defamation Act of 2013 changed some of the libel law landscape in England, and the European Convention on Human Rights can shape the nature of some libel cases in that country,[29] "it is still the case that American defamation law is far more protective of free speech and free press than English law."[30]

"A Touchstone Moment"

Zambarloukos's cinematography shines throughout *Denial*, but it is at its very best when Lipstadt, Richard Rampton (Tom Wilkinson), Rampton's assistant Heather Rogers (Jackie Clune), and historian Robert Jan van Pelt (Mark Gatiss) travel to Auschwitz-Birkenau, in Poland. The perimeter Auschwitz scenes were shot on location, and the crew was permitted to shoot scenes inside the museum. However, the cast could not be filmed inside the museum or within the perimeter of the camps, so scenes involving them were shot on sets constructed in a London studio.[31] Weisz observed in an interview, "I don't know if anyone can come away from" Auschwitz—which she had never before visited—"unaffected."[32] The film's director, Mick Jackson, and Zambarloukos clearly sought to ensure that no one watching *Denial* came away from that cinematic experience emotionally "unaffected" by the images they saw on the screen.[33]

This is entirely consistent with the main themes of the film. As the scenes at Auschwitz seek to underscore, Lipstadt constantly feels as though the real emotional (as opposed to legal and forensic) significance of confronting Holocaust deniers is lost on her legal team and that they are unjustly *denying* her the opportunity to make her authoritative voice on the subject heard. This is why if one criticizes her character, "as written" in the film, as coming across as "little more than an outraged mouthpiece reduced to near silence," one misses a crucial point about the movie.[34]

In the English legal system, one's case is prepared by a team led by a lawyer who is called a solicitor. (For Lipstadt, this was Anthony Julius.) The case is then presented and argued in court by a different lawyer, called a barrister. Lipstadt's case was presented and argued by Rampton. When Lipstadt first meets Rampton, he emphasizes that for a case like this one the lawyer needs to possess a rare quality—an "appetite." This, he explains, requires him to visit Auschwitz. Why? Rampton says, matter-of-factly, "legal reasons." The film immediately cuts to an overhead shot of a fog-shrouded Auschwitz, with the perspective of looking down and along old train tracks. Thus begins a montage of scenes, filmed in color but effectively appearing in a palette of somber blacks and greys; there is deafening silence as the sequence of scenes from Auschwitz appears. This is followed by sad, somber piano music as we begin to see Rampton take photographs of exhibits in the museum. He stands in mesmerized disbelief at what he is seeing. The camera moves from Rampton back to the piles of belongings taken from those imprisoned and murdered. The physical and emotional enormity of what we are witnessing is emphasized by a panning shot along the length of a long glass window behind which are piles and piles of shoes. The camera swings around so we can see the other side of the room (from Rampton's perspective); there are piles of shoes behind the museum glass on both sides of the long corridor.

The scene shifts to an outside shot of the remains of the camps. From an elevated position, we can see the camps laid out in front of us; accompanied by mournful music, the camera stays still for twelve seconds. That does not feel like a long time, because one's mind is constantly trying to process what it is seeing, mentally juxtaposed with the previous scene of the piles and piles of shoes and other belongings. After those twelve seconds pass, we hear Lipstadt say (off camera), "Is he coming?" She is frustrated that Rampton has not joined her and the others. In the next shot, we—unlike those individuals—see Rampton walking around the perimeter fence; the camera follows him as he paces in a methodological manner. The angle shifts as he pauses at one corner to take notes—he is now a small figure in the distance as we look down the length of the fence line at him. This cinematography emphasizes the mental and physical enormity of Auschwitz and the daunting nature of the legal task facing Rampton. (Like Spall, Wilkinson received extensive praise for his work in *Denial*; his acting was described by reviewers as "brilliant" and "effortless.")[35]

Eventually, Rampton's emphasis on legal and forensic elements leads an emotional and clearly overwhelmed Lipstadt to sharply say that she cannot (and will not) view these hallowed grounds without "memorializing." This leads to what one commentator has described as the film's "touchstone moment," when the "fervor and pain" of Lipstadt and Van Pelt "are palpable."[36] Lipstadt quietly walks off to the remains of one of the crematoria. As she recites *El Maleh Rachamim* (the Jewish prayer for the dead) in front of the crumbling steps, we see overlayed behind her, but almost invisible, images of figures descending those steps to their death. Lipstadt is joined by Van Pelt, who removes his woolen hat and retrieves his yarmulke from his pocket. As we continue to hear their voices, the scene changes to another montage of Auschwitz scenes, including a barbed wire fence with raindrops falling from it and train tracks shot from a low angle so as to almost place the audience on them. Finally, we see Rampton walking slowly, looking across the field at Lipstadt and Van Pelt; Rampton is first seen standing behind the tall barbed wire perimeter fence and then from the other side of that fence, a shifting of perspective that now places Lipstadt and Van Pelt behind that fence. The multifaceted symbolism is powerful.

"A Verbal Yellow Star"

"My first reaction was one of extreme reluctance." This is how Oscar-nominated playwright and screenwriter David Hare describes his response when he was asked to write the adapted screenplay for *Denial*. "I have no taste for Holocaust movies," he continues. "It seems both offensive and clumsy to add an extra layer of fiction to suffering which demands no gratuitous intervention. It jars." Convinced that when "[f]aced with the immensity of what happened, sober reportage and direct testimony has nearly always been the most powerful approach," one of the things he insisted upon was "stick[ing] rigidly to the exact words used inside" the courtroom.[37] Indeed, such was Hare's belief in the importance of *not* "offering a boilerplate Hollywood narrative,"[38] he omitted what one commentator has described as the "Dr. Strangelove moment" of the actual trial—the moment when "Irving mistakenly referred to the judge as

'*Mein Fuhrer*,' rather than 'My Lord.'"[39] Including this might have enhanced the audience appeal of the film, attracting moviegoers through the use of marketing that spotlighted this soundbite. However, its inclusion would have detracted from the sobriety of the courtroom scenes. Sometimes less is more. Sometimes you have to leave something out, even though it really happened, in order to achieve the principal—and principled—cinematic goal, which, in *Denial*, was "the imperative of exposing Irving's distortion of history to promote hate."[40]

Literally sticking to the court transcripts elicited mixed responses from the film's reviewers. Some found it to be an engaging cinematic strategy,[41] but others expressed critical opinions along the lines of "the film was not enough of a Hollywood courtroom drama." There was no "emotional flash point" or "courtroom fireworks"—things that "moviegoers have been conditioned . . . to expect," wrote Stephen Holden in the *New York Times*.[42] Similarly, in the *Christian Science Monitor* Peter Rainer described *Denial* as a "workmanlike effort" that "strives not too strenuously to transcend its trappings as a standard-issue courtroom drama."[43] In an interview for an article that appeared in the *Chronicle of Higher Education*, Lipstadt made the following observation: "If someone said, Let's make a movie about a historian, I'd say boring."[44] Maybe the aforementioned reviewers were critical of *Denial* because they viewed it as such a movie. It is not, however, a movie about a historian. It is a movie about words and the importance of preserving facts and the truth—preserving them by utilizing freedom of the (printing) press.

This becomes clear, fifty minutes into the film, when the trial begins in the majestic environs of the High Court of Justice in London. As Zambarloukos explained in an interview, those environs did not lend themselves to dramatic cinematography.[45] Once again, however, this did not matter because of the cinematic focus on the words. As he proceeds with his opening statement (he is acting as his own legal counsel), Irving protests the label "denier": "My Lord; if we were to seek a title for this libel action, I would venture to suggest 'Pictures at an Execution.' My execution." The camera moves from looking directly at him to looking at Lipstadt sitting on the other side of the courtroom. However, instead of focusing entirely on Lipstadt, part of Irving's face remains visible in profile, out of focus on the left-hand side of the screen, as if to accentuate the feeling that even when turning to see Lipstadt's emotions Irving is omnipresent.

Irving continues, "The word 'denier' is particularly evil; for the chosen victim it is like being called a 'wife beater' or a 'pedophile.' It is enough for the label to be attached, for the attachee to be designated a pariah. An outcast from normal society." Speaking the next few words very slowly and deliberately, he says, "It is a verbal yellow star."[46] Again, we see Lipstadt's reaction (total disbelief) framed, in part, by the out-of-focus Irving. Notably, however, the camera then cuts to the screen of the computer of the court reporter who is typing every word said. The words "Yellow Star" appear on the screen in a visually significant representation of the importance of words in this film.

Nothing but the Truth

Denial was a small-budget (approximately $10 million) film that cannot be found anywhere in the listings of top-grossing films of 2016–2017. (It does not even appear in the list of top two hundred films for those years.) In the United States and Canada, it brought in just over $4 million, and only just about $8 million worldwide.[47] Does this mean that the film was a failure? In order to answer that question, it is instructive to consider what Hare wrote in 2016. "Contemplating the Lipstadt/Irving trial may," he suggested, "help" the principally political "charlatans" of our age "to learn" that they (and their supporters) cannot defend their *false* assertions on the basis that those *lies* are their *opinions* which they are freely entitled to express. Just a few years later, we have descended even further into this "post-factual era in which it is apparently permissible for public figures to assert things without evidence," especially in the world of American politics. Therefore, it is difficult to believe that any such "contemplation" will serve as a remedy to politicians (and their supporters) who embrace falsehoods with reckless abandon.[48] *However*, this does not mean that those committed to freedom of truthful expression should abandon their cause. Quite the opposite; pushing back at those who trumpet "alternative facts" by emphasizing what *Denial* can teach us is becoming ever more important in the digital world, because "it is *inevitable* that debates concerning historical denialism raise questions concerning the limits of freedom of speech" in that world.[49] We now live "[i]n an Internet age [where] it is, at first glance, democratic to say that everyone is entitled to their own opinion,"[50] a world in which it is somehow acceptable to spout "alternative facts," even if those "alternative facts," with deliberate intent, incite people to engage in insurrectionist imminent lawless action.

At the posttrial press conference, where she is finally able to break free from the "complete and painful act of self-denial"[51] that the audience has seen dominate her throughout the film, Lipstadt delivers a monologue that offers a compelling response to the "alternative facts are just like other facts" narrative.

"Now some people are saying that the result of this trial will threaten free speech. I don't accept that. I'm not attacking free speech. On the contrary, I've been defending it against someone who wanted to abuse it." Continuing, Lipstadt emphasizes the following: "Freedom of speech means you can say whatever you want; what you can't do is lie and then expect not to be held accountable for it. *Not all opinions are equal*. And some things happen, just like we say they do. Slavery happened. The Black Death happened. The Earth is round, the ice caps are melting . . . Elvis is not alive."

DELIBERATE INTENT

In 1969, the US Supreme Court issued a landmark decision in *Brandenburg v. Ohio*, striking down the Ohio criminal syndicalism statute that Clarence Brandenburg, a Ku Klux Klan (KKK) leader, had been convicted of violating.[52] The law had prohibited the advocacy of unlawful action "as a means of accomplishing industrial or political reform" and voluntarily assembling for the purpose of teaching or advocating such syndicalism.[53] The court's short *per curiam* opinion—an opinion issued by the court as a whole rather than being authored by a specific justice—laid out what has come to be known as the *Brandenburg* test. Under the First Amendment, a government may not "forbid or proscribe advocacy of the use of force or of law violation except where such advocacy is directed to inciting or producing imminent lawless action and is likely to incite or produce such action."[54]

In 1975, legal scholar Gerald Gunther wrote that *Brandenburg* is "the most speech-protective standard yet evolved by the Supreme Court."[55] This is still true. In 1994, historian Bernard Schwartz observed that

> [n]o matter how fiery the advocacy in a newspaper, magazine, *book*, or pamphlet, it is hard to see how it can meet the *Brandenburg* requirement that imminent lawless action is likely to result. . . . Even the most extreme advocacy in the press is now shielded by *Brandenburg*, since print alone is hardly likely to produce imminent lawless action.[56]

In 1997, when a three-judge panel of the Fourth Circuit Court of Appeals announced its decision in *Rice v. Paladin Enterprises*—a wrongful death civil lawsuit—it did just what Schwartz found it hard to imagine.[57] The lawsuit against the publisher Paladin Press was the subject of *Deliberate Intent*, a 2000 made-for-television movie. Like *Denial*, it asks the audience to consider some of the fundamentally problematic moral and legal questions associated with expressions of publishing freedom.

"The Book Was the Key; the Book Tied It All Together"

Very ominous music plays as *Deliberate Intent* opens with parchment scrolling horizontally across the screen. That parchment shows the text of the US

Constitution. We hear a male voice say "This book is dedicated to . . . " The scrolling text then morphs into scenes from a brutal crime, and then we see the cover of a book entitled *Hit Man*. As the unidentified voice runs through multiple steps associated with being a hit man and committing a homicide, we see those steps committed, one-by-one. The movie goes back and forth between the person who is going to commit the crime (we don't see his face) and the soon-to-be victims. After we see the hit man retrieve the gun from the trunk of his car and conceal it in his jacket, we see the outside of a house; the camera is positioned facing the house from the street. As we look at that house, we hear silencer-muffled gunshots, a scream, and then some kind of alarm. We have just witnessed the cinematic reenactment of the 1993 murder of Mildred and Trevor Horn and Janice Saunders. Although we learn from the film that these murders were committed by James Perry (Clark Johnson), who was hired by Trevor's father Lawrence Horn (James McDaniel), and that both men were found guilty of first-degree murder, the focus of the movie quickly becomes the civil lawsuit brought by members of the Horn family against Paladin Press.

As the sound of the alarm heard at the end of the film's opening sequence of scenes dissipates, the screen fades to black. There is an abrupt cut to film of KKK members gathered around a burning cross. A KKK leader is spewing racist and anti-Semitic prose. What we are watching is a video of these events playing on a television. The video (a fictional representation of events leading to Clarence Brandenburg's arrest) is paused as a professor starts speaking; on-screen text tells us this is the "College of William and Mary First Amendment Forum, October 1995." Two other professors sit behind a table on the dais; all three are engaging in a debate with the audience of students about the merits of protecting (or not protecting) the speech of individuals like Brandenburg. The camera swivels from its focus on one of the professors to a man at the back of the room who stands up and says, "Excuse me, does the First Amendment let you advocate anything? What about murder?" Outside, in the bucolic setting of the William and Mary campus, the man who posed that question is waiting for the professor who led the forum. "You and I are going to make history Professor Smolla," the man says. Professor Rodney Smolla (Timothy Hutton) is more than skeptical; he seems rather frustrated that this man—attorney Howard Siegel (Ron Rifkin)—is continuing to try to persuade him to join in representing a group of clients.

Although *Deliberate Intent* is, like *Denial*, based on a true story, it takes far more dramatic license. That dramatic license is evident in the scene where Siegel persuades Smolla to have a beer with him so that he can tell him the facts of the case. In real life, Siegel conveyed those facts to Smolla over the phone.[58] The bar setting makes for far more exciting cinema. For the most part, as we hear Siegel tell the story, we see neither him nor Smolla. Instead, we see a series of flashback scenes showing who the victims were and how the police identified Perry as the shooter and Lawrence Horn as the person who hired him to murder his ex-wife Mildred, his quadriplegic son Trevor, and Trevor's nurse Janice Saunders. Significantly, this part of the film does a very good job of focusing the audience's attention on these horrendous crimes and making it forget about the previous scenes, which had focused on the First Amendment.

Slowly, however, the subject of press freedom is reintroduced into the conversation—literally between Siegel and Smolla, and metaphorically between the film and the audience. One of the flashback scenes shows that after the Maryland police identified a connection between Perry and Lawrence Horn, a search of Perry's residence turns up a large number of how-to crime books. After finding a catalog for Paladin Press, Detective Chris Wittenberger (Kenneth Welsh) makes a phone call to that publisher; this reveals that one of the books Perry purchased from them is *Hit Man: A Technical Manual for Independent Contractors*.[59] Back in the bar, Siegel says to Smolla, "The evidence . . . it was all circumstantial until they found the book; you see, the book was the key; the book tied it all together."

Even though the story Siegel has told is compelling, one of the principal themes of *Deliberate Intent* is the way in which it took a long time for Smolla to overcome his profound hesitancy at getting involved in this litigation. "[I]ndeed," he reflects, "even as late as the actual presentation of the oral argument itself, I was deeply conflicted."[60] An ardent defender of the First Amendment, Smolla readily admits that his ultimate decision to participate in this case—and to thus argue *against* someone (Paladin) hiding behind freedom of the press—instantly turned many of his friends and colleagues against him. This includes Tom Kelley (Cliff DeYoung) who ultimately represented Paladin. Smolla was "pilloried as a traitor to the First Amendment."[61]

"This Is a Book"

The first courtroom scene opens with a shot of a rather austere building; as the camera pans downward, words appear on the screen: "Federal District Court Preliminary Motions, July 22, 1996." There follows an abrupt change of scene. We are now inside the courthouse; however, before we see the actual courtroom, the screen is filled with a copy of *Hit Man* lying on a table. As the camera shows Kelley's hand lifting the book, we hear him say, "Your honor, this is a motion to dismiss this case because . . . " There is a brief, cinematically effective pause as he looks at the book in his hand. Continuing, he says, with a sarcastic tone to his voice, "This is a book, it's not a gun, and it's not a bomb. And therefore, it should be protected under the First Amendment no matter what it says. Why?" As he starts to answer his rhetorical question, the camera moves in a circular manner so that it is now in front of Kelley—this enables the audience to see the people seated in the courtroom behind him, but the focus remains on Kelley, blurring the audience members in the background. "Because," says Kelley, "there's no way to distinguish it from movies, novels, and TV shows that depict crime and how-to details about murder." He proceeds to give examples as disparate as James Bond, *The Silence of the Lambs*, and *NYPD Blue*. It is a classic legal slippery slope argument.[62] Smolla rises from his chair to speak in response. "This suit isn't about censorship." His closing sentence is wrapped in cinematic drama: "It's a book that kills."

This argument fails to persuade the judge, who agrees with Kelley's slippery slope argument. The judge issues the injunction, thereby allowing Paladin to continue publishing *Hit Man*. The film's next shot emphasizes the inevitability of this decision in light of the prevailing principles of press freedom. The scene has shifted to outside on the courthouse steps; on one side of the shot, we see Siegel, Smolla, and the Horn family members walking away, while on the other side we see Peder Lund (Bill MacDonald)—the founder of Paladin—and Kelley standing surrounded by a gaggle of reporters. Paladin, and the media, are literally and legally standing together on the right side.

"This Suit Isn't about Censorship"

As the lawsuit, and film, move to the Fourth Circuit Court of Appeals, the courtroom scenes begin very differently from those at the lower court. We are taken inside the appellate courtroom with a sweeping overhead shot that uses the ornate and austere architecture to visually frame the three judges sitting down below. When Smolla begins to make his argument that *Hit Man* aided and abetted Perry, and is thus immune from First Amendment protection, he immediately encounters resistance and a question from Judge J. Michael Luttig (David Hemblen). As scholarship shows, there are myriad reasons why appellate court judges ask questions of the lawyers appearing before them. One finding of that research is that a judge's line of questioning is by no means a foolproof predictor of their final vote in a case.[63] In *Deliberate Intent*, director Andy Wolk (who has directed numerous crime dramas, including episodes of *NYPD Blue*) intended to present a standard courtroom drama—everything the critics lamented was missing from *Denial*. The camera goes back and forth between Luttig and Smolla in a dramatic, confrontational manner.

With the camera facing him square on and his face filling the frame, Luttig says—it is more of a statement than a question—"Aiding, and abetting, and instructing; that's it, Mr. Smolla." Somber music starts to play as the camera returns to Smolla, who begins to slump at the lectern with an air of defeat. In a flashback, we now see black-and-white snapshots of the victims, of Lawrence

Horn, and of Perry. Returning to the colorized courtroom, the camera goes from Smolla, to the judges, to Siegel, and then back to Luttig, who asks, because counsel seems to be in a daze, "Mr. Smolla, are you still with us?" Still hunched over at the lectern, Smolla looks up defiantly and says, "Your honor, you could say to hell with it." He stands up straight, holding the book up. "Publish the book; price of freedom, right, that's the way it goes. Or, you could prevent this book from being published knowing that Trevor Horn, his mother, and his nurse would still be alive today." He then rhetorically asks why his clients should win, and says the answer is, "The First Amendment." At this point the camera focuses on Siegel, who looks up, astonished. *Hit Man*, Smolla argues, fails the *Brandenburg* test. With dramatically raised voice and forceful body language, Smolla clutches the sides of the lectern and says, "With deliberate intent they steeled James Perry to action, and they cannot hide behind the First Amendment."

The Fourth Circuit's Decision

There are only a small number of US Supreme Court decisions interpreting and/or applying the *Brandenburg* test.[64] In his opinion announcing the Fourth Circuit's ruling against Paladin, Luttig shows considerable respect for that precedent and the important protection of press freedom that it provides. Writing about the Supreme Court's decision in *Brandenburg*, Luttig observes,

> [I]t is evident the Court recognized from our own history that . . . a right to advocate lawlessness is, almost paradoxically, one of the ultimate safeguards of liberty. Even in a society of laws, one of the most indispensable freedoms is that to express in the most impassioned terms the most passionate disagreement with the laws themselves, the institutions of, and created by, law, and the individual officials with whom the laws and institutions are entrusted. Without the freedom to criticize that which constrains, there is no freedom at all.[65]

Significantly, this observation is immediately followed by the word "however."[66] As Luttig explains, "the Court's opinion in *Brandenburg* is, by any measure, elliptical."[67] What is far clearer, however, is that speech aiding and abetting crimes has long been unprotected, that 1969 decision notwithstanding. *Hit Man* "constitutes the archetypal example of speech which, because it methodologically and comprehensively prepares and steels"—note the use of the same verb (to steel) here that Smolla used in the dramatic conclusion to his oral argument in the film—"its audience to specific criminal conduct through exhaustively detailed instructions on the planning, commission, and concealment of criminal conduct, finds no preserve in the First Amendment."[68]

The "'Most Dangerous Publisher in the World'"

After the dramatic courtroom scene, which concludes with Luttig's announcement of the decision in the case—namely, that the case can go to trial—the film shifts to a scene of Smolla waiting for a courthouse elevator to arrive. As the door of the elevator opens, we see—from Smolla's point of view—Lund standing in the elevator, hands in pockets. Smolla enters the elevator, turns to face us, and stands next to Lund. The men briefly look at each other as the doors close. Now inside the elevator, the screen is filled with a waist-up shot of the two men. After a few seconds, Smolla sighs and says (still looking ahead), "How do you do it?" Lund replies (in a rather irritated tone), "Do what, Mr. Smolla?" "Publish that crap, knowing what it's gonna do?" The camera then turns to focus tight in on Lund: "I have no control over what others do with the books that I publish." The camera angle again turns, this time with a focus on Smolla: "You just like to help people along a bit, huh? Tell me sir, are you proud to have published those books?" Again, the camera turns to Lund: "You want to know, Professor, do I have any trouble sleeping at night? No, I don't. I think you got the insomnia market all to yourself." This does not offer a legal explanation for Paladin's "extraordinary stipulations," but the moral explanation is clear for the audience to see.

As *Deliberate Intent* comes to a close, triumphant music begins to play. We see the main characters walk away down the street, viewed from a high camera vantage point. Text begins to appear on the screen. We are told that the US Supreme Court declined to hear Paladin's appeal of the Fourth Circuit's decision[69] and that a jury trial was scheduled for the spring of 1999. "In May, on the eve of the trial Paladin settled." The settlement included a large monetary payment;[70] the publisher agreed to stop selling *Hit Man* and "to turn over all remaining copies to the families." And then comes the line that underscores the press freedom magnitude of this litigation and, inevitably, the controversy that it generated. It "marked the 1st time a publisher has been held financially liable for a crime committed by a reader."

The Fourth Circuit's decision was "highly controversial,"[71] and it has divided scholars. Some have described it as "abominable," a "travesty against free speech," concluding *Brandenburg* should have protected Paladin's publishing freedom.[72] Others see *Hit Man* as a legitimate exception for which the publisher did not deserve to shelter behind the First Amendment.[73] What *Deliberate Intent* does is to bring the *issues* of this important case to a wider audience in an accessible (albeit sometimes excessively dramatized) manner. Importantly, it has the potential to generate, from that audience, profoundly significant questions such as the following: "I think it's fair to ask," writes Barry Yerdon, "'How is *The Hitman* different from a novel about a hitman who uses those procedures to kill people in the story?'"[74] Or, one might add, myriad websites providing "useful" information to prospective assassins (and bombers, and terrorists . . .).

Words Have Consequences

Denial and *Deliberate Intent* both feature timeless principles of press (in this case, publishing) freedom, and force the audience to grapple with thorny moral questions which are by no means confined to any specific time or place. Indeed, as recent news-making events have shown, a knowledge of these principles and questions is exceptionally useful. Whether or not the *Brandenburg* precedent should continue to have legal staying power became a powerful topic of discussion after the January 6, 2021, insurrectionist attack on the United States Capitol.[75] And there is no denying that anti-Semitic attitudes are shockingly pervasive in society, and that similarly shocking are the statistics showing the extent to which young Americans either (a) know little to nothing about the Holocaust, or (b) believe the Holocaust did not happen.[76]

And then consider the 2022 libel lawsuit that the actor Johnny Depp brought against his ex-wife, actress Amber Heard. The case centered on a 2018 op-ed that Heard published in the *Washington Post*, a piece in which she wrote of her experience as a victim of "sexual violence."[77] Although Depp was not named in the piece, he argued that its content clearly referred to him. He contended she had libeled him because she was lying about her experiences. In 2020, Depp lost a similar libel trial in the British courts. He had sued a newspaper publisher, alleging an article falsely stated that he had assaulted Heard when the couple were married. As we saw with the above discussion of *Denial*, it is still easier for plaintiffs to prevail in libel cases in Great Britain than in the United States. Therefore, when one combines Depp's loss in Great Britain, with the high bar set by the *Sullivan* standard in US libel cases, Depp was widely expected to lose on both sides of the Atlantic. However, the Virginia jury ruled in Depp's favor, finding Heard had indeed acted "with 'actual malice'—that is, with knowledge that it was false or with reckless disregard of whether it was false or not."[78] This has led many commentators to express considerable concern about the future of libel law in the United States.[79] Additionally, Depp's victory was decried by many for what it said about societal attitudes toward women who were victims of abuse.[80]

Ultimately, debates about the boundaries of libel law do not seem destined to die out any time soon. "Fake news" labels and campaigns based on "alternative facts" continue to infiltrate US politics, and at least one Supreme Court justice (Clarence Thomas) seems ready to explicitly overrule *Sullivan*. As *New York Times* reporter Adam Liptak observed in a 2021 article, although only a handful of other lower federal court judges have expressed sympathy for Thomas's position, studies show "a marked and previously undocumented uptick in negative depictions of the press by the U.S. Supreme Court."[81] Recall that in *Sullivan*, Goldberg emphasized that "[t]he theory of our Constitution is that every citizen may speak his mind and every newspaper express its view on matters of public concern and may not be barred from speaking or publishing *because those in control of government think that what is said or written is unwise, unfair, false, or malicious*."[82] The two movies analyzed in this chapter squarely address this fundamental theory underpinning the free press clause of the First Amendment.

NOTES

1. Franklin D. Roosevelt, "Message to the Booksellers of America," *Publishers Weekly*, May 9, 1942, 1741.
2. Deborah E. Lipstadt, *Denying the Holocaust: The Growing Assault on Truth and Memory* (New York: Free Press, 1993).
3. Quoted in Deborah E. Lipstadt, *Denial: Holocaust History on Trial*, movie tie-in ed. (New York: Ecco, 2016), 271.
4. Lipstadt, *Denying the Holocaust*, 8, 14, 111, 162, 163, 170, 213, 214, 215, 221, 232, 233.
5. Lipstadt, *Denying the Holocaust*, 161, 179, 180.
6. Lipstadt, *Denying the Holocaust*, 181.
7. Leah Greenblatt, "Denial," *Entertainment Weekly*, October 7, 2016, 41.
8. Stephen Holden, "Review: In 'Denial,' Confronting a Holocaust Revisionist in Court," *New York Times*, September 29, 2016; Peter Rainer, "'Denial' Is Efficient and Dry," *Christian Science Monitor*, September 20, 2016.
9. In the actual speech, Irving said "in" (not "at") "Chappaquiddick." For details of the substance and location of the speech, see Peter Evans, "The Pathology of Denial," in *How Was It Possible? A Holocaust Reader*, ed. Peter Hayes (Lincoln: University of Nebraska Press, 2015), 841; Robert Jan van Pelt, *The Case for Auschwitz: Evidence from the Irving Trial* (Bloomington: Indiana University Press, 2016), 1.
10. Ann Walker, "Film Review: *DENIAL*," *Psychological Perspectives* 61 (2018): 276; Philip Kemp, "Denial," *Sight & Sound*, February 2017, 74–75.
11. Rainer, "'Denial' Is Efficient and Dry."
12. Lipstadt, *Denying the Holocaust*, 221. See also the "About the Book" section of the movie tie-in edition of the book, where Lipstadt answers a frequently asked question: "C-SPAN's BookTV wanted to put you on and then follow your appearance with one by David Irving. What happened?" Lipstadt, *Denial*, 11–13.
13. Helen J. Knowles and Steven B. Lichtman, "Introduction: Oh What a Tangled Web They Weave," in *Judging Free Speech: First Amendment Jurisprudence of US Supreme Court Justices*, ed. Helen J. Knowles and Steven B. Lichtman (New York: Palgrave Macmillan, 2015), 17.
14. 376 U.S. 254 (1964).
15. 376 U.S. at 267.

16. Harry Kalven Jr., "The New York Times Case: A Note on the Central Meaning of the First Amendment," *Supreme Court Review* 1964 (1964): 205.

17. 376 U.S. at 279–80.

18. 376 U.S. at 298–99, italics added (Goldberg, J., joined by Douglas, J., concurring in the result).

19. 388 U.S. 130 (1967).

20. 388 U.S. at 134.

21. Lipstadt, *Denial*, xxi.

22. Lipstadt, *Denying the Holocaust*, 222, italics added.

23. Lipstadt, *Denial*, 32.

24. Bruce D. Brown and Clarissa Pintado, "The Small Steps of the SPEECH Act," *Virginia Journal of International Law Digest* 54 (2014): 2.

25. Lipstadt, *Denial*, 31.

26. Leonard W. Levy, "Did the Zenger Case Really Matter? Freedom of the Press in Colonial New York," *William and Mary Quarterly* 17, no. 1 (January 1960): 35–50.

27. Vincent R. Johnson, "Comparative Defamation Law: England and the United States," *University of Miami International and Comparative Law Review* 24, no. 1 (Fall 2016): 4–6.

28. Johnson, "Comparative Defamation Law," 6.

29. See, for example, "McLibel." (It is worth noting that Richard Rampton was the QC for McDonald's in that case.) Catherine Baksi, "Landmarks in Law: McLibel and the Longest Trial in British Legal History," *Guardian*, July 8, 2019. https://www.theguardian.com/law/2019/jul/08/landmarks-in-law-mclibel-and-the-longest-trial-in-british-legal-history.

30. Johnson, "Comparative Defamation Law," 97.

31. British Society of Cinematographers, "Denial: Haris Zambarloukos in Conversation with Jake Polonsky," 2017, https://vimeo.com/218629269 (last accessed June 20, 2022).

32. Curt Schleier, "A Behind-the-Scenes Look at 'Denial,'" *Hadassah*, September 2016, https://www.hadassahmagazine.org/2016/09/23/behind-scenes-look-denial/.

33. Although Zambarloukos had some time, in advance of shooting, to reconnoiter at Auschwitz, the remainder of the crew had the unenviable task of hitting the ground running at this very emotional location. BSC, "Denial: Haris Zambarloukos in Conversation with Jake Polonsky."

34. Holden, "Review: In 'Denial,' Confronting a Holocaust Revisionist in Court."

35. Rainer, "'Denial' is Efficient and Dry"; Greenblatt, "Denial."

36. Schleier, "A Behind-the-Scenes Look at 'Denial.'"

37. David Hare, "Foreword," in *Denial: Holocaust History on Trial* (New York: Ecco, 2016), xiii, xv. This foreword also appears, verbatim, here: David Hare, "David Hare on Writing Nothing but the Truth about a Holocaust Denier," *Guardian*, September 3, 2016, https://www.theguardian.com/books/2016/sep/03/david-hare-nothing-but-the-truth-about-a-holocaust-denial.

38. Hare, "Foreword," xiv.

39. Kenneth S. Stern, "My Behind-the-Scenes 'Denial' Story," *Jewish Journal*, September 15, 2016, https://jewishjournal.com/culture/arts/189808/my-behind-the-scenes-denial-story/.

40. Stern, "My Behind-the-Scenes 'Denial' Story."

41. Kemp, "Denial."

42. Holden, "Review: In 'Denial,' Confronting a Holocaust Revisionist in Court."

43. Rainer, "'Denial' is Efficient and Dry."

44. Quoted in Marc Parry, "A Holocaust Historian's Trial Hits the Big Screen," *Chronicle of Higher Education* 63, no. 7 (2016), https://www.chronicle.com/article/a-holocaust-historians-trial-hits-the-big-screen/.

45. BSC, "Denial: Haris Zambarloukos in Conversation with Jake Polonsky."

46. In the territory that they occupied during World War II, Nazis required all Jews to wear a "Yellow Star" badge. It "was intended to humiliate the Jews and to mark them out for segregation and discrimination. The policy also made it easier to identify Jews for deportation to camps." British Library, "Learning: Voices of the Holocaust—the Yellow Star," https://www.bl.uk/learning/histcitizen/voices/info/yellowstar/theyellowstar.html (last accessed January 24, 2023).

47. "Denial (2016): Release Info," IBDB, https://www.imdb.com/title/tt4645330/releaseinfo?ref_=ttfc_sa_1 (last accessed June 20, 2022); "Denial (2016): Box Office," IMDB, https://pro.imdb.com/title/tt4645330/boxoffice (last accessed June 20, 2022).

48. Hare, "Foreword," xv–xvi.

49. Galina Nelaeva and Gulnor Sufiyanova, "Review: *Memory and Punishment: Historical Denialism, Free Speech and the Limits of Criminal Law* by Emanuela Fronza," *International and Comparative Law Quarterly* 69 (October 2020): 1035, italics added.

50. Hare, "Foreword," xv.

51. Hare, "Foreword," xiv.

52. 395 U.S. 444 (1969).

53. 395 U.S. at 445.

54. 395 U.S. at 447.

55. Gerald Gunther, "Learned Hand and the Origins of Modern First Amendment Doctrine: Some Fragments of History," *Stanford Law Review* 27, no. 3 (February 1975): 755.

56. Bernard Schwartz, "Holmes versus Hand: Clear and Present Danger or Advocacy of Unlawful Action," *Supreme Court Review* 1994 (1994): 240.

57. 128 F.3d 233 (1997).

58. Rod Smolla, *Deliberate Intent: A Lawyer Tells the True Story of Murder by the Book* (New York: Three Rivers Press, 1999), 2. Unlike the film, Smolla's book does not describe the events using dramatic license.

59. Rex Feral, *Hit Man: A Technical Manual for Independent Contractors* (Boulder, CO: Paladin, 1983).

60. Rodney A. Smolla, "From *Hit Man* to *Encyclopedia of Jihad*: How to Distinguish Freedom of Speech from Terrorist Training," *Loyola of Los Angeles Entertainment Law Review* 22, no. 2 (2002): 487.

61. Smolla, "From *Hit Man* to *Encyclopedia of Jihad*," 485.

62. Slippery slope arguments are commonplace in legal education and legal practice, in both hypotheticals and real-life cases. An example of the latter can be found in *Brown v. Entertainment Merchants Association*, 564 U.S. 786 (2011).

63. For example, see Amanda Frost, "Academic Highlight: Jacobi and Rozema on Predicting Outcomes Based on Interruptions at Oral Argument," *SCOTUSblog*, December 18, 2017, https://www.scotusblog.com/2017/12/academic-highlight-jacobi-rozema-predicting-outcomes-based-interruptions-oral-argument/ (last accessed September 21, 2023).

64. Useful on this point is Joshua Azriel and Jeff DeWitt, "'We Fight Like Hell': Applying the *Brandenburg* Test to Trump's Speech Surrounding the Siege at the U.S. Capitol," *Criminal Law Practitioner* 12, no. 2 (February 2022): 32–34.

65. 128 F.3d at 243.

66. 128 F.3d at 243.

67. 128 F.3d at 264.

68. 128 F.3d at 256.

69. *Paladin Enterprises v. Rice*, *cert. denied sub nom.*, 523 U.S. 1074 (1998).

70. This was "rumored to be around $5 million." Calvin Reid, "Paladin Press Pays Millions to Settle 'Hit Man' Case," *Publishers Weekly* 245, no. 22 (May 31, 1999), https://www.publishersweekly.com/pw/print/19990531/33480-paladin-press-pays-millions-to-settle-hit-man-case.html.

71. Smolla, "From *Hit Man* to *Encyclopedia of Jihad*," 480.

72. Cassandra M. Chin, "Holding the Publisher of a 'Murder Manual' Liable for Aiding and Abetting Murder: A Travesty against Free Speech," *George Mason University Civil Rights Law Journal* 10, no. 1 (1999): 205.

73. Beth A. Fagan, "*Rice v. Paladin Enterprises*: Why *Hit Man* Is beyond the Pale," *Chicago-Kent Law Review* 76, no. 1 (2000): 603–36.

74. Barry Yerdon was a student in my spring 2022 Freedom of Speech class at SUNY Oswego, and this quotation is taken from the screening report about *Deliberate Intent* that he submitted for one of the course assignments.

75. See, for example, Azriel and Jeff DeWitt, "We Fight Like Hell."

76. Generally, see Anti-Defamation League, "ADL Records Dramatic Increase in U.S. Antisemitic Incidents Following Oct. 7 Hamas Massacre," press release, October 24, 2023, https://www.adl.org/resources/press-release/adl-records-dramatic-increase-us-antisemitic-incidents-following-oct-7 (last accessed November 1, 2023); Kit Ramgopal, "Survey Finds 'Shocking' Lack of Holocaust Knowledge among Millennials and Gen Z," NBC News, September 16, 2020, https://www.nbcnews.com/news/world/survey-finds-shocking-lack-holocaust-knowledge-among-millennials-gen-z-n1240031; Gustaf Kilander, "Nearly a Quarter of Young Americans Believe the Holocaust Didn't Happen or Has Been Exaggerated," *Independent*, June 21, 2021, https://www.independent.co.uk/news/world/americas/holocaust-denial-conspiracy-theories-america-b1869838.html.

77. Amber Heard, "I Spoke up Against Sexual Violence—and Faced Our Culture's Wrath. That Has to Change," *Washington Post*, December 18, 2018, https://www.washingtonpost.com/opinions/ive-seen-how-institutions-protect-men-accused-of

-abuse-heres-what-we-can-do/2018/12/18/71fd876a-02ed-11e9-b5df-5d3874f1ac36_story.html.

78. 376 U.S. at 279–80.

79. Katelyn Fossett, "What Was Really at Stake in the Depp-Heard Trial," *Politico*, June 3, 2022, https://www.politico.com/newsletters/women-rule/2022/06/03/what-was-really-at-stake-in-the-depp-heard-trial-00036985.

80. Ashley Fetters Maloy, Karen Heller, and Anne Branigin, "Depp-Heard Verdict Will Have Chilling Impact on #MeToo, Advocates Fear," *Washington Post*, June 2, 2022.

81. Adam Liptak, "Sidebar: The Supreme Court's Increasingly Dim View of the News Media," *New York Times*, April 19, 2021, https://www.nytimes.com/2021/04/19/us/supreme-court-news-media.html.

82. 376 U.S. at 298–99, italics added (Goldberg, J., joined by Douglas, J., concurring in the result).

Chapter 7

Responsibility Matters

Shattered Glass

Helen J. Knowles-Gardner

Inspired by journalist Buzz Bissinger's September 1998 *Vanity Fair* magazine article of the same name,[1] *Shattered Glass*, the only film analyzed in this chapter, tells the true story of the rise and fall of Stephen Glass, "the most sought-after young reporter in the nation's capital."[2] Until the web of lies he wove into the one particular story in 1998 proved to be his downfall, Glass charmed and flattered and ultimately duped his colleagues and editors at the *New Republic* magazine into believing and publishing the fantastical and supposedly true sociopolitical stories he wrote. The story the young associate editor concocted that precipitated his fall from grace was by no means an isolated incident, and *Shattered Glass* asks the audience to consider numerous important critical analytical questions about not only Glass's behavior but also the actions of those who for so long enabled his unethical journalism:

- To what extent does faked (and "fake") news play an important role in a constitutional democracy?
- In news journalism, which is more important: accurately conveying facts, or producing a product that people want to buy/read/watch/consume?
- To what extent does/should the First Amendment give constitutional protection to journalists who use their chosen profession to spread lies?
- What safeguards exist—other than the government—to protect against false reporting? And how effective are they?

Billy Ray, the director of *Shattered Glass* (hereafter SG), envisioned the film being a "little brother to All the President's Men."[3] As discussed below, there are numerous ways in which SG plays cinematic homage to ATPM. In so doing the film addresses the following issues:

- The use of a lead character to do voiceover narration of the true story that a film is telling.
- The use of dialogue to generate audience reactions to particular characters.
- The use of flashbacks to convey a story.

In terms of the ethical and constitutional questions it asks the audience to consider, SG conveys a complex and troubling story. Yet it also presents a story whose main point is very simple. Readers are asked to consider these two elements of the film as they engage with this chapter's analysis.

FACTS MATTER

Facts matter, especially in journalism. It is therefore appropriate that SG opens and closes with on-screen text. Before the music starts to play, the audience is told that "the New Republic Magazine was first published in 1914. It has been a fixture of American political commentary ever since." Indeed, as Glass (Hayden Christensen)—from whose point of view the film is narrated—later tells us, "There are 16,800 magazines in this country, but only one calls itself the in-flight magazine of Air Force One." This statement exaggerates the influence of the magazine if one considers the publication's circulation, but it definitely captures the way in which the staff wanted the magazine to be viewed (thereby accentuating the irony that it is Glass speaking these words).

The opening on-screen text continues. "In May of 1998, its staff was comprised of 15 writer/editors." After a brief pause: "Their median age was 26." After a slightly longer dramatic pause: "The youngest among them was Stephen Glass." The silence accompanying these *facts* is pierced by the introduction of saccharine music that would not feel out of place in a movie based on a fairytale. Shot in slow motion, Glass walks toward us, looking around at the sights of what we come to learn is a convention hall that is hosting a political memorabilia event. Is that a smile, an expression of pride, or a sense of awe on his face? With a shallow depth of field partially blurring the people around him, the focus is on Glass. Everything about this scene is deliberate.

We hear a voiceover (that we soon learn is the voice of Glass):

> There's so many show-offs in journalism, so many braggarts and jerks. They're always selling, always working the room. Always trying to make themselves

> look hotter than they actually are. The good news is, reporters like that make it easy to distinguish yourself. If you're even a little bit humble, a little self-effacing or solicitous, you stand out.

The focus shifts from Glass to close-ups on various convention exhibits—such as "Monicondoms" designed "To Wrap Around Your Slick Willy," and "Oval Office Cigars" labeled as "Rolled On the Thighs of an Intern." There are two ways in which these references to the Clinton presidency are cinematically effective in this scene. First, they provide historically relevant temporal context because they are references to events that happened in the mid-1990s: the sex scandal that broke in 1998 with revelations that President Bill Clinton had been having sexual relations with White House intern Monica Lewinsky for a couple of years. (These revelations led to Clinton's impeachment by the House of Representatives for perjury and obstruction of justice; he was acquitted by the Senate.) Second, they are references that embody the kind of titillating, salacious, designed-to-sell-more-copies things that made Glass's articles so attractive to both his colleagues and his readers—including the political glitterati of Washington, DC.

Even though the focus shifts during this scene, what remains constant is Glass's voiceover, educating us about how journalists should ply their trade.

However, none of this happened. Glass made it all up.

The screen fade-cuts to a granite sign into which is inscribed "Highland Park High School" (Glass's alma mater). Inside the school, the camera moves slowly down a corridor, and the music builds in a triumphant but reflective manner; we see the now suit-and-tie-dressed Glass gazing at a bulletin board covered in clippings of the headlines and articles he has written. The film transitions to a classroom full of students; as the camera pans across the room in rather soft lighting we see the faces of adoring and impressed students. We hear a similarly awestruck female voice (Glass's former teacher Mrs. Duke, played by Caroline Goodall) list Glass's accomplishments, and we witness the exhibiting of sexual tension between Glass, the teacher, and the fawning female students.

None of this happened—except in Glass's imagination.

The opening credits of the film roll.

DIALOGUE MATTERS

Throughout the film, Glass is in constant denial that he has done anything wrong. In his mind, none of the negative things that happen to him are his fault; rather, they can be attributed to the conspiratorial actions of editor Charles (Chuck) Lane (Peter Sarsgaard). From the very first moment that we see Lane and Glass interacting in the movie, we know that their relationship is fraught with tension and underlying distrust. A scene that takes place just ten minutes into the film opens with the camera situated low and behind a seated Glass; we are looking up at him looking up at the wall of magazines. Lane walks into the employees' break room, retrieves food from the refrigerator, and starts to make his lunch at the kitchenette counter, his back to Glass; the two men engage in polite but not friendly conversation about the articles they are working on. When Glass responds to Lane's inquiry, he tells him, nonchalantly, that he is writing about "Young Republicans at the CPAC Conference." He proceeds to discuss the boring details as Lane sits down and reads a newspaper. Glass can see that Lane is not genuinely interested, so he proceeds to regale Lane with details of the boozing and hiring of hookers by the young conservatives. "Sounds great, Steve," says Lane, still unimpressed.

On numerous occasions throughout the film, we learn—from Glass's point of view in his narration of the film—that Glass was much happier with the leadership of Lane's predecessor, Michael Kelly (Hank Azaria). Indeed, although by the end of the film Glass's fall from journalism grace is complete, one is left with the sense that Glass simply cannot accept that he did anything wrong. Throughout the film, Glass deludes himself into believing that everything happening to him is the fault of Lane, who—in his opinion—sought to get Kelly fired in large part so that he could then go after Glass and *personally* terminate him too. When the magazine's publisher, Marty Peretz (Ted Kotcheff), chooses Lane to succeed Kelly, Glass, who hero-worships Kelly, is angry, hurt, and distraught.

Glass's subsequent behavior, and his conspiracy-fueled hatred of Lane, are enabled by the journalist's young, devoted, and adoring colleagues, especially Caitlin Avey (Chloë Sevigny) and Amy Brand (Melanie Lynskey). Cinematically, this is very effectively captured by Glass's repeated utterance, "It's probably nothing," when his colleagues answer the office phones, only to find that they are taking messages for Glass, messages from numerous other high-profile media outlets who have come calling for the journalism hotshot. We are only seven minutes into the film when this first happens. The office administrative assistant Gloria (Linda E. Smith)—who fawns over Glass just like the younger colleagues do—interrupts Glass's meeting with Avey and Brand to say Glass has a call from *Policy Review*. "When d'you start talking to . . . ?" ask the two women. "It's probably nothing" is delivered with apparent humility and nonchalance. It is humility and nonchalance that Glass's colleagues accept as sincere, but the audience is not so sure. There is something about these scenes—something about Glass's mannerisms and the tone of his voice—that begins to instill distrust in the audience; for unlike his colleagues, *we*, the audience, are not his peer employees. We see something else—we see Christensen "sensational as Glass, finding the wonder boy and the weasel in a disturbed kid flying high on a fame he hasn't earned."[4] It is a fame that Avey and Brand believe Glass deserves, and it is a fame they themselves long for. But again, we know better; one can call the cast "lavish and funky,"[5] but that does not really seem to grasp the overall importance of the casting and wardrobe choices in the film: "Christensen sports a slightly oversized pair of spectacles, retreating behind them as if they were mirrors, or translucent walls."[6] Yes, indeed. And we, the audience, see the illusion reflected back at us, even if his smitten colleagues (with the important exception of Lane and, to a lesser extent, Kelly) do not (until it is too late).

What we, the audience—again, unlike Avey and Brand—learn, about fifteen minutes in, is that it is not only Lane who has trust issues with Glass. At the first sign that there is something amiss with one of the young journalist's articles, Kelly is much less trusting than the journalist ever imagines. Kelly asks Glass to come to his office; before Kelly has a chance to say why, Glass asks him, "Are you mad at me?" Kelly simply explains that the organizer of the conservative political conference detailed in "Spring Breakdown" "has made some pretty serious charges" about the piece, and "we need to answer them." Glass brings his notes from the story and stands in the doorway, the embodiment of seeming contriteness and wearing what becomes his trademark puppy/hangdog look.

Just like "It's probably nothing," the phrase "Are you mad at me?" is repeated to great cinematic effect in SG. Readers are encouraged to consider one particular utterance of the line during a scene that takes place at a party Glass is hosting at his apartment. There, Avey confronts Glass about law school. Or, more specifically, why Glass is seemingly set on going to law school even though, as Avey (who here is portrayed as more than just Glass's good friend and coworker) reminds him, it's his parents and not him that want him to go to law school. "Are you mad at me?" asks Glass. Avey's response is priceless and telling: "I told you. I do not respond to 'Are you mad at me?' I'm not your kindergarten teacher." The audience immediately thinks to itself, "Yes, but I bet his high school teacher would respond . . . " And, of course, she wouldn't be mad at him.[7]

Through the use of a flashback, we are now taken to the Washington, DC, hotel room where the events detailed in "Spring Breakdown" took place. As we see what supposedly happened in that room (involving hookers and boozing), we hear an overlay narration, by Glass, that focuses on how he—the dedicated journalist—used proper methods to take meticulous notes about everything he was witnessing. This narration occurs because Glass is using this particular piece as an example to explain to the adoring high school students how an article takes shape—from researching the piece, through the writing of the article, and on to the grueling editorial process. We hear him tell the students, "Now, journalism is about pursuing the truth, and I would never encourage you to do anything sneaky or dishonest in the pursuit of a story. Such as assuming a phony identity." There is a subtle, momentary, cinematically effective pause after "story" and before "such as."

Glass continues, as we now see the flashback of the "Spring Breakdown" events: "Your notes are crucial. You have to record everything you see and hear. Every quote, every detail. All the way down to the mini bottles in the fridge."

When Kelly starts to question him about the veracity of "Spring Breakdown," Glass immediately apologizes in a very dramatic manner; he even offers to resign. He had assumed that there was a mini fridge in the hotel room where the events he described took place because of the presence of the miniature bottles of alcohol. When Glass says that's the only possible issue with the piece, and that there are no other errors or falsities in the article, Kelly appears satisfied.

> Glass: Thanks for backing me.
>
> Kelly, with a warm and sincere smile on his face: It's what editors do.

Glass leaves and is not privy to what happens next, but we, the audience, are. In his now closed-door office, Kelly immediately pulls out a Yellow Pages telephone directory from his desk drawer and calls the hotel to confirm that guests could rent mini fridges if they wanted. One is left with the sense that Kelly's concerns about the veracity of Glass's stories were not assuaged by this information.

When Kelly later informs the magazine's young staff that Peretz has fired him, they immediately assume that Lane conspired to achieve this outcome, and they all make disparaging remarks about the new editor.[8] Shortly thereafter, at an editorial staff meeting, Glass extravagantly regales the young writers, and Lane, with the details of his new piece entitled "Hack Heaven." The scene abruptly shifts from Glass's reenactment of events, complete with a gyrating dance on top of a chair, to the offices of *Forbes Digital* magazine. Adam Penenberg (Steve Zahn) is called into the office of his editor Kambiz Foroohar (Cas Anvar), who tosses Glass's article on the table and demands to know why his journalist didn't get the story. Why was his journalist, who works for a publication devoted to digital technology, beaten to this blockbuster computer hacking story by the *New Republic*'s writer?

Cinematically, what happens next is filmed to great effect. We see a close-up shot of a highlighter pen being used to emphasize names and other such "facts" in the Glass piece. There follows an abrupt cut to an over-the-shoulder shot; Penenberg has the highlighted article propped up next to him, and his computer screen shows the Yahoo! search engine box. There's another abrupt cut as the film focuses on that box and the words "Jukt Micronics" appear as Penenberg types them in. The film again cuts, this time to the journalist's face as he waits for the search results to appear; a cut back to the screen shows: "There were no matches for 'Jukt Micronics.'" After manning the phones and thumbing countless Yellow Pages, Penenberg and his colleague Andy Fox (Rosario Dawson) can find no trace of all of the individuals and organizations named in "Hack Heaven." There is one notable exception: As Penenberg sarcastically says, "There does appear to be a state in the union named Nevada."

The next scene—to which the film very deliberately cuts—emphasizes the irony of the behavioral hold the pathologically lying Glass has over his colleagues. Glass is making the young reporter David Bach (Chad Donella) feel really bad about the piece he has written because, as Glass (with seeming glee) points out, the reporter's facts are all over the place. As Bach leaves, crestfallen, his tail between his legs but still buoyed by Glass's offer to help him with the rewrites, Glass checks his voicemail. He—and, by now, the audience—expect this to be another suitor come calling, the one whose advances Glass dismisses with the aw-shucks "It's probably nothing" line. And at first, the message sounds like that. Penenberg starts out by saying how much he and his colleagues enjoyed "Hack Heaven" and how much they wanted to do a companion piece. Glass looks smug. But then he hears Penenberg say that they are having trouble tracking down one of the individuals referenced in the piece and were wondering if Glass would be able to supply a phone number.

Penenberg is not the only journalist seeking that number; Lane wants it too. Indeed, he wants contact details for all the story's sources. Glass's predictable response? "Did I do something wrong? Are you mad at me?" Nonplussed, Lane casually responds, "No. I just need the phone numbers." There is a shift of scene from the worried (but not terribly so) Glass as Lane walks away, to the *Forbes* offices where more reporters continue to find holes in "Hack Heaven." As upbeat, pulsating music plays, we see the excitement on their faces. They know they are hot on the trail of a major scoop. Fox sums it up, her dialogue accompanied by glee on her face: "Do you know why this is so great? I mean, do you see the irony here?" Yes, she is talking to Penenberg, but it is as though the fourth wall has disappeared and she is actually talking to us, the audience: "The *New Republic*, snobbiest rag in the business. The in-flight magazine of Air Force One. And their star goes out and gets completely snowed by a bunch of hackers. I mean, God couldn't have written this any better." Oh, the irony (of her interpretation of the "facts"), indeed.

"Events Rapidly Overtaking Themselves"

As Todd McCarthy observed in his *Variety* magazine review of SG, Mandy Walker's cinematography creates a "sense of events rapidly overtaking themselves."[9] This is particularly prominent in two scenes near the end of the film. Glass is initially suspended for two years for manufacturing "Hack Heaven." The film fades from a scene where Avey is looking in sadness at the computer screen upon which she has just typed an email to Kelly informing him of this development, to a scene that finds a dejected Glass sitting in a fetal position on the floor of a building, propped up against its interior marble wall. The camera angle shifts to eye level as Kelly and a female coworker (at his new place of employment—which, from Avey's email, we learn is the *National Journal*), deep in conversation, walk toward the camera. "Steve," says a surprised and smiling Kelly as he sees the young man sitting on the floor. Glass, with an awkward and sheepish grin on his face, slowly stands up. The camera turns back to Kelly: "What are you doing here?" There is an immediate cut to a scene with the two men sitting on a set of stairs in the building. The camera is looking up at them, as though it is positioned at the bottom of the stairs. Kelly says nothing as Glass, in a calm but defeated voice, just goes rambling on about how his career is over, and all because Lane was out to get him: "The one guy who's hated me all along." Finally, Kelly intervenes, and as the dialogue progresses, the shot goes back and forth between the two men.

> Kelly: I'm sure that none of this is personal.
>
> Glass: No? Chuck keeps a list in his head . . . everybody who's a Michael Kelly person. A couple of times I said some things I shouldn't have said about you. So now I'm on it. That's why he's so set on killing me now.

At this point, there is an abrupt cut from Glass to Kelly. What does Kelly say next? The audience is half expecting his response, but Glass certainly isn't.

> Kelly: Well, I have to tell you, Steve, he's within his rights. The things you did were fireable offenses.

After some more dialogue, we hear Kelly utter one of the most important lines in the film. The camera is focused on Kelly as he says, "Steve, I have to ask you something. Um . . . "—dramatic pause—"Did you ever cook a piece when I was your boss?" Glass looks at him with a mixture of disbelief, hurt, shock, and betrayal. The camera goes straight back to Kelly: "Did you ever lie to me?" Glass is silent. The camera angle switches very effectively. We are now behind the two men, looking at them looking at each other. Glass silently looks Kelly squarely in the eyes, and then Kelly looks at the floor.

The second scene in which the cinematography gives a "sense of events rapidly overtaking themselves" comes a few minutes later, after the now-fired Glass has left the offices of the *New Republic*. Lane walks into the office break room, where previous issues of the magazine are proudly displayed on wall-mounted racks. Glass has now been fired—rather than just suspended—for concocting "Hack Heaven." The camera shifts from Lane to the magazines (looking at them from the editor's point of view) and then back to Lane, who then walks over and starts removing a large number of the copies with—as the audience clearly grasps—the intention of looking through them to find other falsified Glass articles.

Over the course of the film, the camerawork changes. There is a noticeable shift from scenes shot with a handheld camera to ones where the camera is mounted on a tripod. This gives "[t]he visual image of the magazine . . . stead[ying] itself as the film progresses."[10] As director Billy Ray (making his directorial debut in SG) and adviser Charles Lane (the real Charles Lane) indicate in their audio commentary on the DVD, this evolution was deliberate, giving "'the suggestion . . . that truth as an idea [is] beginning to take hold there'"—at the *New Republic*—"'and that order [is] beginning to be restored.'"[11] The scene in the magazine display room embodies the culmination of this "suggestion." There follows a visually powerful montage of increasingly rapid shots accompanied by intensifying music and Glass's voice reading the articles. (His voice quickly overlays itself as the words of the offending articles literally and symbolically morph into a jumble of text.) We see Lane throw copies of the magazine on the floor, interspersed with shots of Glass's smiling face and the adoring faces of the high schoolers and his colleagues at the magazine. A short while later, the film returns to the school classroom, to the captivated teenagers who are listening to Mrs. Duke. She is reading the titles of Glass's most famous pieces (which we, the audience, now know were entirely fabricated).

These classroom sequences happened only in Glass's imagination. The irony is palpable.[12]

A "Little Brother to All the President's Men"

Director Ray initially viewed the cinematic telling of Bissinger's story as "an opportunity . . . for a satire . . . I thought, this could be like *Network*."[13] (Recall that *Network* is analyzed in chapter 4.) Ultimately, SG was fundamentally "reconceived"[14] in large part because Ray realized the original film would be "glamorizing a media villain."[15] What SG became was a movie that clearly represents a "tip of the cap to Woodward and Bernstein,"[16] envisioned by Ray as being a "little brother to All the President's Men."[17] The director watched ATPM at least "forty-five times before shooting."[18] To journalism professor Matthew C. Ehrlich, the comparison between the two movies is "apt" because "*Shattered Glass* performed much the same role that the Woodward and Bernstein story and other journalism movies had done: It underscored the press's centrality in American life, in particular the notion that self-regulation of the press works."[19]

There are numerous ways in which SG plays cinematic homage to ATPM (for analysis of ATPM, see chapter 3). However, here the analytical spotlight can be shone on two scenes in SG that depict journalism methods in a starkly similar way to its 1976 predecessor. The first scene, which shows the "rectitude" of Chuck Lane, takes place halfway through the film.[20] It is evening, and Lane is at home with his wife and baby. He receives a phone call; it is an irate George Sims. We only hear his voice; we never see the actor—Bill Rowat—who is portraying the fictitious head of the fictitious Jukt Micronics company that Glass created. The camera cuts back and forth between shots of Lane cradling the phone between his ear and shoulder, and the notepad upon which he is rapidly taking notes of the conversation—including one particularly important note—"Young voice," writes Lane.

Sims, supposedly the head of a major software company, is calling to dress down Lane for his subordinate Glass's piece. Before Lane can ask him any questions, Sims says he doesn't have time for the conversation because the company is in the middle of its office party. This raises the suspicions of Lane, but he just keeps scribbling notes while saying "mm-hmm" and listening intently. Sims continues, "Look, if you were calling for a comment on your story, I don't have one, other than to say I wish you hadn't run the stupid thing." As Sims says, "other than . . . ," we see Lane's notepad. Sims abruptly criticizes Glass, saying the reporter should have known that everything in their conversations was off the record. This again does not seem right to either Lane or the audience. When the camera returns to a full-screen shot of Lane's face, he gently says, "I'm just calling to verify some information." Sims, again abruptly, replies, "I'm not verifying anything; bottom line is, I'd like you guys to basically get lost." We can vaguely hear party sounds (office party sounds?) in the background. "Okay?" asks Sims, rhetorically. Before Lane can respond, Sims hangs up. Although there are differences, readers are encouraged to consider the cinematic ways in which this scene harkens back to Carl Bernstein's famous phone conversation with John Mitchell in

ATPM, during which former attorney general Mitchell is asked by Bernstein to comment on an article the *Washington Post* plans to publish the next day, and responds, "Katie Graham's gonna get her tit caught in a big fat wringer if that's published."

The second scene takes place with twenty minutes of the film remaining. Again, it features Lane taking a call at his home in the evening, this time from Bach, who is concerned about what Glass might do to himself as his career unravels. Bach is calling from a building's garage. During the course of the phone conversation, he inadvertently provides Lane with the final piece of *factual* information the editor needs to expose Glass as a journalist who fabricated pieces (rather than just a young, naïve reporter who was duped by his sources). There are important cinematic differences between this scene and the classic Deep Throat garage scenes in ATPM. For example, the lighting of the garage—the way in which Deep Throat and Bob Woodward are cast in very deliberate and ominous shadows—in the 1976 classic is far more suspenseful than in SG. Nevertheless, the point still stands that the garage setting, and the revealing of a key piece of information during this conversation, clearly show Ray's cinematic desire to pay homage to ATPM.

Many of the reviews of SG pick up on the cinematic similarities between the two films, and they are in general agreement that Ray's comparative assessment of his film is "fair."[21] Indeed, writing for the *Christian Science Monitor*, David Sterritt concluded that SG was "the best movie about American journalism since" ATPM.[22] When one considers the fact that almost all the movies analyzed in this volume were made post-1976, this should be regarded as high praise indeed.

It is important to note, however, that it was only when SG was "reconceived"—making Lane the star,[23] the embodiment of journalism's pursuit of the truth—that the film became a twenty-first-century ATPM. As Ray observed, "'You think you're seeing a movie about Stephen Glass, and you realize halfway through you're seeing a movie about Chuck Lane.'"[24] That realization only comes when Kelly is fired and replaced with Lane.

"The Fearless Pursuit and Expression of Truth"

All the President's Men hit theaters less than two years after the resignation of President Richard Nixon. Only five years elapsed between the Glass scandal and the release of *Shattered Glass*. Both films were based on events fresh in the minds of audiences. This is one of the reasons why "half of the journalism industry was chomping at the bit for the film while the other half wished it would go away."[25] But it is not the only reason. The film appeared at a particularly bad time for the industry. Marianne M. Jennings, a professor of legal and ethical studies, has extensively detailed the media scandals that preceded and immediately followed the Glass affair. Although American media history is littered with examples of journalism scandals, particularly those involving falsified materials,[26] 1998 "was a media ethics turning point" that saw major publications—not only the *New Republic* but also the *Boston Globe*—fall "victim . . . [to] the simplest of scandals."[27] And although Stephen Glass's actions "provided the 1998 wake-up call" that the industry needed, the scandals did not stop (perhaps, in part, because journalism was policing itself, and exposing its dirty laundry, with a greater sense of urgency and transparency). Scandals continued to "erupt . . . in a fairly steady stream"; they "were so repetitious: different names and media outlets, same story," and they were not confined to national publications or, indeed, to the print media.[28] As Jennings observes, the five years between 1998 and 2003 were generally "not . . . a pretty sight" for journalism. (During this time, the work of the *Boston Globe* Spotlight team was a rare positive journalistic development; see chapter 9.)[29]

These scandals were *very* fresh in the memories of the industry, because SG opened in theaters (limited release only) in November 2003, barely six months after the Jayson Blair scandal broke at the *New York Times*. As if the rise and fall of Stephen Glass had not served as any wake-up call to more ethical action, the reporter Blair " . . . committed frequent acts of journalistic fraud while covering significant news events in recent months." This "widespread fabrication and plagiarism" was, wrote his colleagues, "a profound betrayal of trust and a low point in the 152-year history of the newspaper."[30] The depth of Blair's betrayal makes for depressing reading:

> He fabricated comments. He concocted scenes. He lifted material from other newspapers and wire services. He selected details from photographs to create the impression he had been somewhere or seen someone, when he had not. And he used these techniques to write falsely about emotionally charged moments in recent history, from the deadly sniper attacks in suburban Washington to the anguish of families grieving for loved ones killed in Iraq.[31]

Jennings reminds us that although "[t]o err is human . . . the course of the road is a choice."[32] The erroneous choices made by Glass and Blair (and also Jack Kelley, whose resignation from *USA Today*—because he too fabricated stories—happened almost at the same time that the SG DVD was released)[33] were just that: *choices*.

Before the final credits roll in SG, two of the lines of information that appear on the black screen are as follows:

> Michael Kelly went on to become editor of The Atlantic Monthly.
>
> In April of 2003, he was killed while covering Operation Iraqi Freedom.

Kelly died alongside Sergeant First Class Wilbert Davis (Third Infantry Division) when the Humvee carrying the two men crashed after taking enemy fire in Baghdad.[34] *This*, says reviewer Anthony Lane (not to be confused with Charles Lane), "is a story, and it makes the rest of 'Shattered Glass' look smaller than ever."[35] Just as with the reviews of *Good Morning, Vietnam* (see chapter 1) written by Henry A. Giroux and Hal Hinson,[36] Anthony Lane's review of SG is based on the belief that the wrong movie was made. The deaths of Kelly and Davis were tragic,[37] but that is an entirely different story from the one told in SG.

After his death, Kelly's best writings from across the course of his career were collected together in a volume entitled *Things Worth Fighting For*.[38] One of those writings, "Master of the Game," first appeared in the *New York Times Magazine* in 1993.[39] In it, Kelly examines one of the ways in which the media's coverage of politicians changed, profoundly, between the 1960s and 1990s. It "is the story of how the idea of image became the faith of Washington, and how the president became the central figure of that faith, the architect and ultimately the victim of the world's most elaborate personality cult."[40] In order to explain to his readers the way in which Watergate (see ATPM, chapter 3) affected (or perhaps effected) this change, Kelly interviewed David Gergen, who joined the Nixon administration staff as a speech writer in 1971:

> Gergen remembers the selling of the Nixon image as a central fact of life. . . . "The great cynicism had already begun when Nixon took office," he says. "It came with Vietnam when a generation of reporters concluded that their government was lying to them. Nixon arrived on the back end of that, and he came carrying this great personal animosity, a lack of trust in the press."[41]

As both his writings and the cinematic portrayal of him by Azaria in SG show, trust and truth were inextricably intertwined in Kelly's journalism. And it is worth noting that they are reflected in the name of the journalism award given in Kelly's memory—an award recognizing "the fearless pursuit and expression of truth."[42] Anthony Lane misses the mark when he suggests that a movie about Kelly's work, rather than Stephen Glass's fabrications, should have been made. For SG is ultimately about Kelly, and everything he held to be important for responsible and ethical journalism, journalism constitutionally protected.

TRUST MATTERS

In ATPM, the "fearless pursuit and expression of truth" is exactly what the pair of *Washington Post* journalists did. One reviewer of SG described Ray and his crew as "haunted by the legend of Bob Woodward and Carl Bernstein." The "saga" of ATPM, observes Robert Sklar,

> hovers over Shattered Glass as a shining example, a challenge, and also something of a mocking irony for the screen retelling of how, a quarter century later, rival reporters exposed the lies of a magazine journalist and helped to rescue not the Republic, but *The New Republic*. It's as if no one can look at the Stephen Glass affair without unconsciously invoking the old Marxian truism that history repeats itself, the first time as tragedy, the second as farce.[43]

Writing about ATPM, journalism professor Michael Schudson says of that 1976 film that it embodied "the central myth of American journalism": namely, that it portrayed the press as "a charter, an inspiration, a reason for being large enough to justify the constitutional protections that journalism enjoys."[44] Ray's deliberate effort to make SG into a "little brother to All the President's Men"[45] naturally opened the film up to the criticism that it, too, was perpetuating this myth. That this came at a time—as discussed above—when the ethics of journalism were coming under sustained attack by the bad examples set by Glass, Blair, et al., inevitably meant that criticisms of SG focused on its mythology-perpetuating element. As mentioned above, in his review of SG for the *New Yorker*, Anthony Lane took serious issue with the idea that the Glass affair was "sufficient grounds for a motion picture." He asked, "[W]hat, pray, is the big deal? Stephen Glass was a faker on the make, a species common to most fields of human endeavor, yet, to judge by the solemnity with which this movie treats his story, the importance of his transgressions puts him somewhere between Ted Bundy and Alger Hiss."[46] Writing for New York's *Daily News*, Jack Mathews similarly asked (rhetorically), "As a former magazine fact checker, he [Glass] knew how to fool his own fact checkers, and he knew how to cajole his editors into trusting him. Where's the movie in this?"[47] Almost two decades after Lane and Mathews's reviews appeared—and, therefore, almost two decades after the release of SG—Rachel Walther also dismissed the relevance and/or importance of the film, but for a different reason. The "awfulness" that the movie's story tells "would likely generate not a scandal" in the 2020s, she concluded; a journalist—or, in fact, any individual—"weav[ing] an elaborate web of deception to cover" their "tracks sounds par for the course in our post-truth era." Continuing, Walther wrote that instead of journalists "[t]he monsters . . .

are those editors, politicians, and readers who cast a blind eye on tall tales and lies in order to reap profits, boost ratings, and gain market share."[48]

Individual Responsibility

Even though these commentators were writing twenty years apart, they all missed an incredibly important point about the significance of SG—then and now—as it pertains to freedom of the press. Yes, some of the polls referenced in the introduction to this volume support the SG reviewers' pessimistic and/or skeptical view of journalism's current state of affairs. (Anthony Lane embodies that view when he says, "[T]he contention of Ray's film is that . . . the noble calling of the reporter, is as sturdy and as polished as ever. . . . Give me a break.")[49] However, journalism has not become Dante's *Divine Comedy*. Journalism has not reached the gates of hell; it is not a business about which we should "abandon all hope." Indeed, it is precisely because public trust in the media is at such a low point that SG is now, more than twenty years later, such an important movie to analyze.

Writing in 2007, W. Lance Bennett, Regina G. Lawrence, and Steven Livingston observed that "[t]he American press is in crisis. The symptoms are widely known and much lamented among journalists, academics, and the general public: diminishing levels of public confidence, dwindling audiences, ratcheting profit pressures, shrinking resources, and increasing negativity, sensationalism, and soft news."[50] These symptoms still plague the press, and inevitably, they negatively affect the degree of First Amendment protection people think journalists should be afforded. In 1786, Thomas Jefferson wrote to a friend that "[o]ur liberty depends on the freedom of the press, and that cannot be limited without being lost."[51] Yet, as law professor Stephen Wermiel observed in a 2019 American Bar Association publication, "[m]ore than two centuries later . . . the role of the news media in our society has become a constant battleground," making it necessary to ask, is "the news media still seen as a pillar of freedom, a bulwark against tyranny?" Wermiel's conclusion was unequivocal: "The First Amendment guarantee of freedom of the press has stood the test of time through vast changes in technology and communications, proliferation of the forms of expression, and dramatic and perpetual changes in societal values. What lies ahead will continue to challenge the strength of this pillar of democracy," but that pillar is still needed.[52] "Similar to other journalism movies," writes Ehrlich, "*Shattered Glass* reaffirms notions of individual responsibility and professional autonomy."[53] Yet these "notions" have become increasingly difficult for the public to accept because of the aforementioned "symptoms" of a "press . . . in crisis." What SG does, however, is not simply "reaffirm" such "notions" but remind us that they are necessary for the very survival of journalism and the press freedoms that are protected by the Constitution.

This can clearly be seen toward the end of the film. Ehrlich observes that "[c]ontrary to some journalists' concerns that *Shattered Glass* denigrated the press by exiling Glass or treating him more sympathetically than he deserved, the movie does the opposite. It exalts the press by denigrating Glass."[54] We see this in the scenes immediately following Lane's firing of Glass. A furious Avey confronts Lane in the building that is home to the magazine. "What the hell did you do to Steve?" she demands. Lane is walking toward the exit doors, exhausted from the previous scenes' confrontations with Glass. He does not immediately respond to Avey. He just keeps walking away from her. He is walking toward us, and we see Avey following him, demanding, "He [Glass] just called me from his car hysterical, and I asked him what was wrong and he said, 'Ask Chuck.'" The camera has now repositioned itself. Avey is out of shot, and we are now following Lane toward the doors. At "ask Chuck," Lane turns to look at Avey, and as he does so, he shouts at her, "I fired him, okay?" Avey continues to refuse to believe that Glass has done anything wrong; she refuses to believe what Lane is telling her—namely, that "Hack Heaven" is not an isolated incident. She now heads toward the doors as he tells her that they are going to have to go back through all of Glass's articles. The camera is now looking at her exiting the building. It is looking over Lane's shoulder as he says, "Make sure you go all the way back, because"—we are now looking directly at Lane, positioned in the right hand third of the screen, hands on hips, as he says—"half of them ran when Mike was still here." Back to the shot over Lane's shoulder, as Avey turns to look at him: "That's what this is; of course. I mean, what are you going to do, Chuck?" She walks toward Lane, sarcastically asking, "Pick us off, one by one? Everybody that was loyal to Mike?" The camera shifts again, as we now look at Lane saying, "Caitlin, when this thing blows, there isn't going to be a magazine anymore." Over his shoulder looking at Avey, arms defiantly crossed again: "Now, if you want to make this about Mike, make it about Mike." Back to looking at Lane: "I don't give a shit. You can resent me. You can hate me. But come Monday morning we're all gonna have to answer for what we let happen here. We're all gonna have an apology to make."

Lane's monologue continues: "He handed us fiction after fiction, and we printed them all as fact." Dramatic pause. "Just because . . . we found him entertaining." Longer pause. "It's indefensible. Don't you know that?"[55]

The film cuts from Lane leaving the building and a dejected and still angry and disbelieving Avey standing in the lobby, to the magazine's meeting room. Text appears on the screen—"Monday, May 11, 1998." The camera pans across the room full of defeated and resentful-looking young staffers seated around the table and focuses on publisher Peretz pacing at the head of the table, arms folded and not looking happy. This scene is reminiscent of one earlier in the film; consequently, when the film cuts to show a somber Lane entering the magazine's offices and asking Gloria (in a very serious voice), "Is everyone in the conference room?" the audience is expecting Lane to receive a very cold reception from his gathered colleagues. Nothing could be farther from the truth.

"A ROSE, BY ANY OTHER WORD"

Of course, what Stephen Glass "handed" his colleagues was faked news. He was by no means the first writer, journalist, or other such literary figure to write fiction and pass it off as nonfiction.[56] And as we have seen, he has certainly not been the last member of the media to attempt such a hoax—think Jayson Blair and Jack Kelley. In his *New Yorker* review, Anthony Lane strongly argued that Glass's faked news was no news at all.[57] Twenty years later, that assessment misses the mark even more than it did in 2003, for a very significant reason: *Shattered Glass* is the story of *faked news* not "fake news," and now more than ever it is important not to let that distinction get lost in the analytical shuffle, because the term "fake news" is such a pervasive component of the contemporary political lexicon.

Of course, one might say that definitionally Glass's work product was indeed fake news because it was false news. However, because of the way in which—in 2023—the term "fake news" is generally understood, labeling Glass's articles as such is deeply problematic. This is because there are now two principal definitions of fake news, and both are easily distinguishable from Glass's unethical journalistic lies.

First, fake news can be defined as

> fabricated information that mimics news media content in form but not in organizational process or intent. Fake-news outlets, in turn, lack the news media's editorial norms and processes for ensuring the accuracy and credibility of information. Fake news overlaps with other information disorders, such as misinformation (false or misleading information) and disinformation (false information that is purposely spread to deceive people).[58]

This type of fake news is clearly becoming more and more prevalent in society, especially on social media platforms. Fed primarily by the "social platforms' structure of rewarding users for habitually sharing information"[59] and "social pressure" that leads people to "share fake news because they don't want to be ostracized from their social circles,"[60] misinformation and disinformation are running rampant on the internet. Although in the case of Glass, the "news media's editorial norms and processes [at the *New Republic*]" put in place to "ensur[e] . . . the accuracy and credibility of information" failed (as SG makes clear) to prevent publication of the offending articles, the fact remains that Glass was working within an industry structured by those "editorial norms and processes." Consequently, his work needs to be distinguished from this first generally accepted definition of fake news.

Today, the second widespread understanding of "fake news" is that it is the media coverage one doesn't like, because that coverage (a) doesn't adhere to one's political views and/or (b) does not present one's political activities in a flattering and fawning light. In other words, the second definition of "fake news" is that which it became commonplace to hear candidate, and then president, Donald J. Trump rail against.[61] Such allegations of "fake news" (they are just that, allegations, hence the use of quotation marks in the discussion of this particular type of "fake news") are also not new; they did not suddenly appear with Trump's presidential campaign.[62] However, what *is* clear is that this "fake news" is also completely different from the faked news work product of Stephen Glass.

What is also clear, however, is that faked news and "fake news" receive the same amount of constitutional protection, and that protection is extensive. This is because any regulatory effort to strike at such misinformation would be an effort to strike at expressions because of their *content*. And the US Supreme Court takes a very dim view of governmental attempts to ban/limit speech simply because the government does not like that speech. Yes, "[l]ies are a problem. In fact," as the Foundation for Individual Rights and Expression observes, "one can persuasively argue that lies are *the* problem." Indeed, "[f]ew behaviors are as corrosive to our social fabric or as foundational to our societal divisions. Lies severely hobble our ability to communicate effectively, our capacity to understand reality, and our attempts at securing social and moral progress. As a result, it's understandable to conclude that using government power to prohibit and eliminate lies is justified."[63] However, such a conclusion completely ignores the long-standing interpretations of the First Amendment. As Justice Anthony M. Kennedy has stated, "[C]ontent-based restrictions . . . have been permitted . . . only when confined to the few 'historic and traditional categories [of expression] long familiar to the bar.'"[64] And "[a]bsent from those few categories . . . is any general exception to the First Amendment for false statements. This comports with the common understanding that some false statements are inevitable if there is to be an open and vigorous expression of views in public and private conversation, expression the First Amendment seeks to guarantee."[65] (It should be noted that in this discussion Kennedy cites both *Brandenburg v. Ohio* and *New York Times v. Sullivan*, the two decisions referenced in the previous chapter.) Constitutionally, faked news and fake news are both protected roses that smell the same.

"IN THE END IT COMES DOWN TO TRUST"

As communications professors Kevin G. Barnhurst and John Nerone observe, movies—and popular culture in general—often approvingly depict the "power" of the newspaper (and the magazine) "to expose and enlighten."[66] *All the President's Men* is of course the perfect example of such a movie. As this chapter has shown, however, *Shattered Glass* is also a powerful depiction of this enlightening power of the press. It is a film that accomplishes these goals by frequently paying cinematic homage to its 1976 big brother. And so it is worth considering the way in which one of the final scenes in SG bears striking similarities to ATPM. Glass and his lawyer are meeting with Lane and one of the magazine's lawyers. Lane says,

> What I'm gonna do is this. I'm going to read to you a list of suspicious titles, one by one. If you raise an objection to a particular title, we'll fact check it again in the hope of removing it from the list. If you remain silent, we'll assume that piece is fabricated, either partially or entirely. And it will stay on. Is that clear to everyone?

As Lane reads a long list of article titles—a list that elicits nothing but silence from Glass—the movie returns to that opening scene of the fictious political convention, and Glass wondering round in awe. Lane's voice is replaced with Glass's:

> You have to know who you are writing for, and you have to know what you're good at. Or record what people do. I found out what moves them, what scares them, and I write that down. That way, they're the ones telling the story. And you know what? Those kind of pieces can win Pulitzers too.[67]

Cut back to the conference room, with a tight focus on Glass. "Steve?" we hear Lane say. Glass was clearly daydreaming. Not for the first time in this film, the irony is palpable.

In her review for the *Guardian*, Aida Edemariam concluded that "[i]n the end it comes down to trust, and that is one of the things Shattered Glass does best."[68] Ehrlich—and Peter Howell, reviewing the film for the *Toronto Star*—echo this sentiment: The film "speaks of ideals regarding truth and democracy that we cannot afford to abandon unless we are prepared to 'retreat to the caves of our prehistoric ancestors.'"[69] Amen.

NOTES

1. Buzz Bissinger, "Shattered Glass," *Vanity Fair*, September 5, 1998, https://www.vanityfair.com/magazine/1998/09/bissinger199809.

2. Bissinger, "Shattered Glass."

3. Peter Travers, "Shattered Glass," *Rolling Stone*, November 13, 2003, 106.

4. Quoted in Travers, "Shattered Glass," 106.

5. Anthony Lane, "Deceived: 'Shattered Glass' and 'The Human Stain,'" *New Yorker*, October 26, 2003, https://www.newyorker.com/magazine/2003/11/03/deceived.

6. Lane, "Deceived."

7. After his disgrace, Glass did in fact go to law school, graduating with honors from Georgetown University Law School. However, he was subsequently rejected for bar admission in both New York and California because of the unethical journalism that SG depicts.

8. Kelly was fired in part because of his criticism of Al Gore, who was a friend of Peretz.

9. Todd McCarthy, "Shattered Glass," *Vanity Fair*, September 3, 2003, https://variety.com/2003/film/awards/shattered-glass-2-1200539582/.

10. Matthew C. Ehrlich, "*Shattered Glass*, Movies, and the Free Press Myth," *Journal of Communication Inquiry* 29, no. 2 (April 2005): 109.

11. Quoted in Ehrlich, "Free Press Myth," 109.

12. Ray originally shot the film as a straightforward story until he decided it wasn't very interesting that way. He raised more money to shoot and add the high school scenes. "Confirm or Deny," *Filmmaker*, https://filmmakermagazine.com/archives/issues/fall2003/features/confirm_deny.php (last accessed November 11, 2023).

13. Quoted in Chris Kaltenbach, "Shattered Glass Changed Paths," *Baltimore Sun*, April 8, 2004.

14. Billy Ray, quoted in Ehrlich, "Free Press Myth," 109.

15. Howard Kurtz, "Stephen Glass: The True Story," *Washington Post*, October 7, 2002.

16. Ray, quoted in Ehrlich, "Free Press Myth," 109.

17. Quoted in Travers, "Shattered Glass."

18. Gal Beckerman, "Facts and Fictions: Shards of Glass," *Columbia Journalism Review* 42, no. 3 (September/October 2003): 55.

19. Ehrlich, "Free Press Myth," 104.

20. "Shattered Glass," November 7, 2003, 2003, https://www.rogerebert.com/reviews/shattered-glass-2003.

21. Travers, "Shattered Glass." *Variety* magazine described the film as "[n]arratively, stylistically and thematically a junior-league 'All the President's Men,'" but this should not be interpreted as a critical description. McCarthy, "Shattered Glass."

22. David Sterritt, "All the News That's Fit to Invent," *Christian Science Monitor*, October 31, 2003, https://www.csmonitor.com/2003/1031/p18s02-almo.html.

23. Lane was a consultant for the film. A. O. Scott, "Film Review: A Young Writer's Ambition, with Loyalty and Betrayal," *New York Times*, October 31, 2003, https:

//www.nytimes.com/2003/10/31/movies/film-review-a-young-writer-s-ambition-with-loyalty-and-betrayal.html.

24. Quoted in Kurtz, "Stephen Glass."

25. The categories were: "Hint-hint, journalism is boring," featuring quotes from the *New York Post*, *Slate* magazine, the *Daily News*, and *OC Weekly*; "Icky, wet description of Stephen Glass," quoting from the *New York Post*, *Hollywood Reporter*, *Journal News* (serving the immediate suburbs surrounding New York City), and *OC Weekly*; "For insiders only," featuring the *New York Times*, the *Star Ledger* (Newark, NJ), and the *Daily News*; "The sobering message," using quotes from filmcritic.com, Reelviews (specifically James Berardinelli), CNN, and the *Christian Science Monitor*; "Headline notables," using quotes from the *Daily News*, CNN, the *New York Post*, *OC Weekly*, and *USA Today*; and "The verdict" with material from *Slate*, the *Star Ledger*, *OC Weekly*, and *USA Today*.

26. Marianne M. Jennings, "Where Are Our Minds and What Are We Thinking—Virtue Ethics for a Perfidious Media," *Notre Dame Journal of Law, Ethics and Public Policy* 19, no. 2 (2005): 641–49.

27. Jennings, "Perfidious Media," 649.

28. Jennings, "Perfidious Media," 649 (quotations), and more generally 649–60.

29. Jennings, "Perfidious Media," 638.

30. Dan Barry et al., "Correcting the Record; *Times* Reporter Who Resigned Leaves Long Trail of Deception," *New York Times*, May 11, 2003, https://www.nytimes.com/2003/05/11/us/correcting-the-record-times-reporter-who-resigned-leaves-long-trail-of-deception.html.

31. Barry et al., "Correcting the Record."

32. Jennings, "Perfidious Media," 639.

33. Blake Morrison, "Ex-*USA Today* Reported Faked Major Stories," *USA Today*, March 19, 2004, http://usatoday30.usatoday.com/news/2004–03–18–2004–03–18_kelleymain_x.htm; Ehrlich, "Free Press Myth," 110.

34. David Carr, "Michael Kelly, 46, Editor and Columnist, Dies in Iraq," *New York Times*, April 5, 2003, https://www.nytimes.com/2003/04/05/us/michael-kelly-46-editor-and-columnist-dies-in-iraq.html.

35. Lane, "Deceived."

36. Henry A. Giroux, "Memory and Pedagogy in the 'Wonderful World of Disney': Beyond the Politics of Innocence," in *From Mouse to Mermaid: The Politics of Film, Gender, and Culture*, ed. Elizabeth Bell, Lynda Haas, and Laura Sells (Bloomington: Indiana University Press, 1995); Hal Hinson, "'Good Morning, Vietnam,'" *Washington Post*, January 15, 1988.

37. For a poignant reflection of Sergeant Davis's life and career, see Louis Romano, "Proud Family Recalls Fallen Soldier," *Washington Post*, April 11, 2003.

38. Michael Kelly, *Things Worth Fighting For: Collected Writings* (New York: Penguin, 2004).

39. Michael Kelly, "Master of the Game," in *Things Worth Fighting For*, 53–79.

40. Kelly, "Master of the Game," 54.

41. Kelly, "Master of the Game," 62. Regarding the aforementioned changes in the media, the reader is encouraged to consult the following: Joe McGinnis, *The Selling*

of the President 1968 (New York: Simon and Schuster, 1969); Theodore H. White, *The Making of the President, 1968* (New York: Atheneum, 1969).

42. "Michael Kelly Award," https://michaelkellyaward.com/about-2/ (last accessed November 11, 2023).

43. Robert Sklar, "Review," *Cinéaste* 29, no. 1 (2003): 23.

44. Michael Schudson, *Watergate In American Memory: How We Remember, Forget, And Reconstruct The Past* (New York: Basic Books, 1992), 124, 26.

45. Quoted in Travers, "Shattered Glass."

46. Lane, "Deceived."

47. Jack Mathews, "Truth under Fire: A Movie about a Reporter Who Invented His Stories Will Inevitably Glamorize Fraudulent Journalism," *Daily News* (New York), September 1, 2002, https://www.nydailynews.com/truth-fire-movie-reporter-invented-stories-inevitably-glamorize-fraudulent-journalism-article-1.498425?outputType=amp.

48. Rachel Walther, "News: Fabulism as Fact in Shattered Glass (2003)," *Medium*, March 27, 2021, https://sleeping-all-day.medium.com/fake-news-fabulism-as-fact-in-shattered-glass-2003-5e72e59ad7ab.

49. Lane, "Deceived."

50. W. Lance Bennett, Regina G. Lawrence, and Steven Livingston, *When the Press Fails: Political Power and the News Media from Iraq to Katrina* (Chicago: University of Chicago Press, 2007), 1.

51. Letter from Thomas Jefferson to James Currie, January 28, 1786, Monticello—Jefferson Quotes & Family Letters, https://tjrs.monticello.org/letter/2141 (last accessed November 5, 2023).

52. Stephen J. Wermiel, "Freedom of the Press: Challenges to this Pillar of Democracy," *Insights on Law and Society* 19, no. 2 (March 26, 2019), https://www.americanbar.org/groups/public_education/publications/insights-on-law-and-society/volume-19/insights-vol-19-issue-2/freedom-of-the-press/.

53. Matthew C. Ehrlich, "Hollywood and Journalistic Truthtelling," *Notre Dame Journal of Law, Ethics and Public Policy* 19, no. 2 (2005): 519–20.

54. Ehrlich, "Free Press Myth," 111–12.

55. After his disgrace, Glass wrote *The Fabulist*, a novel recounting a fictionalized version of these events.

56. See, for example, Madelyn K. Duhon, "Journalist and Hoaxer: William Francis Mannix and the Long History of Faked News" (Master's thesis, Louisiana State University, 2017).

57. Lane, "Deceived."

58. Daniel M. J. Lazer et al., "The Science of Fake News: Addressing Fake News Requires a Multidisciplinary Effort," *Science* 359, no. 6380 (March 9, 2018): 1094.

59. Pamela Madrid, "USC Study Reveals the Key Reason Why Fake News Spreads on Social Media," USC News, January 17, 2023, https://news.usc.edu/204782/usc-study-reveals-the-key-reason-why-fake-news-spreads-on-social-media/.

60. Matthew Asher Lawson, "Americans Share Fake News to Fit in with Social Circles," American Psychological Association, press release, March 9, 2023, https://www.apa.org/news/press/releases/2023/03/fake-news-social-circles. For more

discussion, see M. Asher Lawson, Shikhar Anand, and Hemant Kakkar, "Tribalism and Tribulations: The Social Costs of Not Sharing Fake News," *Journal of Experimental Psychology: General* 152, no. 3 (2023): 611–31.

61. For example, see Angie Drobnic Holan, "The Media's Definition of Fake News vs. Donald Trump's," PolitiFact, October 18, 2017, https://www.politifact.com/article/2017/oct/18/deciding-whats-fake-medias-definition-fake-news-vs/.

62. Keith J. Bybee and Laura E. Jenkins, "Free Speech, Free Press, and Fake News: What if the Marketplace of Ideas Isn't about Identifying Truth?," in *Free Speech Theory: Understanding the Controversies*, ed. Helen J. Knowles and Brandon T. Metroka (New York: Peter Lang, 2020).

63. Angel Eduardo, "Why (Most) Lies are Protected Speech, and Why They Should Stay That Way," Foundation for Individual Rights and Expression, June 29, 2023, https://www.thefire.org/news/why-most-lies-are-protected-speech-and-why-they-should-stay-way.

64. *United States v. Alvarez*, 132 S.Ct. 2537, 2544 (2012), quoting from *Simon & Schuster, Inc. v. Crime Victims Board*, 502 U.S. 105, 127 (1991) (Kennedy, J., concurring in the judgment).

65. 132 S.Ct. at 2544.

66. Kevin G. Barnhurst and John Nerone, *The Form of News: A History* (New York: Guilford, 2001), 1.

67. Relevant here is the Janet Cooke scandal. After she won the Pulitzer in 1981 for a *Washington Post* article that was later discovered to be fabricated, Cooke returned the prize and resigned from the paper. Ironically the article was originally submitted for the Pulitzer by Bob Woodward. Howard Kurtz, "Janet Cooke's Untold Story," *Washington Post*, May 9, 1996, https://www.washingtonpost.com/archive/lifestyle/1996/05/09/janet-cookes-untold-story/23151d68–3abd-449a-a053-d72793939d85/.

68. Aida Edemariam, "The Storyteller," *Guardian*, May 10, 2004, https://www.theguardian.com/media/2004/may/10/pressandpublishing.film.

69. Ehrlich, "Hollywood and Journalistic Truthtelling," 539, quoting Peter Howell, "Big Game of Untruths and Consequences," *Toronto Star*, November 28, 2003.

Chapter 8

Creating Protagonists, Competing Interests, and Uncertain Legal Standards

The People vs. Larry Flynt *and* Citizenfour

Brandon T. Metroka

"Hard cases make bad law." Perhaps most famously expressed in the American context by US Supreme Court Justice Oliver Wendell Holmes, Jr.,[1] this adage generally stands for the proposition that "when a case presents a special hardship, the court is tempted to bend a generally sound law to avoid the hardship, resulting in a law that, though perhaps fine for the case at hand, is unsound as a general rule."[2] As Professor Sepehr Shahshahani explains, even though most definitions of "hard cases" are rather vague, there is a general consensus that such cases typically (a) involve a "special hardship" (which may relate to a pressing public concern), (b) are cases for which an outcome is particularly important, or (c) are close calls for which there is no clear legal answer.[3]

Whatever one's definition of special hardship or hard case, it is reasonable to conclude that hard cases include those involving infamous or larger-than-life figures and those addressing profound, concrete moral considerations—ones that have the potential to interfere with the efficient application of existing legal doctrines. Film depictions of Larry Flynt and Edward Snowden surely fall into these categories. Though from different eras and for different reasons, their respective behaviors and interactions with the law, as captured in the films *The People vs. Larry Flynt* (hereinafter, *The People*) and *Citizenfour*, raise the following questions:

- How have torts, privacy concerns, and government interests served as boundaries for First Amendment press and speech freedoms, including satire?
- How do unresolved questions related to the scope of the term "journalist" relate to the public interest and the issue of government transparency in representative democracy?
- Has the twentieth-century "blurring" of speech and press issues contributed to the difficulty of resolving outstanding questions related to the application of the press clause?

The answers to these questions and review of this chapter's films also highlight the following key themes:

- The issue of objectivity, including how it is defined and affected by documentary filmmakers who are involved in the events captured on film.
- Subversive techniques used by filmmakers (content and form) to create mood, develop characters, and convey the general importance of legal issues.
- The construction of protagonist figures and their lionization (or demonization), and how those constructions can inhibit nuanced, concrete analyses of competing interests in the legal cases they are associated with.

Notably, both films touch upon legal areas marked by varying degrees of ambiguity. *The People*'s depictions of obscenity, illegal interceptions of information, and the relationship between torts and expressive freedoms are classic manifestations of the struggle courts in constitutional democracies have faced when balancing rights against competing interests. *Citizenfour* is an account of how, increasingly, the opaque and ubiquitous surveillance capabilities by government entities—whether through firsthand methods or cooperation with powerful private interests—may chill investigatory journalism practices. Taken together, then, the multifaceted films reviewed in this chapter point toward an overarching question: What kind of democracy do we want?

CREATING LARRY FLYNT

Directed by Milos Forman and released in 1996, *The People* is a whirlwind biopic of the life of infamous *Hustler* magazine publisher Larry Flynt. The principal cast includes Woody Harrelson as the titular protagonist, along with Courtney Love as his wife Althea Leasure (a tragic archetype), Edward Norton as attorney Alan Isaacman, and Brett Harrelson as Jimmy Flynt (his brother). Despite modest box office returns, the film earned numerous accolades, including two Oscar nominations and two Golden Globe Awards.[4] Forman said of the project, "I knew only the sleazy side of Flynt. . . . I knew nothing else about him. . . . I discovered there was a second half to his personality that was admirable, almost noble, and that's what makes him interesting."[5] As for how his own experiences living in a communist regime affected his orientation toward protections against government overreach, Forman added,

> The Founding Fathers were so wise in the way they formulated the First Amendment. There will be no law abridging freedom of speech and freedom of expression. It's so clean and simple. If they wanted to add some loopholes, it would have been very easy, but obviously they knew why they formulated it the way they did.[6]

Both the content and form of *The People* are subversive. In terms of content, it mirrors its principal subject, Flynt, insofar as it courts controversy. As one reviewer, Kathryn Fuller, observes, Flynt is not your "likable, unassuming, Everyman protagonist." Instead, he is an "iconoclastic Everyman that viewers are asked to cheer," even though (or perhaps because) he is "the boorish, crude publisher of *Hustler* and other pornographic magazines."[7] Fuller adds, however, that because encouraging the audience to cheer for Flynt is such a prominent theme of the movie, other opportunities to lean into the less sympathetic epochs of Flynt's life are missed. As a result, while the film makes important free press statements, it rarely forces the viewer to question more critically the value of wide First Amendment protections for publishers.

Additionally, as others have pointed out, the film's liberties with the truth of Flynt's actual life and the contents of *Hustler* gloss over morally reprehensible behaviors. These behaviors go beyond mere parody.[8] Gloria Steinem, for example, noted that the biopic turns a blind eye to the graphic depictions of violence against women occurring under Flynt's watch:

> Suppose Mr. Flynt specialized in such images as a young African-American man trussed up like a deer and tied to the luggage rack of a white hunter's car. Or a nude white man being fed into a meat grinder. (Those are some of the milder ways in which Hustler portrays women.) . . . The truth is, if Larry Flynt had published the same cruel images even of animals, this movie would never have been made.[9]

Similarly, in another review, Karen Sawatzky emphasizes that although the legal consequences of the efforts of some antipornography feminists might be fairly questioned,

> they are part of a rich and creative her story [*sic*] of feminist resistance to male-defined sexuality. Oliver Stone and Milos Forman didn't see fit to include these details in the Larry Flynt story, even though the man himself is known to have invested considerable energy and funds in attempts to trivialize, humiliate and ridicule leaders of the feminist opposition to pornography. These efforts include making Gloria Steinem and Andrea Dworkin characters in cut-and-paste photo spreads in which their images were sexually mutilated.[10]

Turning attention away from content and to form, the film is notable for two disorienting techniques that mirror the chaotic nature of Flynt's life. The first is the use of quick, interspersed cuts of various images to establish a new setting, tone, or motif. The second is the use of abrupt visual or sound cues to signal transitions between scenes, which often advance the narrative by skipping considerable periods of Flynt's life. Indeed, in a preface to an interview with director Forman, one reviewer characterized the script as "more a skillful series of interwoven vignettes than a traditional biopic."[11]

Making an Honest Buck

The People opens with a descending crane shot of a dreary winter forest surrounding a small cabin. The subtitle text reveals this setting as Kentucky in 1952. This technique is used multiple times throughout the film to help the audience keep pace with the many episodes of Flynt's life. The audience hears a woman calling for "Larry" then "Jimmy," with the subsequent shot capturing a preteen boy filling a glass bottle with the clear liquid contents of a barrel. The camera follows him as he transfers the glass bottle contents to one of a collection of small jugs. The next shot captures the boy exiting what is revealed to be a small shed, using his fedora-style hat to wake another, slightly younger boy sleeping near the doorway. The younger boy dutifully takes up the reins of a small wagon loaded with jugs as the older one begins pushing. With the following shot, the title of the film appears in red, white, and blue, the font waving akin to a flag in the breeze as the two boys continue their trek up a sizable hill. Thus, the establishing scene conveys the primary, individual-centric narrative of the film and ties the controversial Flynt, even in his youngest days, simultaneously to patriotic symbols and disreputable activities.

Arriving at their destination, the young entrepreneurs provide a taste of their wares to an older, balding gentleman. As he carefully unfolds two crumpled dollar bills, the camera cuts to a shot of one of the boy's feet, covered in mud and tapping in either impatience or excitement. Upon returning to the site of their moonshine "peddlin'" operation and finding the door locked, the older boy opens it to find "Paw" in something of a stupor lying on the floor.

After Paw tells the older boy to show some respect, the older boy smashes an empty jug over Paw's head. As both boys flee, Paw reaches for a rifle and the camera cuts to a shot of a woman again yelling for Larry and Jimmy to "get on to the house" for supper. This is followed by a quick cut to Paw firing his rifle into the air, and then another cut to the two boys taking cover on a hillside. In response to his younger conspirator's comments, the older boy ends the scene by saying, "I'm just trying to make an honest buck."

The first of many jump cuts in the film occurs at the end of this scene. It quickly fades into a close-up of a man placing dollar bills into the underwear of a female figure, followed by a couple of quick slaps of her backside. The title card reveals that the story has advanced twenty years to Cincinnati, Ohio. Subsequent establishing shots around the venue make clear that we are in a (rather low-energy) strip club, with a tracking shot landing on two figures in stereotypical polyester suits at the bar. As the song fades out, the man on the left signals to "Larry" to work the crowd a bit for the departing performer. After no response from the audience, including several military service members, the first man tries to encourage a reaction through exaggerated applause (resulting in a deadpan, "Thank you, Jimmy," from Larry). The onetime moonshine peddlers now seek their honest bucks in the adult entertainment business, delivering the "finest ladies in southern Ohio."

Subsequent exposition between characters, including Althea Leasure, reveals that the Flynt enterprise is in dire straits. The financial situation does not improve with Larry's idea for a club newsletter featuring full, high-quality photos of the establishment's dancing talent—at least not initially. Flynt's flailing publication finally gains traction when he is offered the opportunity to purchase nude photographs of Jackie Kennedy Onassis, which he publishes in a 1975 issue of *Hustler* magazine. The issue containing the photos is wildly popular and launches Flynt's empire in earnest.

The Obscenity Trials

Flynt's initial First Amendment courtroom experience came after *Hustler* drew the ire of Charles Keating (James Cromwell), founder of Citizens for Decent Literature, and Simon Leis (James Carville), a Cincinnati prosecutor who also belonged to the organization. In an example of humorous casting, Carville, a real-life Democratic strategist, is playing a Republican official. The real-life Leis later supported the prosecution of a local art museum for its installation of homoerotic photographs by Robert Mapplethorpe.[12] A few additional points about this courtroom scene deserve special attention. First, Isaacman (who served as a consultant for the film) represents Flynt in this and most courtroom scenes. This is historically incorrect. It was Paul Cambria who represented Flynt in the Cincinnati, Ohio, and Lawrenceville, Georgia, trials. As explained by Clay Calvert and Robert Richards, "The Isaacman character in the movie, played by actor Ed Norton, was actually a composite of many different attorneys—Cambria included—who [had] represented Flynt over the years."[13] Composites like Norton's Isaacman are commonly used in film; one purpose of this technique is to minimize audience confusion that could result from the inclusion of too many characters. Second, the Cincinnati trial is also notable for the sour demeanor and punitive behavior of the presiding judge, portrayed with apparent relish by the actual Larry Flynt. Finally, the scene foreshadows the assassination attempt on Flynt, as the camera lingers for a moment too long on a nondescript, middle-aged white man who enters the courtroom just before the verdict is read.

Obscenity, which has long been an amorphous target of the American legal system, looms large in Flynt's narrative. In the late 1800s, it was Anthony Comstock leading the charge through the New York Society for the Suppression of Vice.[14] Decades later, as the US Supreme Court became interested in enforcing the Bill of Rights against the states through incremental incorporation (reversing the long-standing interpretation that held the Bill of Rights only limited the actions of the federal government), a confusing body of doctrine flowed from two principal wellsprings: *Roth v. United States* (1957)[15] and *Miller v. California* (1973).[16]

In *Roth*, the Supreme Court considered the constitutionality of both a federal statute and a California law that restricted the distribution (to varying degrees) of obscene materials. Even as the court announced that obscenity did not fall within the scope of First Amendment press and speech protections, it did not equate all depictions of sex with obscenity. According to Justice William J. Brennan, Jr., "[S]ex and obscenity are not synonymous. Obscene material is material which deals with sex in a manner appealing to prurient interest. The portrayal of sex, e.g., in art, literature and scientific works, is not itself sufficient reason to deny material the constitutional protection of freedom of speech and press."[17] As legal scholar Jim Foster has recounted in another volume, Brennan's own clerks were confused by this "prurient interest" standard. After reporting back to him with the dictionary definition of "to itch," Brennan apparently smiled and said, "That's precisely right. If you had an itch you had to scratch it and that was prurient interest."[18]

The court later—and putatively—refined the *Roth* standard for defining obscenity in *Miller v. California.* As part of a mass-mailing effort, Marvin Miller mailed an unsolicited envelope of brochures to an Orange County restaurant. Per the court's description, "The brochures advertise[d] four books entitled 'Intercourse,' 'Man-Woman,' 'Sex Orgies Illustrated,' and 'An Illustrated History of Pornography,' and a film entitled 'Marital Intercourse.'"[19] Under the resulting *Miller* test, obscenity remains outside of the ambit of First Amendment protections. To determine whether material is obscene, the government must demonstrate:

> (a) whether "the average person, applying contemporary community standards" would find that the work, taken as a whole, appeals to the prurient interest; (b) whether the work depicts or describes, in a patently offensive way, sexual conduct specifically defined by the applicable state law; and (c) whether the work, taken as a whole, lacks serious literary, artistic, political, or scientific value.[20]

Of course, the community standards prong of *Miller* raises the question of exactly which contemporary community's standards should apply (and who exactly counts as an "average person," for that matter). Furthermore, replacement of the "utterly without redeeming value" standard with the "lacks serious . . . " prong tipped scales toward more obscenity convictions.[21] *Miller* may offer a brighter-line test for obscenity as compared to *Roth*, but in practice it simply shifts argumentation to a different level of definitional abstraction. This adjustment, which allowed alleged obscenity to be judged by the subnational communities it circulated within, doomed Flynt's chances in conservative areas.

In another example of the film's subversive episodic structure, Flynt's ironic and somewhat flirtatious alliance with the evangelical Ruth Carter Stapleton (Donna Hanover) and his brief conversion to the Christian faith is left somewhat underdeveloped. However, it is followed by one of the more charged moments of the film. Departing a Georgia courthouse following one of multiple obscenity-related legal proceedings Flynt faced, both Isaacman and Flynt are shot by a man previewed in multiple scenes since Flynt's initial Cincinnati courtroom appearance.[22] Flynt's assailant, last depicted in the film leaving the courthouse area as paramedics respond, was never prosecuted for the attempted assassination.[23] At this point, the tone of the film shifts markedly to match the nadir of Flynt's painkiller addiction, depression, and paranoia in the years that followed his paralysis and rejection of God. Visually, it also signals the beginning of the demise of Althea, who appears increasingly gaunt and nearly ghostlike as the narrative progresses.

Revealing Sources

Flynt's antics in the John DeLorean controversy, played mainly for laughs in the film by focusing on Flynt's courtroom outbursts,[24] almost obscure additional legal points about changing interpretations of press clause protections. The first issue concerns the DeLorean tape, acquired by Flynt from an unknown government source and subsequently provided to CBS and other major news networks. This subplot touches on the legal issue of distributing (and airing) recordings illegally taken by another party (an issue also implicated by the events captured in *Citizenfour*).[25] DeLorean, perhaps best known for producing the vehicle at the center of the *Back to the Future* films, was recorded in an attempted entrapment by the FBI. Seeking investors for his faltering automobile company, he was offered a large suitcase containing a small fortune in cocaine (which he declined). As DeLorean's trial was underway, Flynt was held in contempt in a separate proceeding for refusing to identify the source who provided him with the recording.[26]

Flynt's contempt charges, which resulted in a separate cascade of four additional contempt charges for courtroom behavior, including flag desecration and stolen valor for wearing a Purple Heart, appear to have been entirely dismissed by a Ninth Circuit Court of Appeals decision in 1985.[27] A second issue in the background of this ordeal is whether (and if so, how) Flynt's role as a magazine publisher may be relevant for the underdeveloped issue of defining the term "journalist." That question is revisited following the analysis of *Citizenfour* later in this chapter.

Larry Flynt's Revealing Advertisement

Of course, Flynt's most famous interaction with the law is *Hustler Magazine, Inc. v. Falwell* (1987).[28] The death of Althea, Flynt's plea to Isaacman to petition the Supreme Court to review the case,[29] and a reenactment of the oral arguments serve as a sort of unconventional and simultaneous climax and denouement to the film. In yet another example of ironic casting, staunch First Amendment advocate Burt Neuborne appears as Jerry Falwell's lawyer in oral arguments in lower court proceedings. In addition, the film portrays some of the actual exchanges between Isaacman and the US Supreme Court justices as it moves toward Flynt's eventual victory. The case is an important focus of the film, and it was a landmark decision in US constitutional law.

In November 1983, at the direction of Flynt, a parody of a famous Campari advertisement was included on the inside cover of *Hustler*. As Flynt himself later described it, the advertisement followed years of sustained criticism by Falwell that attributed society's "moral decay" to Flynt:

> So we ran a parody ad in Hustler—a takeoff on the then-current Campari ads in which people were interviewed describing "their first time." In the ads, it ultimately became clear that the interviewees were describing their first time sipping Campari. But not in our parody. We had Falwell describing his "first time" as having been with his mother, "drunk off our God-fearing asses," in an outhouse. Apparently, the reverend didn't find the joke funny.[30]

As framed by Chief Justice William H. Rehnquist in his opinion for a unanimous court, the "novel question" in the case was whether the jury award to Falwell for $150,000 in punitive damages, and damages awarded under the tort of intentional infliction of emotional distress (IIED), violated the First Amendment. Specifically, the question for the court was "whether a public figure may recover damages for emotional harm caused by the publication of an ad parody offensive to him, and doubtless gross and repugnant in the eyes of most."[31]

For the court, the basic answer to the question was provided about a quarter of a century prior to Flynt's case. In *New York Times v. Sullivan* (1964), the court held that public officials could not recover damages via defamation or libel torts without a showing of "actual malice" on the part of the publisher. That is, a claimant had to demonstrate that the libelous utterance was published with knowledge of falsity or with "reckless disregard" for the truth; negligence alone would not suffice.[32] Later decisions extended this logic to public figures and preserved a "public-private" distinction that persists to the present day.[33] That *Sullivan*, in the late 2010s and early 2020s, has come under attack by members of the Supreme Court's conservative wing is significant[34] (additional discussion of the importance of *Sullivan* appears in chapter 6).

Thus, the constitutional problem with Falwell's claim and the jury decision recognizing IIED was that sanctioning it would effectively provide an end run around speech and press protections.[35] Simply put, had the court affirmed the jury's decision, public figures could pursue a different tort to achieve the type of result that *Sullivan* expressly ruled out. Protection for outrageous speech, no less than merely negligent falsehoods, provides the "breathing room" necessary for the vitality of First Amendment speech and press protections.[36] While the depiction of Falwell losing his virginity to his mother in an outhouse itself is surely within the realm of the "outrageous" and could reasonably cause emotional distress to affected parties, the advertisement itself explicitly (although in small print) noted that it was an "AD PARODY—NOT TO BE TAKEN SERIOUSLY."[37]

Hustler v. Falwell is more than the film's capstone of Flynt's redemptive arc. It is a landmark case that fits well in any class on expressive freedom or media law. Yet its legacy as the latter may be somewhat misunderstood. As Karen Markin has pointed out, claims for IIED against media organizations persisted—even increased—in the decade following the *Hustler* decision.[38] With reference to countervailing social values, one scholar characterized the decision as "the worst case in the history of the world, maybe the universe" for its assault on civility and human dignity.[39] Another described himself as "concurring" in the court's analysis while also lamenting the decision's failure to adequately consider and protect the interests served by IIED torts.[40] These criticisms notwithstanding, the *Hustler* decision connected the Campari advertisement parody to a tradition of spirited political criticism that often took the form of satirical cartoon.[41] Indeed, parody and satire that could fairly be considered offensive or outrageous has proliferated in multiple new media in the years since. From memes to *Daily Show*–style vignettes, they have also become increasingly important news sources across the US demographic and political spectrums.[42]

Cheering for the Antihero?

As we observed in the introduction to this volume, the biopic genre often includes films that, to varying degrees, deviate from historical truth, and therefore have the potential to reinforce various myths held by a society or culture. As a *VICE* article put it, *The People* "went a long way toward softening Flynt's image as a tawdry yet charismatic freedom fighter, while sanding off the more grotesque aspects of his personality."[43] In an analysis of reviews of the film (including her own impressions), Jennifer Petersen notes how the choice of flag iconography from the start pointed toward the limited conception of speech fetishized by the film.[44]

Beyond the patriarchy and capitalism themes, significant parts of Flynt's legal interactions were also omitted. Approximately four years before oral arguments were held in *Falwell,* Flynt appeared in the courtroom in a different case: *Keeton v. Hustler Magazine* (1984).[45] In an explosive tirade that day, Flynt apparently yelled, "Fuck this court! You denied me counsel of my choice. I won't be judged by nine assholes and one token c—nt—goddamn motherfuckers!" Flynt's FBI file also revealed that an informant described a plot by Flynt to load his wheelchair with C-4 explosives and blow himself and everybody else up (an unconfirmed claim that was characterized by the FBI as "idle chatter").[46]

Some issues repeatedly make appearances in First Amendment press and speech lawsuits, with litigants claiming that they should be afforded constitutional protection. Yet the free press and free speech clauses, taken separately or together, are not absolute no-fly zones for government power. Compelling interests and sufficiently tailored means may override presumptions of unconstitutionality in some contexts. Recall that chapter 1 points out that national security has historically been cited as a compelling public interest, and one that has facilitated government victories during the wartime periods of US history. The remainder of this chapter explores the free press and speech themes that emerge, quite dramatically, in the area of national security in *Citizenfour.*

CITIZENFOUR AND THE NATIONAL SECURITY INTEREST

Released in 2014 by "troublemaker" filmmaker Laura Poitras, *Citizenfour* is a documentary assembled under considerable duress.[47] It illustrates the evolution of journalistic ethics and information gathering, highlighting the emerging necessity of various encryption and surveillance-avoiding tactics. The film captures the leaking of classified documents and sensitive information regarding unchecked, warrantless surveillance by the US government on its own citizens in the aftermath of the September 11, 2001, terror attacks and the ensuing legal regime under the USA PATRIOT Act. For her efforts, Poitras was awarded a Pulitzer Prize for Public Interest, a MacArthur Fellowship, and a George Polk Award for national security reporting.[48] A story by the *Guardian* shortly after the outlet's publication of classified, National Security Agency (NSA) documents contended that Edward Snowden will "go down in history as one of America's most consequential whistleblowers." He was likened to Daniel Ellsberg (leaker of the Pentagon Papers) and Chelsea Manning (leaker of classified and sensitive military documents to WikiLeaks).[49]

Citizenfour begins rather ominously, with white text on a black background describing Poitras's history of conflict with government authorities. The motif is sparse and dark, with what appears to be an ongoing strip of lights passing by as opening credits and narration—both on-screen and in audio form—continue. One notable similarity shared between *The People* and the establishing shots of *Citizenfour* is the disorienting nature of the cuts. Here, they are often to multiple individuals, settings, and email exchanges, and stitched together with captions and additional screens conveying narrative text. This technique, which presents the documentary as something of a thriller, features prominently in the first half of *Citizenfour*, providing the increasingly chilling context at a national and then global level. As Poitras herself has described it, the tunnel shot points the viewer toward a "mystery" and suggests "a journey full of danger and uncertainty."[50]

For example, the viewer learns from a presentation by a former NSA official that the US government's effort to collect "metadata" from the broader population began after the terrorist attacks on September 11, 2001, and that members of Congress appeared uninterested in cabining such surveillance powers. A subsequent cut to a construction site in Utah and later shots of the site's progress toward completion continue as Poitras narrates additional email exchanges with an unnamed contact. All of this occurs as an ominous, one-note synthesizer tone drones on in the background. Again, an abrupt cut to a new setting follows; the viewer is now inside a northern California federal court. Concerned judges look on and offer questions as a prosecutor argues that government data collection and surveillance programs constitute privileged information, and that disclosure of this would pose a grave danger to national security. Another shift occurs and the audience is now in New York, with Jacob Appelbaum explaining the concept of "linkability" (which allows individual personal histories to be tracked and preserved) before a rapt audience. Rounding out the whirlwind, context-laden tour is the infamous 2013 exchange between Director of National Intelligence James Clapper and Senator Ron Wyden (D-OR) during a Senate Intelligence Committee hearing. To Wyden's question, "Does the NSA collect any type of data at all on millions or hundreds of millions of Americans?" Clapper responds, rather uncomfortably, "No sir [pause]. Not wittingly."[51]

During the next segment of the film, the audience is invited to take part in Poitras's complicated journey to meet with the mysterious Citizenfour. At this point, the camera cuts to the "lights-in-tunnel" shot that opened the documentary. The audience learns from Poitras's narration and an eventual caption that the setting has shifted to Hong Kong, and that it is June 3, 2013. Thus begins the filming of the "encounter," which will last for eight days. At this point, the viewer is finally introduced to Citizenfour, previously known only through Poitras's narrated email exchanges. In a hotel room setting, the camera moves between him and journalist Glenn Greenwald, explaining how the interviews and project might unfold. In his initial recorded dialogue, Citizenfour expresses a concern that he does not want the story to become individualized. He explains, "So, for me it all comes down to state power against the people's ability to meaningfully oppose that power. And I'm sitting there, every day, getting paid to design methods to amplify that state power." As he continues to speak extemporaneously about the unchecked growth of the surveillance state and the reach of the government's resources to surveil subjects, the camera occasionally cuts to reverse close-up shots of Greenwald dutifully recording notes. Interspersed in the exchange are exterior shots of a gleaming, glassy building. This is seemingly the hotel where the interview is taking place.[52]

As the interview continues into Tuesday, the setting remains the same but the establishing shot for the scene produces a very different, less polished feel than the first day. The audience view is from behind Citizenfour, seated on a bed (subsequent shots from the opposite angle present him, somewhat disheveled) with Greenwald seated in front of a window on the left side of the shot. Interestingly, this is the first time the audience learns the identity of Citizenfour via a direct question from journalist Ewen MacAskill: "Edward Snowden."

The weeklong interview, as captured and edited by Poitras, oscillates, perhaps intentionally, among feelings of paranoia, seriousness, revelation, and humor. Indeed, some moments manage to capture all these tones simultaneously. Memorably, following the exterior establishing shot for Wednesday and some initial conversations about informational security (i.e., the ability to listen to conversations through common Voice over Internet Protocol (VoIP) phones and the value of "air-gap" laptops), Snowden asks, "Could you pass me my magic mantle of power?" He then proceeds to cover himself in an orange-red sheet while he enters data onto Greenwald's air-gapped laptop. As Poitras swivels the camera back to Greenwald, he inquires, "Is that about the possibility of . . . ," with Snowden interrupting to finish the question, " . . . visual, yeah. Visual collection." After a pause for an apparent moment of reflection and observation of the room, Greenwald half-jokingly comments to nervous chuckles off-camera, "I don't think at this point there's anything in this regard that will shock us."

Creating jarring contrast, a fire alarm goes off six times shortly after, alarming Snowden and creating a sense of unease among the journalists. (Greenwald moves to the window as Snowden confirms with the front desk that the alarms are part of scheduled maintenance.) It is in this setting that Snowden explains the documents he has now provided to the journalists and the sheer scope of the US government's data collection program becomes clear. The scene ends with a cut to another title card indicating that Greenwald published the first story six hours later, with another abrupt cut to a CNN report. There, Greenwald explains the "indiscriminate and sweeping" program, tying it to the USA PATRIOT Act enacted in the traumatic aftermath of September 11.

Poitras's narrative continues Thursday, with a focus on developments in Snowden's personal life. The camera lingers on Snowden as he intensely focuses on typing on his laptop; ambient conversation with Poitras reveals that the US government has questioned his partner about his "illness" and disappearance from work (which occurred while she was away on vacation). This framing serves to humanize Snowden and remind the viewer of the human toll his efforts are starting to exert on those he cares about. As such, he is a different kind of figure than that depicted in *The Post*, where Ellsberg's off-screen presence makes him something of a peripheral character.[53] The camera captures Snowden a bit more unkempt than observed the previous day; he apologizes briefly for his appearance as Greenwald and MacAskill enter the room for another day of interviews.

As stated elsewhere in this volume, there is no such thing as a view from nowhere. Poitras's documentary, intimate in setting and serious in tonality, presents a sympathetic narrative. Regardless of Snowden's actual intentions, a casual viewer would be forgiven for identifying him as the heroic, archetypical protagonist of the story. Much as *Spotlight* (analyzed in chapter 9) depicts all the good that journalism can accomplish in checking secrecy and exposing corrupt public and private institutions, here too Greenwald, MacAskill, and Poitras emerge as exemplars of investigative journalism.[54]

As American as Apple Pie—The National Security Justification

In *Perilous Times*, First Amendment scholar Geoffrey Stone identifies six distinct episodes of US history that feature a willingness to sacrifice expression (and other civil liberties) to the passions of political figures and the broader public. During such periods, dissent becomes disloyalty.[55] Near the end of his historical tour de force, Stone introduces the reader to perhaps the seventh, ongoing episode: the government's execution of the post-9/11 War on Terror. He observes, "Some degree of secrecy in the interest of national security is, of course, essential, especially in wartime. But the Bush administration's obsessive secrecy effectively constrains oversight by both the press and the public and directly undermines the vitality of democratic governance."[56] The rise and extent of the surveillance state captured by *Citizenfour* illustrates how the accumulation of government power, the complexities of a sprawling bureaucracy, and ever-developing mobile technologies combine to create a society that has perhaps too easily ceded fundamental expectations of privacy. This development has transcended administrations and partisan lines. Indeed, the NSA programs exposed by Snowden, along with the sheer value of data collection in both the private and public spheres, harkens back to the old expression, "You can't unring a bell."[57]

Near the end of the film, at a meeting in Berlin, an international team of lawyers explains the nature and source of the charges filed against Snowden by the US government under the Espionage Act of 1917. True to historical form, government leaders of any partisan affiliation have a strong incentive to plead "national security" when faced with accusations of problematic, immoral, or outright unlawful behavior. President Barack Obama was no exception. The problem with Obama's assertion that Snowden was "not a patriot" and his belief that the American people would prefer a "fact-based" discussion about the issues related to untrammeled surveillance is that there was simply no incentive for the government to undertake that project. As the film strongly implies, it was Snowden's (and others') leaks and subsequent press exposure that *forced* such a discussion to begin in earnest.

What was once in shadows was forced into the public sphere, and at considerable cost to all parties involved. Poitras effectively captures the personal dangers to journalists and their families using the detention of Greenwald's partner, David Miranda, at Heathrow Airport following a flight from Brazil. Later, the British High Court ruled that the detention and seizure of encrypted material (related to Greenwald and Poitras's work) was permissible under the Terrorism 2000 Act due to concerns about national security.[58] As for Snowden, the moral picture is far murkier. Unlike Ellsberg, who was also charged under provisions of the Espionage Act but against whom charges were ultimately dropped because governmental misconduct led the judge to declare a mistrial,[59] Snowden has since found refuge in Russia. There is quite a bit of irony in taking refuge in a nation notable for various human rights violations,[60] the initiation of a war with Ukraine that has resulted in the killing of hundreds of thousands of civilians and service members,[61] and increasing hostility toward the United States and other Western democracies.

In the United States, it is not clear that the discussion has or will portend the types of policy solutions desired by Snowden and other privacy advocates. Any attempt to transcend political divisions to better rein in government intrusions on privacy is complicated by the fact that the issues raised by Snowden—like so many other issues in contemporary US politics—appear to code as partisan beliefs. Indeed, some evidence suggests that this occurred nearly a decade prior to his revelations. According to Gallup News, although most Americans disapproved of government surveillance of communications in both 2006 (a few years after the surveillance apparatus began in earnest) and 2013 (just after the Snowden leaks), disapproval appeared to vary based on the identity of the president. That is, more self-identifying Republicans than Democrats supported surveillance efforts in 2006, and the inverse was true in the 2013 poll.[62]

From the perspective of the federal judiciary, decisions under the Fourth Amendment to the Constitution have been mixed. Consider *Smith v. Maryland* (1979), which explicitly created a loophole to traditional court-monitored safeguards via warrant requirements.[63] There, the court held that individuals have no reasonable expectation of privacy in the phone numbers dialed from private home phones. As such, no judicially reviewed and monitored warrant is required for government collection of those records. As Justice Harry A. Blackmun described it, "Th[e] Court consistently has held that a person has no legitimate expectation of privacy in information he voluntarily turns over to third parties."[64] Yet in 2018, the court declined to extend *Smith*'s third-party doctrine in *Carpenter v. United States*.[65] There, the court issued a narrow decision holding that the search and seizure of so-called cell site location information required a judicial warrant.

Further complicating matters is the patchwork system of federal (and, to a lesser extent, state) legislation designed to protect against the sharing of specific types of data. There is no analog to the General Data Protection Regulation, for example, which requires companies operating in Europe "to ask for some permissions to share data and gives individuals rights to access, delete, or control the use of that data."[66] There are some reasons for optimism, however. As far as state legislative efforts go, the International Association of Privacy Professionals reports as of 2023 that six states have enacted legislation designed, with varying degrees, to regulate the policy abyss that allows governments and powerful private interests to act with relative impunity. For example, California's legislation offers a comparatively robust level of protection, including a limited, private right of action against violators.[67]

In terms of federal reforms, Snowden's efforts were not all for naught. Obama's Presidential Policy Directive 28 limited the NSA's collection and monitoring of "bulk" traffic (instead prioritizing "targeted" data collection). Additionally, the USA FREEDOM Act of 2015 placed guardrails on the government's ability to obtain and store phone records. Whether this reform has been a meaningful restriction in practice is open to question.[68] Notably, resistance to renewal due to privacy and other civil liberties concerns has grown from the ideological wings of the political spectrum, creating a "strange bedfellows" coalition of liberals and conservatives.[69]

Citizenfour was generally met positively, with several reviewers noting Poitras's willingness to engage directly with difficult moral and legal issues. Simon Vodrey, for example, points out the film's utilitarian themes: "[S]afety should not automatically outweigh privacy and unbridled expressionism, especially when the public is unaware of the fact that it is sacrificing the latter in the hope of achieving the former."[70] In describing how the film format elevates collections of facts and news reports into compelling narrative, Stuart Klawans's review emphasizes that *Citizenfour* "is more than the record of a historic event. It is, in itself, one of the instruments of that history."[71]

MIRROR IMAGES AND UNRESOLVED PRESS CLAUSE ISSUES

In some ways, the portrayal of Snowden and the themes related to journalism and the law mirror those observed in *The People.* Again, quoting Vodrey: "*Citizenfour* also sheds light on an increasingly important consideration for journalists: the tendency for the media to water down the discussion of complex subject matter where the focus is more on the characters covered in the news than on the news itself."[72] Where *The People*, intentionally or not, may have aggrandized the individual's heroic quest at the expense of the broader legal, political, and moral themes that sometimes feel like background pieces for Flynt's subversive antics, Snowden repeatedly forswore any spotlight desires. He expressed fear that individualizing the narrative would detract from the broader legal, political, and moral issues at stake. Some of the cinematic differences may be attributable to choice of form. One reviewer commented that Poitras's use of "cinema verité" allows her to privilege "the performativity and temporality of speaking, questioning, writing, witnessing, and whistleblowing." These exchanges represent the richness of human communication and interactions in the face of "a state surveillance apparatus that is on the fast track to reducing, controlling, and ignoring them."[73] But, as noted earlier in this chapter, even documentaries necessarily create narratives.

One important theme raised by each film is the question of who qualifies as a member of the press—or, more specifically, as a journalist (something also discussed in chapter 4). First Amendment scholar Eugene Volokh emphasizes that the weight of historical evidence and precedent from the ratification period until the early 1970s supports a "press-as-technology" interpretation of the clause rather than a more limited "press-as-industry" reading.[74] Moving forward, court decisions and rapidly changing technologies in the twentieth century enlarged the original protection for *speech* (literally, speaking) to myriad forms of *expression*. The free press clause—perhaps due to the increasingly antiquated status of its namesake medium—seems far more limited in application. Yet Volokh's historical review suggests that the First Amendment's text, purpose, original meaning, and subsequent precedents, taken together, support an "all speakers view" of the free press and free speech clauses. In this understanding, "communicators are treated the same whether or not they use mass communications. 'The freedom of speech, or of the press,' the theory goes, provides the same protection for the rights to 'speak,' 'write,' and 'print.'"[75]

If Volokh's interpretation is correct, then a more expansive definition of "journalist" *may* also follow—one that might apply to both Flynt and Snowden, but at the cost of conceptual stretching of the term. On the question of determining press "membership" as a matter of legal principle, consider the difficulties faced by previous federal courts on the matter. As Calvert explains, the first US appeals court to attempt to clearly define the attributes of a journalist (the logical antecedent to any case concerning application of so-called journalistic privilege) was the Third Circuit Court of Appeals in *In re Madden* (1998).[76] The case concerned a professional wrestling organization employee who revealed various tips and insider information via a promotional, pay-per-minute, 900-number, and who subsequently claimed journalistic privilege (refusal to reveal sources) in a civil trial proceeding. The so-called *Madden* test for determining whether a claimant is a journalist has three parts, all of which must be satisfied. First, "the claimant was engaged in investigative reporting"; second, "the claimant was gathering news"; and finally, "the claimant possessed the intent at the inception of the newsgathering process to disseminate the news to the public."[77]

The application of the *Madden* standard to individuals like Flynt and Snowden demonstrates how tidy legal standards in the abstract become quagmires in practice. First, consider Snowden's on-camera explanation of why he did not choose to openly (and simply, without discrimination) disclose classified documents about the NSA's program:

> Honestly, I don't want to be the person making the decisions on what should be public and what shouldn't. Which is why, rather than publishing these on my own, or putting them out openly, I'm running them through journalists. So that my bias, you know, and my things—because clearly I have some strongly held views—are removed from that equation, and the public interest is being represented in the most responsible manner.

Under the *Madden* definition, Snowden clearly intended to make a newsworthy issue (routine and growing surveillance, without court-imposed safeguards) accessible to the public. Yet Snowden is not the conventional disseminator of information to the masses here; he intentionally chose to forgo that route. As Peter Scheer, executive director of the First Amendment Coalition, explains, constitutional and statutory protections for journalists (those who gather and disseminate news, with reference to the first two prongs of *Madden*), rather than the sources, "may seem unfair, arbitrary, even offensive." But the distinction is a necessary one because the legal structure in this area requires "that government investigator must 'exhaust all alternative means' for identifying a leaker before they can force a journalist to name a source."[78] This explanation, Scheer notes, is not quite on point in the case of Snowden, as he agreed to reveal himself to the public fairly quickly (creating an interesting tension with his explicit claims to not want the story to be individualized to him).[79]

As far as protections go for a leaker or "whistleblower," legal doctrines that attempt to tease out speech as a government employee or as a citizen on matters of public concern and other statutory protections appear of limited application in Snowden's case. (Snowden was employed by an NSA contractor.)[80] While it is true that he "reasonably believe[d]" his leaks would illustrate "an abuse of authority" or "substantial and specific danger[s] to public safety," the federal Whistleblower Protection Act (WPA) also extends its protections to disclosures that are neither "prohibited by law nor required to be kept secret by Executive Order."[81] Snowden was clearly alarmed by the profound moral and privacy implications of the lack of a clear policy or coherent legal structure preventing government data collection efforts, but the disclosures ran afoul of the qualifying language in the WPA.

In contrast, recall Flynt's position in *The People*'s portrayal of the DeLorean case. There, he was something of an intermediate leaker. He received information from an undisclosed source and then leaked the tape to a CBS news station and other outlets. This example may fit more easily under the first two prongs of *Madden* but more uncomfortably within the third: the intent to disseminate news gathered and whether it was present at the inception of the effort. Flynt, with a history of contrarianism, controversial behaviors, and manifestations of mental health struggles, may not have had any firm intent in that episode. In fact, the overturning of his contempt convictions was based in part on his inability to stand trial.

These questions are not simply academic ones, nor have they been resolved. In 2021, the Washington Supreme Court ruled against YouTuber Brian Green in a case that again attempted to meaningfully define the term journalist. Green, who operated the channel "Libertys [*sic*] Champion" and often focused on perceived corruption and court cases in Pierce County, was denied a Washington Public Records Act request because he did not belong to a corporate media entity.[82] Whether or not one agrees with tying the definition of journalist to that specific standard, it is undeniably and incredibly narrow. As other chapters in this volume have suggested, a democratically relevant press clause must somehow take account of the changing ways in which news can be gathered and disseminated.[83]

CONCLUSION: ODD PAIRINGS AND BAD LAW?

At first glance, the pairing of *The People* and *Citizenfour* may seem an odd one. Yet it is in sometimes glaring contrasts that abstract First Amendment considerations often become concrete. Ironically, both films contain elements that suggest the irrelevance or impotence of press freedoms in a modern era. In *The People*, press freedom is sometimes mere background context in the (re)creation of a larger-than-life figure. There, as some reviewers noted, the press freedom depicted at times feels less like a right and more like a fetish, perhaps a privilege accessible primarily to those with material means. How democratic—and how good for democracy—is such an institution, particularly when one of its excesses is the type of material promulgated by such outlets as *Hustler*? In *Citizenfour*, however, traditional "fourth estate" press freedom is exercised in the service of protecting citizens from government overreach at the global level. And yet, the efforts of the investigative vanguard depicted by Poitras feels increasingly diminutive in the face of a sprawling, worldwide network that exceeds even the idealized panopticon in its scope and capabilities.[84]

In terms of form, both depictions illustrate how the film medium can distort or mythologize the actual effects of legal decisions. According to historian Robert Rosenstone, whether intentionally or inadvertently, film has the power to "plunge us into the drama of confrontations" in legal settings and favors "visual and emotional data while simultaneously playing down the analytical." As such, Rosenstone further cautions that even documentary history style films should always be viewed as presenting a truth that is "not reflected, but created."[85] In an era where most people get their history not from written records but increasingly from edited audiovisual media, such representations of important legal cases and considerations deserve our careful scrutiny.

Additional similarities in the legal depictions are present but somewhat understated. Both films occur during an era when the US Supreme Court has decided to elevate and utilize the free speech clause despite plausible framings available under its free press clause counterpart. Additionally, the blurring of speech and press protections is present in each of the depictions reviewed in this chapter. As First Amendment scholar Michael Kent Curtis notes, "In America, freedom of the press and of speech are linked in the First Amendment and in many state bills of rights."[86] Indeed, in mid-twentieth-century US Supreme Court rhetoric, the freedoms of speech and press were "traveling companions" at a rate similar to mentions of the speech clause alone. Yet the fading away of the press clause as a separate source of constitutional protection from the speech clause has, quite recently, also been empirically documented.[87] This historical retreat may be an underlying cause of some of the outstanding and underdeveloped issues under free press clause precedents. To wit, Sonja West and RonNell Jones have identified nearly a dozen unresolved legal issues under or with implications for the free press clause.[88] The consequences of defining the term "journalist" fall within this underdeveloped area of study.

Supreme Court Justice Felix Frankfurter once observed, "It is a fair summary of history to say that the safeguards of liberty have frequently been forged in controversies involving not very nice people."[89] Do the doctrinal conflicts that emerge from controversies involving lionized—or demonized—individuals represent the type of "bad law" alluded to at the beginning of this chapter? The answers to this question are for the reader, and indeed all citizens of the global society, to decide. Though privacy-based doctrines have historically conflicted with various press newsgathering and publishing freedoms (as illustrated in *The People*), the more recent work of Glenn Greenwald and others demonstrates how the exercise of press freedoms can complement—and maybe even buttress—privacy expectations. Despite the victories for journalism depicted in the two films reviewed here, the future of the press, its investigatory methods, and its relationship to such fundamental values as privacy is troublingly unclear.

NOTES

1. *Northern Securities Co. v. United States*, 193 U.S. 197, 400–401 (1904) (Holmes, J., dissenting).

2. Sepehr Shahshahani, "Hard Cases Make Bad Law? A Theoretical Investigation," *Journal of Legal Studies* 51, no. 1 (2022): 139.

3. Shahshahani, "Hard Cases Make Bad Law?" 139–40.

4. "The People vs. Larry Flynt," IMDB, https://www.imdb.com/title/tt0117318/ (accessed May 1, 2023).

5. Richard Porton, "Porn Again: The People vs. Larry Flynt," *Cinéaste* 22, no. 4 (1997): 31.

6. Porton, "Porn Again," 32.

7. Kathryn Fuller, "Review: The People vs. Larry Flynt by Oliver Stone and Milos Forman," *Journal of American History* 84, no. 3 (1997): 1185.

8. Jared Hohlt, "Reality vs. Larry Flynt: Exactly How Airbrushed is the Movie's Hero?" *Slate*, January 25, 1997, https://slate.com/news-and-politics/1997/01/reality-vs-larry-flynt.html.

9. Gloria Steinem, "Hollywood Cleans up Hustler," *New York Times*, January 7, 1997, https://www.nytimes.com/1997/01/07/opinion/hollywood-cleans-up-hustler.html.

10. Karen Sawatzky, "The People vs. Larry Flynt," *Canadian Dimension* 31, no. 2 (March–April 1997): 39.

11. Porton, "Porn Again."

12. Associated Press, "Ex-Prosecutor Who Took on Larry Flynt to Retire," *San Diego Tribune*, September 16, 2011, https://www.sandiegouniontribune.com/sdut-ex-prosecutor-who-took-on-larry-flynt-to-retire-2011sep16-story.html.

13. Clay Calvert and Robert D. Richards, "Adult Entertainment and the First Amendment: A Dialogue and Analysis with the Industry's Leading Litigator," *Vanderbilt Journal of Entertainment and Technology Law* 6, no. 2 (2004): 147.

14. At the time of this writing, the so-called Comstock Act of 1873 has received new attention as a potential vehicle by right-wing, anti-choice interests to further impede access to the abortion medication mifepristone, including in states that recognize the right to choose following the US Supreme Court's controversial decision to eliminate the federal version in *Dobbs v. Jackson Women's Health Organization* (2022). See Moira Donegan, "An Anti-Obscenity Law From 1873 Was Discarded for Decades. Now the Anti-Abortion Movement Wants It Back," *Guardian*, April 19, 2023, https://www.theguardian.com/commentisfree/2023/apr/19/comstock-act-censorship-anti-abortion-obscenity.

15. 354 U.S. 476 (1957).

16. 413 U.S. 15 (1973).

17. 354 U.S. at 487.

18. Seth Stern and Stephen Wermiel, *Justice Brennan: Liberal Champion* (New York: Houghton Mifflin Harcourt, 2010), 124. This quotation and explanation appear in James C. Foster, "Justice Civility: William J. Brennan Jr.'s Free Speech Jurisprudence," in *Judging Free Speech: First Amendment Jurisprudence of US Supreme Court Justices*, ed. Helen J. Knowles and Steven B. Lichtman (New York: Palgrave Macmillan, 2015), 128.

19. 413 U.S. at 18.

20. 413 U.S. at 24.

21. *Jacobellis v. Ohio*, 378 U.S. 184, 191 (1964).

22. Isaacman was not Flynt's attorney at the time. As described by Paul Cambria, Flynt's counsel at the time, "They actually shot him and our local counsel right in front of me," Cambria added, "I was on the phone with my secretary back in Buffalo when they shot him." Ryan Whalen, "Hustler Founder Flynt's Attorney Paul Cambria Reflects on His Legacy," Spectrum News, February 11, 2021, https://spectrumlocalnews.com/nys/buffalo/news/2021/02/11/hustler-founder-flynt-s-attorney-paul-cambria-reflects-on-his-legacy.

23. According to a *New York Times* extended obituary piece following Flynt's death, Joseph Paul Franklin was a white supremacist who objected to *Hustler*'s portrayal of interracial couples. He was captured in 1980 and later executed in Missouri after confessing to multiple murders. See Robert D. McFadden, "Larry Flynt, Who Built a Porn Empire with Hustler, Dies at 78," *New York Times*, February 10, 2021, https://www.nytimes.com/2021/02/10/business/media/larry-flynt-dead-hustler-magazine.html.

24. Associated Press, "Around the Nation: Flynt Goes to Prison for Contempt of Court," *New York Times*, February 2, 1984, https://www.nytimes.com/1984/02/02/us/around-the-nation-flynt-goes-to-prison-for-contempt-of-court.html.

25. See, for example, *Bartnicki v. Vopper*, 532 U.S. 514 (2001).

26. The outburst that follows in this ongoing courtroom vignette, including the wearing of a flag diaper and a "FUCK THIS COURT" shirt, appear to be a reference to Flynt's first appearance at the US Supreme Court in *Keeton v. Hustler Magazine*.

27. 756 F.2d 1352, 1358 (1985).

28. 485 U.S. 46 (1988).

29. In the lower court trial scene, Falwell's attorney (Norman Roy Grutman) is played by law professor Burt Neuborne, a strong First Amendment advocate and signatory of an amicus brief in support of Flynt in the subsequent SCOTUS case. See "Neuborne Goes Hollywood," *NYU Law Magazine*, 2004, https://blogs.law.nyu.edu/magazine/2004/neuborne-goes-hollywood/ (last accessed June 12, 2024).

30. Larry Flynt, "My Friend, Jerry Falwell," *Los Angeles Times*, May 20, 2007, https://www.latimes.com/la-op-flynt20may20-story.html.

31. 485 U.S. at 50.

32. 376 U.S. 254 (1964).

33. See *Curtis Publishing Co. v. Butts*, 388 U.S. 130 (1967) and *Gertz v. Robert Welch, Inc.*, 418 U.S. 323 (1974).

34. Adam Liptak, "Clarence Thomas Renews Call for Reconsideration of Landmark Libel Ruling," *New York Times*, October 10, 2023, https://www.nytimes.com/2023/10/10/us/clarence-thomas-libel-supreme-court.html.

35. Arlen W. Langvardt, "Stopping the End-Run by Public Plaintiffs: Falwell and the Refortification of Defamation Law's Constitutional Aspects," *American Business Law Journal* 26 (1988): 665–708.

36. 376 U.S. at 270–73.

37. The advertisement, designed by Terry Abrahamson at the direction of Mike Salisbury, is easily located via web searches. See Adam Langer, "Too Lewd for Larry," *Chicago Reader*, January 30, 1997, https://chicagoreader.com/news-politics/too-lewd-for-larry/. See also Dan Kennedy, "How Larry Flynt Beat Jerry Falwell and

Expanded Legal Protections for Parody," *Media Nation*, February 11, 2021, https://dankennedy.net/2021/02/11/how-larry-flynt-beat-jerry-falwell-and-expanded-legal-protections-for-parody/. The advertisement originally appeared in the November 1983 issue of *Hustler*.

38. Karen Markin, "The Truth Hurts: Intentional Infliction of Emotional Distress as a Cause of Action against the Media," *Communication Law & Policy* 5, no. 4 (2000): 469–503.

39. John M. Kang, "Symposium: The Worst Supreme Court Case Ever?: *Hustler v. Falwell*: Worst Case in the History of the World, Maybe the Universe," *Nevada Law Journal* 12, no. 3 (2012): 582–83.

40. Paul A. LeBel, "Emotional Distress, the First Amendment, and This Kind of Speech: A Heretical Perspective on *Hustler Magazine v. Falwell*," *University of Colorado Law Review* 60 (1989): 315–56.

41. 485 U.S. at 53–55.

42. Daniel Merino, "How Trump's America Changed Political Satire—for Both Liberals and Conservatives," *The Conversation*, September 4, 2020, https://theconversation.com/how-trumps-america-changed-political-satire-for-both-liberals-and-conservatives-145145. The extent to which "Gen Z" news consumers are more sophisticated in distinguishing underlying assumptions as fact, falsehood, or opinion has not been answered definitively. See, for example, Kalhan Rosenblatt, "Gen Z Isn't Immune to Misinformation. These Zoomers Are Making Sure Their Peers Don't Get Fooled," NBC News, March 11, 2022, https://www.nbcnews.com/pop-culture/pop-culture-news/ukraine-conflict-shows-gen-z-isnt-immune-misinformation-online-rcna19606.

43. Irving Alpert, "'Fuck This Court': We Obtained Larry Flynt's FBI File and It's Pretty Wild," *VICE*, May 13, 2021, https://www.vice.com/en/article/m7evg4/larry-flynt-fbi-file-hustler.

44. Jennifer Petersen, "Freedom of Expression as Liberal Fantasy: The Debate over *The People vs. Larry Flynt*," *Media Culture & Society* 29, no. 3 (2007): 381–82.

45. 465 U.S. 770 (1984).

46. Alpert, "'Fuck This Court.'" According to the *VICE* review of the file, Flynt also sent Associate Justice Sandra Day O'Connor copies of *Hustler* in the months leading up to oral arguments in *Keeton*.

47. Agence-France Presse, "Laura Poitras: 'Good Journalism Is Trouble-Making," France24, March 10, 2023, https://www.france24.com/en/live-news/20230310-laura-poitras-good-journalism-is-trouble-making.

48. Alex Danchev, "Troublemakers: Laura Poitras and the Problem of Dissent," *International Affairs* 91, no. 2 (March 2015): 381.

49. Glenn Greenwald, Ewen MacAskill, and Laura Poitras, "Edward Snowden: The Whistleblower behind the NSA Surveillance Revelations," *Guardian*, June 11, 2013, https://www.theguardian.com/world/2013/jun/09/edward-snowden-nsa-whistleblower-surveillance. For a deeply personal account of Manning's experiences, see Emma Brockes, "Chelsea Manning: 'I Struggle With the So-Called Free World Compared with Life in Prison,'" Guardian, October 22, 2022, https://www

.theguardian.com/us-news/2022/oct/22/chelsea-manning-leaked-military-documents -free-world-prison.

50. Richard Porton, "Birth of a Whistle-Blower," *Utne Reader*, August 6, 2021, https://www.utne.com/politics/whistle-blower-zm0z15uzsau/.

51. YouTube, "'Does the NSA Collect Any Type of Data at all on Millions or Hundreds of Millions of Americans?'—Video," *Guardian*, June 6, 2013, https://www .theguardian.com/world/video/2013/jun/07/privacy-wyden-clapper-nsa-video.

52. Both the access and "live" recording of Snowden's life as the consequences of his whistleblowing unfolded are very unusual—and compelling—for a documentary. I am grateful for Bruce's observation of this feature of Poitras's work in *Citizenfour*.

53. I am grateful to Bruce and Helen for this observation.

54. In 2014, Greenwald and MacAskill (*Guardian*) and Barton Gellman (*Washington Post*) were awarded the Pulitzer Prize for their series of stories on the NSA programs leaked by Snowden.

55. Geoffrey R. Stone, *Perilous Times: Free Speech in Wartime, From the Sedition Act of 1798 to the War on Terrorism* (New York: Norton, 2004), 12–13.

56. Stone, *Perilous Times*, 557.

57. Origins unknown, though some sources refer to an Oregon Supreme Court case. See, for example, Roger Carlton, "You Definitely Can't Unring a Bell," *Graham Star*, June 25, 2020, https://www.grahamstar.com/opinion/you-definitely-cant-unring-bell. The case is *State v. Rader* (1912).

58. Alan Travis, Matthew Taylor, and Patrick Wintour, "David Miranda Detention at Heathrow Airport Was Lawful, High Court Rules," *Guardian*, February 19, 2014, https://www.theguardian.com/world/2014/feb/19/david-miranda-detention-lawful -court-glenn-greenwald.

59. Alex Kingsbury, "The Man Who Leaked the Pentagon Papers Is Scared," *New York Times*, March 24, 2023, https://www.nytimes.com/2023/03/24/opinion/ international-world/ellsberg-nuclear-war-ukraine.html.

60. "Russia: Events of 2021," Human Rights Watch, https://www.hrw.org/world -report/2022/country-chapters/russia#493dd1 (last accessed May 23, 2023).

61. Guy Faulconbridge, "Ukraine War, Already With up to 354,000 Casualties, Likely to Last Past 2023—U.S. Documents," Reuters, April 12, 2023, https://www .reuters.com/world/europe/ukraine-war-already-with-up-354000-casualties-likely -drag-us-documents-2023-04-12/.

62. Frank Newport, "Americans Disapprove of Government Surveillance Programs," Gallup News, June 12, 2013, https://news.gallup.com/poll/163043/americans -disapprove-government-surveillance-programs.aspx.

63. 442 U.S. 735 (1979).

64. 442 U.S. at 743–44.

65. 138 S.Ct. 2206 (2018).

66. Thomas Klosowski, "The State of Consumer Data Privacy Laws in the US (and Why It Matters)," *New York Times*, September 6, 2021, https://www.nytimes.com/ wirecutter/blog/state-of-privacy-laws-in-us/.

67. Klosowski, "The State of Consumer Data Privacy Laws"; "US State Privacy Legislation Tracker," International Association of Privacy Professionals, updated May

26, 2023, https://iapp.org/resources/article/us-state-privacy-legislation-tracker/ (last accessed June 3, 2023).

68. Sean Gallagher, "The Snowden Legacy, Part One: What's Changed, Really?" *Ars Technicia*, November 21, 2018, https://arstechnica.com/tech-policy/2018/11/the-snowden-legacy-part-one-whats-changed-really/.

69. Ryan Tarenelli, "Congress Starts Work on Renewal of Controversial Surveillance Law," *Roll Call*, April 27, 2023, https://rollcall.com/2023/04/27/congress-starts-work-on-renewal-of-controversial-surveillance-law/.

70. Simon Vodrey, "Digital Media Reviews: *Citizenfour*," *American Journalism* 34, no. 1 (2017): 121.

71. Stuart Klawans, "What Are Movies Good For?" *Nation*, October 21, 2014, https://www.thenation.com/article/archive/what-are-movies-good/.

72. Vodrey, "Digital Media Reviews," 122.

73. Lisa Parks, "Cover Your Webcam: Unencrypting Laura Poitras's *Citizenfour*," *Film Quarterly* 68, no. 3 (2015): 14.

74. Eugene Volokh, "'The Freedom . . . of the Press,' From 1791 to 1868 to Now—Freedom for the Press as an Industry, or the Press as a Technology?," *University of Pennsylvania Law Review* 160 (2012): 459–540.

75. Volokh, "'The Freedom . . . of the Press,'" 505.

76. 151 F.3d 125 (3d Cir. 1998).

77. Clay Calvert, "And You Call Yourself a Journalist? Wrestling with a Definition of 'Journalist' in the Law," *Dickinson Law Review* 103, no. 2 (1998–1999): 426.

78. Peter Scheer, "The First Amendment Protects Journalists using Snowden's Documents. But What about Snowden?" First Amendment Coalition, October 21, 2013, https://firstamendmentcoalition.org/2013/10/the-first-amendment-protects-news-organizations-using-snowdens-documents-to-report-on-nsa-what-about-snowden/.

79. Similar questions have been raised about WikiLeaks founder Julian Assange. See, for example, Seth Stern, "Is Julian Assange a 'Journalist'? Here's Why It Doesn't Matter," Freedom of the Press Foundation, October 20, 2023, https://freedom.press/news/is-julian-assange-a-journalist-heres-why-it-doesnt-matter/; and Trevor Timm, "If You Care about Press Freedom, Make Some Noise about Julian Assange," *Guardian*, May 4, 2023, https://www.theguardian.com/media/2023/may/04/julian-assange-us-justice-department-wikileaks.

80. Dave Davies, "Edward Snowden Speaks Out: 'I Haven't and I Won't' Cooperate with Russia," NPR, September 19, 2019, https://www.npr.org/2019/09/19/761918152/exiled-nsa-contractor-edward-snowden-i-haven-t-and-i-won-t-cooperate-with-russia.

81. L. Paige Whitaker, "The Whistleblower Protection Act: An Overview," Congressional Research Service, March 12, 2007, https://sgp.fas.org/crs/natsec/RL33918.pdf.

82. Ilya Shapiro, Trevor Burrus, Thomas A. Berry, and Gregory Mill, "*Green v. Pierce County, Washington*," CATO Institute, November 23, 2021, https://www.cato.org/legal-briefs/green-v-pierce-county-washington.

83. *Green v. Pierce County*, October 22, 2021 (Petition of Certiorari), https://www.supremecourt.gov/DocketPDF/21/21–614/197287/20211022140222589_green_cert_petition.pdf, 1

84. Thomas McMullan, "What Does the Panopticon Mean in the Age of Digital Surveillance?" *Guardian*, July 23, 2015, https://www.theguardian.com/technology/2015/jul/23/panopticon-digital-surveillance-jeremy-bentham.

85. Robert A. Rosenstone, "History in Images/History in Words: Reflections on the Possibility of Really Putting History onto Film," *American Historical Review* 93, no. 5 (1988): 1179.

86. Michael Kent Curtis, *Free Speech, 'The People's Darling Privilege': Struggles for Freedom of Expression in American History* (Durham, NC: Duke University Press, 2000), 49.

87. Sonja R. West and RonNell Anderson Jones, "The Disappearing Freedom of the Press," *Washington & Lee Law Review* 79, no. 4 (2022): 1377–462.

88. West and Anderson Jones, "The Disappearing Freedom," 1448–49.

89. *United States v. Rabinowitz*, 339 U.S. 56, 69 (1950) (Frankfurter, J., dissenting).

Chapter 9

A Tale of One Press Clause and Two Journalisms

Spotlight *and* Out in the Night

Brandon T. Metroka

As alluded to in the introduction by way of Thomas Jefferson's famous quotes, the press, with its ability to not only inform, but inform the *behavior* of, the masses, has long been subject to charges of irresponsibility and generated fears of its ability to undermine powerful institutions. Such institutions include, but are not limited to, those constitutive of the US form of republican democracy.[1] As the multiple portrayals and individual-centric stories in this volume illustrate, there are times when the press, despite the mythic virtue associated with its unique constitutional guarantee and its evolving, within-profession standards, has given in to sensationalism and acted short of professional and moral expectations. (*Shattered Glass*—discussed in chapter 7—is a particularly stark example of this.) Still, others are exemplars of elements of the press shining a light on corruption of or oppression by powerful institutions (see, for example, *All the President's Men*, discussed in chapter 3). What explains these disparate tendencies observed of the press in action?

The first film examined in this chapter, *Spotlight*, depicts the exposure of the Catholic Church's decades-long cover-up of child abuse at the hands of priests (initially in Boston, but then nationally and internationally), while the second, *Out in the Night,* reviews the events of August 26, 2006, when seven Black lesbians were attacked in the West Village of New York City. In the first film, members of the *Boston Globe*'s "Spotlight" team are presented as ideal-types of the investigative journalism tradition, illuminating the evils wrought by powerful institutions against vulnerable, relatively powerless

Catholic boys and their families. In the second film, however, tabloid-style journalism falls woefully short in its sensational, dehumanizing treatment of the New York City victims.

The themes explored in this chapter invite consideration of the following questions:

- How, like other provisions in the US Constitution, has the meaning of the free press clause been informed by underlying theories and extralegal considerations?[2]
- What is the relationship among practices of the modern press—whether of the serious, investigative variety or tabloid-style sensationalism—and the much-maligned yellow journalism of the late nineteenth and early twentieth centuries?
- What role does the press play in the construction and reinforcement of various subgroups within broader society?

When considering the answers to these questions, the two films analyzed in this chapter highlight the following issues:

- The scope of the free press clause freedom, including the nature of protection for "low value" as opposed to "high value" news, as well as "infotainment."
- Differential treatments of various populations, and their ongoing social construction(s) by various social institutions.
- Cinematic techniques commonly used within the dramatization and documentary forms, including visual motifs, to capture qualitatively divergent forms of journalism and its effects.
- Potential avenues by which the mainstream press may maintain relevance and its legitimacy for the modern era, including the use of traditional investigative methods.

SERIOUS JOURNALISM IN *SPOTLIGHT*

Released in 2015 to critical acclaim and some commercial success, the Academy Award–winning *Spotlight* chronicles the diligence, tenacity, and pressures faced by the *Boston Globe*'s "Spotlight" division in the early 2000s as they worked to expose the Boston Archdiocese's decades-long cover-up of child sexual abuse by priests.[3] The team's reporting revealed the vast, international reach of the abuse and complicity of high-ranking church officials, triggering a wave of legal actions that continues through to today.[4] Spotlight, created in 1970 under editor-in-chief Thomas Winship "to provide in-depth reporting on the big stories of the day,"[5] has often focused on exposing government corruption—resulting in three Pulitzer Prizes since the team's inception.

Importantly, the Spotlight team was and is something of an aberration in journalism. According to the Knight Case Studies Initiative at the Journalism School of Columbia University:

> The Spotlight Team enjoyed unusual autonomy and freedom within the news operation. It typically spent weeks and months reporting stories, which tended to focus on governmental corruption and organized crime. . . . Such units were prohibitively expensive; many newspapers could not afford them. Spotlight investigations occupied four of the *Globe*'s best journalists, who otherwise would have produced hundreds of other stories a year.[6]

In recent years, the *Boston Globe* has not been immune from adverse trends in newspaper coverage and distribution across the United States. As revealed in the Northwestern University Medill School's 2023 Report of the State of the Local News, cuts of thousands of journalist positions at "major metro dailies" like the *Globe* have had the effect of reducing investigative and "beat" reporting and have occurred as these papers have considerably cut circulation to areas outside of their respective cities.[7]

The film *Spotlight* focuses on the four main members of the team during the period leading up to publication of articles about the Archdiocese's cover-up: editor Walter "Robby" Robinson (Michael Keaton), Michael Rezendes (Mark Ruffalo), Sacha Pfeiffer (Rachel McAdams), and Matt Carroll (Brian d'Arcy James).[8] Additional characters cast in the film include the newly hired editor-in-chief Marty Baron (Liev Schreiber), Assistant Editor Benjamin Bradlee Jr. (John Slattery),[9] plaintiff attorneys Mitchell Garabedian (Stanley Tucci) and Erick MacLeish (Billy Crudup), church attorney Jim Sullivan (Jamey Sheridan), and Survivors Network of Those Assaulted by Priests (SNAP) leader Phil Saviano (Neal Huff).

Much as in *All the President's Men*, the journalists of *Spotlight* are clearly the heroes of the story told by the film. Cowriter and director Tom McCarthy confirms, "At the beginning of this they were our heroes. They still are our heroes. Those reporters are heroes. The work was heroic; that's once-in-a-generation reporting. It has a world impact, that story. We're still feeling it."[10] Yet, despite this overture and the apparent focus on the work of these journalists individually and as a team, the film consistently and increasingly gestures toward the role that cultural and institutional structures play in channeling individual behavior. The press itself is not immune from this increasingly explicit critique.

In many respects, the work of the real Spotlight team confirms long-standing, mythical imagery of the serious, muckraking, truth-seeking journalist.[11] A review of the Spotlight section of the *Boston Globe* in May 2022, for example, revealed an ongoing focus on local social, economic, and political issues that members of an engaged, enlightened community *should* care about.[12] The cinematic techniques employed in *Spotlight* convey the ethos of investigative journalism via the use of classic camera and editing techniques.[13] In doing so, the film maintains forward momentum while also conveying a sense of growing dread. As McCarthy explains, "We were trying to represent this as true to life as possible. We weren't overdramatizing a lot of things. We weren't sensationalizing or sentimentalizing." He continues, "So we knew to some degree these would be talkie [*sic*], dry scenes and pace and transitions were going to be really crucial to what ended up on screen."[14] In her review of the film, Ann Hornaday of the *Washington Post* adds, "Restraint . . . defines the film's aesthetic as well."[15]

The filmmakers largely achieve these objectives through two common yet effective techniques. The first and more obvious of the two is scattered throughout the film: It is the use of the "walk and talk," an objective viewpoint technique perhaps most famously employed throughout the run of Aaron Sorkin's *The West Wing*. These tracking (or "dolly") shots infuse the aforementioned overly talky scenes with an element of action, creating motion that helps keep the viewer engaged in what could otherwise be a static scene. Indeed, the walk and talk shot serves multiple purposes in narrative development, including conveying a sense of business on the part of the performers; creating an active, fluid (rather than static and dry) space for exposition; and highlighting the set and production design.[16]

The second technique is more subtle, yet hints of it are apparent in the opening sequence. The film opens with the viewer closely following a Boston police officer down a nondescript, rather drab hallway with the text "Boston, MA—1976" fading in then out as the tracking shot continues. Tinsel hanging from a reception desk and a small tree in the background reveal that it is the Christmas season, creating contrast with the ominous piano score and the scene's establishing focus. The dialogue between two on-screen actors—an older cop returning from an off-screen break room (Joe Stapleton) and a younger cop staffing the desk (Tim Whalen)—quickly provides a great deal of narrative context to the viewer. In response to the younger cop's inquiries about the distraught mother who is apparently in the break room, the older cop lights a cigarette and, with an eyebrow raise and nod, makes a suggestive and knowing comment: "I guess Father was helping out."

At this point, a third character is revealed: Assistant District Attorney Burke. Alert yet with telltale facial indications of exhaustion, he enters the station and is provided with an update by the older cop. The exchange has the feel of a well-rehearsed routine, the quick questions and answers conveying to the viewer that this has happened before. After the younger cop remarks, "It's gonna be hard to keep the papers away from the arraignment," his seasoned partner scoffs incredulously, "What arraignment?"

At this point, the dialogue ends and the young cop focuses on something off-screen. The camera appears to shift to a subjective viewpoint—we now see what he sees. A priest, revealed to be Father Geoghan (we know this from the older cop's off-screen dialogue), can be seen through open blinds. He is seated in the break room, motionless and eyes closed. This shot quickly transitions to a different room in the precinct, the camera slowly panning right to left from two younger boys (viewed from the rear) to an opening door, whereupon Burke enters. Near-whispered dialogue between the bishop (revealed in the previous exchange with Burke) and the boys' mother, Sheila, quickly establishes the pressure brought to bear on the victims of abuse: "Now Sheila, you know what good work the church does in the community. I give you my personal guarantee that I'm going to take Father out of the parish and this will never happen again."

The scene ends with a close-up of the young cop, now outside the precinct and smoking a cigarette himself, as the bishop and Father Geoghan quickly exit the building and enter the rear of a black sedan. The car pulls away, pausing under an unusually bright streetlamp (an obvious visual metaphor) at a nearby intersection before leaving the area. As the scene fades to black and reveals the film's title card, the viewer is nearly over the shoulder of the young cop, who has, much as the viewer in two short minutes, quickly learned how things are done in the tight-knit, Catholic community of Boston.[17]

Creating Investigative Journalism via Cinematic Technique: The Slow Build

The recurring cinematic technique previewed in the opening sequence is the shift from objective to performer's viewpoints, which often take the form of a series of shot/reverse shots of a scene's performers that become increasingly close up. Objective viewpoints are those where the viewer is akin to a spectator with VIP seating, watching the story unfold through carefully scripted angles, shots, and movements. Comparatively, the performer's viewpoint combines the objective and subjective. As Roy P. Madsen describes it:

> [I]t keeps the viewer outside the dramatic action, looking in, and he never has the direct participation effect of eye-to-eye contact. The camera is placed so close to one of the performers, however, that the viewer sees the dramatic action very nearly as the performer does. While the viewer remains a spectator, he comes to identify strongly with the given player by looking, quite literally,

> over his shoulder. During a buildup of emotional intensity, a filmmaker may progressively change from an objective viewpoint to a performer's viewpoint to a subjective viewpoint, to make the dramatic action progressively more heightened and personal to the viewer.[18]

In this way, the filmmakers create pacing and suspense even as they depict the serious, tedious work of investigative journalism. These techniques frequently reinforce the themes of corruption and pressure on "outside" groups and identities challenging entrenched, powerful community institutions. Consider newly hired editor Marty Baron's meeting with Cardinal Law (Len Cariou) early in the film. Baron, who in an earlier scene set the Spotlight team agenda against some resistance by Bradlee, is invited to a meeting with the cardinal at "Lake Street," referring to the physical address of the Archdiocese. Following an establishing shot outside of the imposing structure, the camera cuts to a focus on Cardinal Law's hands, held together as if praying, while he describes his fondness for "the newspaper business."

At the moment the conversation takes on a more ominous tone, the camera mirrors the change. Law observes from his own experience with the *Mississippi Register* that managing a newspaper entails a great deal of responsibility, sharing his efforts with the Evers brothers and resulting reputation as a "meddling outsider."[19] As he does so, Baron appears to shift uncomfortably.

At this point, the shots begin alternating between close-ups of each actor, elevating the tension further as Law makes the comparison more explicit and ominous: "Tough seat to sit in, especially in a small town. I think you'll find that Boston's still a small town too, Marty . . . in many ways." From here, the camera abruptly cuts to a long shot of the entire room, with Law's assistant Maureen entering and carrying a small package. The transition acts as a pressure valve of sorts, immediately relieving much—but not all—of the built-up tension. The exchange concludes with Law giving Baron the wrapped package delivered by Maureen. "Think of it as a cardinal's guide to the city of Boston," Law tells the rattled editor. A concluding shot of Baron, now in his car, reveals that the gift is a copy of the *Catholic Church Catechism.* Baron is Jewish.[20] Whether the cardinal was ignorant of Baron's faith or applying some not-so-subtle pressure is for the viewer to decide.

As the Spotlight team begins its assignment, it revisits previous reporting on priests accused of sexual abuse of children. These early stages of the investigation emphasize skepticism on the part of the team; the institutional malfeasance they eventually discover and expose feels little more than an itch at this point. A meeting between the full team and Phil Saviano, founder of SNAP, serves as the initial spark for the team's investigative efforts despite some apparent reservations. The scene begins with a long shot of Robinson's office, with Saviano's back to the door and the Spotlight team gathered around him.

As Saviano describes the meaning of growing up Catholic while in poverty, he moves from the abstract to the concrete in retelling how priests use the symbolic power of God to earn the trust and acquiescence of children (and their families). As Saviano pleads with the team to listen, to take him seriously, the filmmakers use the camera to cue the viewer to do the same: "This is not just Boston. It's the whole country. It's the whole world. And it goes right up to the Vatican." Saviano's dialogue is interrupted by questions from Rezendes and Robinson, who (along with Pfeiffer) express considerable skepticism. The sequence ends with wide-angle shots of the team reflecting on the information and its source: "Well . . . what do you think?"

The role of the investigative journalist as a relative outsider—a throughline in the film, and like Woodward and Bernstein in ATPM—is conveyed similarly. Later, during a dinner meeting between victims' lawyer Garabedian and Rezendes, the film again emphasizes the institutional, insider/outsider nature of the problem. What begins as a conversation about work-life balance and innocuous comments about background becomes a more pointed comment about outsider status and its relationship to insular communities. Garabedian remarks, "This city—these people—making the rest of us feel like we don't belong. . . . But they're no better than us. Look at how they treat their children. Mark my words, Mr. Rezendes: If it takes a village to raise a child, it takes a village to abuse one." A cut to an annual Catholic charity ball, with festive atmosphere, simultaneously serves the pressure-release function and continuity from the previous scene, as Robinson's gaze falls on a visibly uncomfortable Baron—alone in a crowd.

Slowly but surely, the team begins to realize the veracity of Saviano's claims and the scope of the church's efforts to cover up abuse. Gathered around a speaker phone to listen to former priest and researcher Richard Sipes's (Richard Jenkins) estimates of pedophile priests, a gradual camera zoom-out conveys a sense of isolation and smallness on the part of the investigative journalists (perhaps an intentional nod to ATPM). Just as the investigation gathers steam, with Rezendes learning of the existence of court documents proving knowledge of systematic abuse at the highest levels of the church, the intervening event of the 9/11 terrorist attacks temporarily shifts focus and resources from Spotlight's efforts. The sequence that follows, capturing the newsroom gathered around small televisions to watch coverage of the attacks' aftermath and Cardinal Law's call for unity, includes Bradlee's decision to reallocate resources because of the attacks. More than any other pressure valve moment in the film, the sequence imparts how the necessities of the news cycle interact with limited resources to forestall the efforts—and eventual fruits—of investigative journalism.[21]

Shadows on the Spotlight

Spotlight captures the best that the fourth estate can be—inquisitive, tireless, and driven to expose a systemic, multilayered evil. The effects of the considerable efforts of members of Spotlight, exposing the decades-long, seemingly willful blindness across institutions and communities, cannot be overstated. Indeed, the film ends with a five-screen list of locations where abuse was discovered in the aftermath of the team's initial article, "Church Allowed Abuse for Years," published on January 6, 2002.[22]

That said, the film does not absolve the press from culpability even as it largely works to uphold the heroic journalist myth.[23] Earlier reporting on the abuse operated using the "a few bad apples" framework. There was an opportunity to show the magnitude of the abuse, but it was a missed opportunity because the focus was on the trees, not the forest. As Josh Singer, who wrote the original screenplay for *Spotlight* (for which he won an Academy Award)[24] explained,

> We literally started going back through the clips and saying, "How was this story played with but not gotten [right away]?" . . . It turns out there were a bunch of things floating around. You've got all sorts of beat reporters and they're running hard and stuff falls through the cracks. It was interesting to see what the bits and pieces were.[25]

This discovery is incorporated into the film, underscoring its function as a dramatization: Retrospectively, *Spotlight* shines a cinematic spotlight on the journalistic shortcomings that would have been more difficult to weave into a stenographic account of the events depicted.[26]

As such, the culpability scene in the newsroom just before the initial article's publication takes on particular significance. That scene reflects the filmmakers' own investigative efforts during the film's development.[27] In his review, Alexander Nazaryan notes Keaton's depiction of Robinson's growing guilt as the sheer scope of the abuse became clear, as under his watch the *Globe* had buried an important revelation of abuse in 1993. As the film builds toward its conclusion, multiple scenes convey Robinson increasingly grappling with and reflecting upon his own dereliction of duty: interactions with members of his own staff (Pfeiffer and Carroll), church representative Pete Conley (Paul Guilfoyle), and friend and church attorney Jim Sullivan. In another nod toward antihero elements of the film, Nazaryan also focuses on Mark Ruffalo's turn as Rezendes and offers that the filmmakers did not paint him as "righteous iconoclast" and instead as "just a guy doing his job."[28] The fallibility of human institutions looms large even as the viewer may drift toward focusing on individual-level failures.[29]

Additionally, rapid social and technological change underscores the rarity and perhaps bygone nature of the type and process of journalism depicted in *Spotlight.* Though generally lauded, a great deal of praise for the film came from within the profession itself. Whether that praise is an indication of the fulfillment of McCarthy and Singer's desire to emphasize the heroic possibilities of journalism is an open question. As Bishop puts it:

> [T]he methods used by the Globe reporters—poring through old diocesan directories and doggedly tracking down people—come off as antiquated. The relative anonymity of the Spotlight journalists and their sheer tenacity and dedication to truth are still necessary professional attributes, but they are also positioned in this coverage as hallmarks of journalism's halcyon days.[30]

Through careful and tedious archival reviews and in-person interviews, the Spotlight team demonstrated how media may reestablish the "cultural authority" to describe news events, which "exists only when people believe journalists are credible."[31] That said, the somewhat tepid box office performance of the film—and praise largely from critics and media elites—makes that assumption questionable. If the mass public did not turn out to see and internalize the depictions of journalism at its finest, does the film really burnish the credibility of its principal subjects?

PRESS SENSATIONALISM AND ITS HUMAN COST IN *OUT IN THE NIGHT*

In the early hours of August 26, 2006, four young, Black lesbians—Renata Hill, Patreese Johnson, Terrain Dandridge, and Venice Brown—were attacked in Manhattan's West Village. They fought back, and were subsequently arrested, leading to sensationalized media coverage that dubbed them the "Gang of Killer Lesbians." In media descriptions, they are known as the New Jersey Four.[32] Nine years later, in an interview for NPR, Hill made the following observation: "We went out that night as family, as friends. . . . We are always going to protect one another in a dangerous situation, and we have that right. I don't regret it, but it's like why didn't the media talk to us and get another side of the story?"[33]

Released in 2014, the year before the NPR interview, *Out in the Night* is a documentary film that does present that other side. Made by blair dorosh-walther, it tells the perspective of the New Jersey Four, who maintained their innocence and claimed self-defense during the altercation. (Three other women involved accepted plea deals in the aftermath of the events of that night.) Through interviews with family members, reporters, lawyers, community organizers, and the defendants themselves, dorosh-walther recounts the events of the evening in question, including the criminal trials, the appeals, and the consequences of the framing choices made by journalists. If *Spotlight* is best understood as a depiction of journalism's potential at its apogee—critical, investigative collaborations in service of exposing institutional corruption—*Out in the Night* reveals the shadowy side of press freedoms. As explored in the analysis that follows, due to a lack of conceptual and doctrinal nuance, tabloid sensationalism is also subject to the protective ambit afforded by the free press clause. Furthermore, it also plays an important role in the social construction of various populations.

Even if the label "documentary" conjures a sense of objective reality more so than the designation of "dramatization" (as in *Spotlight*), Pierre Sorlin reminds us "that filmmakers make personal choices, even in the most 'neutral' documentaries."[34] This reference to neutrality underscores the problematic "view from nowhere" expectation—failing to realize that viewpoint necessarily varies by one's position or station in life—that continues to influence journalism and perhaps, by extension, documentary viewers.[35] No less than any other, documentary filmmakers create a reality for the viewer and rely on common editing techniques in the construction of that reality. In creating *Out in the Night*, dorosh-walther (who is gender nonconforming) observes:

> I went to school for film, but I initially didn't think that I should tell this story, I didn't think a white director should, which is why the first two years I didn't think about it as a film. But then when their appeals were approaching in 2008 and there was just not as much happening in the news about the case, it was just one of those stories I couldn't get out of my mind.[36]

As the story unfolds, then, the viewer gets to know the women as individuals—much as *Spotlight* humanizes the long-voiceless, faceless victims of sexual abuse.

Of course, dorosh-walther did not have a dedicated ensemble and institutional resources comparable to those of the *Boston Globe* or other institutional behemoths. New Day Films, the distributor for the film, characterizes itself as a "democratic filmmaker collective" for which all members volunteer time to run the business—in addition to supporting one another's substantive documentary projects.[37] The fact that the narrative context for the New Jersey Four was constructed and seized upon primarily by tabloid—rather than "serious"—journalism outlets suggests that news treatment varies with broader cultural attitudes toward specific identities.[38] *Spotlight* and *Out in the Night* are similar in that they both shine a light on systemic injustices that persist and operate to marginalize relatively powerless groups within broader communities. The key difference, of course, is that the motifs of courage and heroism in *Out in the Night* surround the women who acted in self-defense and their lives after the attack. The focus is not on the journalists. Indeed, here, members of the press function as the villains of the story.

Creating Sensationalism through Cinematic Technique: Blaring Headlines

The opening credit sequence is a montage, featuring a series of blurry nighttime shots linked together to convey the journey, from Newark, New Jersey, to New York City, taken by Patreese, Renata, Venice, and Terrain on that August 2006 evening. The sequence invites the viewer to take that journey with them, as images from various points between and within the two cities transition to security camera footage outside the IFC Center in the West Village. They are interspersed with cuts to news article headlines published in the aftermath of the incident. Voiceovers provide additional audio context, as the sequence ends with a shot of four Polaroid-style photos arrayed, the four women's names captioned on the photos.

Variants of this technique convey the extent of the sensationalistic, homophobic press headlines that followed the arrests of the women. The audience is shown a brief ABC-affiliate television report referring to the attack by "a group of seven women yesterday in Manhattan," but the camera then cuts—with purpose and effectiveness—to the start of a series of newspaper articles and commentary. "ATTACK OF THE KILLER LESBIANS," blares the *New York Post*. As the headline moves closer to the viewer, reporter Laura Italiano provides the voiceover: "The headline writers had a very good time. We went at this for war."[39] As she speaks, the body of the article flies in from the bottom of the screen. The viewer now sees that Italiano was the author of the *Post* story. She takes credit—now on-screen herself—for the phrase "seething sapphic septet," and emphasizes her belief in "the accuracy" of that phrase, "which I still stand by." She adds, as the article reappears on screen, "I don't think it's a stretch to say they were out for blood." The highlighted phrase on screen characterizes the group as "seven bloodthirsty young lesbians."

The montage continues with a new article titled "The Case of the Lesbian Beatdown," this time from the pages of New York's *Daily News*. The opening phrase "A POSSE of lesbians charged . . . " is visible to the viewer as the off-screen commentator states: "At that point I knew it was just gonna be a gay thing." A cut reveals the speaker as Terrain's mother, Kimma, who continues, "But, of course, you being a woman . . . then being Black, and then the nerve of you to be gay." As Kimma's reflection proceeds, the camera again cuts back to the press clipping montage, with "Jersey girl gang gets lockup in beatdown" now slowly rotating counterclockwise as a highlighted area slowly moves toward an accompanying photo of Terrain. The next article is titled "'Crotching Tiger,'" with the word "UGLY" noticeable in the caption of the photo array featuring Terrain, Patreese, and a blurred photo of the twenty-eight year-old male who initiated the fight. "'I'm a man!' lesbian growled during fight" rotates clockwise in the next shot, slowly filling the screen.

The film moves on to the women's trial, where they are charged with felonies for "gang" assault. The news clip montage returns with "GIRLS GONE WILDING: Lesbians locked up in W. Village beating"[40] approaching the viewer, the introductory passage highlighted for additional effect: "A GANG OF PETITE but ornery lesbians pummeled and stabbed a DVD bootlegger." Notably, the language used to describe the New Jersey Four is similar (and in some cases, identical, as in the term "wilding") to that used in the hysteria surrounding the "Central Park Five" teens wrongfully convicted of the horrific sexual assault of Trisha Meili in New York City's Central Park. As Jelani Cobb observed of contemporaneous news coverage (and as noted in Ken Burns's 2012 documentary), that is not the only relevant and unfortunate comparison:

> A month later, the Times noted that there had been reports of twenty-eight other actual or attempted first-degree rapes in the city that week, but almost all those victims were black or Latina women, and none of their cases generated the city-wide outrage that the Central Park attack did. While headlines demanded justice for Meili, who was an investment banker at Salomon Brothers, the case of a thirty-eight-year-old black woman who had been raped and thrown off the roof of a building in Brooklyn was treated as something of a municipal footnote.[41]

The next cut is to a broadcast of *The O'Reilly Factor* on Fox News, with a graphic titled "Lesbian Gang Epidemic?" positioned next to host Bill O'Reilly, ticking off a series of examples of alleged "lesbian gangs" threatening the public order: "In Tennessee, authorities say a lesbian gang called GTO, Gays Taking Over, are involved in raping young girls. And in Philadelphia, a lesbian gang called DTO, Dykes Taking Over, are allegedly terrorizing people as well." Cutting to later in the segment in a split-screen exchange with a guest, O'Reilly continues, increasingly incredulous: "This is a lower socioeconomic crew, all right, who identify themselves as lesbian or gay. And they band together, just like some of the ethnic gangs do to do harm?" These particularly extreme claims were debunked in the following days by reporters affiliated with the Southern Poverty Law Center (SPLC).[42]

Important legal context appears in the next collection of visuals paired with voiceovers, with defense lawyers Susan Tipograph and Lori Cohen explaining how the headlines emphasizing the word "gang" presented an inaccurate narrative and image of the women charged.[43] As courthouse statuary appears on screen, Tipograph explains how a juror feared retribution by an organized gang, followed by Renata responding that she is not and has never been a gang member. Against a downward panning shot of a New York courthouse, Cohen offers additional information about the gang assault charge and the elements of proof required. From here, the press-clipping montage continues. "'HATED BY LEZ GANG': Straight-bash claim" appears first, floating slowly to the left of the screen as "Lesbian gang-stab shocker" flies in from below to take up the middle third of the frame. "Woman in Gang Assault Trial Says Man Started the Fight" by the *New York Times* is next, then quickly covered by "Jersey girl gang gets lockup in beatdown," which now covers two-thirds of the frame. The camera lingers on a final headline clipping, "GAL GANG."

Together, these montage sequences leave no doubt that this journalism in no way intended to cover the events with integrity or objectivity.

Following a presentation of surveillance camera footage that strongly supported the defense's case in the group's criminal trial, a series of Polaroid-style photos of the women fades onto screen, describing the respective charges and, later, the sentences they received. Voiceovers from members of each woman's family, followed by close-up shots as their comments continue, convey regret, grief, and outrage. For example, Mollie (Renata's mother) intones, "The media doesn't tell the whole story. They didn't tell how my daughter was attacked. How she was choked. It's called gay-bashing, but they won't call it that. . . . And my daughter is in jail for eight years for defending herself." Patreese's brother, Anthony, laments that his concern for her safety—advising her to carry a knife—contributed to her incarceration. Tanisha, Patreese's sister, breaks down into tears as her young daughter, sitting on her lap, turns around and silently stares at her mother with a look of concern. dorosh-walther ends this portion of the documentary by returning to the news-clipping montage motif. A percussive cut follows, and the viewer is left with an empty, black screen.

Although the tabloid journalism that followed the New Jersey Four dominates the film, dorosh-walther also reviews contemporaneous journalism critical of their treatment. Reva McEachern, a reporter with the *New Jersey Star-Ledger*, appears first, noting that "the only people who have been considered the villains in this case were the seven women who were, you know, attacked and followed." The shot of McEachern cuts to another news article montage, though these headlines are markedly different. As they scroll from the bottom of the screen, the viewer reads "No Justice When Women Fight Back," "Be Killed or Be Caged" (published in the *Advocate*), "The Whole System Failed Trayvon Martin," "The Case of CeCe McDonald: Murder—or Self-Defense Against a Hate Crime?," and "Where Was 'Stand Your Ground' for Marissa Alexander?"[44] After McEachern reappears on the screen to provide an additional voiceover explaining that the right to self-defense is often denied Black individuals, the camera cuts again to the original press-clipping montage motif used early in the film. Her own article headline, "Young, black, lesbian . . . and always on guard," appears. A final cut back to McEachern, who has finished explaining that these identities are often presumed guilty until proven innocent, lingers for effect.

The Contrast with *Spotlight*'s Journalism

The documentary techniques employed in *Out in the Night* simultaneously simplify a large amount of complex information for the viewer and present a tragedy that is both individualized and systemic.[45] As a sort of fun-house mirror to the work of journalists like those on the Spotlight team, headlines that sensationalize conflict by perpetuating harmful racial and gender-based stereotypes at the expense of careful, deliberate coverage destroy individuals and families. Such headlines also poison and reinforce broader social attitudes toward entire group identities. Even comparatively anodyne headlines, such as "Man Is Stabbed in Attack after Admiring Stranger,"[46] which appeared in the *New York Times*, conjure up incomplete narratives that further contribute to individual and systemic harms (i.e., victim-blaming).[47]

More broadly, the documentary points toward two (arguably) problematic truths about the press. By now, the first should be clear to readers of this volume: Any theory of the press as the fourth estate must account for the fact that "the press" is a business industry with a concurrent goal of generating profits. Sensational, tabloid-style accounts sell papers, and this motive—as noted in multiple accounts in this volume—can conflict with those emphasizing and serving broader public goods.

Less obvious but related, however, is the second truth. There is no single theory of the press or journalism ethics under the free press clause.[48] What one group of scholars have deemed the "libertarian" theory of the press (particularly in the United States and Great Britain), emphasizing its duty and right to freely check against authoritarian tendencies in the government (a role that motion pictures also can and do perform), is often pitted against the so-called social responsibility theory.[49] Subscribers to the latter theory might be fairly characterized as disillusioned onetime believers in the promise of the marketplace of ideas (see chapter 2). According to Fred S. Siebert, Theodore Peterson, and Wilbur Schramm, a social responsibility theory of the press "accepts the role of the press in servicing the political system, in enlightening the public, in safeguarding the liberties of the individual; but it represents the opinion that the press has been deficient in performing those tasks. . . . It accepts the role of the press in furnishing entertainment but with the proviso that the entertainment be 'good' entertainment."[50]

Out in the Night received generally positive reviews from critics. Describing it as "humanizing" in contrast to "New York's hysterical tabloid journalism and stealthily discriminatory criminal justice system," Steven Boone at RogerEbert.com offers that "[t]his film could help influence the ongoing LGBT civil rights struggle. Everyone should see it."[51] Writing for the *Guardian,* AM Brune emphasizes the investigative nature of the film, highlighting "key evidence not presented during the original trial, including camera shots showing Buckle ripping the dreadlocks out of Brown's head, a photograph of the scar on Buckle's stomach presented during the trial—a trauma incurred during from [*sic*] elective gallbladder surgery, not the stabbing."[52] Michael Nordine at IndieWire had similar praise for the film's indictment of media coverage, but felt that the accompanying editorializing came at the expense of a richer look at minoritized, neglected communities and issues related to the criminal process.[53] Somewhat ironically then, the film's emphasis on the proliferation of blaring, dehumanizing headlines and sensational cacophony to the exclusion of more deliberative, serious investigative coverage is a microcosm of what actually occurred in the case of the New Jersey Four.

ANALYSIS: DIFFERENT JOURNALISMS, FOR DIFFERENT IDENTITIES?

Although not an obvious pairing, *Spotlight* and *Out in the Night* provide several interesting points of comparison and contrast. Despite clear differences in form (dramatization versus documentary), financial resources, and distribution, both films function as commentary about the relationship between journalism and systemic institutional problems. *Spotlight* offers a glimpse into the potential of serious journalism despite opposition from insular communities, institutional power, and market demands. The headlines in the aftermath of the attack on the New Jersey Four, by contrast, convey the less-than-heroic tendencies of tabloid journalism: sensational headlines reflect and reinforce harmful attitudes at the intersection of race, gender, class, and sexuality.[54] Why the subjects of the latter film were left largely to tabloid accounts while the subjects of the former benefited (and rightly so) from the work of serious investigative journalism is a question worth additional exploration, especially if the cultural authority of the media's work under the free press clause depends on the rigor and internal checks on the ethics of the reporting process (as examined in additional detail in chapter 7).[55]

Initially, it is worth noting that multiple studies have found evidence that press coverage of crimes often lacks explanatory or humanizing context, may generate fear and cultivate punitive tendencies among the public (especially among subjects who watch local television news), and may reinforce negative racial stereotypes.[56] Indeed, one study found that fear and crime-hyping local news reporting had its strongest effects on white subjects who lived near predominantly Black neighborhoods.[57] Furthermore, political science research on the concept of target populations offers some additional clues. According to authors Anne Schneider and Helen Ingram, the "social construction of target populations refers to the cultural characterizations or popular images of the persons of groups whose behavior and well-being are affected by public policy." From here, Schneider and Ingram offer a typology of target populations. For example, "dependent" populations are constructed as "deserving" of sympathy and benefits but lack the political (or institutional) power to gain them (e.g., children and mothers).[58] In contrast, some populations fall into the category of "deviants," used to describe those who lack political power and are often excluded and minoritized elements of society.

Though Schneider and Ingram are interested in explaining how such constructions affect policy outcomes, the concept easily travels to explorations of press themes because the characterizations are "normative and evaluative, portraying groups in positive or negative terms through symbolic language, metaphors, and stories."[59] In the course of reporting, journalists are "carriers" of social constructions who obviously can and do influence the portrayals of various groups in the broader population,[60] with effects that can manifest in those groups' orientations toward government (i.e., views on the legitimacy of the criminal justice system) and political participation (i.e., sense of efficacy). Regardless of the objects and effects of reporting, one important point remains. "Serious" and "tabloid" journalism—to use the useful ideal-type dichotomy about which the expressive freedom scholar Rodney Smolla has written—are *both* protected by the free press clause of the First Amendment.[61] Although at least one prominent legal scholar has made such an argument for the free speech clause, there is no "low value" versus "high value" press content distinction.[62]

According to Smolla, characteristics of "serious" journalism include thoughtful presentation; emphases on political, social, scientific, artistic, and financial issues; respect for the line between public and private life; strong sourcing and documentation; and the avoidance of sensationalism in reporting facts (i.e., no gossip, rumors, or innuendo). Conversely, sensationalism is offered as the primary trait of tabloid journalism—"with glaring headlines and graphic photographs, and content permeated with exaggeration and hyperbole." When important political or social issues are covered, "they are covered in a sensational manner." The additional attributes of minimal sourcing and documentation, the failure to recognize and maintain the boundary between the public and private, and the use of "surreptitious" newsgathering techniques (including the use of "paparazzi") stand tabloid journalism in stark contrast with serious journalism.[63]

Interestingly, the common ancestor to the modern forms of sensational, tabloid *and* serious, investigative journalism may be the historically maligned "yellow journalism" (also discussed in chapter 2). The insult was (putatively) coined in 1897 by *New York Press* editor Ervin Wardman following and in reference to the publication of a series of comics featuring artist R. F. Outcault's "Yellow Kid" character, "an irreverent, jug-eared child of the New York City tenements."[64] Though often used as a synonym for sensationalist journalism (which Smolla identified as a core component of the tabloid style), more nuanced definitions exist. For example, under W. Joseph Campbell's more extensive definition, yellow journalism has attributes that include "crusades against monopolies and municipal corruption."[65] So, to the extent that serious investigative journalism continues to evince a concern for the relatively powerless vis-à-vis the powerful, yellow journalism can be fairly characterized as a common ancestor to both types of journalism. On a similar note, in terms of legal doctrine, so too can the examples of journalism covered here be traced to both the "original" understanding of the free press clause as a majoritarian function (somewhat popular editors and publishers speaking truth to power) and post–Fourteenth Amendment, libertarian emphases (protection for the unpopular dissenters).[66]

Echoes of these attributes are apparent in *Spotlight* and *Out in the Night*, but not in equal measures. While the former portrays tendencies toward uncovering corruption in the halls of power, the latter showcases the worst of the sensationalist attributes. These divergent exercises of press freedom are driven by long-standing profit-seeking incentives that, due in part to rapid technological change, continue to inhibit the pursuit of the traditional watchdog role of the press oriented toward the public good. Still, the benefits of investigative journalism and its orientation toward exposing malfeasance in powerful institutions, appear necessary for preserving democratic ideals. Perhaps New York University law professor Stephen Gillers offers a useful path forward with his observation that our discussions of the role of the press must begin with the law, but we cannot end there. Instead, we must sincerely ask "what freedom of press *should* be in order to best serve democracy, not simply what courts happen to say about it at the moment."[67]

NOTES

1. Thomas M. Keck, Brandon T. Metroka, and Richard Price, "The Judicial Protection of Anti-Judicial Speech," *American University International Law Review* 33, no. 4 (2018): 693–769.

2. For a useful explanation of the difference between the Constitution, constitutionalism, and a constitution ("small-c"), see James C. Foster, "No Neutrality: Hobbesian Constitutionalism in the Internet Age," in *Free Speech Theory: Understanding the Controversies*, ed. Helen J. Knowles and Brandon T. Metroka (New York: Peter Lang, 2020), 33–62.

3. "Spotlight," IMDB, https://www.imdb.com/title/tt1895587/ (last accessed May 19, 2022).

4. For an example of continuing litigation, see Adam Klasfeld, "Federal Bankruptcy Judge Rejects Catholic Diocese's Bid to Stop State Litigation on Child Sex Abuse, Excoriates 'Heavy-Handed Threat' to Survivors," *Law & Crime*, May 23, 2022, https://lawandcrime.com/high-profile/federal-bankruptcy-judge-rejects-catholic-dioceses-bid-to-stop-state-litigation-on-child-sex-abuse-excoriates-heavy-handed-threat-to-survivors/. For an example of systematic abuse and corruption of this type outside of the Catholic Church, see David French, "The Southern Baptist Horror (How Many Bad Apples Must We Pluck before We Recognize That the Orchard Is Diseased?)," *Atlantic*, May 23, 2022, https://www.theatlantic.com/ideas/archive/2022/05/southern-baptist-evangelical-allegations-cover-up/629954/. For the original report, see "Report of the Independent Investigation: The Southern Baptist Convention's Executive Committee's Response to Sexual Abuse Allegations and an Audit of the Procedures and Actions of the Credentials Committee," updated May 15, 2022, https://static1.squarespace.com/static/6108172d83d55d3c9db4dd67/t/628bfccb599a375bece1f66c/1653341391218/Guidepost+Solutions+Independent+Investigation+Report_.pdf (last accessed May 29, 2023).

5. "Five Decades in the Spotlight: A Selected Timeline of Groundbreaking Investigations," *Boston Globe*, September 23, 2021, https://www.bostonglobe.com/2021/09/23/magazine/five-decades-spotlight-selected-timeline-groundbreaking-investigations/.

6. Knight Case Studies Initiative, "The Spotlight Team," The Journalism School, Columbia University, 2012, https://ccnmtl.columbia.edu/projects/caseconsortium/casestudies/14/casestudy/www/layout/case_id_14_id_142.html (last accessed May 29, 2023).

7. Penelope Muse Abernathy, "The State of Local News: 2023 Report," Northwestern University: Medill Local News Initiative, https://localnewsinitiative.northwestern.edu/projects/state-of-local-news/2023/report/#vanishing-newspapers (last accessed November 16, 2023).

8. Olivia Truffaut-Wong, "Where the 'Spotlight' Journos Are Now," *Bustle*, November 6, 2015, https://www.bustle.com/articles/121285-where-are-the-spotlight-journalists-now-the-boston-globe-team-is-still-hard-at-work. These members of the team were complimentary of the mannerisms of their respective actor counterparts.

9. Benjamin Bradlee Jr. is the son of Benjamin Bradlee, the former editor of the *Washington Post* known for his role in the publication of the Pentagon Papers. The elder Bradlee is portrayed in both of the films analyzed in chapter 3.

10. Kristopher Tapley, "Tom McCarthy and Josh Singer on Wrangling the Story of 'Spotlight,'" *Variety*, September 14, 2015, https://variety.com/2015/film/in-contention/tom-mccarthy-and-josh-singer-on-wrangling-the-story-of-spotlight-1201593027/.

11. Matthew C. Ehrlich, "Hollywood and Journalistic Truthtelling," *Notre Dame Journal of Law, Ethics and Public Policy* 19, no. 2 (2005): 519–40.

12. At the time of this writing, the following headlines and links appear prominently at the *Globe's* Spotlight page: "Unfinished Justice" (effects of a Massachusetts statute imprisoning for life terms those who never actually killed anyone); "How Brigham Health Helped Create a Chinese Hospital for Elites—and Almost Nobody Came" (questionable use of funds and resources including a Harvard teaching hospital); "Some Dana Farber Cancer Institute Trustees Stood to Profit from Their Philanthropic Role" (examining conflicts of interest that occur when those with financial investments exert influence on hospital operations); and a three-part series from 2020 investigating the inequities associated with end-of-life care, including those at the intersection of race and economic status. "Spotlight," *Boston Globe*, last updated May 20, 2022, https://www.bostonglobe.com/metro/investigations/spotlight/ (last accessed May 20, 2022).

13. While considered "classic" techniques, Bordwell has argued that their frequency of use in the modern era has created an aesthetic of "intensified continuity." See David Bordwell, "Intensified Continuity Visual Style in Contemporary American Film," *Film Quarterly* 55, no. 3 (2002): 16–28.

14. Tapley, "Tom McCarthy and Josh Singer on Wrangling the Story of 'Spotlight.'"

15. Ann Hornaday, "'Spotlight' Joins 'All the President's Men' in the Pantheon of Great Journalism Movies," *Washington Post*, November 12, 2015, https://www.washingtonpost.com/goingoutguide/movies/spotlight-joins-all-the-presidents-men-in-the-pantheon-of-great-journalism-movies/2015/11/12/a4e9e7a6–86ed-11e5-be39–0034bb576eee_story.html.

16. Rachel Wilson, "The Walk and Talk: Crafting Exposition That Won't Bore Your Audience," Premium Beat, January 9, 2018, https://www.premiumbeat.com/blog/create-walk-and-talk-scene/.

17. David F. Pierre Jr., creator of TheMediaReport.com and a section titled "The Media and the Catholic Sex Abuse Story: Separating Fact from Fiction," takes issue with the opening scene and other elements of the film dramatization that did not actually occur, either as depicted or at all. "'Based on Actual Events'? Except the Very First Scene From 'Spotlight' Is Completely Bogus," TheMediaReport.com, November 25, 2015, http://www.themediareport.com/2015/11/25/spotlight-fabricated-scene/. A series of articles critical of media coverage of child sexual abuse within the Catholic Church is also available at https://www.catholicworldreport.com/author/pierre-david/.

18. Roy P. Madsen, *The Impact of Film: How Ideas are Communicated Through Cinema and Television* (New York: Macmillan, 1973), 74.

19. Medgar Evers, a leading figure in the 1960s US civil rights movement, was assassinated outside of his house with a high-powered rifle (shot in the back) on June 12, 1963. White supremacist Byron De La Beckwith IV was finally convicted of Evers's murder more than three decades later in a third trial in 1994. Charles Evers continued his brother's work in the aftermath of the assassination and later became an elected representative and, just prior to his death, a supporter of Donald Trump. Olesia Plokhii, "Charles Evers, Brother of Slain Civil Rights Activist, Dies at 97," *Washington Post*, July 22, 2020, https://www.washingtonpost.com/local/obituaries/charles-evers-brother-of-slain-civil-rights-activist-dies-at-97/2020/07/22/09bf3d40–52c3–11e8–9c91–7dab596e8252_story.html.

20. See also Michael Sragow, "Deep Focus: Spotlight," *Film Comment*, November 5, 2015, https://www.filmcomment.com/blog/deep-focus-spotlight/.

21. This trade-off situation is one of several in the film, including instances where members of the team wrestle with publishing findings before being scooped by a rival (the subplot of Rezendes's pursuit of Garabedian's sealed motions) or growing concern to inform the community about the dangers posed by priests living in the community, often near schools and/or within residential neighborhoods (Pfeiffer and Carroll's interactions with Robinson). For an extended discussion of the investigative journalism tension between empiricism (just the facts) and moral gatekeeping, see Theodore L. Glasser and James S. Ettema, "Investigative Journalism and the Moral Order," *Critical Studies in Mass Communication* 6, no. 1 (1989): 1–20.

22. The article was published on the Feast of the Epiphany, a holy day in the Catholic Church. Michael Rezendes, "Church Allowed Abuse by Priest for Years," *Boston Globe*, January 6, 2002, https://www.bostonglobe.com/news/special-reports/2002/01/06/church-allowed-abuse-priest-for-years/cSHfGkTIrAT25qKGvBuDNM/story.html.

23. Myth, as used here, does not denote "falsehood." See Ehrlich, "Hollywood and Journalistic Truthtelling," 160; Ronald Bishop, "'Not an Ounce of Hollywood Bullshit': A Narrative Analysis of News Media Coverage of Spotlight's Oscar Win," *Journal of Communication Inquiry* 44, no. 2 (2020): 157–77.

24. Incidentally, he also cowrote the screenplay for *The Post*.

25. Kristen Page-Kirby, "Researching Spotlight Made the Film's Makers into Journalists," *Washington Post*, November 10, 2015, https://www.washingtonpost.com/express/wp/2015/11/10/researching-spotlight-made-the-films-makers-into-journalists/. See also Hornaday, "Pantheon of Great Journalism Movies."

26. Stephen Engelberg, "'Spotlight' Gets Investigative Journalism Right," ProPublica, February 25, 2016, https://www.propublica.org/article/spotlight-gets-investigative-journalism-right.

27. Jeff Labrecque, "Spotlight Players Confront the Clue That Became the Movie's Key Twist," *Entertainment Weekly*, November 23, 2015, https://ew.com/article/2015/11/23/spotlight-boston-globe-key-clue/.

28. Alexander Nazaryan, "Review: 'Spotlight' Explores the Sins of the Fathers," *Newsweek*, October 8, 2015, https://www.newsweek.com/review-spotlight-revisits-boston-globe-pedophile-priest-case-380849. See also Bishop, "Not an Ounce."

29. For a review of some of the Catholic Church's responses to the film as well as some of the themes explored here, see "Vatican Paper Lauds Spotlight as Brave, Not Anti-Catholic," Catholic News Agency, February 29, 2016, https://www.catholicnewsagency.com/news/33496/vatican-paper-lauds-spotlight-as-brave-not-anti-catholic.

30. Bishop, "'Not an Ounce.'"

31. Samuel P. Winch, "Ethical Challenges for Investigative Journalism," in *The Big Chill: Investigative Reporting in the Current Media Environment*, ed. Marilyn S. Greenwald and Joseph Bernt (Ames: Iowa State University Press, 2000), 122.

32. "About," *Out in the Night* website, https://www.outinthenight.com/about-2 (last accessed May 29, 2023).

33. Nicole Pasulka, "How 4 Gay Black Women Fought Back against Sexual Harassment—and Landed in Jail," *Code Sw!tch*, June 30, 2015, https://www.npr.org/sections/codeswitch/2015/06/30/418634390/how-4-gay-black-women-fought-back-against-a-sexual-harasser-and-landed-in-jail.

34. Pierre Sorlin, "Documentaries: A Gold Mine Historians Should Begin to Exploit," in *Using Visual Evidence*, ed. Richard Howells and Robert Matson (New York: McGraw-Hill, 2009), 119.

35. Gina Baleria, "What Is Neutrality Bias, and Why Do We Need to Address It?" Routledge, September 15, 2021, https://www.routledge.com/blog/article/what-is-neutrality-bias-and-why-do-we-need-to-address-it.

36. "Out in the Night: Filmmaker Interview," *POV*, June 22, 2015, http://archive.pov.org/outinthenight/interview/.

37. "Who Runs New Day," accessed June 16, 2024, https://www.newday.com/about/who-runs-new-day.

38. Newspaper depictions of Black lesbian women as uniquely violent compared to other identities is a long-standing theme. See Cookie Woolner, "'Women Slain in Queer Love Brawl': African American Women, Same-Sex Desire, and Violence in the Urban North, 1920–1929," *Journal of African American History* 100, no. 3 (2015): 406–27.

39. Italiano resigned from the *New York Post* in 2021 following the publication of a story that incorrectly claimed that unaccompanied minors temporarily held at a facility in Southern California were given Vice President Kamala Harris's children's book *Superheroes Are Everywhere.* See Aayush Sharma, "Who Is Laura Italiano? NY Post Journalist Resigns over 'Incorrect Story' on Kamala Harris, Says Was 'Ordered,'" *meaww*, April 27, 2021, https://meaww.com/who-is-laura-italiano-ny-post-journalist-hands-over-resignation-over-incorrect-story-kamala-harris; Jim Waterson, "New York Post Reporter Quits Citing Pressure to Write Incorrect Story about Kamala Harris," *Guardian*, April 28, 2021, https://www.theguardian.com/us-news/2021/apr/28/new-york-post-reporter-quits-over-incorrect-story-about-kamala-harris-book.

40. For a review of recent miniseries and the lasting effects of the case, see Elizabeth Hinton, "How the 'Central Park Five' Changed the History of American Law," *Atlantic*, June 2, 2019, https://www.theatlantic.com/entertainment/archive/2019/06/when-they-see-us-shows-cases-impact-us-policy/590779/.

41. Jelani Cobb, "The Central Park Five, Criminal Justice, and Donald Trump," *New Yorker*, April 19, 2019, https://www.newyorker.com/news/daily-comment/the-central-park-five-criminal-justice-and-donald-trump.

42. Investigative reporters for the SPLC fact-checked these claims in the aftermath of the O'Reilly interview, which led to a "weak clarification" by O'Reilly two days later. See Mark Potok, "How I Got Fox News to Tell the Truth about 'Violent Lesbian Gangs,'" *Daily Beast*, May 30, 2017, https://www.thedailybeast.com/how-i-got-fox-news-to-tell-the-truth-about-violent-lesbian-gangs; Susy Buchanan and David Holthouse, "Rod Wheeler Claims on the O'Reilly Factor Lesbian Gangs Are Raping Young Girls," *Intelligence Report*, October 1, 2007, https://www.splcenter.org/fighting-hate/intelligence-report/2007/rod-wheeler-claims-o'reilly-factor-lesbian-gangs-are-raping-young-girls.

43. Although considerable research has examined the relationship between Supreme Court decisions and media coverage (or salience), far less has examined news coverage of lower court proceedings. For some details, see Gene Policinski, "Setting the Docket: News Media Coverage of Our Courts—Past, Present and an Uncertain Future," *Missouri Law Review* 79 (2014): 1007–19.

44. George Zimmerman's killing of Trayvon Martin, an unarmed Black teenager wearing a hoodie and returning from a trip to a local convenience store, marked the beginning of the Black Lives Matter movement. Police and civilian killings of Black men (e.g., Ahmaud Arbery, Philando Castile, George Floyd), women (e.g., Breonna Taylor), and children (e.g., Tamir Rice) continue to occur. See Deepti Hajela, "Trayvon Martin, 10 Years Later: Teen's Death Changes Nation," Associated Press, February 24 2022, https://apnews.com/article/Trayvon-Martin-death-10-years-later-c68f12130b2992d9c1ba31ec1a398cdd. See also Alia Chughtai, "Know Their Names: Black People Killed by the Police in the U.S.," Al Jazeera, 2020, https://interactive.aljazeera.com/aje/2020/know-their-names/index.html (last accessed June 12, 2024).

45. The literature on these interrelated themes continues to grow. On institutional racism as it relates to incarceration and its effects, see, for example, Michelle Alexander, *The New Jim Crow: Mass Incarceration in the Age of Colorblindness* (New York: New Press, 2010). On how government "redlining" decisions contributed to the racial wealth gap and poverty in the present day, see Richard Rothstein, *The Color of Law: A Forgotten History of How Our Government Segregated America* (New York: Liveright Publishing, 2017). For an example of an individual-level story that captures broader racial disparities in the criminal justice system (and its effects), see Danielle Allen, *Cuz: Or the Life and Times of Michael A* (New York: Liveright Publishing, 2017).

46. Cara Buckley and Kate Hammer, "Man Is Stabbed in Attack after Admiring a Stranger," *New York Times*, August 19, 2006, https://www.nytimes.com/2006/08/19/nyregion/19stab.html. The article ends with: "It's not a crime to say hello to a human being," Mr. Buckle said. "Now, I think I'll know which girls not to talk to."

47. On how institutional structures privilege racial and sexual harassment ("free speech"), see Laura Beth Nielsen, *License to Harass: Law, Hierarchy, and Offensive Public Speech* (Princeton, NJ: Princeton University Press, 2004).

48. See, for example, Fred S. Siebert, Theodore Peterson, and Wilbur Schramm, *Four Theories of the Press* (Urbana: University of Illinois Press, 1984), 1: "The thesis of this volume is that the press always takes on the form and coloration of the social and political structures within which it operates."

49. Siebert, Peterson, and Schramm, *Four Theories of the Press*, 56.

50. Siebert, Peterson, and Schramm, *Four Theories of the Press*, 74.

51. Steven Boone, "Overturning Perceptions: 2014 Los Angeles Film Festival Preview," RogerEbert.com, June 9, 2014, https://www.rogerebert.com/festivals/overturning-perceptions-2014-los-angeles-film-festival-preview.

52. AM Brune, "Out in the Night: New York City's Racism and Anti-Gay Bias Plays out on Screen," *Guardian*, April 27, 2015, https://www.theguardian.com/world/2015/apr/27/out-in-the-night-new-york-racism-anti-gay-bias.

53. Michael Nordine, "LAFF Review: 'Out in the Night' Indicts the Media and the Justice System but Comes up Short as a Movie," IndieWire, June 13, 2014, https://www.indiewire.com/criticism/culture/laff-review-out-in-the-night-indicts-the-media-and-the-justice-system-but-comes-up-short-as-a-movie-25397/.

54. See, for example, George Comstock and Erica Scharrer, *The Psychology of Media and Politics* (Boston: Elsevier Academic Press, 2005), 250: "vicarious learning."

55. Nicole Pasulka, "The 'Criminal' Black Lesbian: Where Does This Damaging Stereotype Come From?" *Code Sw!tch*, March 17, 2016, https://www.npr.org/sections/codeswitch/2016/03/17/456541972/the-criminal-black-lesbian-where-does-this-damaging-stereotype-come-from.

56. Michael O'Hear, "Violent Crime and Media Coverage in One City: A Statistical Snapshot," *Marquette Law Review* 103, no. 3 (2020): 1012.

57. A. J. Baranauskas and K. M. Drakulich, "Media Construction of Crime Revisited: Media Types, Consumer Contexts, and Frames of Crime and Justice," *Criminology* 4, no. 56 (2018): 679–714.

58. Anne Schneider and Helen Ingram, "Social Construction of Target Populations: Implications for Politics and Policy," *American Political Science Review* 87, no. 2 (1993): 338.

59. Schneider and Ingram, "Social Construction of Target Populations," 334.

60. Schneider and Ingram, "Social Construction of Target Populations," 343.

61. "Tabloid" journalism refers to both the form of the publication (smaller than the standard "broadsheet" associated with comparatively "serious" journalism outlets) and content. Rodney A. Smolla, "Will Tabloid Journalism Ruin the First Amendment for the Rest of Us?" *DePaul Journal of Art and Entertainment Law* 9, no. 1 (1998): 1–6.

62. See, for example, Cass Sunstein, *Democracy and the Problem of Free Speech* (New York: Free Press, 1995), 121–65.

63. Smolla, "Will Tabloid Journalism," 2.

64. W. Joseph Campbell, *Yellow Journalism: Puncturing the Myths, Defining the Legacies* (Westport, CT: Praeger, 2001), 25–34.

65. Campbell, *Yellow Journalism*, 7–8.

66. Akhil Reed Amar, *The Bill of Rights: Creation and Reconstruction* (New Haven, CT: Yale University Press, 1998), 236–37. Admittedly, this comparison is much more tenuous regarding this chapter's examples as hypotheticals, as it is more difficult to frame Marty Baron and Spotlight as "popular" figures—at least in light of the outsider role they played in examining the Catholic Church in Boston.

67. Stephen Gillers, *Journalism under Fire: Protecting the Future of Investigative Reporting* (New York: Columbia University Press, 2018), 2 (also see chapter 3, "What Does the Press Clause Demand of the Press?").

Chapter 10

Mainstream Press Negligence and Its Effects

The Normal Heart *and* Tongues Untied

Brandon T. Metroka

Visual literacy—the ability to comprehend and evaluate images—can enhance our awareness of the ways that filmmakers have used creative elements and techniques to evoke desired impressions or reactions.[1] The techniques employed in *The Normal Heart* and *Tongues Untied* demonstrate how *cinematic* editorial choices (including those relating to coverage and tone) can highlight *journalistic* editorial choices about "newsworthiness."[2] In so doing, the cinematic choices retroactively give dignity and respect to subjects who were persecuted, stigmatized, and dehumanized by a decades-long government campaign to destroy their livelihoods and lives.[3] And this was persecution, stigmatization, and dehumanization that the mainstream media at best ignored and at worst perpetuated.

As this chapter shows, the press freedoms so often lionized by society (and championed by many of the movies analyzed in previous chapters) for exposing uncomfortable truths also leave the media free to keep those truths hidden when it suits their moral and capitalistic bottom lines. The consequences can be devastating; the impact of the governmental and mainstream media action/inaction conveyed in *The Normal Heart* and *Tongues Untied* fell most heavily on those with very little insulating social capital or popular support. It is therefore ironic that it was the failure or refusal of the mainstream media to use its First Amendment–protected power to publish newsworthy events that created group consciousnesses with affinities for innovation, direct action, and more radical forms of participation in political processes. As such, this chapter invites consideration of the following questions:

- To what extent can the HIV/AIDS crises, still ongoing, function as case studies for examining the effects of press negligence?
- When the mainstream media exercises its freedom to *not* cover something, is such a decision primarily driven by financial or sociopolitical factors, or something else?
- How should the mainstream media react when films like *The Normal Heart* and *Tongues Untied* retroactively demonstrate that media's complicity in or failure to shed light on governmental dehumanization of entire groups in society?
- To what extent do *The Normal Heart* and *Tongues Untied* send complementary and contrasting messages about the oppressive treatment of marginalized groups in society?

When considering the answers to these questions, it will become clear that the two films analyzed in this chapter highlight the following issues:

- Power dynamics within the media and society.
- The differences between mainstream media and journalism's "others."
- The negatives and positives of the power that the First Amendment affords the institutional press.
- Government funding of controversial media (i.e., the role of the National Endowment for the Arts [NEA]).
- Methodological diversity in studying the effects of legal provisions (top-down versus bottom-up approaches).
- Societal and systemic oppression of individuals and groups.
- The power of media beyond the institutional press, including experimental documentary and editing techniques, to create narratives of validation and empowerment.

"Oppression" is a particularly prevalent theme in this chapter (as in chapter 9). Here, the term is used broadly, and reflects the definition offered up by political theorist Iris Marion Young: "[I]n this extended structural sense oppression refers to the vast and deep injustices some groups suffer as a consequence of often unconscious assumptions and reactions of well-meaning people in ordinary interactions, media and cultural stereotypes, and structural features of bureaucratic hierarchies and market mechanisms—in short, the normal processes of everyday life."[4]

Cinematic depictions of these "processes of everyday life"—and how they relate to press freedoms—are the focal points of this chapter.

HISTORICAL BACKGROUND: "THE NEGLIGENT, NON-INTEREST OF THE STRAIGHT PRESS" IN THE US HIV/AIDS CRISES IN THE 1980S

An article published in the *Los Angeles Times* in June 1981 reported, "Researchers are investigating mysterious outbreaks of pneumonia that have occurred among male homosexuals in Los Angeles and several other cities across the nation."[5] About a month later, an article in the *New York Times* observed of the growing diagnoses of the mystery condition: "[D]octors said that most cases had involved homosexual men who have had multiple and frequent sexual encounters with different partners, as many as 10 sexual encounters each night up to four times a week."[6] These quotations mark the publication of the first major mainstream newspaper articles on what later became known as the HIV/AIDS (human immunodeficiency virus/ acquired immunodeficiency syndrome) crises in the United States.[7] The retrovirus responsible for the disease now known as AIDS—initially known as "gay cancer" or "gay plague" and later as gay-related immunodeficiency (GRID)—has since infected tens of millions of individuals globally, including heterosexuals.[8]

The disease—and underlying virus—does not discriminate. In 2011, Lawrence Altman reflected upon his 1981 *New York Times* article, quoted above, and suggested an ethical obligation of journalists to provide ongoing coverage of the issue because "[a]s AIDS has become entrenched in the United States and elsewhere, a new generation has grown up with little if any knowledge of those dark early days." This is problematic, he explained, because "AIDS still presents extraordinary challenges—*not least to journalists trying to chronicle the epidemic's unfolding story*, to remind a new generation of the importance of safe sex, and to follow the sometimes halting effort to make effective drugs available to all who need them."[9]

It would be a mistake to assume, however, that the aforementioned mainstream news articles represented the first coverage by any print media of the AIDS crisis. They were preceded by an article published without the support of any mainstream press institution. Writing in the *New York Native,* a biweekly gay publication, in May 1981, Dr. Lawrence Mass discussed a conversation with city health officials, who (perhaps due to lack of clear information and to avoid causing panic) downplayed the reality and risks of what was then being identified as gay cancer.[10] As the activist and playwright Larry Kramer observed a short time later,

> If all of this had been happening to any other community for two long years, there would have been, long ago, such an outcry from that community and its members that the government of this city and this country would not know what

> had hit them. Why isn't every gay man in this city so scared shitless that he is screaming for action? Does every gay man in New York want to die?[11]

Kramer's observation has empirical support:

> In 1981, the New York Times published only three stories on AIDS, and just three stories in 1982, none of which made the front page. (The Times didn't put AIDS on the front page until the following year.) By contrast, the cyanide-laced Tylenol pills that killed seven people in 1982 resulted in a massive media panic, with the New York Times covering the story every single day that October.[12]

Once the mainstream press started paying attention, the tone of the coverage appeared less than sympathetic to victims:

> The public went from ignoring AIDS to panicking over it. A poll conducted by the *New York Daily News* in 1985 found that 42 percent of respondents wanted people with AIDS to be quarantined. News reports featured stories of nurses quitting rather than treating AIDS patients, prison guards demanding special protective suits to deal with infected prisoners, and funeral directors refusing to embalm dead people with AIDS. The CDC [Centers for Disease Control] published a report about how AIDS was transmitted in September 1983, but misinformation was clearly still running rampant.[13]

Public opinion, contemporaneous with the crisis during the 1980s, captures the (shocking) widespread acceptability of the condemnation and shaming. In 1987, "roughly half of Americans agreed that it was people's own fault if they got AIDS (51%) and that most people with AIDS had only themselves to blame (46%)." Indeed, "[b]etween 43% and 44% of Americans in 1987 and 1988 believed that AIDS might be God's punishment for immoral sexual behavior." And further, "most Americans also agreed that people with AIDS should be made to carry a card noting they had the virus, and one in three agreed that employers should be allowed to fire employees who had AIDS. Twenty-one percent of Americans said people with AIDS should be isolated from the rest of society."[14]

THE NORMAL HEART—FIGHTING WITHIN OR AGAINST THE SYSTEM?

Kramer's observation about media coverage of AIDS came two years before he penned his heavily autobiographical 1985 play, *The Normal Heart*. Written shortly after Kramer's ejection from the Gay Men's Health Crisis (GMHC), a support and resource-providing organization for gay men (especially those with HIV/AIDS) of which Kramer was a founding member,[15] the play enjoyed a nine-month run at the Public Theatre in New York City.[16] Nearly thirty years later, and reflecting the fact that depictions of AIDS in film had become increasingly socially acceptable, the play became an Emmy Award–winning HBO Films production in 2014.[17] The main plot of the film can be understood as the GMHC's foundational narrative, taking some creative license with characters in Kramer's ambit yet also providing an accurate portrayal of the group's challenges, services, and mission.

Prior to the onset of the HIV/AIDS crises in the United States, Kramer had a well-established reputation as an "irascible . . . bombastic" screenwriter and producer, even earning the ire of the gay community with his denunciation of the "hedonism" of what might today be called hookup culture.[18] Indeed, the opening sequence of the film captures this period of Kramer's life—and the abrupt onset of the pandemic within the gay community—via common and disorienting narrative editing techniques that convey an increasingly palpable sense of unease.[19]

In that opening sequence, Ned Weeks (Mark Ruffalo), a character based on Kramer himself, is traveling to Fire Island Pines, New York, via ferry. The year—"1981"—is superimposed against the ocean, with a ferry entering the shot. Subsequent shots decrease the distance to the ferry as the camera pans around the vessel. Somewhat abruptly, the viewer sees Ned in close-up. Taken together, the editing techniques in the establishing sequence fake toward a gradual, pondering introduction before immersing the viewer in the bustle of the trip via shifts between subjective and performer's viewpoints.[20] As the viewer walks with Ned from the ferry to meet his friend Craig Donner (Johnathan Groff), editorial cuts allow the viewer to see events from Ned's own perspective, thereby drawing the audience's attention to the notice Weeks pays to physically fit gay men in various stages of undress and acts of physical intimacy. The camera stays with Ned's expressions throughout these scenes, including in close-ups, communicating discomfort and hesitation to the viewer.[21]

Viewers are introduced to the HIV/AIDS pandemic in the latter part of the opening sequence via the unexpected collapse of Craig (who is also Bruce Niles's boyfriend, played by Taylor Kitsch), on the beach during his birthday celebration. Later, while departing the beach house and celebratory atmosphere of the party, the camera lens sharpens into focus on Ned approaching and observing (and then, apparently, joining) a group of men engaged in sexual intercourse against a darker, washed-out backdrop of the surrounding woodlands—portending the crisis to follow and again capturing Kramer's feelings prior to the crisis. Against the notable tonal shift in visuals, the opening sequence ends with Ned reading the now (in)famous *New York Times* article by Altman. The following scene, in the office of Dr. Brookner

(Julia Roberts), also relies heavily on color (drab browns and greens) as Ned meets a departing patient expressing concern about the noticeable lesions marking his body.

Director Ryan Murphy has a reputation for centering queer storylines and characters (i.e., *Pose, American Horror Story, Glee*). One pop culture publication offered that Murphy's storylines and direction tend to favor "underdog" characters as well as "glamorous" set pieces. Another emphasized "the sheer force and variety and chutzpah of his creations, which are linked by a singular storytelling aesthetic: stylized extremity and rude humor, shock conjoined with sincerity, and serious themes wrapped in circus-bright packaging." However, the best metaphor for *The Normal Heart's* style might be the article's prior description of Murphy's own mood as "shift[ing] unexpectedly, like a wonky thermostat—now warm, now icy."[22] Kramer's play, with its focus on Ned's relationships within the GMHC, his brother, and his lover Felix, initially seems well tailored to fairly static office- and home-type backdrops rather than the "pure eye-candy" and "color" of sets on *American Horror Story* and *Glee*.[23] Yet the frequently varying aesthetic of the film is appropriate to the subject material and works effectively, contributing to the overall sense of unease and tension. Bouncing between the idyllic beaches of Fire Island and the drab interior of Dr. Brookner's clinic creates an anxious, ominous mood.

Ned's initial challenge is to disseminate information concerning the rise of the so-called gay cancer among otherwise healthy men to (a) a skeptical, even hostile, gay community, and (b) to try to convince the mainstream press in New York City to give the emerging disease attention. As the film, and the pandemic, progresses, within-group hostility toward disease mitigation is gradually supplanted by the sadness, helplessness, isolation, and rage (conveyed primarily and convincingly by Ruffalo) that increasingly permeates the community as friends and lovers waste away from AIDS.[24] As to the attempt to get mainstream press coverage, Ned's trip to the *New York Times* offices is the introductory scene for his eventual lover, fashion reporter Felix Turner (Matt Bomer). Felix—himself a closeted gay man and, unbeknownst to Ned initially, a former bathhouse partner—conveys the challenges the gay community faces in gaining an agenda foothold, and the risks to individuals who might try: "No one here will write about it, and I can't."[25] A short time later, Ned's indictment of the media and social apathy takes the form of rumination on the causes of the Holocaust in World War II, delivered at his "first" date with Felix at his apartment. The scene is notable for the intense despair conveyed, the indictment of the institutional press, and the ignorance of gay men to their own vulnerability due, in part, to the liberating power of sex. Felix dryly responds, "This is turning out to be a very romantic evening."

Giving What the Press Wouldn't, Thirty Years Later

Though some reviews of *The Normal Heart* thought it too melodramatic or overwritten at times (the characters offering angst-ridden, extended, soliloquy-like lines laden with statistics and various metaphors),[26] this feature may be attributable to the film's origins as a theatrical play, where such techniques are more common due to the constraints of the stage medium. Combined with the regular use of subjective and performer's viewpoints, tilted camera angles (the scene following Ned's meeting with an unnamed White House official), and effective use of shadows and lighting, feelings of discomfort, guilt, and shame are almost certainly the film's desired emotional responses. For example, Mickey's (Joe Mantello) anguished pleas against Ned's media interview tactics and criticism of closeted men, and his own near-conspiratorial (and suicidal) despair and culminating physical rage near the end of the film are less directed to Ned than to the viewer of the film, similar to Ned's continued angry incredulity at gay men being rendered invisible.

In both the film adaptation and the actual crises as they unfolded, humanizing and empathetic coverage by the press is conspicuously absent.[27] In *The Normal Heart*, several sequences are constructed to humanize the suffering of the individuals afflicted by the crisis and to indict those unable or unwilling to do. Ned and Felix "marrying" one another in the latter's final moments in a hospital bed, with his now-supportive brother Ben (Alfred Molina) and Dr. Brookner observing, is an important example of the use of extreme close-ups to produce overpowering emotion within the viewer.[28] However, one specific sequence in the film may be the most likely to stir viewers for its emotion-laden content because it is enhanced via a series of close-up shots, dolly shots, ominous lighting decisions, and a combination of subjective and performer's viewpoint techniques that make the viewer feel present with the characters and party to the trauma and misery.[29] In doing so, it is a sequence that provides, decades after the initial press coverage of the pandemic and perhaps as a corrective to modern "AIDS Amnesia,"[30] the empathy and humanity sorely needed but conspicuously absent from that early press reporting. For that reason, it receives extended attention here.

The film conveys the loss of Bruce's partner, Albert (Finn Wittrock), through a flashback sequence recounting his final days and an attempted trip to visit his mother ("His mother wanted to see him in Phoenix before he died"). While flashback sequences may disorient viewers by creating breaks in the "presentness" of the film depiction, thereby interrupting progression to a climax,[31] the technique is used here to intensely emotional effect. During the sequence, Bruce's retelling to Ned provides context to the viewer as it is interspersed among the events unfolding in the flashback. Beginning with Bruce and Albert's experience on the plane prior to takeoff, the camera lingers on the uncomfortable look of the female flight attendant standing near the door but only a couple of rows from the clearly distressed Bruce and clearly sick Albert. A close-up shot of the pilot follows. Even though the pilot's words are inaudible over Bruce's narration, a close-up shot makes clear his unwillingness to fly the plane. A second pilot enters the scene and gives a quick but knowing glance to Bruce, agreeing to take the flight. The viewer experiences Albert's final moments in a series of quick shots from and cuts to various positions in the plane cabin, with Bruce trying to calm him, now in audible and visible hysterics, among horrified (audibly gasping) passengers and concerned flight attendants. These edits create a sudden and intense sense of unease and anxiety and convey Albert's own dissociated state of being. As Bruce intones, "He doesn't recognize me, he doesn't know where we're going, that we're going to see his mother in Phoenix—nothing. He just becomes . . . " Albert violently and unexpectedly vomits on the back of his seat.

As the viewer learns that Albert did not survive long enough to meet his mother at the hospital in Phoenix, the film uses tracking shots to follow his lifeless body, carted by an ambulance technician clad in hazmat gear, to a nurse's reception station area inside the hospital. The objective viewpoint for the audience in this scene is alongside and then directly over the hospital gurney, perhaps suggesting (or inviting) the audience member to take the perspective of the now-deceased Albert as his body approaches Bruce and his distraught mother. The viewpoint then switches to that of Albert's mother (and/or Bruce), first lingering on the faces of the ambulance techs, who leave the gurney and hurry away without word or acknowledgement, then a quick, wide, side-profile shot through a hallway window of Bruce and Albert's mother moving toward Albert's body, and ending with a shaky zoom-in on Albert's face for a close-up. A mirrored close-up of Bruce and Albert's mother, in shock and grief, is quickly followed by another cut back to the close-up of Albert's face. The scene's punctuation mark is the tossing of a sheet over Albert's head, followed by an abrupt cut to darkness (an edit signifying finality and death).

The indignities that Albert (and others like him) faced in life did not end with death. The film conveys the reality of this indignity and distress with a panning shot transition from the *seeming* finality of the previous shot. As with the passage from the flight to the hospital scene, jump cuts are used to logically move the narrative forward, but without direct continuity, first to what appears to be the hospital morgue via an establishing shot notable for its gloominess. Again, Bruce provides commentary: "The hospital doctors refused to examine him and give him a cause of death on his death certificate. Without the death certificate, the undertakers will not take him and neither will the police." As Bruce delivers this line, the viewer first sees a concerned and shocked mother in a medium shot (and on the other side of diamond-gridded windows typical of hospital environments), against a nearby wall with arms folded tightly and silently sobbing as an orderly and Bruce work to stuff Albert's body into a common black kitchen garbage bag ("and puts him the alley with the rest of the garbage"). The next cut is to a scene outside an industrial door entrance at the hospital, bathed in intense yellow from a nearby security light that adds additional unease to a shot of the orderly demanding fifty dollars for providing Albert's body.

The viewer perspective here is at considerable distance, but it is now from behind the silhouetted figure of Albert's mother, who is grabbing a car door handle and visibly heaving and shaking as Bruce gives in to the orderly's demands. The transition to the next shot, of Bruce wheeling Albert's garbage-bag clad figure to the car, is accompanied by a rising wail on his mother's part as she opens the door and helps Bruce load her son's corpse into the back seat. The next cut is to bright daylight, with a hand holding up a bag of Albert's ashes in the foreground and a close-up of Bruce, asking "Is that all of him?" A wide shot establishes that the viewer has moved to the rear of a nondescript funeral home, with Bruce ready to accept Albert's remains and the silhouetted figure of his mother visible in the car. The final close-up of the scene conveys the growing contempt Bruce (and perhaps the viewer) by now feels, as we hear the demands of the mortician: "You want it? Three thousand dollars." The sequence ends with a short, gradual zoom-in on Albert, now nothing but ashes in a clear plastic bag, held by his mother with a distant look next to Bruce in the car.

Beyond Doctrine . . .

What does *The Normal Heart* contribute to our understanding of the press? It is perhaps useful to consider answers to this question through an analytical lens that draws on law and society literature. That is because this chapter adopts a more "bottom-up" approach that stands in contrast to earlier chapters that focus on films depicting media elites, press institutions, or journalists actively engaged in their professions. Those are films that feature the press "in action"—they are accounts that tend to be "top-down," focusing on media elites or journalist exemplars and often with accompanying emphasis on doctrinal free press clause connections. *The Normal Heart* (and, as we will see, also *Tongues Untied*) lends itself to analysis through a law and society lens because the film captures the way in which individuals perceive and organize under the power of law, and in turn, participate in its ongoing transformation.[32] As Josh Wilson describes it, the law and society framework expands inquiry beyond legal formalism and mere contestation through litigation and courts. Instead, scholars adopting this approach also recognize that "legal power is intimately intertwined with what individuals believe, the stories that they tell, and the ways that they choose to behave."[33]

In the realm of the free speech clause, scholars have demonstrated how this framework reveals the power of legal symbols beyond doctrine and decree. Wilson, for example, explores how pro-choice and pro-life activists draw upon the symbolic power of legal pronouncements to organize their activities (thereby reifying the legitimacy of state power).[34] Similarly, Laura Beth Nielsen captures how purveyors of offensive and harassing speech in public areas, despite the harms perceived by the subjects of such speech and others, benefit from the default, normalizing tendencies of free speech frames.[35] The films analyzed in this chapter ask the viewer (and you, the reader) to consider the adoption of this framework to begin to interrogate effects of actions under the free *press* clause.

Notably, even as *The Normal Heart* focuses the viewer upon the suffering wrought by the ongoing global HIV/AIDS crises, it also captures the absence of the institution. In contrast with the numerous other depictions of this volume, the mainstream press is, at best, a complicit purveyor of indifference. Contemporary audiences may justifiably view the editorial choices made during the period depicted as inexplicably tone-deaf. But even as the press has a social responsibility to inform, it is and always has been a business—the bottom line matters. The disease's early manifestations in a minoritized group, already pervasively shunned and shamed, likely made it an easy decision to forgo publication coverage, let alone coverage with humanizing, empathetic qualities. Indeed, one film reviewer suggests that despite the advances in treatment and public attitudes since the early 1980s,[36] AIDS amnesia and the effects of media silence remain, but with overdue focus on the racial dimensions of inequity:

> Today, Hispanic and African American populations are disproportionately affected. . . . These are not the faces of the gay community we see on TV, which skew overwhelmingly white, urban, affluent, and more often than not male. As AIDS now hits these less visible communities the hardest, are we all that surprised to see it follow a trend familiar to these communities: less funding, less outrage, and less coverage in the mainstream media?[37]

As the 1980s unfurled, racial minorities and nongay individuals claimed a growing share of new diagnoses.[38] This trend, along with the important question of whether activists—once a consciousness and ability to "name" and "blame" manifests[39]—should work to change policy and public attitudes via working within the system or by defying it, are useful segues to the experimental documentary *Tongues Untied*.

TONGUES UNTIED—BREAKING THE SILENCE THAT DESTROYS

A 2022 selection to the National Film Registry of the Library of Congress,[40] Marlon Riggs's *Tongues Untied* (1989) is a documentary-style production that drew considerable controversy—particularly, the ire of conservative interests (including the American Family Association)—because it was made with the financial support of the National Endowment for the Arts.[41] In 1992, presidential candidate Patrick Buchanan—who challenged incumbent Republican president George H. W. Bush in the 1992 GOP primaries and delivered a (in)famous "culture war" speech at that year's GOP National Convention—released an advertisement critical of Bush. The advertisement referenced the $5,000 in NEA funding that *Tongues Untied* had received. "In the last three years," it said, "the Bush administration has invested our tax dollars in pornographic and blasphemous art, too shocking to show. This so-called art has glorified homosexuality, exploited children, and perverted the image of Jesus Christ."[42] In short, conservatives and others like Buchanan may have viewed the film as an opportunity to cultivate and reap the combined political harvest of homophobia, racism, HIV/AIDS stigma, and anti-intellectualism.[43]

In sharp contrast, Riggs viewed *Tongues Untied* as a deeply personal opportunity to affirm and center the "experiences of Black gay men and the search for identity," creating his own media product to fill a too-familiar silence.[44] In an interview with Ron Simmons, Riggs observed of Black filmmaking themes that depictions of being gay within the Black community were notably absent.[45]

As if to immediately and forcefully interrupt the silence imposed on Black gay men (the documentary's overriding but not exclusive emphasis), *Tongues Untied* opens with a montage of live-action shots, played at slower speeds, of Black men in public settings. Before the first image is visible, a chant of "Brother to Brother" begins against a completely black background and repeats throughout the opening forty-five-second sequence. The black background gives way to the back of a Black man's head, donning headphones, apparently in a public setting. Following this establishing shot, the opening sequence is broken into a series of scenes of approximately fourteen seconds long, punctuated by returns to the black screen and brief pauses in the ongoing chant. The chant modulates from a single voice to multiple voices in each sequence. At some points, a Black face is superimposed on the ongoing montage with the mouth visibly completing the chant, fading in and out of the visual. All scenes included in the montage are presented to the viewer through a black-and-white filter.

If the opening sequence can be understood as a call for, or expression of, solidarity among Black men, the sequence following it can be understood, in part, as an initial expression of the isolation that gay men feel within that discrete group. Less than a minute into the film, the scene fades to white, and off-screen narration begins, with new scenes—initially in full color—of a basketball game fading into view: "Silence is what I hear after the handshake and slap of five. After 'what's happenin' homeboy?' 'What's up, cuz?' 'How ya feel girlfriend?' 'Blood.' 'Miss thang.'" The change in audio expressions, from what might be fairly coded as stereotypical heterosexual men to women (or men whose gender expressions meet heteronormative, social expectations of women), is the first nod to the stigma that Black gay men like Riggs endure from broader social communities.[46]

The shift from lighthearted scenes, such as the explanation of various "diva snaps" in the roughly 3.5 minute "Snap Expression," to the increasingly malignant recounting, by Riggs himself, of oppression along both racial and sexual orientation continuums, is quite jarring. In the latter sequence, "Marginalization," Riggs recounts the progressive alienation he experienced within the Black male community due to his sexuality, followed by the race-based hatred and slurs directed at him from the white community, and then class- and race-based accusations from Black teenagers ("Uncle Tom"). The sequence is primarily shots of Riggs, speaking against an empty black background, retelling the story of his life from early childhood to attending a prestigious school in Augusta, Georgia, interrupted by cuts to extreme close-ups of the lower portions of Black and white faces declaring the phrases noted above, with voice intonation conveying contempt above all else. The sequence ends with Riggs confessing his growing isolation because of the continued othering of his identities. At this point, the viewer is provided with an extreme close-up of Riggs's face, partially out of frame, as he continues to describe his alienation and trauma in an increasingly quavering voice and as the shot slowly fades to black.[47]

The following sequence features Riggs's move to San Francisco and his tasting "snow" and immersion in "vanilla." White gay men appear on the screen, accompanied by increasingly overdubbed chants of "let me taste it" and "let me lick it" in echoed whispers, followed by a sound that initially evokes heartbeats. The audio continues to play against a montage of men strolling about San Francisco's Castro District, with the camera eventually lingering on a physically fit white male eating while suggestively rubbing his own torso. As the heartbeats transform into ominous drums, Riggs observes how he was progressively internalizing hatred of his identities as he describes how white identities were privileged in various gay media, and how the Black identities depicted were often stereotypical, demeaning, and outright racist.[48]

At this point, and again in purposeful, abrupt contrast to the preceding series of shots, the montage shifts to racist magazine advertisements of Black women in harmful stereotypical and exploitative "Mammy" depictions; a magazine cover or advertisement with a "SLAVES FOR SALE" heading and a Black man in chains (also the submissive sadomasochism partner); a rough drawing or etching of a white man whipping a fleeing Black man from behind with his erect penis; and finally a comic-book-style depiction of a Black man with enormous genitalia, sculpted physique, and other exaggerated features, apparently covered in semen, with a speech bubble conveying stereotypical and objectifying assumptions about Black men's education, motivations, and bodies.

HIV/AIDS appears forcefully during the "Homophobia" sequence, which again uses the editing technique of cuts between extreme close-ups of Black faces (only mouths visible) voicing religious objections to being gay ("homosexuality") and what one might describe as "family-oriented" discrimination against gays ("I don't want him around me or my kids, period"). Periodically, the camera focuses on a close-up of Essex Hemphill as the chant of "Silence is my . . . " from the film's post-introductory sequence takes audio precedence.[49] Eventually, one of the nonreligious characters offers, "Yeah, man, like this AIDS shit, all the innocent victims, man. Mommas and babies dying 'cause of dope fiends and f—ts." This statement cuts to comedian Eddie Murphy and actors from Spike Lee's *School Daze* (1988) performing routines contemptuous of gay men, then cutting back to the close-up, silent image of Hemphill as the audio again returns to the conclusion of the "Silence is my . . . " chorus:

> Each joke levels us a little more, and we sit silently—sometimes join in the laughter, as if deep down, we too believe we are the lowest among the low.

Layers of Inequalities

The theoretical structure underpinning the documentary's narrative merits discussion as well. The concept of "intersectionality" was initially coined and explored by Kimberlé Crenshaw in her 1989 article "Demarginalizing the Intersection of Race and Sex: A Black Feminist Critique of Antidiscrimination Doctrine, Feminist Theory and Antiracist Politics." By centering the experiences of Black women, Crenshaw illustrates how race discrimination cases often erase their oppression by emphasizing "sex- or class-privileged Blacks," and sex discrimination discussions "focus . . . on race- and class-privileged women."[50] However, Crenshaw's conceptual insight may travel to other identities that have been erased or ignored due to intersecting power structures. Black gay men experience a distinct but similar problem: Sexual orientation discrimination issues tend to privilege white, socioeconomically advantaged identities, all while an additive layer of oppression arises within the identity of Black men, there subject to dominant heteronormative conceptions of "maleness."[51] In "Black Macho Revisited: Reflections of a SNAP! Queen," Riggs makes the traumas concrete: "From black gay men, this burden of (mis)representation is compounded. We are saddled by historic caricatures of the black male, now fused with newer notions of the Negro f——t. The resultant dehumanization is multilayered, and profound."[52]

As Crenshaw's accessible "basement" metaphor demonstrates, the two scenarios are not identical in terms of the degree and nature of erasure experienced.[53] Certainly, the concept of intersectionality should not be carelessly wrenched from its important contextual foundations, thereby further contributing to the social and legal erasure experienced by Black women.[54] But, as Riggs's work illustrates, the framework has potential application to power dynamics beyond its original focus, underscoring its continued salience—and perhaps explaining the hostility it continues to receive, particularly from the contemporary right wing of US politics.[55]

The final precredits sequence of the documentary directly addresses the stigma of being HIV/AIDS-positive, the final layer of silencing.[56] The techniques are familiar to the viewer by now: close-ups of Hemphill narrating in poetic form, his lip-synchronous, close-up shots interspersed with cuts to a close-up of a Black man, unnamed in the film, providing an insistent chant, with short exclamations of sexual pleasure increasingly punctuating the chant. Hemphill describes, in a vocal and visual delivery symbolizing the approach to sexual climax, how AIDS corrupts the purity and pleasure of the act of lovemaking ("This nut might . . . kill us").

Most notable is the visual montage that immediately follows: obituaries of Black men who died from HIV/AIDS and its complications, an approach that is far more direct than the symbolic Rolodex that features increasingly in *The Normal Heart,* maintained by Tommy Boatwright of the GMHC (Jim Parsons). As "friends, faces . . . disappear" from Riggs's life, an ominous clock ticking grows louder. The "revolution" that Riggs calls for at the conclusion of the segment, which segues into the credits sequence, calls for Black men to love other Black men and to cast off the internalized hatred of their own bodies, their own identities, perpetuated by broader society (white supremacy) and from within the Black male community (homophobia masquerading as masculinity). Empowered by the strength of Harriet Tubman, Frederick Douglass, Dr. Martin Luther King Jr., and others, represented by still and live images, the closing montage is a call for Black gay men to draw from the accumulated historical strength of overcoming racist violence. It empowers them to claim ownership in a narrative that previously excluded them, from within the gay community on account of race and from the Black male community on account of gender expectations and sexual orientation.

Similar to *The Normal Heart* in theme but with its own distinct emphases and unique delivery, Riggs's work is notable for effectively blending common editing and compositional techniques—the quick, interspersed cuts; the audio shifts from narrator to poetic reading to cacophonies; the fades to darkness; the close-ups; the lingering images; the montages—that make concrete the abstractions about the intersectional stigmatization of Black gay men for the uninitiated viewer.[57] In short, to convey the incredible degree of isolation, to convey being rendered invisible. Through this composition, Riggs's work demonstrates the power of established media, and depictions therein, for maintaining social identity expectations, which are generally established and imposed by relatively privileged identities. Through this experimental, documentary form of media—again in the relative "silence" of dedicated institutional press coverage—he exposes and then subverts many norms in the service of centering and affirming a minoritized identity. As Riggs later explained,

> What's encouraging is the degree to which you're seeing marginalized communities making use of this medium, both as a tool and an art form. . . . People are breathing new life into the form, as well as exploring new kinds of subjects with documentary, so I think it has a long and healthy life ahead even though public TV stations may not show it, and 60 Minutes may not broadcast it.[58]

FROM CONSCIOUSNESS TO VISIBILITY, WITHOUT THE FOURTH ESTATE

The individual and institutional editorial and publication decisions of the mainstream press are not the sole causes of all that followed in the HIV/AIDS crises in the United States (and the world), and coverage did indeed increase as time went on. Seemingly gone are the days when a White House press conference on the subject would be punctuated by laughter and dismissiveness, but the stigma and discrimination that beget dehumanization remain.[59] And the choice to not exercise a constitutional prerogative is still a choice. Of course, the power to decide what is newsworthy—a notoriously slippery term to define—will aways be part of the constitutionally protected press freedom. But the choice to *not* exercise the power of publication is an action with significant effects, too. After all, if the actions of the press are meaningless or without consequential value, it makes little sense to single out this institution for constitutional protection in the first place.

Media indifference and its effects may prove difficult to examine because they may be conceived of as little more than tough-to-assess, negative counterfactuals: How would this situation be different without these actions or this coverage?[60] That said, some historical events are quite notable for the lack of attention received despite checking off the common criteria for newsworthiness.[61] The 1980s HIV/AIDS crises in the United States, taken together, represent an unfortunate exemplar of this category.[62] *The Normal Heart* and *Tongues Untied* both explore a period of relative media indifference in the earlier years of those crises in the United States. Since those early days, there have been some well-known Hollywood film portrayals of individuals struggling with HIV/AIDS that highlight the social discrimination that follows an HIV-positive diagnosis.[63] But those films do not offer direct or obvious connections to media issues and resulting opportunities to explore the consequences of actions (or inaction) of the media. And these consequences should not be taken lightly. They include the fueling of stigma and dehumanization, the relationship between which, as Isabel Wilkerson describes it, is as follows:

> To dehumanize another human being is not merely to declare that someone is not human, and it does not happen by accident. . . . It takes energy and reinforcement to deny what is self-evident in another member of one's own species. It is harder to dehumanize a single person standing in front of you, wiping away tears at the loss of a loved one, just as you would. . . . Which is why people and groups who seek power and division do not bother with dehumanizing an individual. Better to attach a stigma, a taint of pollution to an entire group.[64]

The Normal Heart depicts the galvanization of a marginalized group identity (initially, mostly white gay men) in the face of erasure. Somewhat paradoxically, it was the failure of elite mainstream media to exercise its legal right to publish that helped to awaken a newfound social and political consciousness within that group. It depicts a turn to direct action and organization despite, or against, negligent institutions and a comparative lack of legal symbols, resources, and remedies.[65] Whether ironically or all-too-predictably, the GMHC's use of nonconventional media and "shock" tactics to inform the gay community and broader society about HIV/AIDS privileged some identities over others at the intersection of sexuality, gender, race, and HIV-positive/AIDS status.[66] Although breakdowns of early data suffer from apparent nonsystematic collection and disclosure, CDC reporting suggests that by 1985 (the year of the first run of Kramer's play), approximately 40 percent of HIV/AIDS diagnoses were among Black, non-Hispanic (~25 percent) and Hispanic (~15 percent) identities.[67] Despite this trend, the rise of the GMHC as depicted in the film adaptation of Kramer's 1985 play centers gay white identities in the HIV/AIDS narrative at the expense of BIPOC identities.[68] More recent efforts and interpretations of the play, including its casting, have been more diligent in centering these experiences.[69]

These dynamics, captured in each film analyzed here and which press decisions reflect and reinforce, in turn form and reinforce group identities.[70] *Tongues Untied* is an important example of how the power of the non-institutional press or experimental media can—perhaps must—be harnessed to affirm the identities and lives of those at the intersection of multiple, historically minoritized identities. Ultimately, these are not stories of victimization—they are ongoing narratives of empowerment.

NOTES

1. I am grateful to Dr. Robert Matson, University of Pittsburgh at Johnstown, for this working definition.

2. For a general but accessible, recent overview of the relationship between media and political behavior/identity formation, see Ezra Klein, *Why We're Polarized* (New York: Avid Reader, 2020), 139–70. The ability of the press (media) to affect identity formation is well documented; a Google Scholar search of "media influence on identity formation" produced dozens of examples of scholarship in this area.

3. See, for example, Eric Cervini, *The Deviant's War: The Homosexual vs. the United States of America* (New York: Farrar, Straus, and Giroux, 2020); Carlos A. Ball, *The First Amendment and LGBT Equality: A Contentious History* (Cambridge, MA: Harvard University Press, 2017), 15–25.

4. Iris Marion Young, *Justice and the Politics of Difference* (Princeton, NJ: Princeton University Press, 2011), 41.

5. Harry Nelson, "Outbreaks of Pneumonia among Gay Males Studied," *Los Angeles Times*, June 5, 1981, https://www.newspapers.com/clip/20691026/the-los-angeles-times/.

6. Lawrence K. Altman, "Rare Cancer Seen in 41 Homosexuals," *New York Times*, July 3, 1981, https://www.nytimes.com/1981/07/03/us/rare-cancer-seen-in-41-homosexuals.html.

7. Erin Blakemore, "This Was the First Major News Article on HIV/AIDS," *Smithsonian*, July 3, 2017, https://www.smithsonianmag.com/smart-news/was-first-major-news-article-hivaids-180963913/. Blakemore emphasizes the *New York Times* article, although the *Los Angeles Times* piece was published about a month prior.

8. "Global HIV & AIDS Statistics—Fact Sheet," UNAIDS, https://www.unaids.org/en/resources/fact-sheet (last accessed October 14, 2023). While HIV/AIDS is not a disease exclusive to or defining of any one race, gender, or sexual orientation, the effects have been disparate. For example, "[i]n 2020, key populations (sex workers and their clients, gay men and other men who have sex with men, people who inject drugs, transgender people) and their sexual partners accounted for 65% of HIV infections globally." Sub-Saharan African nations also account for many new cases, reflective of the substantial challenges facing that region. For an account of how

systemic and institutional structures produce disparate effects among subgroups of the population, see Steven W. Thrasher, *The Viral Underclass: The Human Toll When Inequality and Disease Collide* (New York: Celadon Books, 2022).

9. Lawrence K. Altman, "30 Years In, We Are Still Learning from AIDS," *New York Times*, May 30, 2011, italics added.

10. Lawrence Mass, "Disease Rumors Largely Unfounded," *New York Native*, May 18, 1981, https://gaycitynews.com/disease-rumors-largely-unfounded/. Mass became one of the founding members of the GMHC. As he described the article decades later, "The piece is largely this little interview with Steven Freeman; it was trying to allay any panic and trying to emphasize that we still just didn't know enough to make any conclusions, or to initiate any sweeping advisories at that moment. Clearly, there would have to be follow up on this, but, at least, for that moment, that's what we knew." See Mathew Rodriguez, "Before the Storm: The Inside Story of the Earliest News Coverage on HIV/AIDS," *The Body*, May 18, 2021, https://www.thebody.com/article/larry-mass-earliest-hiv-aids-news-coverage.

11. Larry Kramer, "1,112 and Counting," *New York Native*, March 27, 1983, https://www.losangelesblade.com/2020/05/27/march-27–1983–1112-and-counting/.

12. Harmon Leon, "How the Media, the White House, and Everyone Else Failed AIDS Victims in the 80s," *VICE*, December 1, 2016, https://www.vice.com/en/article/9b8q4y/aids-failure-1980s-reagan.

13. Leon, "Failed AIDS Victims in the 80s."

14. Justin McCarthy, "Gallup Vault: Fear and Anxiety During the 1980S AIDS Crisis," Gallup, June 28, 2019, https://news.gallup.com/vault/259643/gallup-vault-fear-anxiety-during-1980s-aids-crisis.aspx.

15. "History," Gay Men's Health Crisis, https://www.gmhc.org/history/ (last accessed April 4, 2023).

16. Isaac Butler, "Making an Art or Artlessness," *Slate*, May 27, 2020, https://slate.com/culture/2020/05/larry-kramer-normal-heart-play.html.

17. "The Normal Heart: Awards and Nominations," Academy of Television Arts and Sciences, https://www.emmys.com/shows/normal-heart (last accessed April 4, 2023). On portrayals of the AIDS crisis, HBO Films also released *Angels in America* to critical acclaim just over a decade prior to *The Normal Heart*; it too was originally a play (by Tony Kushner), though the time between it and film adaptation was considerably less (nearly thirty years for *The Normal Heart*, just over a decade for *Angels in America*). See, for example, Barry Garron, "'Angels in America': THR's 2003 Review," *Hollywood Reporter*, December 7, 2018, https://www.hollywoodreporter.com/tv/tv-news/angels-america-review-2003-hbo-tv-adaptation-1153657/.

18. Lillian Faderman, *The Gay Revolution: The Story of the Struggle* (New York: Simon and Schuster, 2016), 418.

19. Roy P. Madsen, *The Impact of Film: How Ideas are Communicated Through Cinema and Television* (New York: Macmillan, 1973), 45. Note also that the opening sequence of the film did not appear in the original play.

20. Madsen, *The Impact of Film*, 71–74.

21. Madsen, *The Impact of Film*, 34–38.

22. Emily Nussbaum, "How Ryan Murphy Became the Most Powerful Man in TV," *New Yorker*, May 7, 2018, https://www.newyorker.com/magazine/2018/05/14/how-ryan-murphy-became-the-most-powerful-man-in-tv.

23. Kaitlin Reilly, "The Hallmarks of a Ryan Murphy Show," *Refinery29*, September 27, 2019, https://www.refinery29.com/en-us/2018/06/200555/ryan-murphy-tv-shows-themes.

24. For a chronology and narrative of the pandemic's early days from a variety of perspectives—including of those slowly succumbing to the disease—see Randy Shilts, *And the Band Played On: Politics, People, and the AIDS Epidemic* (New York: St. Martin's Griffin, 2007).

25. Felix Turner may have been modeled after *New York Times* reporter John Duka, though Kramer denied the comparison. Dan Shaw, "Who Was John Duka? Looking for the Heart of *The Normal Heart*," *Vulture*, May 16, 2014, https://www.vulture.com/2014/05/looking-for-the-heart-of-the-normal-heart.html.

26. Brian Lowry, writing for *Variety,* noted Murphy's "characteristic lack of subtlety," by "throwing in moments that drift toward an 'American Horror Story' vibe, such as a subway sequence where dramatic lighting flashes in and out on lesion-pocked face," and yielding "speeches that probably played better live." Matt Seitz, for *Vulture,* found the film rightfully and necessarily unapologetic but also opined, "It is imprecise in its effects and sometimes clumsy and overbearing, and there are times when you might wish it would just shut the hell up (particularly when a character launches into yet another statistics-laced speech that sounds far too obviously "written"). See Lowry, "TV Review: 'The Normal Heart,'" *Variety*, May 21, 2014, https://variety.com/2014/tv/reviews/tv-review-the-normal-heart-1201183609/; Seitz, "HBO's Messy, Powerful, The Normal Heart Rages against AIDS Amnesia," *Vulture*, May 23, 2014, https://www.vulture.com/2014/05/tv-review-hbo-the-normal-heart.html.

27. See Shilts, *And the Band Played On*, 183–84.

28. The quotations around "marrying" are only to remind readers that same-sex marriage, as a matter of law, was not recognized by any state during the period depicted in the film.

29. Madsen, *The Impact of Film*, 27–52.

30. "Are We Suffering from AIDS Amnesia?" *Newsweek*, June 26, 2009, https://www.newsweek.com/are-we-suffering-aids-amnesia-222476.

31. Madsen, *The Impact of Film*, 48–49.

32. See, for example, William L. F. Felstiner, Richard L. Abel, and Austin Sarat, "The Emergence and Transformation of Disputes: Naming, Blaming, Claiming . . . " *Law & Society Review* 15, no. 3–4 (1980–81): 631–54.

33. Joshua C. Wilson, *The Street Politics of Abortion* (Stanford, CA: Stanford University Press, 2013), 17.

34. Wilson, *Street Politics of Abortion*, 111–30.

35. Laura Beth Nielsen, *License to Harass* (Princeton, NJ: Princeton University Press, 2004), 1–16.

36. The death of lead-role celebrity Rock Hudson from AIDS in 1985 changed mainstream news coverage approaches and may have also played a role in softening

attitudes toward those suffering from the disease. See Kat Eschner, "The Hollywood Star Who Confronted the AIDS 'Silent Pandemic,'" *Smithsonian*, October 2, 2017, https://www.smithsonianmag.com/smart-news/hollywood-star-who-confronted-aids-silent-epidemic-180965059/; and Shilts, *And the Band Played On*, 573–82.

37. Eric Sasson, "The Media Forgets That AIDS Is Still an Epidemic, but Hollywood Doesn't," *New Republic*, May 25, 2014, https://newrepublic.com/article/117897/hbos-normal-heart-reminds-us-aids-still-epidemic.

38. Centers for Disease Control, "HIV and AIDS: United States, 1981–2000," updated June 1, 2001, https://www.cdc.gov/mmwr/preview/mmwrhtml/mm5021a2.htm (last accessed October 14, 2023).

39. See Felstiner, Abel, and Sarat, "The Emergence and Transformation of Disputes," 631–36.

40. Library of Congress, "25 Eclectic Films Chosen for National Film Registry," December 14, 2022, https://newsroom.loc.gov/news/25-eclectic-films-chosen-for-national-film-registry/s/8c41f7a1-b9d9-4f9e-b252-4795b73a4aaf (last accessed April 4, 2023).

41. Walter Goodman, "Review/Television; Growing up Black and Homosexual in America," *New York Times*, July 15, 1991. See also Charles Stephens, "Why Black Gay Filmmaker Marlon Riggs Matters Now," *Advocate*, February 27, 2017, https://www.advocate.com/current-issue/2017/2/27/why-black-gay-filmmaker-marlon-riggs-matters-now.

42. "User Clip: Pat Buchanan Ad Featuring Tongues Untied," C-SPAN, February 28, 1992, https://www.c-span.org/video/?c4679699/user-clip-pat-buchanan-ad-featuring-tongues-untied. After its release, Riggs claimed copyright infringement and the advertisement was withdrawn soon after. In a distinct but related matter, standards of decency and respect considered in determining recipients for NEA funding were later upheld by the US Supreme Court in the First Amendment case *National Endowment for the Arts v. Finley*, 524 U.S. 569 (1998).

43. For Riggs's response, see Marlon Riggs, "Meet the New Willie Horton," *New York Times*, March 6, 1992, https://www.nytimes.com/1992/03/06/opinion/meet-the-new-willie-horton.html.

44. Tambay Obenson, "Marlon Riggs Shakes the Establishment: How a Personal Film on Black Gay Sexuality Stirred up National Debate," IndieWire, September 29, 2020, https://www.indiewire.com/2020/09/marlon-riggs-tongues-untied-controversy-1234582898/.

45. Ron Simmons, "*Tongues Untied*: An Interview with Marlon Riggs," in *Brother to Brother: New Writing by Black Gay Men*, ed. Essex Hemphill (New Orleans: RedBone Press, 2007), 236.

46. The concept of "intersectionality" was initially coined and explored by Kimberlé Crenshaw in 1989. See Kimberlé Crenshaw, "Demarginalizing the Intersection of Race and Sex: A Black Feminist Critique of Antidiscrimination Doctrine, Feminist Theory and Antiracist Politics," *University of Chicago Legal Forum* 8, no. 1 (1989): 139–67.

47. The voiceover is a reading of portions of Riggs's poem, "Tongues Untied," as featured in Hemphill's (and Beam's) collection, *Brother to Brother.* See Simmons, "An Interview with Marlon Riggs," 249–51.

48. This spoken dialogue in the film is also from Riggs, "Tongues Untied," in *Brother to Brother*, 252.

49. The emphasis on silence here echoes the famous "Silence=Death" poster designed by Avram Finkelstein and its eponymous collective in the mid-1980s. The poster, intentionally designed in the style of an advertisement (the "folk language of capitalism"), was adopted by what would become the group ACT UP. See Ivana Cruz, "The Story behind Silence=Death, an Icon of the LGBTQ+ Rights Movement," *W*, June 27, 2022, https://www.wmagazine.com/culture/avram-finkelstein-silence-equals-death-image-poster-act-up-interview.

50. Crenshaw, "Demarginalizing the Intersection of Race and Sex," 150–57.

51. Other scholars have more recently drawn on the concept of intersectionality to explain the health effects of the marginalization of gay Black men. See, for example, K. Quinn, L. Bowleg, and J. Dickson-Gomez, "'The Fear of Being Black Plus the Fear of Being Gay': The Effects of Intersectional Stigma on PrEP Use Among Young Black Gay, Bisexual, and Other Men Who Have Sex With Men," *Social Science and Medicine* 232 (2019): 86–93. For a review of the article's main findings and emphasis on the intersectional nature of the problem, see Krishen Samuel, "Being Black and Gay: How Intersectional Stigma Impacts on the Uptake of PrEP," aidsmap, May 17, 2019, https://www.aidsmap.com/news/may-2019/being-black-and-gay-how-intersectional-stigma-impacts-uptake-prep.

52. Marlon Riggs, "Black Macho Revisited: Reflections of a SNAP! Queen," in *Brother to Brother: New Writing by Black Gay Men*, ed. Essex Hemphill (New Orleans: RedBone Press, 2007), 326.

53. Crenshaw, "Demarginalizing the Intersection of Race and Sex," 151–52.

54. In a review of Hemphill's edited volume *Brother to Brother* and Riggs's contribution to the volume, "Tongues Untied," Arthur Flannigan-Saint-Aubin views these works as creating little space for the Black gay male reader and appear to be directed instead at white homosexuals and Black heterosexuals. He also argues for a reading of these works that is informed by feminist theory. See Arthur Flannigan-Saint-Aubin, "Black Gay Male Discourse: Reading Race and Sexuality Between the Lines," in *American Sexual Politics: Sex, Gender, and Race Since the Civil War*, ed. John C. Fout and Maura Shaw Tantillo (Chicago: University of Chicago Press, 1993): 381–403.

55. One author explicitly described some of Riggs's work as "early foundational texts of intersectionality . . . critiquing the contours and borders of black identity and imagining broader and more inclusive possibilities of our race." Specifically, Riggs viewed the backlash to *Tongues Untied* as a manifestation of white fear of Black sexuality and characterized himself as "the new Willie Horton." See Stephens, "Why Black Gay Filmmaker Marlon Riggs Matters Now."

56. Marlon Riggs and Essex Hemphill, featured prominently in the film, both died from AIDS complications, in 1995 and 1994, respectively.

57. For a useful review of these various editing techniques and what they are likely to evoke on the part of the viewer, see Madsen, *The Impact of Film*, 27–52.

58. Robert Anbian, "An Interview with Marlon Riggs: Tongues Untied Lets Loose Angry, Loving Words," 1990, https://newsreel.org/guides/Riggs-Guide/Release-Print-Riggs-Interview-1990.pdf (last accessed June 15, 2024).

59. Faderman, *The Gay Revolution*, 417–18. See also "Reagan Administration's Chilling Response to AIDS Crisis," YouTube, December 1, 2015, https://www.youtube.com/watch?v=yAzDn7tE1lU.

60. A theoretical basis for this problem can be found in Peter Bachrach and Morton Baratz's critique of then-prevailing elite and pluralist-oriented explanations for observable exercises of power. See Peter Bachrach and Morton S. Baratz, "Two Faces of Power," *American Political Science Review* 56, no. 4 (1962): 947–52.

61. Megan Hodgkiss, "Newsworthiness Guidelines for a Socially Responsible Press: Aligning Definitions at the Intersection of Journalism, Ethics, and the Law" (PhD Dissertation, Georgia State University, 2017), https://scholarworks.gsu.edu/communication_diss/88/.

62. Comparable dynamics and concerns outside of the US were unfolding during this period as well. See Shilts, *And the Band Played On*, 35–37, 193, 391–92, 499–501, 564–66.

63. Examples include *Philadelphia* (1993), *Precious* (2009), and *Dallas Buyer's Club* (2014).

64. Isabel Wilkerson, *Caste: The Origins of Our Discontents* (New York: Random House, 2020), 141.

65. See generally Patricia Ewick and Susan Silbey, *The Common Place of Law: Stories from Everyday Life* (Chicago: University of Chicago Press, 1998).

66. Kramer's play and adaptation is not the only one that can be critiqued on this point. See, for example, Steven Thrasher, "Why Is 'Angels in America' Still the Most Prominent Story Being Told about AIDS?" *Buzzfeed News*, March 25, 2018, https://www.buzzfeednews.com/article/steventhrasher/angels-in-america.

67. "U.S. HIV and AIDS Cases Reported Through December 1995," *HIV/AIDS Surveillance Report* 7, no. 2 (1995): 1. https://stacks.cdc.gov/pdfjs/web/viewer.html?file=https://stacks.cdc.gov/view/cdc/149062/cdc_149062_DS1.pdf.

68. This problem continues. See, for example, Shehzad Mansoor Bajowala, "The Invisibility of Intersectionality: Being Black and LGBTQ+," *The Acronym*, September 8, 2020, https://sites.imsa.edu/acronym/2020/09/08/the-invisibility-of-intersectionality-being-black-and-lgbtq/.

69. See, for example, Tracy E. Gilchrist, "The Normal Heart Stars BIPOC, LGBTQ+ Cast for ONE Archives World AIDS Day Encore," *Advocate*, November 23, 2021, https://www.advocate.com/theater/2021/4/30/normal-heart-stars-bipoc-lgbtq-cast-one-archives-performance; and Kirsten Chuba, "'The Normal Heart' Virtual Reading Set with Sterling K. Brown, Laverne Cox: 'It Doesn't Have to be about All White Gay Men,'" *Hollywood Reporter*, May 4, 2021, https://www

.hollywoodreporter.com/lifestyle/lifestyle-news/the-normal-heart-virual-sterling-k-brown-laverne-cox-4175871/.

70. Young, *Justice and the Politics of Difference*, 44.

Conclusion

The Cost of a Free Press

Helen J. Knowles-Gardner, Bruce E. Altschuler, and Brandon T. Metroka

Each of the films discussed in this book tells a story about what we now call the media. With a seemingly infinite number of possible stories available, how do moviemakers decide which ones are worth the large sums of money required to produce them? How do they tell their stories? How do these movies relate to the First Amendment and the law in general? Can we connect these films to the public's opinion of the media? These questions are representative of the analytical inquiries we have undertaken in this volume.

Bill Nichols believes that "film is central to the representation of values and beliefs, customs and practices in modern culture."[1] It tells stories through narrative but also by additional means such as visual images, the camera's viewpoint, music, and a variety of other nonverbal devices. Storytelling is also a fundamentally important part of the law. As such, film is a particularly appropriate and educational way in which to convey complex (and often controversial) principles of First Amendment freedom of the press law to diverse audiences. Stephen Pasky astutely observes that all legal rules are "literally a form of narrative in which the essential elements of a story—events, characters, and plot—have been reduced to general terms."[2] These legal rules originate in stories that stress some factors while omitting or minimizing others (as do movies). Don Rushing extends this to litigation, where each party tells a story whose purpose is to convince the judge or jury that it is preferable to the different narrative offered up by opposing counsel. "Virtually every argument you make in litigation can be reduced to a story," writes Rushing.[3] The law, in our case the law of freedom of the press, is a natural subject for films.

SELECTIVE STORYTELLING

Of course, as we have seen, *which* movies get made—and exactly *how* they tell their stories—is not simply dependent upon the quality of potential narratives out there and the interests of filmmakers. Most newspapers, television stations, and networks are private companies whose primary goal is to make a profit. Movies are also covered by the First Amendment, but only since 1952.[4] It isn't surprising that groups with the fewest resources are the least likely to receive press coverage and the least likely to be the subjects of movies.

What kind of stories are filmmakers likely to expect to be profitable enough to attract the large investments necessary to produce them? Because movies need to attract a large enough audience to make a profit, producers often try to avoid taking a position that would alienate one side or another on controversial issues (which, in the context of legal films, frequently sets them apart from the legal actors whose stories they are telling). One way for filmmakers to avoid this is for them to make movies that focus on individual stories and create characters that audiences will root for. Bob Woodward and Carl Bernstein have become symbols of heroic investigative reporters. Deborah Lipstadt defends her work against a Holocaust denier in court. Edward R. Murrow takes on a powerful demagogic senator. Adrian Cronauer advocates for ordinary soldiers despite opposition from the top brass. The Spotlight team tirelessly investigates powerful institutions, including the church. Chuck Lane and Michael Kelly both pursue journalistic integrity by exposing the fabrications of their colleague Stephen Glass. Even the mentally unbalanced Howard Beale is remembered for his iconic "I'm mad as hell and I'm not going to take this anymore" speech. Box office appeal will also be enhanced if movies are entertaining rather than simply civics lessons.

The movies in this book apply these guidelines in a variety of ways. The very first, *Good Morning, Vietnam*, uses the comedic talents of Robin Williams along with poignant, engaging, and entertaining music to make a serious point. *Network* paints a dystopian future for the media, but in the form of a satire that includes comedic elements and attention-grabbing speeches. And *The China Syndrome* and *All the President's Men* are structured as thrillers rather than political diatribes.

At the same time, most of these films are either based on real events or are documentaries. Even a fictional film such as *Citizen Kane* has a protagonist so similar to media mogul William Randolph Hearst that the real Hearst did everything in his power to prevent this less-than-flattering portrayal from being shown.

Nevertheless, mainstream Hollywood studios have often been reluctant to finance such serious movies. Despite the efforts of prominent director Ridley Scott, no studio was willing to finance *RKO 281*, forcing him to step aside in favor of a less prominent director. Additionally, the film was recast in order to obtain financing from HBO for a smaller-budget cable television film. Orson Welles was able to make *Citizen Kane* only because of his unprecedented contract with RKO, a freedom he would lose soon thereafter.

Given the financial constraints and pressures of the moviemaking industry (and media in general), it is unsurprising that so many films about press freedom feature white men as their protagonists. As the films that we have discussed clearly show, even where more recent films have made advances regarding the diversity of the individuals featured in the stories they tell, many stubborn stereotypes remain. And this is not simply because many of the events depicted took place in a past where discrimination (understood and defined broadly) met a very different social fate than is often the case today.

Take, for example, the role of women in the films to which we have devoted chapters. Yes, on the one hand we can applaud *The Post*, which was made in 2017 in part to highlight *Washington Post* publisher Katharine Graham's role in the dramatic press freedom events surrounding the Pentagon Papers case. This is certainly a cinematic advancement over *All the President's Men*, in which Graham was nowhere to be seen. And then there is 2016's *Denial*, which features a female lead. However, because she is an American defending herself in British courts, it is her male lawyers who take the lead in defending her case. To be sure, Kimberly Wells ultimately becomes a strong and tenacious female investigative reporter in *The China Syndrome*, but only by overcoming the obstacles of a heavily sexist workplace. And of course, the original script for the film did not even have a woman playing her role; instead, the tenacious investigative reporter was supposed to be a man (played by Richard Dreyfus). Certainly not least, there's the portrayal of Larry Flynt that glosses over or outright ignores his publication's misogynistic, violent depictions of women.

Other groups have been even less visible than women. Numerous reviewers and commentators have identified the problematic racial elements of *Good Morning, Vietnam*, from the portrayal of Vietnamese nationals to the character of Edward Garlick.[5] But the invisibility of—or visibility in an entirely negative light—of other groups dominates the films discussed in chapters 9 and 10. For example, *Out in the Night*, a documentary with limited distribution, told the story of a group of Black lesbians who found that the mainstream media and courts had turned them from victims of an assault into violent criminals. *The Normal Heart* is another HBO film, in this case about activists confronting media and a government that had ignored the AIDS epidemic affecting primarily gay men. Although the play it was based on ran in

1985, the cable television film was not made until 2014, when the public had become more sympathetic to the subject matter. Indeed, the support received by *Tongues Untied* from public broadcasting became a political issue in the 1992 Republican presidential primaries, discouraging future public funding for projects with controversial subjects. How should the government determine what role, if any, it should play in financing films on issues of public concern? All three films point toward ways in which various intersecting identities constitutive of the broader public are constructed by media coverage, and how alternative forms of media may be harnessed to push back against mainstream or otherwise uncritical accounts.

CHECKS AND BALANCES

One of the main reasons for originally singling out the press for protection was to ensure its ability to hold government accountable, what Vincent Blasi has called the checking function of the press.[6] As the famed broadcaster Walter Cronkite once observed, "Freedom of the press is not just important to democracy, it is democracy."[7]

Several of our films focus on how investigative reporting exposes misconduct and corruption both by government and other powerful groups. In *All the President's Men*, local *Washington Post* reporters expose the Nixon administration's corruption and what became known as the Watergate scandal. Their reporting led to further investigations that eventually forced Nixon to resign to avoid likely impeachment and removal from office. Despite fears that cuts in the budgets of media, particularly newspapers, would lead to far fewer investigative reports, more recent films suggest that reporters continue to perform their valuable checking role of uncovering misconduct. *Spotlight* shows a *Boston Globe* team exposing sexual abuse by priests who had been protected not only by the Catholic Church but also by police and public officials. *Out in the Night* is itself a piece of investigative journalism, calling out the police and mainstream media for unjust treatment of a group of Black lesbians who were assault victims yet were prosecuted for defending themselves against their attackers. In *Citizenfour*, director Laura Poitras becomes part of the story of Edward Snowden, a whistleblower who revealed a government program of surveillance of American citizens. This story is particularly dramatic because it shows Poitras and Snowden actually working on the story when Snowden was traveling around the world to avoid prosecution.

The court's main role has been to prevent prior restraints that stop the public from learning about the government misconduct these stories have exposed. Probably the most famous of these cases was the publication of the Pentagon Papers, the subject of *The Post*. The movie argues that because of the risk of criminal prosecution by the Nixon administration and the financial risks to her newspaper, *Washington Post* publisher Katharine Graham demonstrated extraordinary courage in deciding to authorize publication of the Papers, raising the question of whether other news media leaders will be willing to take such risks in the future.

While protecting the press against government interference, the courts have declined to give the media the right to protect the confidentiality of their sources. The most famous of these sources was "Deep Throat," so memorably dramatized in *All the President's Men*. The film made him even more memorable by inventing his often-quoted phrase, "Follow the money." Most states have moved to fill this void by enacting "shield laws" protecting this confidentiality, thus proving that it is not only the First Amendment that is needed to protect freedom of the press in its checking function. However, efforts to pass a federal shield law have yet to succeed.

DO EXCEPTIONS PROVE THE RULE?

Despite the absolute language of the Constitution ("Congress shall make no law . . . abridging the freedom of speech, or of the press"), the courts have allowed exceptions to free speech and the press. People who are damaged by false statements can try to collect damages for libel in court. As explained in chapter 6, the Supreme Court has provided extra protection for speech about public officials even if it proves false. As Justice William J. Brennan, Jr. explained in *New York Times v. Sullivan* (and as the court has elaborated upon in subsequent cases), the media should be free to criticize and hold accountable public officials and public figures; penalizing such criticisms when they contain mistakes should be limited to exceptional circumstances when the making of the mistakes was accompanied by "'actual malice'—that is, with knowledge that it was false or with reckless disregard of whether it was false."[8] As a result, very few libel suits by public officials or public figures against the press have succeeded. However, because American media outlets are now available throughout the world, public figures have sued Americans in other countries whose libel laws are more favorable to plaintiffs. *Denial* provides an example of how British courts treat libel cases. American historian Deborah Lipstadt was forced to provide evidence for the truth of her writing about the Holocaust in a court that used a very different standard of proof than American courts do.

National security has proven to be a particularly thorny issue for the American legal system to deal with. Although a majority of the Supreme Court upheld the right of the *New York Times* and the *Washington Post* to publish the top-secret Pentagon Papers, it also held that there is a very narrow national security exception that could justify a prior restraint. Because *The Post* told the story as one of the individual courage of Graham and her newspaper's reporters and editors, it paid little attention to the underlying legal issues. In *Good Morning, Vietnam*, Cronauer was fired for violating military broadcast guidelines while serving in a combat zone during the undeclared Vietnam conflict. The filmmakers preferred to tell a version of Cronauer's personal story instead of exploring the legal issues of the possible conflict between national security and the First Amendment. Because Snowden of *Citizenfour* evaded prosecution when Russia gave him sanctuary, whatever issues his case might raise have yet to be resolved in court.

Deliberate Intent addresses the question of whether a book can be so harmful that its publisher is liable for the damage it causes. Rodney Smolla, well known as an ardent First Amendment advocate, takes the opposite side in *Deliberate Intent*, arguing that the book *Hit Man* bore responsibility for a murder by providing instructions on how to get away with such a crime. The rarity of this bizarre exception to the First Amendment gave it curiosity appeal to audiences.

A final exception is obscenity. Larry Flynt is so widely reviled by much of the public that he is probably the least appealing protagonist of any of the films discussed in the preceding chapters. Indeed, the label "protagonist" itself may not resonate with many viewers or readers. That is the point of *The People vs. Larry Flynt*, which suggests that even a publisher of crude, sexually explicit material deserves First Amendment protection, and in some ways, even audience sympathy. Who could have guessed that the publication of an obscene parody advertisement in a smut magazine would lead to one of the court's strongest statements of speech and press freedoms in the *Falwell* case?[9]

PROFIT AND LOSS

Because media companies are largely privately owned enterprises whose primary goal is earning a profit, they often have to deal with conflicts between informing the public and making money. *The Post* demonstrated this most starkly when Graham had to decide whether to publish the Pentagon Papers at a time when the paper's publisher was about to issue stock as a public corporation. The company's lawyers, worried about the effect a criminal prosecution would have, urged her not to publish. Her decision to go against their advice helped the newspaper's reputation without harming its bottom line or her company's television stations. Although Murrow and his bosses at CBS also decided to go ahead with his programs critical of Senator McCarthy, their story is more complex. In exchange for his freedom, Murrow had to host *Person to Person*, a fluffy celebrity interview program. Eventually his news program, *See It Now*, lost advertisers, resulting in a less desirable time slot, fewer programs per season, and ultimately, cancellation. In *The China Syndrome*, a television reporter consigned to lightweight news features suddenly found herself reporting on the serious story of a nuclear reactor accident. Much of the film's suspense focuses on whether her determination to report the story accurately will prevail over her station management's desire not to alienate sponsors.

As the press morphed into the media, with audiences moving from print to television to social media for their news, revenues grew. Television news, once a loss leader, became profitable. Opinionated cable news emerged. Facebook and other social media companies became among the largest corporations in the world. *Network* predicted a world in which television's insatiable greed for ratings and profits would overtake its interest in providing important news to the public. Even though many of the most prominent figures of the time ridiculed its depictions of news as entertainment as alarmist exaggeration, much of what it predicted has come true. The gentler *The Social Network* shows how an undergraduate's project originally meant to provide students with a way to communicate with their friends and family grew into a giant corporation that has become a main source of news for much of the public while supplying advertisers with considerable data about potential customers and generating profits for Facebook (now Meta).

FAKE NEWS

All the President's Men represented the high-water mark for public approval of the press. Since then, as documented in several chapters, the public has rated the media less and less favorably. Some moviemakers, most notably Steven Spielberg, hoped to make films that would rehabilitate the media in the public's view. However, even a popular movie like *The Post* has had no long-term (and not much short-term) impact on public opinion. The news media has simply lost much of its credibility.

Symptomatic of the problem is the growth of the concept of "fake news." Chapter 7 quoted a commonly cited definition as "fabricated information that mimics news media content in form but not in organizational process or intent."[10] Its outlets lack the editorial safeguards for checking accuracy. The difference between what might be termed, for want of a better term, real and fake news is the intent and process of the publisher.

Fake news has existed for a long time. Charles Foster Kane's "You provide the prose poems; I'll provide the war" was a deliberate reflection of a supposedly similar declaration by real life media mogul William Randolph Hearst, also about inventing stories to sensationalize events in Cuba in the late nineteenth century.

Despite the previously mentioned safeguards, there have been dramatic failures at even the most prestigious publications. *Shattered Glass* demonstrated how Stephen Glass defeated the editorial processes of the *New Republic* to publish numerous fabricated stories. It took what the film portrays as the dedicated efforts of conscientious editor Chuck Lane to uncover Glass's deceptions and ultimately retract the false articles. Even Ben Bradlee, the *Washington Post* editor celebrated in *All the President's Men* and *The Post*, was deceived by reporter Janet Cooke, whose story "Jimmy's World," about an eight-year-old heroin addict who in fact did not exist, won a Pulitzer Prize in 1981. When the newspaper learned the truth, it returned the prize. According to his biographer, Jeff Himmelman, Bradlee thought that "by far, this was the big black eye of his career." To Howard Kurtz, "it was a harbinger of all kinds of journalistic scandals to come."[11] After the *New York Times* discovered at least thirty-six examples of fraud in reporter Jayson Blair's stories, Steven Roberts noted that "there are no official methods of accountability in journalism—no review boards, no licensing procedures."[12] The First Amendment prevents the same kind of licensing used for other professions, such as doctors or lawyers, from being used by government to license reporters or others involved in dissemination of the news. This, of course, points toward another legal question without definitive answer touched upon in chapter 8: Who exactly is a journalist—or member of "the press"—anyway?

Chapter 7, by contrast, discusses a different use of the term "fake news" that applies it to any coverage one doesn't like. It is a phrase frequently used by Donald Trump as part of his campaign to discredit the mainstream media, a goal he freely admitted to in an interview cited in chapter 3. Although most presidents have grumbled about negative press coverage, direct public attacks are a fairly recent phenomenon that some scholars suggest started during the Nixon administration with a 1969 speech in Des Moines by Vice President Spiro Agnew criticizing the media as biased in favor of liberalism. Despite, according to Dale Cressman, being "seemingly tame" compared to Trump's rhetoric, the speech was "an inflection point in the relationship between journalists and the president," making it more adversarial.[13] Nixon told his staff that it was "good politics to kick the press around."[14]

Network and *The Social Network* show how, as television and social media have provided more of the public's information, the processes and intent that filtered out misinformation and lies have become a relatively small part of the news universe. As one article observed, studies of fact checking's effectiveness have proved "at best mixed" because much of the public tends to view and believe information consistent with their preconceptions.[15]

Artificial intelligence (AI) may make the problem dramatically worse. According to a study by Jack Brewster of NewsGuard, during the last half of 2023, the number of websites with false AI-created articles increased from 49 to 603. He found that "some of these sites are generating hundreds if not thousands of articles a day."[16]

The films in this book are, for the most part, either celebrations of freedom of the press or relatively friendly criticisms of the media's flaws. In contrast, public approval of the news media has become increasingly unfavorable since *All the President's Men*'s celebration of the press's role in the downfall of President Nixon. Because, with the relatively narrow exception of libel, the First Amendment's guarantee of a free press protects both true and false stories, reversing this trend will likely prove extremely difficult, particularly given the political and financial incentives facing government and the media.

The simplicity of the First Amendment's command that "Congress shall make no law . . . abridging the freedom of speech, or of the press" would seem to limit the ability of filmmakers to tell interesting press freedom stories. If neither the federal government nor the states (since the ratification of the Fourteenth Amendment in 1868) shall make any law restricting press freedom, then where is the drama? Where is the suspense? Are there really any audience attention-grabbing stories to be told? Quite apart from the fact that no US Supreme Court justice has ever hewed to an absolutist position that the First Amendment's "no law" actually means "no law,"[17] the movies analyzed in this volume demonstrate that within this subject matter there are plenty of suspenseful, dramatic, and absorbing stories to be found and told by the world of cinema. Indeed, there was no shortage of movies for us to choose from when compiling this volume about filming the First.

NOTES

1. Bill Nichols, *Engaging Cinema: An Introduction to Film* Studies (New York: Norton, 2010), xix.

2. Stephen Paskey, "The Law Is Made of Stories: Erasing the False Dichotomy between Stories and Legal Rules," *Legal Communication and Rhetoric* 11 (2014): 52.

3. Don G. Rushing, "Storytelling," *Litigation Chicago* 49 (Spring 2023): 18.

4. *Burstyn v. Wilson*, 343 U.S. 495 (1952).

5. Hal Hinson, "'Good Morning, Vietnam,'" *Washington Post*, January 15, 1988; Carla A. Fellers, "'What a Wonderful World': The Rhetoric of the Official and the Unofficial in Good Morning, Vietnam," *War, Literature & the Arts: An International Journal of the Humanities* 17, no. 1/2 (November 2005): 232–41.

6. Vincent Blasi, "The Checking Value in First Amendment Theory," *American Bar Foundation Research Journal* 3, no. 3 (July 1977): 521–649.

7. This famous quote appears in a generally very informative and interesting newspaper editorial "Freedom of the Press Is Never Your Enemy," *Newnan Times-Herald* (Newnan, GA), August 15, 2018, https://www.times-herald.com/opinion/freedom-of-the-press-is-never-your-enemy/article_48e593e0-c366-5156-9c74-b8f3d88c096a.html.

8. *New York Times v. Sullivan*, 376 U.S. 254, 280 (1964).

9. *Hustler v. Falwell,* 485 U.S. 46 (1988).

10. Daniel M. J. Lazer et al., "The Science of Fake News: Addressing Fake News Requires a Multidisciplinary Effort," *Science* 359, no. 6380 (March 9, 2018): 1094.

11. Mike Sager, "The Fabulist Who Changed Journalism," *Columbia Journalism Review*, June 1, 2016, https://www.cjr.org/the_feature/the_fabulist_who_changed_journalism.php.

12. Howard Kurtz, "N.Y. Times Uncovers Dozens of Faked Stories by Reporter," *Washington Post*, May 11, 2003.

13. Dale L. Cressman, "Agnew, ABC and Richard Nixon's War on Television," *Journalism History* 46 (December 2020): 2.

14. Jill Lepore, "Does Journalism Have a Future?" *New Yorker*, January 21, 2019, https://www.newyorker.com/magazine/2019/01/28/does-journalism-have-a-future.

15. Lazer et al., "The Science of Fake News," 1095.

16. Pranshu Verma, "The Rise of AI Fake News is Creating a 'Misinformation Superspreader,'" *Washington Post*, December 17, 2023.

17. Although Justice Hugo Black declared himself an absolutist, he did find some expression unprotected by the First Amendment. See Michael Paris and Kevin J. McMahon, "Absolutism and Democracy: Hugo L. Black's Free Speech Jurisprudence," in *Judging Free Speech: First Amendment Jurisprudence of US Supreme Court Justices*, ed. Helen J. Knowles and Steven B. Lichtman (New York: Palgrave Macmillan, 2015), 75–97.

Bibliography

Adair, Gilbert. *Hollywood's Vietnam*. London: Heinemann, 1989.

———. *Vietnam on Film: From the Green Berets to Apocalypse Now*. New York: Proteus, 1981.

Alexander, Michelle. *The New Jim Crow: Mass Incarceration in the Age of Colorblindness*. New York: New Press, 2010.

Allen, Danielle. *Cuz: Or the Life and Times of Michael A*. New York: Liveright Publishing, 2017.

Alterman, Eric. "All Rupert, All the Time." *Nation*, August 13, 2007, 10.

Altschuler, Bruce E. "Is the Pentagon Papers Case Relevant in the Age of Wikileaks?" *Political Science Quarterly* 130 (Fall 2015): 401–23.

Amar, Akhil Reed. *The Bill of Rights: Creation and Reconstruction*. New Haven, CT: Yale University Press, 1998.

Anderson, C. W., Leonard Downie Jr., and Michael Schudson. *The News Media: What Everyone Needs to Know*. New York: Oxford University Press, 2016.

Andrews, Peter, and Edward Sorel. "The Press." *American Heritage*, October 1994, 36–54.

"The Awareness Doctrine." *Harvard Law Review* 135 (2022): 1907–28.

Azriel, Joshua, and Jeff DeWitt. "'We Fight Like Hell': Applying the *Brandenburg* Test to Trump's Speech Surrounding the Siege at the U.S. Capitol." *Criminal Law Practitioner* 12, no. 2 (February 2022): 23–56.

Baccanti, Anna. *Screening the Creative Process: Genius, Gender, and the Contemporary Biopic*. Paderborn, Germany: Brill | Fink, 2023.

Bachrach, Peter, and Morton S. Baratz. "Two Faces of Power." *American Political Science Review* 56, no. 4 (1962): 947–52.

Ball, Carlos A. *The First Amendment and LGBT Equality: A Contentious History*. Cambridge, MA: Harvard University Press, 2017.

Baranauskas, A. J., and K. M. Drakulich. "Media Construction of Crime Revisited: Media Types, Consumer Contexts, and Frames of Crime and Justice." *Criminology* 4, no. 56 (2018): 679–714.

Barnhurst, Kevin G., and John Nerone. *The Form of News: A History*. New York: Guilford, 2001.

Bayley, Edwin R. *Joe McCarthy and the Press*. Madison: University of Wisconsin Press, 1981.

Bazin, André. *Orson Welles: A Critical View*. Venice, CA: Acrobat Books, 1992.

Beckerman, Gal. "Facts and Fictions: Shards of Glass." *Columbia Journalism Review* 42, no. 3 (September/October 2003): 54–55.

Bennett, W. Lance, Regina G. Lawrence, and Steven Livingston. *When the Press Fails: Political Power and the News Media from Iraq to Katrina*. Chicago: University of Chicago Press, 2007.

Bickel, Alexander M. *The Morality of Consent*. New Haven, CT: Yale University Press, 1975.

Biddle, Francis. *In Brief Authority*. New York: Doubleday, 1962.

Bishop, Ronald. "'Not an Ounce of Hollywood Bullshit': A Narrative Analysis of News Media Coverage of Spotlight's Oscar Win." *Journal of Communication Inquiry* 44, no. 2 (2020): 157–77.

Blasi, Vincent. "The Checking Value in First Amendment Theory." *American Bar Foundation Research Journal* 3, no. 3 (July 1977): 521–649.

Bluestone, Cheryl. "Feature Films as a Teaching Tool." *College Teaching* 48, no. 4 (2000): 141–46.

Bordwell, David. "Intensified Continuity Visual Style in Contemporary American Film." *Film Quarterly* 55, no. 3 (2002): 16–28.

Boynton, Robert S. "Checkbook Journalism Revisited." *Columbia Journalism Review* 46, no. 5 (January/February 2008): 12–14.

Bradlee, Ben. *A Good Life: Newspapering and Other Adventures*. New York: Simon and Schuster, 1995.

Brown, Bruce D., and Clarissa Pintado. "The Small Steps of the SPEECH Act." *Virginia Journal of International Law Digest* 54 (2014): 1–14.

Bybee, Keith J., and Laura E. Jenkins. "Free Speech, Free Press, and Fake News: What If the Marketplace of Ideas Isn't about Identifying Truth?" In *Free Speech Theory: Understanding the Controversies*, edited by Helen J. Knowles and Brandon T. Metroka, 95–118. New York: Peter Lang, 2020.

Callow, Simon. *Orson Welles. Vol. 1: The Road to Xanadu*. New York: Viking, 1996.

Calvert, Clay. "And You Call Yourself a Journalist? Wrestling with a Definition of 'Journalist' in the Law." *Dickinson Law Review* 103, no. 2 (1998–1999): 411–51.

Calvert, Clay, and Robert D. Richards. "Adult Entertainment and the First Amendment: A Dialogue and Analysis with the Industry's Leading Litigator." *Vanderbilt Journal of Entertainment and Technology Law* 6, no. 2 (2004): 147–79.

Campbell, W. Joseph. *Yellow Journalism: Puncturing the Myths, Defining the Legacies*. Westport, CT: Praeger, 2001.

Canby, Vincent. "Chayefsky's 'Network' Bites Hard as a Film Satire of TV Industry." *New York Times*, November 15, 1976.

Candeub, Adam, and Eugene Volokh. "Interpreting 47 U.S.C. §230(C) (2)." *Journal of Free Speech Law* 1 (2021): 175–90.

Carringer, Robert L. *The Making of Citizen Kane*. Berkeley: University of California Press, 1985.

Cervini, Eric. *The Deviant's War: The Homosexual vs. the United States of America*. New York: Farrar, Straus and Giroux, 2020.

Chadwick, Alex. "'Citizen Kane' Actress Lets Out 'Secret.'" *Weekend All Things Considered*, April 27, 1991.

Chayefsky, Paddy. *The Collected Works of Paddy Chayefsky: The Screenplays*, vol. 2. New York: Applause Books, 2000.

Chin, Cassandra M. "Holding the Publisher of a 'Murder Manual' Liable for Aiding and Abetting Murder: A Travesty against Free Speech." *George Mason University Civil Rights Law Journal* 10, no. 1 (1999): 205–26.

Citron, Danielle Keats. *The Fight for Privacy: Protecting Dignity, Identity, and Love in the Digital Age*. New York: Norton, 2022.

Collins, Ronald K. L., and Sam Chaltain. *We Must Not Be Afraid to Be Free: Stories of Free Expression in America*. New York: Oxford University Press, 2011.

Comstock, George, and Erica Scharrer. *The Psychology of Media and Politics*. Boston: Elsevier Academic Press, 2005.

Crenshaw, Kimberlé. "Demarginalizing the Intersection of Race and Sex: A Black Feminist Critique of Antidiscrimination Doctrine, Feminist Theory and Antiracist Politics." *University of Chicago Legal Forum* 8, no. 1 (1989): 139–67.

Cressman, Dale L. "Agnew, ABC and Richard Nixon's War on Television." *Journalism History* 46 (December 2020): 1–27.

Cronauer, Adrian. "The Twenty-Third Charles L. Decker Lecture in Administrative and Civil Law." *Military Law Review* 183 (2005): 176–86.

Curtis, Michael Kent. *Free Speech, 'The People's Darling Privilege': Struggles for Freedom of Expression in American History*. Durham, NC: Duke University Press, 2000.

Danchev, Alex. "Troublemakers: Laura Poitras and the Problem of Dissent." *International Affairs* 91, no. 2 (March 2015): 381–92.

Day, Christian C., Michael P. Walls, and Lisa A. Dolak. "Riding the Rapids: Financing the Leveraged Transaction without Getting Wet." *Syracuse Law Review* 41, no. 2 (1990): 661–740.

Donovan, Robert J. *Tumultuous Years: The Presidency of Harry S. Truman, 1949–1953*. Columbia: University of Missouri Press, 1996.

Drabble, Margaret, ed. *The Oxford Companion to English Literature*. 5th ed. Oxford: Oxford University Press, 1985.

Duhon, Madelyn K. "Journalist and Hoaxer: William Francis Mannix and the Long History of Faked News." Master's thesis, Louisiana State University, 2017.

Ebert, Robert. *Roger Ebert's Movie Home Companion: 1988 Edition*. Kansas City, MO: Andrews McMeel, 1987.

Edwards, Bob. *Edward R. Murrow and the Birth of Broadcast Journalism*. New York: Wiley, 2004.

Ehrlich, Matthew C. "Hollywood and Journalistic Truthtelling." *Notre Dame Journal of Law, Ethics and Public Policy* 19, no. 2 (2005): 519–40.

———. "Radio Prototype: Edward R. Murrow and Fred Friendly's Hear It Now." *Journal of Broadcasting and Electronic Media* 51, no. 3 (2007): 438–56.

———. "*Shattered Glass*, Movies, and the Free Press Myth." *Journal of Communication Inquiry* 29, no. 2 (April 2005): 103–18.

Emerson, Thomas I. *The System of Freedom of Expression*. New York: Random House, 1970.

Evans, Peter. "The Pathology of Denial." In *How Was It Possible? A Holocaust Reader*, edited by Peter Hayes, 821–41. Lincoln: University of Nebraska Press, 2015.

Ewick, Patricia, and Susan Silbey. *The Common Place of Law: Stories from Everyday Life*. Chicago: University of Chicago Press, 1998.

Faderman, Lillian. *The Gay Revolution: The Story of the Struggle*. New York: Simon and Schuster, 2016.

Fagan, Beth A. "*Rice v. Paladin Enterprises*: Why *Hit Man* Is Beyond the Pale." *Chicago-Kent Law Review* 76, no. 1 (2000): 603–36.

Faulkner, Richard. *Pershing's Crusaders: The American Soldier in World War I*. Lawrence: University Press of Kansas, 2017.

Feeney, Mark. *Nixon at the Movies: A Book About Belief*. Chicago: University of Chicago Press, 2004.

Fellers, Carla A. "'What a Wonderful World': The Rhetoric of the Official and the Unofficial in *Good Morning, Vietnam*." *War, Literature & the Arts: An International Journal of the Humanities* 17, no. 1/2 (November 2005): 232–41.

Felstiner, William L. F., Richard L. Abel, and Austin Sarat. "The Emergence and Transformation of Disputes: Naming, Blaming, Claiming . . . " *Law & Society Review* 15, no. 3–4 (1980–81): 631–54.

Feral, Rex. *Hit Man: A Technical Manual for Independent Contractors*. Boulder, CO: Paladin, 1983.

Flannigan-Saint-Aubin, Arthur. "Black Gay Male Discourse: Reading Race and Sexuality between the Lines." In *American Sexual Politics: Sex, Gender, and Race Since the Civil War*, edited by John C. Fout and Maura Shaw Tantillo, 381–403. Chicago: University of Chicago Press, 1993.

Foster, James C. "Justice Civility: William J. Brennan Jr.'s Free Speech Jurisprudence," in *Judging Free Speech: First Amendment Jurisprudence of US Supreme Court Justices*, edited by Helen J. Knowles and Steven B. Lichtman, 123–46. New York: Palgrave Macmillan, 2015.

———. "No Neutrality: Hobbesian Constitutionalism in the Internet Age." In *Free Speech Theory: Understanding the Controversies*, edited by Helen J. Knowles and Brandon T. Metroka, 33–62. New York: Peter Lang, 2020.

Frenkel, Sheera, and Cecilia Kang. *An Ugly Truth: Inside Facebook's Battle for Domination*. New York: Harper, 2021.

Frost, Jacqueline B. *Conversations with Contemporary Cinematographers: The Eye behind the Lens*. London: Routledge, 2021.

Fuller, Kathryn. "Review: *The People vs. Larry Flynt* by Oliver Stone and Milos Forman." *Journal of American History* 84, no. 3 (1997): 1185.

George, Alexander L., and Andrew Bennett. *Case Studies and Theory Development in the Social Sciences*. Cambridge, MA: MIT Press, 2005.

Ghiglione, Loren. *CBS's Don Hollenbeck: An Honest Reporter in the Age of McCarthyism*. New York: Columbia University Press, 2008.

Gillers, Stephen. *Journalism Under Fire: Protecting the Future of Investigative Reporting*. New York: Columbia University Press, 2018.

Gilman, Owen W., Jr. "Vietnam, Chaos, and the Dark Art of Improvisation." In *Inventing Vietnam: The War in Film and Television*, edited by Michael A. Anderegg, 231–50. Philadelphia: Temple University Press, 1991.

Giroux, Henry A. "Memory and Pedagogy in the 'Wonderful World of Disney': Beyond the Politics of Innocence." In *From Mouse to Mermaid: The Politics of Film, Gender, and Culture*, edited by Elizabeth Bell, Lynda Haas, and Laura Sells, 43–61. Bloomington: Indiana University Press, 1995.

Glasser, Theodore L., and James S. Ettema. "Investigative Journalism and the Moral Order." *Critical Studies in Mass Communication* 6, no. 1 (1989): 1–20.

Goldman, William. *Adventures in the Screen Trade: A Personal View of Hollywood and the Screenwriting*. New York: Warner Books, 1983.

Goodman, Ezra. *The Fifty-Year Decline and Fall of Hollywood*. New York: Simon and Schuster, 1961.

Gragg, Larry. "Order vs. Liberty." *American History* 33 (October 1998): 24–32.

Graham, Katherine. *Personal History*. New York: Vintage, 2011.

Greenbaum, Dov. "Is It Really Possible to Do the Kessel Run in Less than Twelve Parsecs and Should It Matter: Science and Film and Its Policy Implications." *Vanderbilt Journal of Entertainment and Technology Law* 11, no. 2 (2009): 249–334.

Greenblatt, Leah. "Denial." *Entertainment Weekly*, October 7, 2016, 41.

Gronke, Paul, and Timothy Cook. "Disdaining the Media: The American Public's Changing Attitudes toward the News." In *Media Power in Politics*, 6th ed., edited by Doris A. Graber. Washington, DC: CQ Press, 2011.

Gunther, Gerald. "Learned Hand and the Origins of Modern First Amendment Doctrine: Some Fragments of History." *Stanford Law Review* 27, no. 3 (February 1975): 719–74.

Hamilton, James T. *Democracy's Detectives: The Economics of Investigative Journalism*. Cambridge, MA: Harvard University Press, 2016.

Hare, David. "Foreword." In *Denial: Holocaust History on Trial*, by Deborah E. Lipstadt, xiii–xvi. New York: Ecco, 2016.

Hoberman, J. "RKO 281." *Film Comment*, January/February, 2000, 75–77.

Holzer, Harold. *The Presidents vs. the Press*. New York: Dutton, 2020.

Horowitz, Susan. "Paddy Chayefsky Speaks Out." *Saturday Review*, November 13, 1976, 45–47.

Howells, Richard. *Visual Culture*, 3rd ed. Medford, MA: Polity Press, 2019.

Itzkoff, Dave. *Mad as Hell: The Making of Network and the Fateful Vision of the Angriest Man in Movies*. New York: Times Books, 2014.

Irons, Peter. *The Courage of Their Convictions: Sixteen Americans Who Fought Their Way to the Supreme Court*. New York: Penguin, 1988.

Jennings, Marianne M. "Where Are Our Minds and What Are We Thinking—Virtue Ethics for a Perfidious Media." *Notre Dame Journal of Law, Ethics and Public Policy* 19, no. 2 (2005): 637–704.

Johnson, Vincent R. "Comparative Defamation Law: England and the United States." *University of Miami International and Comparative Law Review* 24, no. 1 (Fall 2016): 1–97.

Kalven, Harry, Jr. "The New York Times Case: A Note on 'The Central Meaning of the First Amendment.'" *Supreme Court Review* 1964 (1964): 191–221.

Kang, John M. "Symposium: The Worst Supreme Court Case Ever? *Hustler v. Falwell*: Worst Case in the History of the World, Maybe the Universe." *Nevada Law Journal* 12, no. 3 (2012): 582–90.

Karnow, Stanley. *Vietnam: A History*. 2nd ed. New York: Penguin, 1997.

Keck, Thomas M., Brandon T. Metroka, and Richard Price. "The Judicial Protection of Anti-Judicial Speech." *American University International Law Review* 33, no. 4 (2018): 693–769.

Kelly, Michael. "Master of the Game." In *Things Worth Fighting For: Collected Writings*, 53–79. New York: Penguin, 2004.

———. *Things Worth Fighting For: Collected Writings*. New York: Penguin, 2004.

Kemp, Philip. "Denial." *Sight and Sound*, February 2017, 74–75.

Klein, Ezra. *Why We're Polarized*. New York: Avid Reader, 2020.

Knowles, Helen J. *Making Minimum Wage: Elsie Parrish Versus the West Coast Hotel Company*. Norman: University of Oklahoma Press, 2021.

Knowles, Helen J., and Steven B. Lichtman. "Introduction: Oh What a Tangled Web They Weave." In *Judging Free Speech: First Amendment Jurisprudence of US Supreme Court Justices*, edited by Helen J. Knowles and Steven B. Lichtman, 1–26. New York: Palgrave Macmillan, 2015.

Knowles, Helen J., and Steven B. Lichtman, eds. *Judging Free Speech: First Amendment Jurisprudence of US Supreme Court Justices*. New York: Palgrave Macmillan, 2015.

Knowles, Helen J., and Brandon T. Metroka, eds. *Free Speech Theory: Understanding the Controversies*. New York: Peter Lang, 2020.

Knowles, Helen J., and Brandon T. Metroka. "Introduction: Why Free Speech Theory Matters." In *Free Speech Theory: Understanding the Controversies*, edited by Helen J. Knowles and Brandon T. Metroka,1–32. New York: Peter Lang, 2020.

Kolker, Robert P. *Film, Form, and Culture*. 4th ed. New York: Routledge, 2015.

Koresky, Michael. "Liberty Films." *Film Comment* 54, no. 1 (January–February 2018): 52–56.

Kunz, Don. "Barry Levinson's Good Morning, Vietnam." *War, Literature & the Arts: An International Journal of the Humanities* 14, no. 1/2 (March 2002): 230–37.

Lair, Meredith H. *Armed with Abundance: Consumerism & Soldiering in the Vietnam War*. Chapel Hill: University of North Carolina Press, 2011.

Langvardt, Arlen W. "Stopping the End-Run by Public Plaintiffs: Falwell and the Refortification of Defamation Law's Constitutional Aspects." *American Business Law Journal* 26 (1988): 665–708.

Lawson, M. Asher, Shikhar Anand, and Hemant Kakkar. "Tribalism and Tribulations: The Social Costs of Not Sharing Fake News." *Journal of Experimental Psychology: General* 152, no. 3 (2023): 611–31.

Lazer, Daniel M. J., et al. "The Science of Fake News: Addressing Fake News Requires a Multidisciplinary Effort." *Science* 359, no. 6380 (March 9, 2018): 1094–96.

LeBel, Paul A. "Emotional Distress, the First Amendment, and This Kind of Speech: A Heretical Perspective on *Hustler Magazine v. Falwell*." *University of Colorado Law Review* 60 (1989): 315–56.

Lebo, Harlan. *Citizen Kane: A Filmmaker's Journey*. New York: Thomas Dunne, 2016.

Levy, Leonard W. "Did the Zenger Case Really Matter? Freedom of the Press in Colonial New York." *William and Mary Quarterly* 17, no. 1 (January 1960): 35–50.

Levy, Steven. *Facebook: The Inside Story*. New York: Blue Rider Press, 2020.

Lipstadt, Deborah E. *Denial: Holocaust History on Trial*. Movie tie-in ed. New York: Ecco, 2016.

———. *Denying the Holocaust: The Growing Assault on Truth and Memory*. New York: Free Press, 1993.

Lopate, Phillip. "The Medium and Its Conscience: George Clooney's Good Night, and Good Luck Recreates One of the Most Dramatic Chapters in Television History." *Film Comment*, September–October 2005, 30–34, 37.

Lumet, Sidney. *Making Movies*. New York: Vintage, 1996.

Macnab, Geoffrey. "Good Night, and Good Luck." *Sight and Sound* 15, no. 11 (2005): 26.

Madsen, Roy P. *The Impact of Film: How Ideas Are Communicated through Cinema and Television*. New York: Macmillan, 1973.

Mahler, Jonathan. "What Rupert Wrought," *New York*, April 11, 2005, 28–36.

Marantz, Andrew. *Antisocial: Online Extremists, Techno-Utopians, and the Hijacking of the American Conversation*. New York: Viking, 2019.

Markin, Karen. "The Truth Hurts: Intentional Infliction of Emotional Distress as a Cause of Action against the Media." *Communication Law & Policy* 5, no. 4 (2000): 469–503.

McGinnis, Joe. *The Selling of the President 1968*. New York: Simon and Schuster, 1969.

McLuhan, Marshall. *Understanding Media: The Extensions of Man*. New York: McGraw-Hill, 1964.

McMullen, Wayne J. "*The China Syndrome*: Corruption to the Core." *Literature/Film Quarterly* 23, no. 1 (1995): 55–62.

McNair, Brian. "Journalism at the Movies." *Journalism Practice* 5, no. 3 (2011): 366–75.

McNamara, Robert S. *In Retrospect: The Tragedy and Lessons of Vietnam*. New York: Crown, 1995.

Meeks, Lindsey. "Defining the Enemy: How Donald Trump Frames the News Media." *Journalism & Mass Communication Quarterly* 97, no. 1 (2020): 211–34.

Meiklejohn, Alexander. "The Barenblatt Opinion." *University of Chicago Law Review* 27 (1960): 329–40.

Mezrich, Ben. *The Accidental Billionaires: The Founding of Facebook: A Tale of Sex, Money, Genius and Betrayal a Tale of Sex, Money, Genius and Betrayal*. New York: Doubleday, 2009.

Morris, James McGrath. "Man of the World." *Wilson Quarterly* 34, no. 1 (2010): 28–33.

Mulvey, Laura. *Citizen Kane*. 2nd ed. London: British Film Institute, 2012.

Nasaw, David. *The Chief: The Life of William Randolph Hearst*. Boston: Houghton Mifflin, 2000.

Nelaeva, Galina, and Gulnor Sufiyanova. "Review: *Memory and Punishment: Historical Denialism, Free Speech and the Limits of Criminal Law* by Emanuela Fronza." *International and Comparative Law Quarterly* 69 (October 2020): 1035–37.

Nichols, Bill. *Engaging Cinema: An Introduction to Film Studies*. New York: Norton, 2010.

Nielsen, Laura Beth. *License to Harass: Law, Hierarchy, and Offensive Public Speech*. Princeton, NJ: Princeton University Press, 2004.

O'Hear, Michael. "Violent Crime and Media Coverage in One City: A Statistical Snapshot." *Marquette Law Review* 103, no. 3 (2020): 1007–33.

The Oxford American Dictionary and Language Guide. New York: Oxford University Press, 1999.

Pakula, Alan J., and Richard Thompson. "Mr. Pakula Goes to Washington." *Film Comment* 12, no. 5 (September–October 1976): 12–19.

Palmer, William J. *The Films of the Eighties: A Social History*. Carbondale: Southern Illinois University Press, 1993.

Paris, Michael, and Kevin J. McMahon. "Absolutism and Democracy: Hugo L. Black's Free Speech Jurisprudence." In *Judging Free Speech: First Amendment Jurisprudence of US Supreme Court Justices*, edited by Helen J. Knowles and Steven B. Lichtman, 75–97. New York: Palgrave Macmillan, 2015.

Parks, Lisa. "Cover Your Webcam: Unencrypting Laura Poitras's *Citizenfour*." *Film Quarterly* 68, no. 3 (2015): 11–16.

Paskey, Stephen. "The Law Is Made of Stories: Erasing the False Dichotomy between Stories and Legal Rules." *Legal Communication and Rhetoric: JALWD* 11 (2014): 51–82.

Pautz, Michelle C. "*Argo* and *Zero Dark Thirty*: Film, Government, and Audiences." *PS: Political Science & Politics* 48, no. 1 (2015): 120–28.

Petersen, Jennifer. "Freedom of Expression as Liberal Fantasy: The Debate over *The People vs. Larry Flynt*." *Media Culture & Society* 29, no. 3 (2007): 377–94.

Policinski, Gene. "Setting the Docket: News Media Coverage of Our Courts—Past, Present and an Uncertain Future." *Missouri Law Review* 79 (2014): 1007–19.

Porton, Richard. "Porn Again: The People vs. Larry Flynt." *Cinéaste* 22, no. 4 (1997): 28–32.

Quinn, K., L. Bowleg, and J. Dickson-Gomez. "'The Fear of Being Black Plus the Fear of Being Gay': The Effects of Intersectional Stigma on Prep Use among Young Black Gay, Bisexual, and Other Men Who Have Sex with Men." *Social Science and Medicine* 232 (2019): 86–93.

Ramsey, E. Michele. "Protecting Patriarchy: The Myths of Capitalism and Patriotism in *The People vs Larry Flynt*." *Feminist Media Studies* 5, no. 2 (2005): 197–213.

Rehnquist, William H. *All the Laws but One: Civil Liberties in Wartime*. New York: Vintage, 1998.

Riggs, Marlon. "Black Macho Revisited: Reflections of a Snap! Queen." In *Brother to Brother: New Writing by Black Gay Men*, edited by Essex Hemphill, 324–30. New Orleans: RedBone Press, 2007.

Rollins, Peter C. "Using Popular Culture to Study the Vietnam War: Perils and Possibilities." In *Why We Fought: America's Wars in Film and History*, edited by Peter C. Rollins and John E. O'Connor, 367–89. Lexington: University Press of Kentucky, 2008.

Roosevelt, Franklin D. "Message to the Booksellers of America." *Publishers Weekly*, May 9, 1942: 1741.

Rosenstone, Robert A. "History in Images/History in Words: Reflections on the Possibility of Really Putting History onto Film." *American Historical Review* 93, no. 5 (1988): 1173–85.

Rothstein, Richard. *The Color of Law: A Forgotten History of How Our Government Segregated America*. New York: Liveright Publishing, 2017.

Rushing, Don G. "Storytelling." *Litigation Chicago* 49, no. 3 (Spring 2023): 18–21.

Sawatzky, Karen. "The People vs. Larry Flynt." *Canadian Dimension* 31, no. 2 (March–April 1997): 39.

Schneider, Anne, and Helen Ingram. "Social Construction of Target Populations: Implications for Politics and Policy." *American Political Science Review* 87, no. 2 (1993): 334–47.

Schudson, Michael. *Discovering the News: A Social History of American Newspapers*. New York: Basic Books, 1978.

———. *Watergate in American Memory: How We Remember, Forget, and Reconstruct the Past*. New York: Basic Books, 1992.

Schwartz, Bernard. "Holmes versus Hand: Clear and Present Danger or Advocacy of Unlawful Action." *Supreme Court Review* 1994 (1994): 209–45.

Segal, Victoria. "Small-Screen Hero: A Tale of Anti-McCarthy Pluck Sets High Standards for TV." *New Statesman*, February 20, 2006: 48.

Shahshahani, Sepehr. "Hard Cases Make Bad Law? A Theoretical Investigation." *Journal of Legal Studies* 51, no. 1 (2022): 133–75.

Shaw, Tony. "'Rotten to the Core': Exposing America's Energy-Media Complex in *The China Syndrome*." *Cinema Journal* 52, no. 2 (Winter 2013): 93–113.

Sheehan, Neil. *A Bright Shining Lie: John Paul Vann and America in Vietnam*. New York: Random House, 1988.

Shilts, Randy. *And the Band Played On: Politics, People, and the AIDS Epidemic*. New York: St. Martin's Griffin, 2007.

Siebert, Fred S., Theodore Peterson, and Wilbur Schramm. *Four Theories of the Press*. Urbana: University of Illinois Press, 1984.

Silver, Charles. *An Auteurist History of Film*. New York: Museum of Modern Art, 2016.

Simmons, Ron. "*Tongues Untied*: An Interview with Marlon Riggs." In *Brother to Brother: New Writing by Black Gay Men*, edited by Essex Hemphill, 234–48. New Orleans: RedBone Press, 2007.

Sklar, Robert. "Review." *Cinéaste* 29, no. 1 (2010): 23–25.

———. "Review." *Cinéaste* 36, no. 1 (2010): 46–48.

Smolla, Rod. *Deliberate Intent: A Lawyer Tells the True Story of Murder by the Book*. New York: Three Rivers Press, 1999.

Smolla, Rodney A. "From *Hit Man* to *Encyclopedia of Jihad*: How to Distinguish Freedom of Speech from Terrorist Training." *Loyola of Los Angeles Entertainment Law Review* 22, no. 2 (2002): 479–90.

———. "Will Tabloid Journalism Ruin the First Amendment for the Rest of Us?" *DePaul Journal of Art and Entertainment Law* 9, no. 1 (1998): 1–6.

Sorlin, Pierre. "Documentaries: A Gold Mine Historians Should Begin to Exploit." In *Using Visual Evidence*, edited by Richard Howells and Robert Matson, 107–22. New York: McGraw-Hill, 2009.

Stelter, Brian. *Hoax: Donald Trump, Fox News, and the Dangerous Distortion of Truth*. New York: One Signal, 2020.

Stern, Seth, and Stephen Wermiel. *Justice Brennan: Liberal Champion*. New York: Houghton Mifflin Harcourt, 2010.

Stone, Geoffrey R. *Perilous Times: Free Speech in Wartime, from the Sedition Act of 1798 to the War on Terrorism*. New York: Norton, 2004.

Street, John. *Mass Media, Politics & Democracy*. 2nd ed. London: Red Globe Press, 2019.

Street, Sarah. "Citizen Kane." *History Today*, March 1996, 48–52.

Sunstein, Cass. *Democracy and the Problem of Free Speech*. New York: Free Press, 1995.

Taibbi, Matt. *Hate Inc.: Why Today's Media Makes Us Despise One Another*. New York: OR Books, 2019.

Thomson, David. *The New Biographical Dictionary of Film*. 6th ed. New York: Knopf, 2014.

Thrasher, Steven W. *The Viral Underclass: The Human Toll When Inequality and Disease Collide*. New York: Celadon Books, 2022.

Travers, Peter. "Shattered Glass." *Rolling Stone*, November 13, 2003, 106.

Turow, Joseph. *Media Today: Mass Communication in a Converging World*. New York: Routledge, 2017.

Tye, Larry. *Demagogue: The Life and Long Shadow of Senator Joe McCarthy*. Boston: Houghton Mifflin Harcourt, 2020.

Ungar, Sanford J. *The Papers & the Papers: An Account of the Legal and Political Battle over the Pentagon Papers*. Boston: Dutton, 1972.

Urofsky, Melvin I. "The Court at War and the War at the Court." *Journal of Supreme Court History* 1996, no. 1 (1996): 1–18.

van Pelt, Robert Jan. *The Case for Auschwitz: Evidence from the Irving Trial*. Bloomington: Indiana University Press, 2016.

Vodrey, Simon. "Digital Media Reviews: *Citizenfour*." *American Journalism* 34, no. 1 (2017): 121–22.

Volokh, Eugene. "'The Freedom . . . of the Press,' from 1791 to 1868 to Now—Freedom for the Press as an Industry, or the Press as a Technology?" *University of Pennsylvania Law Review* 160 (2012): 459–540.

Vuic, Kara Dixon. "The Guys in the Rear, with the Beer." *Reviews in American History* 41, no. 1 (March 2013): 140–44.

Walker, Ann. "Film Review: *Denial*." *Psychological Perspectives* 61 (2018): 276–78.

Weinberg, Jonathan. "Broadcasting and Speech." *California Law Review* 81 (1993): 1101–206.

Welles, Orson, and Peter Bogdanovich. *This Is Orson Welles*. New York: Da Capo Press, 1998.

West, Darrell M. *The Rise and Fall of the Media Establishment*. New York: Palgrave, 2001.

West, Sonja R., and RonNell Anderson Jones. "The Disappearing Freedom of the Press." *Washington & Lee Law Review* 79, no. 4 (2022): 1377–462.

White, Theodore H. *The Making of the President, 1968*. New York: Atheneum, 1969.

Wilkerson, Isabel. *Caste: The Origins of Our Discontents*. New York: Random House, 2020.

Wilson, Joshua C. *The Street Politics of Abortion*. Stanford, CA: Stanford University Press, 2013.

Winch, Samuel P. "Ethical Challenges for Investigative Journalism." In *The Big Chill: Investigative Reporting in the Current Media Environment*, edited by Marilyn S. Greenwald and Joseph Bernt, 121–36. Ames: Iowa State University Press, 2000.

Woodward, Bob, and Carl Bernstein. *All the President's Men*. 1974; repr. New York: Simon and Schuster, 2012.

Woolner, Cookie. "'Women Slain in Queer Love Brawl': African American Women, Same-Sex Desire, and Violence in the Urban North, 1920–1929." *Journal of African American History* 100, no. 3 (2015): 406–27.

Wu, Tim. *The Attention Merchants: The Epic Scramble to Get Inside Our Heads*. New York: Knopf, 2016.

Wulf, Steve. "On the Record." *Entertainment Weekly*, February 22, 2002, 74–77.

Young, Iris Marion. *Justice and the Politics of Difference*. Princeton, NJ: Princeton University Press, 2011.

Index

About the Authors

Bruce E. Altschuler is professor emeritus of political science at SUNY Oswego. He is the author or coauthor of nine books, most recently *Lights, Camera, Execution: Cinematic Portrayals of Capital Punishment*, as well as numerous articles in professional journals.

Helen J. Knowles-Gardner is research director at the Institute for Free Speech. She has written extensively about various aspects of American law and politics, including coediting/coauthoring two other books about freedom of speech: *Judging Free Speech: First Amendment Jurisprudence of US Supreme Court Justices* and *Free Speech Theory: Understanding the Controversies*.

Brandon T. Metroka is associate professor of political science and Pre-Law Program coordinator at University of the Incarnate Word in San Antonio, Texas. He is the coeditor of *Free Speech Theory: Understanding the Controversies* and has authored or coauthored articles appearing in *Justice System Journal*, *American University International Law Review*, and *Washington & Lee Law Review*.

www.ingramcontent.com/pod-product-compliance
Ingram Content Group UK Ltd.
Pitfield, Milton Keynes, MK11 3LW, UK
UKHW041450071026
15587UKWH00010B/742

9 781793 650443